D1562994

Reprints of Economic Classics

AMERICAN POLITICAL IDEAS

Also published by
Reprints of Economic Classics

by Charles E. Merriam

A History of American Political Theories (1903)

AMERICAN POLITICAL IDEAS

STUDIES IN THE DEVELOPMENT OF AMERICAN POLITICAL THOUGHT 1865-1917

BY

CHARLES EDWARD MERRIAM, Ph.D.
Professor of Political Science, University of Chicago

REPRINTS OF ECONOMIC CLASSICS

AUGUSTUS M. KELLEY · PUBLISHERS
NEW YORK 1969

First Edition 1920
(New York: The Macmillan Company, 1920)

Reprinted 1969 by
Augustus M. Kelley · Publishers
New York, New York 10010

SBN 678 00511 7

Library of Congress Catalogue Card Number
68-56259

PRINTED IN THE UNITED STATES OF AMERICA
by SENTRY PRESS, NEW YORK, N. Y. 10019

TO
THE MEMORY OF
MY MOTHER

PREFACE

In 1903, the writer presented " A History of American Political Theories." That study, with the exception of one chapter on " Recent Tendencies," dealt with the development of political thought down to the Civil War. The present volume is an attempt to outline some of the chief tendencies in our fundamental political thinking from the close of the Civil War to the beginning of the American participation in the recent war. The purpose of the writer is to trace the broad currents of American political thought in their relation to the social, economic and political tendencies of the time. Sometimes these ideas have been best expressed in political institutions; sometimes in laws, judicial decisions, administration, or customs; again, in the utterances of statesmen and publicists or leaders of various causes; sometimes by the formal statements of the systematic philosophers. This study traces the main lines, the typical forms of political ideas, in their relation to each other and to the conditions out of which they grew. Some of these doctrines are thinly disguised pleas for group interests; others are parts of the great process by which the experience and counsel of the leaders, statesmen and sages are woven into the web of social and political control; others are relatively impartial and technical studies of social or political science. All are indirectly parts of the progressive adaptation of democratic ideas to new economic and social conditions.

This study is the outgrowth of investigations begun in the Seminar on American political philosophy given by Professor Dunning, in Columbia University, 1896-97, and the writer wishes to acknowledge his deep sense of obligation for the inspiration then given, and for subsequent encouragement in the prosecution of this work. I am also indebted to my colleagues, Professors Freund, Small, and Dodd for counsel and help; and particularly to Mr. Harold F. Gosnell, Fellow in the Department of Political Science in the University of Chicago, for aid in the reading of proof.

CHARLES EDWARD MERRIAM.

CONTENTS

AMERICAN POLITICAL IDEAS

CHAPTER I

THE BACKGROUND OF AMERICAN POLITICAL THOUGHT

IT is important at the outset to sketch briefly the fundamental conditions under which the American political thinking of the last half-century has been carried on — to inquire into the outstanding factors of our growth since the Civil War. What are the new conditions out of which new political interpretations are shaped or new ideas have sprung? What are the new forces that have led men to frame new formulas, and new philosophies? [1]

The nineteenth century was full of new political forces and forms. Individualism of the eighteenth-century type deepened into the nineteenth-century *laissez faire*, and still

[1] This period is reviewed in Hart's "American Nation Series," Group V, vols. 22–26, and in " the Yale Chronicles of America " series, particularly in the volumes by Fish, Ford and Hendricks; in James Rhodes' "History of the United States." See also Beard's Contemporary American History"; Frederic L. Paxson, "The New Nation," 1915. See also F. A. Cleveland, "The Growth of Democracy in the United States," 1898; Henry Jones Ford, "The Rise and Growth of American Politics," 1898; C. E. Merriam, "History of American Political Theories," 1903; Albert Bushnell Hart, "National Ideals Historically Traced," 1907; James Schouler, "Ideals of the Republic," 1908; E. D. Adams, "The Power of Ideals in American History," 1913.

further developed into the unanticipated doctrines of philosophical anarchism. Democracy, the revolutionary ferment of the seventeenth and eighteenth centuries, took the new form of Liberalism in its varying shades, and at times passed over into the garb of Collectivism and of Socialism. About the mid-century Nationalism appeared as a distinct political doctrine, on the basis of which were made states of the type of America, Italy and Germany, while many smaller nationalities lifted up their heads. With the expansion of European powers, rose the familiar figure of Imperialism, and with the rapid expansion of transportation and communication, Internationalism appeared on the horizon of the national state. Democracy, representative government, constitutionalism, universal suffrage, developed in the Orient as well as in the Occident. But there also arose a new Aristocracy clothed in forms appropriate to modern life and philosophy; now in the garb of the divine right of the industrial aristocracy, the precedence of the captain of industry. And again in the amazing combination of the throne and modern industrialism seen in the German state, militarism appeared equipped with all the devices of modern science and philosophy, and with all the weapons of a modern mechanical age. On the other hand came the opposing theories of organized Pacifism, speaking through great philosophers and prophets of every state.

Old formulas of freedom were used for the defence of new and strange causes by unfamiliar hands. New formulas were created for the defence of what were really old causes. Individualism, anarchy, socialism, imperialism, militarism and pacifism, democracy and aristocracy, were all swept into the current along with the new-found forces of industrialism, education, science, feminism and urbanism, with all their long train of implications and complications. Never was there a time of greater ferment in the thoughts of men, of sharper paradox, of more mystifying confusion in the use of terms and formulas, presumably well understood and established. All the new political doctrines and dogmas invoked in turn the support of history, science and statistics, psychology and philosophy, to sanction their new propaganda of attack or defence.

One of the most striking features in the wide range of philosophy and politics of the century was the development of Liberalism to meet the new conditions of human life.[2] The transition from political to industrial liberalism was one of the central features of the age, shattering political parties, shaking the foundations of the state, and breaking up political philosophies. In the seventeenth and eighteenth, and the early part of the nineteenth century, the forces of Democracy were directed against political Absolutism, against the rule of arbitrary personal power, against entrenched political privilege, against institutionalized political inequality. Democracy battled for representation, first for the right to be heard, and then for the right to be obeyed under parliamentary government. Democracy contended for equality before the law, as against systems of institutionalized inequality and privilege; for constitutions, written or unwritten, as

[2] W. A. Dunning, "A Century of Politics," *North American Review*, 179, 801-14; "History of Political Theories," Vol. III; E. Barker, " Political Thought in England "; C. Delisle Burns, " Political Ideals."

solemn guarantees of a general understanding of a public policy regarding the fundamentals of public life. This was the great struggle carried on in England, America, and France, and throughout the continent, though not everywhere with uniform success.

In the later stages there was a struggle for more perfect recognition of the principles of democracy, nowhere yet completely carried out to their fullest extent. There followed great battles, bloodless battles as a rule, for broader suffrage, for more nearly equal representation, for more complete control over the acts and agencies of government, for a closer hold on legislation, administration, and on the judgments of the courts, if these ran contrary to popular will. Thus England had its great contests over reform in the House of Commons, over Chartism, over extension of the right to vote, over the veto power of the House of Lords. America had its battles to widen the circle of the land-owner and the tax-payer, over the abolition of the status of slavery, over the gradual extension of the principle of democratic control through the governmental system.

Toward the mid-century, however, Liberalism and Democracy came face to face with a new set of problems dividing the forces that had been united and requiring extensive realignment upon many fronts. Sometimes Conservatives became Liberals, and Liberals in many instances became Conservatives. In the politics and philosophy of all countries significant and far-reaching readjustments were made under the stress of new situations. The new problem was the interpretation of the formulas and the ideals of the historic democracy in terms of the new social and industrial conditions appearing in the nineteenth and twentieth centuries. It was agreed that democracy meant the abolition of political absolutism and all forms of political privilege, and the setting up of some form of parliamentary and responsible government. But beyond that there was the problem of the significance of democracy under the new conditions that had sprung up in the modern state, around the factory, in industrial life, transformed as it was by new organizations of capital, credit, labor and mechanics. What did democracy mean in the days of the union, the railroad, the trust and of modern business organization? After popular sovereignty had been fully established, what was to be the theoretical and practical program of democracy? What should be the social and industrial function of the people's government under the new regime? What should be the interpretation of liberty and equality in the midst of these new and strange social forces? What should be the conception of political and social justice in the midst of an environment without precedent? Should the democracy adopt a policy of indifference — an attitude of *laissez-faire* toward the struggles of its citizens, leaving to a beneficent competition the ultimate solution of all difficulties? Or should democracy press on and establish a complete co-operative commonwealth in the industrial sense of the term? Or should the democracy endeavor to find some middle ground between unrestrained individualism and all-inclusive collectivism? These were the overshadowing problems of the last half-century. They were not confined to any latitude or longitude — they were the common property of all the great industrial

states of the western world.[3]   They taxed the ingenuity
of statesmen, the precedents of jurists, and the subtleties
of philosophy, wherever the new democracy came in contact with the new life conditions thrust forward by the
vigorous social and economic forces of our time.

Democracy was challenged and attacked by thinkers of
various schools. Sir Henry Maine [4] criticized the assumptions of democracy, while Lecky [5] questioned the fundamental connection between democracy and liberty. The
German writers developed varying theories justifying
monarchical government, and sharply criticized the practical operations of democratic government. Nietzsche's
doctrines were the nearest approach to a political theory
of aristocracy, and they were widely influential, particularly in the German circles. Socialism challenged the
results thus far obtained by democracy under modern
conditions. Syndicalism [6] and Anarchism [7] openly denied the validity of the democratic system.

One of the outstanding theoretical features of the time
was the concerted assault made from many different quarters upon militarism. Of all the numerous and varied
attacks upon war by far the most notable was that of
Count Tolstoi, who both in philosophy and in fiction developed the pacifist doctrines in widely influential fashion.
Tolstoi and Nietzsche in fact stand as the two opposite
poles in the theory of the time — one reflecting the influ-

[3] L. T. Hobhouse, "Liberalism," especially Ch. VI, on the "Heart
of Liberalism." John A. Hobson, "The Crisis of Liberalism."
[4] "Popular Government."
[5] "Democracy and Liberty."
[6] P. F. Brissenden, "The I. W. W."
[7] Zenker, "Anarchism."

ence in philosophy of the principles of ruthless competition and the other an underlying theory of compassion — one elaborating a philosophy of aggression, aristocracy and militarism, and the other a doctrine of non-resistance, communism and pacifism.

While there was bitter and protracted controversy between aristocracy and democracy as forms of government, and between the opposing doctrines of pacifism and militarism, on the whole the characteristic feature of the time was the rise of social issues. Through the machinery of government, industrial and social questions were constantly thrust forward. Men were concerned about the economic basis of their life in relation to the legal and political forms of government. Democracy was still a cherished ideal, but democracy being assumed, the question of its practical application to social and industrial conditions came to be of paramount importance. Thus to the battle still raging between political aristocracy and democracy, and between localism, nationalism and internationalism, there was added the controversy between democracy and oligarchy in the industrial world. As between nations, the struggle was one in which race played the principal role, while within nations the contest was between classes for economic and political power. So it happened that both race and class fought, sometimes together and sometimes against each other, for authority, for moral, legal and political justification of their position, for political ideals and for political institutions expressing these ideals. Nationalism and socialism were the most significant factors of the time, struggling with the crosscurrents of democracy and aristocracy, militarism and pacifism for domination. As the issues were variously defined from time to time, classes and races fell upon one side or the other of the line. Toward the end of the period aristocracy tended to retreat before political democracy, yet at the very close of the period aristocracy gathered its forces for a powerful effort. Likewise militarism retreated before the pacifist forces of the time, yet militarism also rallied for a gigantic effort at the end of this era. The forces of industrial democracy fighting as Socialism or Liberalism made rapid progress in institutions and in theories, but the structure of economic society remained distinctly aristocratic and the theory of the time was divided between the upholders of the old regime and various types of radical and moderate opponents.

One of the most interesting features of the time was the contest between capital and labor for the possession of the institutions and the theories of democracy. Capitalism strove to appear as the defender of individual liberty and the guardian of democratic doctrines, using for this purpose the narrower and more technical legal and political arguments, charging its opponents with betrayal of the individual, with disregard of democracy, and designs ultimately leading to practical slavery under a socialistic regime. On the other hand, the influences working for industrial democracy charged capitalism with the betrayal of representative institutions through corruption and undue influence, with adroit attempts to turn the defenses of liberty into the safeguards of oppression, with intention to preserve and maintain oligarchic and autocratic interests under the guise of democratic institutions. The capitalistic strategists strove to maneuver the opposition into a position where it must abandon the doctrine of liberty or even democracy, while the progressive influences relying less upon technical and legal arguments, undertook to show that actually and practically capitalism and plutocracy were controlling the lives and fortunes of men through ingenious interpretations of outgrown laws. Both were in turn obliged to yield to the demands of Nationalism, when the nation spoke, or the middle class when fully aroused.

Some of the great social changes underlying these developing ideas were common to the world, but some were peculiar to America. A brief survey of the situation will indicate the most significant forces affecting the growth and form of American political thought. The foremost of the fundamental social changes wrought by a half-century is the mass-fact of the rapid expansion of population. During the first years of our Republic, a vast territorial domain had been acquired, but this wide-reaching territory had not been peopled. During the last half-century the range of territory stretching from Atlantic to Pacific was settled. Wave after wave of migration swept to the West, across the Mississippi, over the Missouri, beyond the mountains, along the coast, until finally the frontier disappeared. We must now reckon also with the over-seas dependencies, Porto Rico, Hawaii and the Philippine Islands. In 1870 the population of the United States was less than 40,000,000; by 1917 it was approximately 100,000,000. The addition of these multitudes and the shifting of this population from one section

to another, particularly from the east to the west, was
one of the significant features in the development of our
Republic during the last fifty years.

Equally notable was the amazing concentration of
population in great urban centers. This phenomenon
was common to all the great industrial states of the world,
but nowhere was it more pronounced than in America.
In 1870 the urban population was twenty-one per cent. of
the total; by 1917 approximately fifty per cent. of the
population was found in urban centers. In many of the
states more than one-half of the entire population had
become urban.[8] In the last fifty years the United States
ceased to be a rural democracy, and was transformed into
a half-rural, half-urban Republic. In this process fundamental changes were made in the life and labor of men.
In their housing conditions, in their working surroundings, in their facilities for leisure, and in many other ways
far-reaching changes in human life were made. Not only
were readjustments necessary within the city itself, but
under the new conditions reconciliations of the ideals of
the urban and rural communities were distinct features in
the nation's life. The early prophets and statesmen of
the Republic had thought of democracy as agrarian in its
composition and rural in its tendencies, but by the end of
the century the rush of population to great urban centers
had changed in great part this portion of the foundations
upon which the earlier philosophies had rested.

[8] In Rhode Island 96.7 per cent. of the population was urban in
1910; in Massachusetts 92.8 per cent.; in Connecticut 89.7 per cent.;
in New York 78.8 per cent.; in New Jersey 75.2 per cent.; in Illinois
61.7 per cent.; and in Pennsylvania 60.4 per cent.

During the last half-century the composition of the population underwent a fundamental change. The immigration movement had begun before the Civil War, particularly after the Irish potato famine in 1840, and the German revolution in 1848, but the full tide of immigration did not begin until after the Civil War. In 1851-60, the immigrants numbered 2,598,214. In 1861–70 they numbered 2,314,824; in 1871-80, 2,812,191; in 1881-90, 5,246,613; in 1891–1900, 3,687,564; in 1901–10, 8,795,-386. From 1820 to 1910, the total immigration was 27,-918,992. By 1910 the total foreign born population of the United States was 13,000,000, while the population of foreign parentage was approximately 20,000,000 more.

In the early part of the period the immigration came largely from England, Ireland, Germany and the Scandinavian countries. In the later part of the period the great proportion of those who entered were from Italy, Austria and Russia, introducing a variation in race elements. Furthermore, the new population manifested a strong tendency to center in the urban communities, in even larger percentages than the native born population. Thus, heterogeneity of population appears as one of the striking factors in the development of the United States since the Civil War.

This period was characterized by material prosperity on a vast scale.[9] The wealth of the country increased by leaps and bounds. Agriculture and trade expanded at a marvelous rate in almost every portion of the nation.

[9] H. C. Emery, "Economic Development of United States" in "Cambridge Modern History," VII, Ch. 22.

Manufacturing in particular developed at a pace never before known. This was particularly true of the northern section at the outset of the period, but in the south as well during the latter part of it. Roughly speaking, it may be said that during the first generation of our history the republic was characteristically an agricultural state. During the next stage of our growth the power was divided between the agricultural and commercial interests. Following the Civil War the balance definitely inclined toward the predominance of trade, while during the latter part of the period the wage-worker appeared for the first time as an organized and formidable factor. During the last part of the century the great national economic forces were those of agriculture, commerce, and labor. Their influence upon the party politics and the political philosophy of the time is one of the fundamental points in any discussion of this period. Their inter-relationship is one of the keys to the comprehension of our national philosophy, explaining many phenomena otherwise inexplicable.

Another of the striking social characteristics of this period was the growth of great individual fortunes.[10] Some of these large aggregations were the result of increases in land value, particularly in the urban centers, but in the main they were the outgrowth of activities directed through the corporation or " trust," in such cases, as oil, steel, lumber, railroads and other conspicuous illustrations. Banking and stock exchange speculation also added to the list. The report of the Federal Industrial

[10] See Anna Youngman, "The Economic Causes of Great Fortunes "; also G. Myers, "History of the Great American Fortunes."

Relations Commission appointed in 1913 presented the following conclusions regarding the distribution of wealth: The " rich," including 2 per cent. of the people, own 60 per cent. of the wealth; the " middle class," 33 per cent. of the people, own 35 per cent. of the wealth; the poor, 65 per cent. of the people, own 5 per cent. of the wealth.[11] The tendency to concentrate vast wealth in the hands of a few corporations and relatively few owners, was marked by all observers and constituted one of the basic movements of the time. It profoundly affected the assumptions both of the many and of the few, and forced substantial modifications of theoretical belief and of practical policy as well.

In addition to these fundamental tendencies, the expansion of population, diversification of types and concentration of settlement, there emerged from the general struggle deeply significant types of organized activity. These new groupings became active forces in the social, economic and political life of the nation. On the one side, there appeared an unparalleled concentration of activity in corporate form; on the other, the unprecedented concentration of labor in the trades unions. Prior to the Civil War the corporation was not unknown, but as an effective instrument of business it was little known.[12] Following the War, however, this form of industrial organization developed at an astonishing rate. The public utility in the city, the railroad in the state and nation, and

[11] See "Report of Industrial Relations Commission," Vol. I, p. 33. See also, Willford I. King, "The Wealth and Income of the People of the United States."

[12] See Victor S. Clark, "History of Manufactures in the United States."

other large combinations in the industrial world, appeared with startling rapidity. Steel, sugar, oil, whiskey, lumber, coal, and a hundred other products were organized in large corporate form. Out of the ordinary corporation, in the course of time came the trust, the holding company, the combination of corporations, in doubly concentrated form. The growth of these gigantic organizations constitutes one of the most striking features in the development of American life. Into their hands flowed the control of billions of money, and the employment of millions of men. With their growth and activities there came an inevitable series of legal and political problems which demanded the attention of the lawyer, the statesman, the economist and the philosopher.

On the other hand, the trades union developed formidable power simultaneously with the corporation. Not unknown before the War, but practically regarded as an outlaw, the labor union had been unable to make perceptible headway. It was only after the Civil War that laws against combinations of labor were repealed and that the trades union obtained a definite legal position from which its efforts might be directed. In 1881 the American Federation of Labor was organized, and this organization, with its various subsidiary and collateral branches, expanded at a rapid rate, until in 1910 it reached a membership estimated at three million. The individual laborer in many states no longer stood alone; he was associated with his fellows, organized, equipped and led to vigorous industrial battle. As in the case of the corporation and the holding company, here was a new-comer in the national field, requiring readjustments of fundamental political presupposition-changes in law and in custom. In the midst of the labor struggle legal and political theories often melted like wax, and were as easily molded.

Our political and industrial development has carried us far from our earlier views. In the trial of the journeyman boot and shoe makers in 1806 for criminal conspiracy, based on their organization to increase their wages, the court said: " A combination of working men to raise their wages may be considered in a two-fold point of view — one is to benefit themselves, the other is to injure those who do not join their society. The rule of law condemns both." [13]

On the other hand, the Philadelphia mechanics of the Vulcan Iron Works petitioned the Legislature as follows, in 1826: " The grant of particular privileges to any body of men for the purpose of carrying on business beyond the reach of individual enterprise operates most unjustly upon those individuals who upon their own responsibility and without legislative aid are engaged in the same pursuits." This they used against the creation of corporations.[14]

In the field of agriculture as well, large-scale combinations were formed, although not with the same coherence or permanence as in the case of corporate wealth, or of labor. The Granger movement in the early seventies grew with miraculous speed, and for a time obtained great political power and industrial prestige. The Farmers'

[13] Cited by Wright in " Industrial Evolution of the United States." (p. 283.)

[14] Cited by Clarke, *op. cit.*, pp. 251, 281. See also arguments on relative merits of corporate and individual enterprises, p. 459.

Alliance in the late eighties also spread like wildfire, and for a time became a formidable political party movement, but neither possessed the tenacity and coherence of either trade unionism or corporations. At the very close of this period appeared the Non-Partisan League, an association of farmers organized in party form for political action.

Another great transformation in the underlying conditions of the time was the entrance of women into industry and professions. Prior to the War their chief industry had been domestic in nature, although some had entered the mills and participated in various forms of commercial life. After the Civil War, however, both trades and professions, generally speaking, were gradually opened to both sexes, and a great influx of women followed. In 1880 the number of women engaged in gainful occupations was two and a half million [15]; in 1910 the number reached a total of 8,000,000.[16] Not only did women enter the activities of industry, but also in still larger numbers the field of education. Prior to the War, institutions of higher learning were almost entirely closed to women, while the opportunities of the common schools were not equally shared. During this period facilities for education have been opened practically upon an equivalent basis to both sexes. Education and economics combined, then, to create another social and political force of fundamental importance requiring new interpretations

[15] 2,647,157 or 14.7 per cent.

[16] In 1910, 38,167,336 persons ten years of age and over, were engaged in gainful occupations in continental United States. Of these, 30,091,564 were men and 8,075,772, women. See Edith Abbott, *Women in Industry*.

and new adjustments and new formulas of political action. Of fundamental importance in a consideration of the growth and tendencies of American political thought is an analysis of the general background, the *hinterland*, of American ideas in the broadest sense, and particularly as they relate to the specifically social and political forces and reasoning of the time. The political is obviously not a thing of itself, but is interwoven with all the strands of life; a resultant of the action of many forces and reacting upon them all, directly in some instances and remotely in others. Family, church, state, business, arts and sciences, education, all types of association and all forms and forces are bound up together in the social aggregate. What is " political " is a part of the social life and ideals of the community, past and present, in most highly concentrated form. Political theory is usually an integral part of the instincts, the ideals, the institutions, the general philosophy and point of view of the community, or of the dominant influences in it.

Unquestionably the strongest note in American life during the last half century has been that struck by what is termed " business "— the activities of commercial life centering around the new industrial system of the time. In this the chief new factor was the appearance and leadership of large scale industry. This has set the pace for American energy and thought and has been the touchstone by which the initiation of social policies and ideas has been tested. What effect will they have upon the growth and development of the system of pecuniary profit, was the crucial question applied to them all; to political movements and ideas, to political parties and their leaders, to every new effort in the social field. Yet back of this were found two other systems which from time to time expressed themselves vigorously and effectively. These were the ideals and institutions of the agrarian group and those of the labor group. The rural influence had been dominant in the early days of the Republic and had shared the throne until the time of the Civil War after which the commercial interest was for the time predominant. But the agricultural elements were still powerful in national life and great deference was paid to their ideas of social policy. This was in many instances a mere lip service, but none the less the fact that close attention was given to their demands and ideals was itself significant. The rural group had an individuality of its own, not only as distinguished from the other groups here, but as distinguished from the rural group anywhere else in the world. They possessed a degree of independence, traditionally at least, that marked them as a special type of the agricultural producer. They were sharply distinguished from the activities and the points of view of the strictly commercial class, and from the machine activities of the laboring class.[17]

On the one hand his ownership of property and his relations to labor or " help " tended to identify the farmer with the commercial group, but on the other hand, his exploitation by monopoly in various forms tended to align him against the dominant group of " business." As to the property rights of individual landowners he was

[17] See Mr. Bryan's description of the "business man" in the Democratic National Convention of 1896 as including practically all groups.

an individualist, but as to the regulation of railroad monopoly he was on the side of collectivism, which he did not call by that name. As to his relations to his few employees he was individualistic, but as to competition which destroyed the small business and affected the prices in his community he was on the collectivist side. He was distinctly anti-trust, but by no means pro-labor union. He was not a friend either of monopoly or of strikes. The agrarian influence was a powerful one, not only by reason of the political strength involved in its action, but by virtue of the survival of agrarian tradition in the minds of the large numbers of the business and labor group recruited from the farming class, and unable to free themselves wholly from the traditional point of view of the rural group. Long accustomed to political power and deference, the farming interest still retained large elements of authority both in the nation and in the individual units of political power. The farming group was to a large extent free from the influences which characterized the commercial group on the one hand and the " machine technology " of the laboring class on the other, although influenced more and more by both machinery and by system as the end of this period approached. There were also evidences of a growing division between conservative and liberal groups of farmers.

Associated with the farming group were the smaller merchants and the considerable group of persons employed, but not organized, and the bulk of the various professions. Taken together, they constituted the middle class in America, a shifting, not always clearly defined group, ill organized, but nevertheless traditionally and actually powerful. Its membership constantly tended toward the ranks of labor or of capital. Many of them were both laborer and capitalist. Their ideas of law, justice, equality, liberty were an important factor in the determination of the final result. They were on the whole on the side of individualism as against socialism, and democracy as against plutocracy; and on the side of collectivism where necessary to curb monopoly or unfair competition as they conceived it; but not for the type of collectivism implied in the labor theory and ideal of industry administered by the standardized union association of men, in which all stood upon the same level of production and compensation regardless of individual differences in capacity. They were for a progressive income tax, but not for a single tax on land; for an inheritance tax to prevent swollen fortunes, but not for common ownership of capital.

The development of the labor group in the United States is of deep significance. Interwoven closely with it are the factors of urbanism and industrialism. After the Civil War manufacturing advanced at a rapid rate and increasingly larger numbers of men were employed in new types of industry under altogether novel conditions. The large scale industry, the "machine technology," the dominance of the tool over the man, the startling developments of the new urban conditions, child labor and the labor of women revolutionized the conditions of life for thousands of human beings, who were suddenly brought face to face with situations of the most puzzling variety and complexity. Conditions of life and labor were turned upside down. The ways of life were altered in a few years, while the ways of thought and the types of organization followed far in the rear. There developed new standards, new norms of conduct, new demands, new philosophies to match these new environments. And all the while the movement of many of the more energetic and the more intelligent to other groups was depleting the ranks of those who were left behind.

The machine process made the man no longer the master of his tool. It brought the new and often impersonal master who remained unseen, the true invisible government of the industrial world. It took away the opportunity for the exercise of the trader's ordinary powers of bargain and dicker, so far as the individual was concerned. It took away from many the creative opportunity and instinct of the earlier handicrafts, and of the rural group even now. Men under these conditions were thrown at first on the mercy of the employer, who was himself subject to the most vigorous and often the most unfair competition; or upon their own unorganized resources. Out of this situation came the union and the principle of collective bargaining, the standardization of the condition and rewards of labor for large groups of men, and the bitter process of struggle for the right to organize and the right to act under new conditions. The outstanding features of this situation was the development of new centers of economic and political power in the unions, the abandonment of unlimited individual enterprise and the substitution of the fraternal and collective idea that all go up or down together within the limits of the organization, the subtle influences of the machine technology upon the underlying type and mode of philosophy, the substitution of a more matter of fact philosophy for the earlier theories of the conventional and the authoritative.

The far-reaching influence of this new situation upon ideas of social justice, equality, liberty, and democracy can scarcely be overestimated. It cut straight across the path of earlier individualistic conceptions and traditions. Collectivism tended to dominate the labor type of thought, especially as developed under urban conditions where large groups of men were massed together and where the contrasts between poverty and wealth were most sharply marked. Relief from impending regimentation of life was sometimes found in super-socialistic and anarchistic theories of individual liberty after and beyond the maintenance of human living standards and measures necessary for the securing of industrial democracy, but inevitably these ultimate purposes must be subordinated to the immediate necessity for the creation of a type of discipline essential to the winning of victories in industrial warfare. The individual must be subordinated to the group in sharp contests with the common foe.

This new group was found arrayed in battle line in all contests where the issue seemed to be industrial plutocracy with the farmer and the small business man, but not necessarily against monopoly as such or against the general integration of economic force upon which its allies looked with hate and fear. It was for many types of community regulation in general, but not for the compulsory arbitration of strikes or the requirement of continued labor in public utilities or any other industries. This it identified with "involuntary servitude," invoking an earlier legal concept of liberty, as had its competitors in the application of the principle of freedom of contract, and the liberty of the individual.

From time to time the labor group lost touch and sympathy with the agrarian and middle class group through the employment of violence or corruption in strikes, and in the standardization of the labor day, conditions of labor and compensation, which ran counter to the traditions and present day practices of the rural group. But they were fundamentally united in opposition to the growth and establishment of any system of industrial oligarchy and to the ruthless practices of the dominant commercial group. Social philosophy made a deep impression upon the laboring group, but not the socialist political propaganda. The absence of fixed classes as compared with the European countries, the quick and frequent transitions from class to class, the general mobility of persons and property, took away the class basis of solidarity upon which the Marxian socialism was founded and to which it owes much of its strength abroad. The philosophy and methods of the English trades unions tended to prevail as against the Continental modes of thought and organization. Contact with the soil as against contact with the machine, life in daily contact with the vital forces of nature and life with the power-directed machine, the relative isolation of the rural toiler and the mass contact of the factory employee, unquestionably tended to shape different views of life and different ways of thought, but no sufficient analysis has been made of these fundamental changes; and perhaps sufficient time has not yet elapsed to make this study possible or to indicate clear lines of differentiation, particularly in a highly mobile society such as ours. The commercial or "business" group came into predominance after the Civil War. That controversy was not only a victory for free labor as against slave labor; but eventually a triumph for manufacturing as against agricultural labor. The outstanding feature of the last half century was the great expansion of manufacturing and trade,[18] and the new types of concentrated organization. While the agricultural interest also expanded, it was overshadowed by the more striking and significant development of the arts of manufacture. In number of employees, amount of capital invested, in value of output, the new type of activity showed the greatest advance. Not only was this true, but "business" underwent important alterations. Large scale industries appeared and made rapid inroads on the smaller business enterprises which found themselves crowded to the wall somewhat as the feudal chiefs went down before the national rulers. The technical man was to a great extent displaced as the active and directing head of the enterprise, and his place was taken by the capitalist, often without detailed knowledge of the industry in its technical aspects. The process of combination of industries became so much the order of the day that the commercial leadership was to a large extent taken by those whose chief function was that of consolidation, of merging and uniting scattered industries in centralized form. Transportation, monopolies and

[18] See E. L. Bogart, "Economic History of the U. S." (1907).

credit interlocked in unprecedented form. And for these services the largest material rewards were often paid. Toward the end of this period another fundamental change was seen in the marked development of foreign trade. " The balance of trade," as it was called, shifted and turned in favor of the United States, and attention was directed as never before to the expansion of industry in outside territory.

These changes are hastily sketched only for the purpose of showing that the type of " business " which now came into the ascendancy was widely different from the earlier forms of commercial organization and activity in many of its features. While the pecuniary system remained the same in its broadest outlines, the business man of a century ago was now old-fashioned and unadapted to the new competitive conditions of the later day. Large scale organization, quick consolidation, accounting, advertising, credit, " system "— all were changed, and a new world commercially was created. And above all the appearance and activities of the corporation and the super-corporation characterized the period.

It was this new type of so-called " big business " that assumed the leadership in the industrial as well as in the political world. A government traditionally weak and already corrupt was often swept aside except where it was useful for privilege or immunity, and then it was either controlled through the party machine or corrupted in more direct form. Thus Mr. Taft says, " The great corporations found it useful first to restrain hostile legislation and then to secure affirmative legislation giving them undue advantage in the conduct of their business. The time came when it was possible in some great corporations for the officers and directors to issue, with the same nonchalance and certainty of their being complied with, orders for steel rails or industrial equipment, on the one hand, or for the delivery of delegations in a state, county or national political convention, on the other. In the early years of this century the people became fully aroused to the fact that they were almost in the grasp of a plutocracy." [19]

The activities of this new and small commercial group were not uncontested. They were bitterly fought by the farmers where their interests came in conflict as in the case of the railroad rates; and they were drawn into the sharpest of conflicts with organized labor during the whole period. Of equal significance was the opposition of the smaller business men, much greater numerically, who as independent producers were often driven from the field, and who defended themselves with the greatest vigor, although with little success so far as their immediate objects were concerned. Combinations of the farmer, the labor group and the endangered small producers or merchants frequently overthrew the rule of the larger business in states and in the United States; but while these allied groups were able to score political triumphs and force the enactment of laws, they were not able to obtain consistent administration and enforcement of the policies for which they fought. The Interstate Commerce Act and the Anti-Trust Law, the great national monu-

[19] "Economic and Political Summary of the Generation Just Closing," in *Journal of the National Institute of Social Sciences,* p. 64 (1915).

ments to the efforts of these allies, were rendered largely ineffective, and did not materially affect the general consolidating tendencies of the times. That this was due, partly, to the weakness of administrative agencies, but also in great measure to the failure to interpret correctly the economic tendencies of the time and to formulate an appropriate program cannot be denied. The novelty of the situation, the rapidity of current change, the weakness of government, the prevailing and traditional opposition to governmental interference with individual liberty in the political sense of the term, or with that type of it represented by individual freedom of competition: — all conspired to make effective action impossible at this stage of the politico-economic development. In the meantime "business," that is large scale business, wanted chiefly non-interference, which it was able to obtain either from governmental inertia or when necessary by the process of influence, intimidation or of corruption.

This was not a government for which a ruling group assumed a grave responsibility of a paternal kind as was the case in contemporary England or in Germany. It was a situation in which the ruling powers wished to be let alone, employing the government only occasionally as in the case of the tariff, yet feeling that the government was at their disposal whenever required; but not frequently requiring it, and not much disposed to build up an effective government which might prove troublesome when set up and put in action. To this the prevailing popular opposition to economic concentration and the corrupt tendencies of politics of the spoils type contributed. Thus a prevailing type of thought regarding the government tended to a certain kind of contempt for it, not the type of theoretical dislike entertained by the anarchist, but a feeling that energetic government internally was more likely to make trouble than otherwise in the evolution of the nation's industries, just as labor was thought of frequently as a potential source of " trouble." Government was a necessity, but it was a corrupt, ignorant and weak thing, to be roughly handled and sharply spoken to when contact with it became necessary — useful in times when force was needed at home or abroad for the protection of persons or property, but dangerous in that when once galvanized into action it showed a tendency to continue its activities. Its enthronement and its abdication were both awkward. Thus the political *mores* of the leading group was divided against itself. On the one hand, it preached patriotism, devotion to the state in international affairs, and in internal affairs respect for law and order as often as it became necessary to call upon the government for protection of persons and property in industrial disputes; but on the other hand the broader social interests of the state, the majesty of the public purpose, the supremacy of the common interest against the special, could not be too vigorously emphasized. Nor could corruption be too strongly condemned, nor spoils politics too vigorously assailed; for these were instruments of control under the given situation and with the given purposes and methods accepted as practically necessary, although theoretically indefensible. Thus there came to be a hopeless conflict in ideals within the inmost mind and heart of those who held the power.[20] The new

[20] See H. G. Wells, " Social Forces," p. 335.

group had no roots running back deep into the past;—
neither the sanctions of ancestral origin, the solid backing
of established religion, the lure of the *jure divino,* or traditional responsibility for the government; — only the
fact of present day power in unaccustomed and busy
hands. They did not have time to " transform their
might into right " or the obedience they claimed into duty;
to create the " higher conservatism " of Europe. Ruthlessness, then, was a characteristic method, brutal exercise
of power as power, unwillingness to appeal to ethics or
theory or systematic interpretation of events, for all
types of ethics, theory and interpretation were hostile to
the current methods : and the appeal would be made in vain
to these jurisdictions. Without the prevalence of spoils
politics, with a government possessed of more vigor and
initiative, with other theories in the public mind regarding
economic concentration, a different position might have
been taken. And as the end of the period approached
there came a change in the view taken by large scale
" business " as on the other hand there was a change in the
democratic theory of large scale enterprise; and as the
grip of spoils politics tended to weaken somewhat, and as
the government grew in strength, and energy and leadership, the " higher conservatism " tended to appear, and
the coarser type of earlier conservatism, developed during
through alliance with corrupt politics, to give way.

Many of the conspicuous features of the earlier periods
of American history survived during the last half-century.
Some of the characteristics noted by De Tocqueville [21] in
1835 were commented upon by Bryce [22] in 1888, and

[21] " Democracy in America." [22] " The American Commonwealth."

Muensterberg [23] and Wells [24] twenty years later.   In reviewing the predictions made by Hamilton and De Tocqueville, Lord Bryce indicates the defects in the prophecy of
these publicists. [25]

Among the fundamental features were the absence of
an official governing group resting upon an hereditary or
class basis as in European countries.   The beginnings of
a large class of administrators were found in the expansion of governmental activities, but there was no trace
here of the hereditary system or position based upon class
connection.   The American merit system was open to all
without social discrimination and without particular preliminary requirements of a financial nature.   The professional " politician " on the other hand, was not recruited from any special class or group to the exclusion of
others.

Another striking feature of American political life was
the almost complete absence of the military caste or class
conspicuous in nearly all of the contemporary European
states, and often so powerful in the determination of
national policies.   The powerful military equipment
created during the strenuous years of the Civil War was
completely disbanded and its members quietly took their
places again in the ranks of civil life.   Individual officers
became prominent in public affairs, and associations of
veterans, North and South, exerted a considerable influ-

[23] " The Americans " and in " American Traits."
[24] " The Future in America."   See also Paul de Rousiers, " La
Vie Americaine," 1892; Angelo Mosso, " La Democrazia nella
Religione e nella Scienza " (1908), ch. 8, 10.
[25] Bryce, " Constitutions," p. 358.

ence in politics, but this was the voice of civilians, not of soldiers. Nor was the ceremonialism and formalism of the European governments introduced in America during this period. Another continuing feature of American life was the general freedom of occupation and trade. The exceptional mobility and versatility which characterized the national life during the early generations of its existence remained, though in less pronounced degree during the period under discussion. Nowhere was mobility of land, mobility of labor, and interchange of occupation more notable than here. It is true that specialization of activity under the stress of the division of labor tended more and more to limit this freedom, but for the time being the same tendency endured, little diminished from its original course. Taken in connection with the constantly shifting population from section to section, and from rural region to urban community, together with the great influx of immigration, the effect of this general tendency was very great. On the one hand, it operated to make the crystallization of fixed classes and of class points of view difficult, while on the other hand it tended to prevent or delay the formation of those necessary "common understandings" upon which all successful government rests in last analysis. As the limit of free land was reached, as the organization of trades unions was perfected, as combinations of capital became more and more powerful, as the many types of specialized occupation developed, the mobility of life tended to diminish; but on the whole, during this period, had not yet so far diminished as to reduce seriously the importance of this characteristic, so long distinctive of American economic and social life.

A powerful democratizing influence at work throughout this period was that of education — perhaps the most powerful of all. The school system expanded rapidly and also made notable advances in the quantity and quality of work. In no field of social activity was more rapid progress made than in that of public education. In the South this movement was delayed, but toward the latter part of the period remarkable advances were made here. Free and compulsory in character, the school system was a ceaseless factor in democratization. At the same time, high schools, colleges and universities sprang up in all parts of the country, and helped in the general enlightenment of the community. It would be impossible to discuss here the details of this comprehensive and important movement, but it is important to note the development of public education — everywhere the corner-stone of free government.[26]

The school, the magazine, the book, all developed with the very greatest rapidity; and they all pointed in the general direction of intelligent consideration of democratic problems. At the same time, the expansion of leisure through the shortening of the hours of labor opened the way to education for thousands. In the same way the enormous growth of the press aided in the great processes of democratic discussion, although toward the end of the period portions of the daily press tended to fall

[26] See C. H. Judd, "The Evolution of a Democratic School System," 1918; E. P. Cubberly, "Public School Administration," 1916; "Public Education in the United States," 1919.

under the special control of particular interests. Mr. Hart says, "The great newspaper is no longer a voice — it is a property." Yet a democratic circulation is the basis of power in any case.

Another early American characteristic continuing through this period was the separation of church and state. This was accomplished during the Jacksonian democracy, and no change was made in the last half of the century in the status then established. To the previous diversity of religious sects, there was added during the last fifty years a large infusion of the Catholic element, and of the Jewish also, particularly during the last quarter of the century. This very multiplicity of religions tended to preserve the spirit of toleration and to maintain the doctrine of the separation of the church from the state. In the rapid development of the far reaching system of public education the same principle held through. No provision was made or even seriously considered for the allotment of school money to any particular denomination or creed. Educational facilities supplied by particular religious faiths were maintained at private expense, although in some instances payments of public money were made to various charitable or correctional institutions under religious auspices. Almost the only evidence of the union of the church and state was seen in the general immunity from taxation accorded to properties held and utilized for religious purposes.

In short, there were working in America in the main the same forces that were operating in the Occident generally, the same influences of modern Industrialism, of Urbanism, of Feminism, with the challenging need of interpreting democracy in new terms to meet the changing situations. Imperialism, Militarism, Socialism, were less active as political agencies here than elsewhere. Only during the last years of the period did they become factors of material importance. Militarism scarcely troubled us, while the figure of Pacificism loomed large, as the Great War drew nearer. Our population was less homogeneous than that of most, though not all European states, and was further complicated by the race problem of the South. The migratory movement of our population within the nation was without a parallel elsewhere. Our educational system was more democratic.

In comparison with the earlier years of American development, the most striking changes were those brought about by the rapid concentration of a heterogeneous population, the swift increase in manufacturing and commerce, the new types of industrial organization both of capital and labor. America had ceased to be a rural, agricultural state, and had become a partly rural, partly urban, nation, with industries partly agricultural, but partly commercial, with capital, labor and agriculture organized in varying degrees of compactness. A mighty process of urban and industrial concentration was going on, under the forms and traditions of rural democracy. Industrially, geographically, socially and politically the sources and seat of power were shifting.

CHAPTER II

AT the close of the Civil War the two great problems which had absorbed the attention of publicists and political philosophers since the birth of the Republic, lost their hold upon popular interest. Whether the nation could endure and whether the institution of slavery should survive : — these were no longer urgent questions for the statesman. Detailed political readjustments and revisions touching the Union and slavery were necessary, but as major issues they were definitely laid aside. The international duties and obligations of the United States were not regarded as pressing problems for half a century, except at the close of the Spanish war. Hence the way was clear for the intimate consideration of the internal problems of democracy. Swift and far reaching changes in the industrial and social world, made a reconsideration of the scope and structure of democracy all the more urgently necessary; made it, indeed, impossible to avoid meeting the new problems face to face and earnestly undertaking their solution.

In the American Revolution the chief political problems had been those of independence, primarily an international question, and the establishment of popular government instead of hereditary rule. The problems were stated in terms of the natural law philosophy then

35

in vogue throughout the world; in fact the identical philosophy which had been invoked by the English revolutionists against the old regime in the seventeenth century. The natural rights of the colonists were closely related to the ancient rights of British subjects. The construction of the local governments of the states carried with it necessarily a broad discussion of structural problems, and the outcome was the abolition of the hereditary principle, whether applied to the head of the state, or to any subordinate branch, and the erection of a Republican edifice. The intense localism of the time, together with the fear of possible recurrence to monarchy, induced the establishment of a system of checks and balances on a scale hitherto unequaled. But in the main the Revolutionary issues were not class questions. They turned primarily upon economic and political independence of a distant nation, and the measures and safeguards, whether federal or local, which were necessary to guarantee American independence, and to ensure representative and responsible government.

Under Jefferson, the spirit of democracy, rather than any particular program, triumphed over various tendencies which might have meant a return to the spirit and purpose of English institutions, unless checked by vigorous, and perhaps undisciplined expression of the democratic sentiment. The Jeffersonian democracy rested upon an agrarian foundation, as distinguished from the commercial interests with which the Federalists were more closely identified. Yet Jefferson neither outlined nor executed any striking program in the evolution of democratic institutions, although he gave a powerful impetus to the development of democratic spirit. He was a prophet and preacher of democracy, rather than a builder of democratic institutions.

The later democracy, incarnated in the dramatic personality of " King Andrew Jackson," more nearly represented a section and a class — the south and west, together with the smaller tradesmen and mechanics, against the mercantile east. During this era there was no change in the general principles of democracy, but their practical application was very greatly broadened. Human personality was substituted for the property qualification for voting and office-holding, and provision was made for popular referendum upon amendments in the organic law of the states. The popular election of many different offices was established by various constitutional amendments. The life term of the judges was changed to a limited tenure. The position of the executive, both constitutionally and politically, was greatly strengthened. On the economic side, the center of interest was the attack upon the United States Bank, as a general representative of the power of wealth in politics and industry.

The bitter controversy over slavery covering the generation prior to the Civil War, reduced the formulas of democracy to extremely simple terms, so plain, in fact, that there could be little real discussion of their significance. On any democratic basis, the entire deprivation of the civil rights of any group of adult citizens, and their permanent assignment to the status of property, was wholly indefensible. The fine-drawn theoretical argument in favor of slavery advanced by Calhoun and others, was after all a specious anachronism which could not

survive either the assaults of democracy, or the stern
verdict carried by the economic advantages of free
labor in the United States. During this struggle many
really divergent forces readily combined upon the formula of anti-slavery, or slavery restriction in some modified form. When the battle lines were so plainly drawn
between freedom and slavery, there was no occasion for
refinement in the principles of democracy. An adequate
rallying point was the general belief that all men are entitled to certain civil rights which should everywhere be
respected, and the specific application was made to the
status of the colored man. The union of slavery and
secession hastened the downfall of both. The overwhelming tendency of the time, the world over, was
toward nationalism and the abolition of slavery. The
battle in behalf of localism in the form of " states
rights " and secession, with the institution of slavery,
against the powerful forces of national union and the
world sentiment against human slavery, resulted in the
victory of Union and Liberty.

But with these issues settled, the way was clear for the
more minute discussion of internal democracy. It is
now fifty years that our statesmen and philosophers have
wrestled with the perplexing problems arising from the
development of democracy under urban and industrial
conditions. In this half-century many different ap-
proaches to this question have been made by many different minds. The new interpretations were as many
and varied in their scope and their shades as were the
rapidly shifting situations out of which they came. At
times the lines of demarcation were sharp and clean-cut

in their cleavage, and again they were as delicate and elusive in their finer *nuances*. Party and personal, sectional and class, relations often added to the inherent difficulties of evolving a principle. At all times liberty, equality and justice had been the despair of those who sought to confine them within the close walls of exclusive and permanent statement, and for our modern democratic theorists the task was not easy. They were, it is true, relieved from some of the ever-present European embarrassments of international relationships, alliances and dependencies, past, present and prospective. On the other hand, they were obliged to face the difficulties peculiar to America. Before entering on a detailed analysis of American political thought, it will be useful to pass in review the types of general interpretations of democracy, in their broadest form.

The earliest attempt at a formulation of an aggressive democratic political program after the War followed the precedents set by Jackson in his day. Historically, the great movement of the Jacksonian democracy had centered concretely around the attack upon the United States Bank, as the stronghold of financial aristocracy and political power. Nothing was more natural after the War than to restate this earlier doctrine in the language of the new day. The protest against contraction of the currency, the demand for larger issues of paper, or as it was called " people's money," was an easy and ready continuation of the old warfare against the bank, the " money power " and the industrial aristocracy against which Jackson had so vigorously and so successfully tilted in his day.

The Greenback Party was formed around the demand

for currency based primarily upon fiat or credit of the government, and was attractive not only as a monetary program, but also as an appeal to the latent democratic unrest caused by the development of industrial conditions. When this issue fell into desuetude, the currency dogma assumed the form of a demand for the free and unlimited coinage of silver, in which the same appeal was made as in the previous currency controversy, although on a larger scale. Ultimately this policy became the nucleus of a great political campaign under the effective leadership of Bryan. The struggle terminated in the definite adoption of the gold standard, and this seemed to close the alliance continued for nearly a generation between democratic sentiment and a particular currency specific.

At bottom, however, the new doctrine obtained its strength not from the currency program presented, but as a tentative formulation of democratic sentiment. It contained a sharp note of appeal to the agrarian element, burdened by debt, but also reached the working men of the great cities, and the smaller business men threatened by the encroachments of industrial combinations. It was neither " fiat money " nor " free silver " that constituted the prime element of cohesion among these diverse factors. It was not by accident that the opponents of monopoly in general or of the railways in particular, were ready to unite with the Greenbackers in a political movement,[1] nor that many of the various elements of social unrest and political protest, both rural and urban, centered around the later currency doctrines. In some instances

[1] See the excellent study, *Third Party Movements*, by Fred E. Haynes. S. J. Buck's, " The Granger Movement."

doubt of the adequacy of the silver program was openly announced, and in more instances might be readily inferred. It was not merely belief in the economic soundness of these money programs that gave the movements their real power. It was the widespread confidence in the minds and hearts of many that this was the cause of the people; that here the battle lines were being drawn between the many and the few. It was an affair of the heart as well as of the head — a matter of democratic sympathy, as well as intellectual calculation. In short, the currency campaigns were efforts to interpret democracy in terms of money, following the earlier efforts of the *ante bellum* days.

In the first part of the period, however, the desire to preserve the Union and the fruits of the war proved far stronger than any considerations of economic or party creed, and hence the currency demand was easily brushed aside by the larger national parties, and, when isolated, was unable to make its way alone. In the latter part of the period, however, the continued side-tracking of the currency question proved to be no longer possible. The phenomenal growth of the Populist Party was a factor that could not be ignored. The democracy surrendered to the new propagandists and the nation was compelled to meet the issues squarely. The weakness of the currency plan proposed, however, made it impossible to draw clearly the lines of democracy, inasmuch as many fundamental democrats were unwilling to accept the free silver premises as sound, and reluctantly withheld their support from the party. The passage of the Federal Reserve Act in 1913 by a Democratic Congress under the influence of a Democratic President, assisted by Mr. Bryan, may be said to mark the last of the series of attempts to construct a democratic program out of currency material.

Another attempt to formulate a program of social, economic and political reform centered around the ownership of land.   Henry George's brilliant study.   " Progress and Poverty," published in 1879, laid the responsibility for modern political and economic ills at the door of the system of taxation.   Nothing, he believed, could be accomplished until the system under which public revenues are collected from improvements on land and from labor is utterly abolished.   In their stead he proposed to substitute the single tax upon the site value of land. This he contended would accomplish several purposes. It would provide a simple and effective source of public revenue in place of the inefficient and unjust system now in vogue, and, furthermore, it would reduce the congestion of population in large cities by compelling the building upon vacant lots.   It would make impossible the acquisition of large fortunes through the increase in value of the land held, and finally, it would inaugurate a whole series of beneficent economic and social reforms.   These considerations he discussed with great keenness, vigor, and persuasive power.   Following Henry George came a long series of disciples who presented the philosophy of the single tax with great enthusiasm and effectiveness.[2]

The very large number of independent land owners in the United States, however, made it difficult to secure

[2] Among the more conspicuous of these was Louis F. Post, " Social Service," and other works; also T. G. Shearman, " Natural Taxation."

widespread adherence to the new doctrine. In the rural communities the single tax theory was coldly received. In the urban centers, on the other hand, the constitutional limitations under which practically all cities operate, prevented the adoption, or in most cases even the serious consideration of any system of taxing the large increases in urban values.[3] In fact, the land increment tax made much more rapid progress in England and Germany than in the United States, largely owing to the fact that in these countries the landlords are few and tenancy the order of the day.

No systematic political philosophy or program was contained in the theory of George. Entire reliance was placed upon the new system of land taxation, which it was confidently assumed would prove the solution of social as well as governmental problems. Yet throughout his writings ran a strong current of democratic sympathy and democratic idealism, which beyond doubt, was as broadly influential as his arguments in the field of public finance. His goal was as attractive to many as the road he indicated.

In some instances the single tax passed over into the field of land nationalization — the general ownership of all the land by the state or government through some one of its units, and in other cases, by an easy process of transition, developed into the socialistic doctrine. In the main, however, socialism and the single tax were antagonistic, and upon more than one occasion sharp criticisms were passed between the leaders of these movements. The single taxer naturally believed that socialism stood in

[3] See "Report of New York City Commission on Taxation," 1916.

the way of the more rapid advance of his doctrine; while on the other hand, the thorough-going socialist looked upon the single tax propaganda as an irritating obstacle in the way of the complete triumph of his plan for the regeneration of society.

Another type of thought took the form of a demand for political changes, particularly as a result of the developments of urban conditions and of political parties. In this group men like Tilden and Hughes were conspicuous figures. Corrupt and unrepresentative government furnished the basis for a widespread movement against the spoils system, against electoral fraud and trickery. The spirit of this effort was that of protest against the control of cities, parties and various agencies of government by small groups of spoilsmen, with largely selfish purposes. The concrete demands were made for the merit system in public service and for the Australian ballot in the earlier period, and for direct primaries, the short ballot, simplified city government in the later period, and " good " or " honest " government generally.

In the earlier period these demands were often separated from any specific relation to economic causes, and they were generally grouped together under the head of " political reform," as civil service reform, party reform, municipal reform, or sometimes they were characterized by the term " good government." It the latter part of the period the connection between " bad government " and economic disorder was more frequently announced, and there came a division in the forces of " reform." The term " progressive " came to be more commonly applied to the group of measures, directed toward reorganization of the political machinery.

In great part it may be said this legislation was designed to secure an easier and more effective expression of the will of the democracy, without considering very carefully the economic consequences. Men of diverse industrial interests often found common ground in these movements, although in the main the greatest impetus was given by the middle class, rather than by the laboring group or the very rich. As economic lines became clearer, the forces formerly allied tended to fall apart, on such definite issues as public utility policies in cities, and economic applications of the idea of " good government " elsewhere: and while they combined again from time to time, the earlier fusion became more and more difficult to effect and maintain, as the social and economic purposes of democracy came more and more into prominence. Nevertheless, there was no more conspicuous type of political thought and action than this " reform " movement upon which so much individual and organized effort was expended. On the whole, its effect on public education and political morality was probably greater than the direct effect of the elaborate program of changes in political machinery, important and significant as were these modifications.[4]

[4] " The Education of Henry Adams," p. 280: " The political dilemma was as clear in 1870 as it was likely to be in 1970. The system of 1789 had broken down and with it the 18th century fabric of a priori or moral principles. Politicians had tacitly given it up. Grant's administration marked the avowal. Such a system, or want of system, might last centuries if tempered by an occasional

The over-shadowing social feature of this period was, however, the concentration of economic power in corporate form. This movement had begun in the early part of the nineteenth century, but had not attained its full dimensions until the last half of the century.[5] The observation of this process gave rise to various movements. On the one hand there was the effort to prevent the concentration, again the effort to control concentration, and again an effort to correct abuses which arose from the unequal terms upon which the individual employer or the small business man was obliged to compete with the large corporate employer. Roughly speaking, the first of these were championed by the agrarian or middle-class commerical groups, while the latter were espoused by the representatives of organized labor. From time to time these groups made common cause in various undertakings. Generally speaking, they were more ready to combine upon personalities than upon specific measures.

The movement toward regulation of large scale industrial corporations began shortly after the Civil War. The immediate impulse to it was the industrial depression occurring in the early seventies. By far the most conspicuous of large-scale industries was the railroad, which was for a generation the storm center of political interest and action. In this movement the Grange, a national

revolution or civil war; but as a machine it was, or soon would be, the poorest in the world — the clumsiest — the most inefficient."

[5] See Cushman K. Davis, " Modern Feudalism," cited in Holmes " Minnesota," IV, p. 60. Charles Francis Adams's " A Chapter of Erie " is a notable analysis of a railroad situation. *North American Review.* 1869. Vol. 109, p. 30.

organization of farmers, was particularly active, and was for some time exceedingly effective from a political point of view. Material progress was made in the awakening of public sentiment, and various regulative laws were enacted by state legislatures, although practically the process of consolidation was not seriously retarded. In the case of Munn vs. Illinois [6] the Supreme Court held that businesses "affected with a public interest" were subject to public regulation; and thus laid the broad foundation for a program of public control. Not until 1887, however, was a plan of national regulation of railroads adopted, in the form of the Interstate Commerce Act, which was designed to lay the basis of a comprehensive policy of railroad control.

Measures for the general regulation of other corporations followed on the heels of the Interstate Commerce Act. In 1890 the Sherman Anti-Trust Law was passed, presumably the beginning of a far-reaching policy of corporate regulation. Specific enforcement of the Act was, however, long delayed, and when obtained its results were not wholly satisfactory. In 1914 the Clayton Law was passed providing for the creation of a Federal Trade Commission, with broad regulative powers of an unusual character, and authorizing the prohibitition of unfair competitive practices, and a general policy of detailed supervision over abuses arising in the course of trade.

Party movements reflecting the anti-corporation view began almost immediately after the War. The first of these was the Anti-Monopoly Party, which was also

[6] 94 U. S. 113.

allied with the Greenbackers, however, and whose program was confused with the currency program both in the public mind and in the personnel of its own leadership. Following the decline of this party there came the United Workingmen's party, which was based upon somewhat the same principle of opposition to corporate combinations, together with a developed program for the improvement of the condition of the workers. After the collapse of this movement, came the Populist party, with a radical program appealing primarily to the agricultural interests, but also enlisting the interest of the workers in the industrial centers. The Populist movement was swallowed up by the Democratic party in the free silver campaign in 1896, and with that defeat it collapsed. A more complete formulation of a policy was made by the Progressive party. The chief emphasis was laid, however, upon the machinery of the government and upon beneficent social legislation, while the anti-trust program was neither sharply formulated nor widely understood.

Many different, and at times confusing, phases of the movement for corporate regulation developed. They may be grouped as follows:

1. The demand for the recognition of the right of the government to regulate the affairs of individuals or corporations where they conflict with public interest, particularly of railways. This was the basis of the Granger movement and the Granger legislation and of later regulatory movements.

2. The demand for prohibition of the consolidation of industrial concerns in monopoly form. This was the

basis of many state laws and of the federal law of 1890 prohibiting combinations in restraint of trade.

3. The demand for the prohibition of unfair competitive practices on the part of corporations or others — the attempt to eliminate what was termed " unfair competition." The underlying theory here is that competition, as such, is beneficent and benevolent, except in individual cases, where bad practices should be exposed and ended.

4. The demand for the recognition of the large-scale industry as a permanent factor in industrial organization, with provision for full publicity of affairs, regulation of stock issues, working conditions, limitation of profits, and price fixing. The latter doctrine has been applied particularly in the case of municipal utilities and of railroads.

5. The demand for the governmental ownership of railroads, municipal public utilities, so-called " natural monopolies," and of all other industrial combinations where monopoly is established.

6. The demand for the collective ownership of all large-scale or basic means of production and distribution.

7. The demand for a policy of *laissez faire* in regard to industrial enterprise — first, on the ground that these were private businesses; later on the ground that the specific remedies proposed were inadequate, unconstitutional or inappropriate; later on the grounds of stress of international competition; and continuously on the theory that private enterprise should not be subjected to governmental interference, except in the most extreme cases.

These various points of view were not always clearly

stated or sharply distinguished, and in fact they were frequently intermingled in the same mind or in the same movement; or obscured by parties or personalities. Bryan, Roosevelt, La Follette and Wilson, represented the mingling of many points of view upon this problem, and sometimes their personalities illuminated and then again obscured, mercifully perhaps, the broad differences of opinion among their often heterogeneous followers.

At the outset many diverse elements co-operated in the attempt to curb corporate combination, but as time went on, wide variations in diagnosis and prescription appeared. These variations took the shape of political and economic theories, and of legislative and party programs. The socialists held and the labor unions inclined to believe that the checking of the growth of large scale industry was impossible, but insisted that steps should be taken to mitigate the incidental evils in the one case by the governmental ownership of industries, and in the other by a series of laws designed to protect the workers, and by industrial organization and action for purposes of collective bargaining. Likewise, many employers, sometimes characterized as "Civic Federationists" believed that large-scale production was inevitable but that strenuous efforts should be put forth to meet all the evils arising from the new situation, while retaining all the benefits of the new type of production. On the whole, the general opinion gradually shifted to the position that combination was inevitable, and that public policy should be directed toward the adequate regulation of large combinations or toward their public ownership. The idea made most rapid progress in the municipalities, where under intensive conditions typical symptoms developed more quickly than elsewhere.

In addition to the struggles to interpret democracy in terms of currency and credit, of land and the single tax, of political reform, in the narrow sense, there was through a considerable part of the period an effort to construe democratic progress in terms of the tariff. This movement was notably strong in the '80's and '90's, between the Greenback and the Free Silver campaigns. The tariff was held to be the means of enriching the few at the expense of the many, the " mother of trusts," the means of governmental corruption. Free trade or tariff revision was hailed as the remedy. Protectionism was proclaimed, however, as the cause of high wages, the protector of labor, the source of commerical development, the bulwark of national prosperity. The issue was overshadowed by the currency, railroad and monopoly problems, and did not effectively function as an interpreter of democratic sentiment.

With these preliminaries in view it was now possible to scrutinize intelligently the different interpretations made in view of and in terms of the overshadowing industrial and social fact of concentration. They do not correspond consistently to party lines or divisions, but are broad cleavages in interest and opinion. First came what might perhaps be called the theory of reaction — the defense of the industrial process in terms of political philosophy. This was not often expressed in systematic form. Possibly it would not have been acknowledged as a philosophy at all if written large and systematically. But it was a doctrine which had adherents who, if not numerous, were powerful and aggressive, and often dominated both local and national affairs, and from time to time statements were made which seemed to embody this theory. A great railroad chief once said, " The public be damned!" A great coal baron referred to the divine right of the coal miner and owner. " The rights of the laboring man will be protected and cared for, not by labor and agitation but by the Christian men to whom God in his infinite wisdom has given control of the property interests of this country." From these statements may be discerned the outcroppings of a life philosophy which dominated the activities of many men. From one point of view this was the theory of cynical and indifferent and selfish disregard of the interests of the rest of the community — what we now term an " anti-social " point of view. Fundamentally, however, it was a belief that the elect of the industrial leaders should not be subjected to interference by the rest of the people, but should be allowed to work out the salvation of the economic world.

On the whole, it was believed that the leaders if left undisturbed would accomplish more for their fellows than the industrially inferior would be able to do for themselves. It was the philosophy of exploitation, over-capitalization, cut-throat competition and political corruption employed to obtain or hold economic privilege or immunity. It was the philosophy of power and ruthlessness, based partly upon sheer selfishness and partly upon the conviction that the few should determine the life course of the many, with or without their consent. It was the American version of Nietzsche's " superman " in trade, and Bernhardi's " ruthlessness " in business —

the translation in terms of industrialism of the doctrine of the divine right and duty of the political ruler and the autocratic power and obligation of the military commander. But far from assuming its real rôle, this doctrine was not uncommonly clothed in the most correct garb of authority, morality, liberty and jurisprudence.[7] Ross thus characterized it: " A brutal selfishness as old as the Ice Age struts about in phrases borrowed from the Darwinists and bids us see in the prosperity of the wicked the success of the adapted." [8]

The systematic theory of conservatism developed more slowly. During the first quarter of the half century the democratic arguments were often so ill-formulated that they were early brushed aside as communistic, socialistic or anarchistic. However, as the industrial tendency of the time became more and more pronounced, and as the industrial and social sides of the democratic philosophy and program became more evident, the conservative theory also began to develop more clearly. The new interpretation of democracy corresponding to the new conditions was expounded by numerous authorities; sometimes by jurists and courts; sometimes by statesmen; sometimes by systematic economists and philosophers. There was, it is true, no such elaborate defence of action as was seen in England in Mallock's " Aristocracy and Evolution," or in Lord Hugh Cecil's diplomatic " Conservatism." A closer analogy is found in some of the developments of thought in France where economic con-

---

[7] Victor Yarros, " Theoretical and Practical Nietzsche-ism," *American Jour. Soc.* VI, 682.

[8] *Social Psychology*, 282.

ditions more closely resembled those in America.[9] The writings of the eminent sociologist, Herbert Spencer, particularly "The Man versus The State," were the common authority at this time, particularly in the earlier part of the period.

The conservative position turned upon two points. First, the theory of *laissez faire* as the foundation of national and personal prosperity; and second, the doctrine of the strictest limitation of the powers of government in behalf of personal and property rights. Individualism was stated in language not much different from that employed in England during the earlier part of the century, although from time to time the later arguments drawn from the Darwinian theory of the survival of the fittest were employed. Briefly stated, this theory assumes that there are certain natural laws of trade, whose operation will bring about the greatest welfare of the individual and the community. Progress depends upon the operation of free competition which is the great regulator of economic life. It ensures the survival of the fittest, the elimination of the unfit. Interference with the law of competition is paternalism or socialism. It results in the stifling of the impulses of human progress. Consequently, the ideal government is one in which the minimum of political control is found, and the maximum of opportunity for the individual man.[10] Hence it follows that all efforts to expand the functions of government should be discouraged, especially where they interfere with trade or with property rights. For it may be as-

[9] Henri Michel, "L'Idee de l'Etat."
[10] For fuller discussion on this point see Chap. XI.

sumed that if free competition is left to work its way, the elements of good will survive, and the others will disappear. There is an order of nature which will work constantly for the betterment of the race, if only men will permit its operation with the minimum of interruption. Sometimes the natural rights of man as developed in legal form in the seventeenth and eighteenth centuries were relied upon: sometimes the economic theory of *laissez faire* developed by the Manchester school of English economists, and again the language and spirit of the Darwinian doctrine of evolutionary struggle. In any event, individual liberty and property served as a defence against the encroaching tendencies of the government. As time went on and the specific abuses arising under the industrial system were more clearly outlined, it was conceded that a certain *quantum* of regulation might be necessary, but it was stoutly contended that this should be reduced to the very lowest degree. The hereditary and religious influence which led English and German Conservatives to develop a program of social reform met with belated recognition here. Only at the close of the period did the outlines of such a course begin to appear.

Senator Root for example, showed his appreciation of this situation when he said:

" The individualism which was the formula of reform in the early 19th century was democracy's reaction against the law and custom that made the status to which men were born a controlling factor in their lives."

" Now, however," said he, " the power of organization has massed both capital and labor in such vast operations that in many directions, affecting great bodies of people, the right of contract can no longer be at once individual and free. . . .

Accordingly, democracy turns again to government to furnish by law the protection which the individual can no longer secure through his freedom of contract, and to compel the vast multitude, upon whose cooperation all of us are dependent, to do their necessary part in the life of the community." [12]

At the same time there was vigorous opposition to new devices for the development of democracy in the structure of the government. The basis of this opposition was the belief that the tyranny of the majority over the minority is one of the great dangers that menace the pathway of a republic. History showed, it was contended, that an unchecked democracy would inevitably become unmindful of the rights of individuals, and particularly the rights of property. Therefore, it is essential to maintain elaborate safeguards against hasty action or against the tyrannically minded majority. The extension of the suffrage to women was not looked upon with favor. Constitutions should not be too easily amendable. Checks and balances should be preserved. The initiative and referendum, it was believed, would utterly destroy representative government. The recall of judges or the recall of judicial decisions, would break down the independence of the courts, and destroy the last safeguard of property. An essential part of the conservative program was the defence of individual rights through the courts as independent interpreters of the law.

Throughout the entire period this group constantly minimized the amount of economic distress and political and social discontent and on the other hand the possibility of progress through political methods. Movements in the

[12] Addresses on Government and Citizenship, p. 539.

direction of fundamental social change were characterized as " foreign " and " un-American," as the work of agitators and malcontents, as the " philosophy of failure." In the currency and the tariff campaigns strong emphasis was placed on the prosperity of the American workingman, and the economic welfare of the entire country as a result of the existing economic and political order. Down to 1900 it was deemed sufficient to " stand pat," satisfied with the economic and social conditions, as the highest development of modern civilization, and to denounce the dissatisfied as unsuccessful or unpatriotic or both. In the latter part of the period however this tendency was partly abandoned and it was conceded that certain changes were desirable and necessary, but that they should be made slowly and under the auspices of the group already in power. Increased governmental efficiency and broader industrial welfare began to enter into the program of the conservative who, as a generation earlier in England, began to see the importance of change and the equal importance of making the change himself.

The theory of Liberalism also developed slowly. At first, it was allied, as already indicated, with the currency program of the Greenbackers, and later with the propaganda of free silver. This alliance between democrats and currency reformers lasted for more than a generation. The democratic movement was also delayed by the divergent policies and interests of the agrarian and industrial elements, and by the numerous divisions within each of them. The Grange movement proved to be temporary in character, although revived later in the powerful organization known as " The Farmers' Alliance."

The labor movement struggled for many years with a broad division between trades unionists and socialists, with further internal divisions between the socialists and the anarchists on the one hand, and between the Knights of Labor and the American Federation of Labor on the other. Out of this array of personalities, factions, parties, policies and philosophies, came a more coherent program of democratic action and of fundamental philosophy, interpreting the needs of the time. At no time, however, and particularly in the latter part of the period, was a complete agreement reached, and the clash of person‧ alities, principles and parties was often confusing to the observer, and always delayed the forward movement of liberalism.

The earlier Liberals quickly sounded the alarm against the political corporation and corrupt combinations. That the center of the controversy would be the industrial situation was evident almost as soon as the war was over. Wendell Phillips, the great orator of the abolition movement, promptly entered the lists against the new enemies of democracy. " Land has ruled England for six hundred years," he said. " The corporations of America mean to rule it in the same way, and unless some power more radical than that of ordinary politics is found will rule it inevitably." [13]

The central feature in the new system he believed would be the railroads. " Take a power like the Pennsylvania Central Railroad and the New York Central Railroad and there is no legislative independence that can exist in its sight. As well expect a green vine to flourish

[13] " Speeches," Volume 2, p. 157. 1871.

in a dark cellar as to expect honesty to exist under the shadow of those upas trees." [14]   The specifics advocated were the eight hour day, which he defended at length, and a drastic progressive income tax.

Henry Ward Beecher denounced in most scathing terms the current standards of business ethics and politics.   The disclosures regarding Tammany Hall, he said, showed that the culprits were only boils and carbuncles, symptoms of general decline.   " There is," the eloquent pastor said, " some of your blood and some of mine in every one of those thieving rascals.   Furthermore, business has been the anvil on which have been beaten out these superlative villains."   The central point in political control is the railroads.   " We have," said Beecher, " as much to fear now from the great corporated money institutions which spread themselves from ocean to ocean, and which are every year coming more and more into the command of treasure literally uncountable, as we have to fear from slavery." [15]   Let things go on, he warned, for ten years as they have for the past twenty and the councils of this nation will issue from the directors' rooms of our great railroad corporations.   It will make no difference, he said, who is in the White House — some Vanderbilt or Scott will be our president.[16]

The fear of the control of democracy by the " money power " in some form — at first that of railroad combin-

---

[14] *Op. cit.*, 175.

[15] " Cause and Cure of Corruption in Public Affairs, Sermons," Vol. VII, p. 66, 69.   1871.   Compare D. C. Cloud, " Monopolies and the People."   1873 (4th ed.).

[16] But in 1878 he denounced socialism, labor unions and European social philosophy.   P. 820, " Red Letter Life of The Republic."

ations and later that of industrial combinations of various types — was widespread. Unceasing alarms were sounded, warning the nation of the impending danger of corporate control over the many by the few. Henry D. Lloyd, in his " Wealth Against Commonwealth " (1894), launched a sweeping indictment against industrial combinations as seen in the oil industry.[17]   Washington Gladden was likewise vigorous in his attacks.[18]

The connecting link between the older liberalism and the new is found in William Jennings Bryan, who throughout his political career struggled for democratic ideals. " The great issue," he said, " in this country today is Democracy against Plutocracy.   I have been accused of having but one idea — silver.   A while back it was said I had only one ; then it was tariff reform.   But there is an issue greater than the silver issue, the tariff issue or the trust issue.   It is the issue between the democracy and plutocracy — whether this is to be a government by the people as administered by officers chosen by the people and administered in behalf of the people, or whether government by the moneyed element of the country in the interest of predatory wealth.[19]   Political liberty, he declared, could not long endure under the industrial system which permitted powerful magnates to control the means of livelihood of the rest of the people.[20]

[17] See also, " Man, The Social Creator," 1906.   " Men, The Workers," 1909.

[18] " The New Idolatry."   " Social Facts and Forces."

[19] Speeches, Vol. II, p. 59.   See also pp. 100–119.

[20] Vol. II–88.   In his famous income tax speech in 1894 he said: " They call that man a statesman whose ear is attuned to catch the slightest pulsation of a pocketbook and denounce as a demagogue

Toward the end of the period there appeared a new democratic movement differing in spirit and technique from any that had preceded it. The significant features in this new development were the broader basis of information; a demand for important modifications in the form of the government, including the Constitution and the courts; the appearance of a more pronounced social spirit modifying the traditional individualism, although by no means abandoning it; and the formulation of a specific and somewhat comprehensive social democratic program. Underneath it lay significant changes in philosophy and point of view. It came at the end of a long period of desperate struggle for railroad control, for corporate regulation, for the elimination of corruption from political life, and of sundry movements for currency reform, tariff reform, single tax, and various forms of social idealism. Its personnel included such publicists as La Follette, Roosevelt, Wilson. There came a series of statesmen who perceived the relation between the industrial problem and politics, and attempted to hew out a democratic program on new lines of democratic philosophy. Thus we find Mr. La Follette declaring " the supreme issue involving all others is the encroachment of a powerful few on the rights of the many." [21]   Mr. Roosevelt declared that one of the greatest issues of the day was whether " property shall be the servant and not the master of the commonwealth." " We are face to face with new conceptions of property and human welfare and

any one who dares to listen to the heart-beat of humanity." Speeches I-177.

[21] " Autobiography," p. 760.

we must undertake a policy of far more active interference with social and economic conditions in this country than we have yet had." Woodrow Wilson denounced the union of special privilege and political corruption. " Every community is vaguely aware that there is a definite connection between the political machine and large scale business. Were Jefferson living," said he, " he would see what we see,— that the law in our day must come to the assistance of the individual. . . . Freedom to-day is something more than being let alone. The program of the government of freedom must in these days be positive and not negative merely." [22]

Behind many conflicting programs and plans, there was a common instinctive opposition to the rapid advances in power of the few who were gradually gaining ascendancy in the industrial world and were transforming their economic power into political. This was the common bond that often united apparently incongruous elements upon a theory or program. They agreed upon the necessity for materially extending the functions of the state, although not always upon the precise direction in which the extension should run. They agreed upon a policy of curbing the power of great combinations of wealth, but not upon a concrete method in which this plan could be carried into effect. It was not clear whether they desired to prohibit combinations, to permit and regulate them, or to place them under governmental operation. They agreed upon a policy of social legislation for the protection of the worker, especially in the latter part of this period, although the precise limits of

[22] " The New Freedom," p. 284.

the plan were the subject of controversy. Among many of the Liberal group there was a strong demand for the governmental ownership of industries which assumed monopoly form, as in the case of urban utilities and of railroads in particular.

There was a nearer approach to agreement on the political program dealing with the structure of government and democratic political leadership. The extension of suffrage to women, the initiative, referendum and recall, more flexible methods of amending constitutions, opposition to any check and balance system so constituted as to make reasonably prompt action by a majority impossible: — were widely proclaimed. There was a general disposition to emphasize the urgent need of a government sufficiently strong and sufficiently flexible to meet the changing conditions of industry and society.

It is evident that there was a cleavage between liberal at d conservative elements upon the question of a structure of the government and the nature and extent of its social program. The currency and tariff controversies delayed but could not prevent this. The divergent interests of urban and agrarian workers offered a serious obstacle to unified theory and practice. Generally speaking, if the farmers and the city workers and the small shop keepers were united they ruled, but divided, as they often were by section, party, race, religion, they fell. But this struggle cannot be understood unless it is read in the light of the great social and industrial conflict reaching throughout the nation and the world. It was partly a battle over platforms and programs, partly a war over specific material objects, partly a struggle over the possession of the ideals of justice and right — a mixed battle over the distribution and possession of material goods, and the precious justification of courses of conduct which make up the idealism of man,— the struggle of democratic ideals with new industrial and social forces.

The labor movement also produced its interpretation of democracy and social progress [23] in various forms. Of these the most conspicuous were the trades union movement [24] and the socialistic movement. Of the trades unionists there were those who favored political action, and those who were doubtful of its practical utility. The Knights of Labor representing the political action group, and also the fusing of unions with others not in the unionized crafts, obtained its maximum strength in the '80's. The American Federation of Labor represented the strict trades union movement, beginning in the '80's and steadily increasing in numbers and power.

Samuel Gompers, the philosopher and practical leader of the trades union movement for a generation, was equally distrustful of political and governmental appeals on the one hand, and of Socialism and Anarchism on the other.[25] An excellent statement of his theory is found in his presidential address of 1898. He did not expect, he said, to wake up any fine morning and find the millennium. The trades unions did not anticipate, in view of the slow development seen in history, that millions " will turn philosopher in the twinkling of an eye." In spite of all discouragements, they would keep on perfecting their or-

[23] Commons and Associates, " History of Labor in the United States."

[24] See R. F. Hoxie, " Trade Unionism in the United States."

[25] " Labor and the Common Welfare," 1920.

ganization and increasing their power. An admirable statement of his views is contained in the following passage.

" The toilers of our country look to you to devise the ways and means by which a more thorough organization of the wage-earners may be accomplished, and to save our children in their infancy from being forced into the maelstrom of wage slavery. Let us see to it that they are not dwarfed in body and mind, or brought to a premature death by early drudgery, to give them the sunshine of the school room and playground instead of the factory and the workshop. To protect the workers in their inalienable rights to a higher and better life; to protect them, not only as equals before the law, but also in their rights to the product of their labor; to protect their lives, their limbs, their health, their homes, their firesides, their liberties as men, as workers, and as citizens; to overcome and conquer prejudice and antagonism; to secure to them the right to live, and the opportunity to maintain that life; the right to be full sharers in the abundance which is the result of their brain and brawn, and the civilization of which they are the founders and the mainstay; to this the workers are entitled beyond the cavil of a doubt. With nothing else ought they, or will they, be satisfied. The attainment of these is the glorious mission of the trade unions. No higher or nobler mission ever fell to the lot of a people than that committed to the working class, a class of which we have the honor to be members."

From time to time Gompers opposed political and party action, fearing to rely too much upon the power of the government or of the entanglements of party, and con-

stantly going back to the necessity of developing industrial organization and power. " Much of our misery as
enforced wage workers," said he, " springs not so much
from any power exerted by the upper or ruling classes
as it is the result of the ignorance of so many in our own
class, who accept conditions of their own volition." [26]
Nor did he believe that the tendency toward industrial
combination could be checked by law.[27]   He denounced
both Anarchism,[28] and Socialism [29] at various times, but
he was no less tender toward political parties and the
governmental system as operated.   In short, his theory
was that of industrial organization and action rather than
political or governmental.   For our purposes, it is not
important whether this was the expression of a fixed philosophy or of an adroit policy.   At any rate, it was the
practical working theory of millions of working men.[30]

At the same time, outside the ranks of organized labor,
there were many movements for the amelioration of labor
conditions.   These assumed a wide variety of forms,—
profit sharing, arbitration, voluntary and compulsory,
modified types of collective bargaining, prohibition of
child labor, establishment of a minimum wage and working conditions for special groups, such as women; and a
multitude of ingenious devices offered as partial or total
solutions of the labor problem.

There was also the socialistic interpretation of democracy in terms of the collective ownership of the means of

[26] " Proceedings," 1898, p. 15.
[27] *Ibid.*   1899, p. 15.
[28] *Ibid.*   1901, p. 212.   Federation resolution.
[29] *Ibid.*   1895, p. 65 : 1898, p. 109.
[30] " Labor in Europe and America," 1910.

production and distribution and reaching out toward
ideals of industrial democracy, not always clearly defined.
During the ante-bellum period, Socialism had been adopted
by the idealists, by the intellectuals, and by certain men of
religious zeal, by leaders like Emerson, Channing, Greeley.
But the many tentative experiments failed and the leaders
lost their social point of view. After the Revolution of
1848 and especially after the Commune of 1870, Socialism
lost much of its earlier support. Its chief strength for a
generation after the Civil War lay with various national-
istic groups, notably those of German origin, and almost
entirely in the laboring class. Socialism encountered
many vicissitudes after the War, until it reached a party
organization and a definite stature.

From the outset there were revolutionary socialists,
and evolutionary socialists. The former group affiliated
with the Anarchists and Communists. The French
Commune in 1870, and the Anarchist affair in Chicago
in 1886, left them with no general support. The evolutionary socialists were, as a rule, state socialists, believing in the use of the government as a means of general
"socialization." Organized labor, under the powerful
leadership of Gompers, opposed the Socialist party activity, and as a political force during this period it was
not effective. Its most conspicuous figure was Eugene
Debs, who was not a political philosopher of systematic
tendencies, but an effective popular orator and agitator.
But philosophers were not wanting.

Socialistic interpretation of politics did not at first
make great headway in America. Labor was not actively
interested in its philosophy or program. Independent

parties and reforms, together with various labor movements, made heavy inroads on it, and until the latter part of the period it made no appreciable advance. The influence of Socialism in shaping American political thought was considerable, however, especially in the latter half of the period, when Collectivism loomed larger on the social horizon and when the general tendencies toward social reform began to be effective. Down to 1890, Socialism was only feebly felt, but after that time the influence of the socialistic philosophy radiated more and more widely both in the circles of organized labor and in the middle classes. Advertised by writers like Edward Bellamy in his famous " Looking Backward," introduced in fiction by Howells, and championed by a vigorous group of defenders, it made its way into the thought of the nation little by little, particularly in the great urban and industrial centers.

Toward the end of the period, syndicalism and industrial unionism appeared in the shape of the Industrial Workers of the World, opposing both political socialism and trades-unionism. They proclaimed the impossibility of political democracy and the futility of all political methods. They proposed the industry as a whole in place of the special craft as a basis for industrial organization, to recruit the unskilled worker, to abandon the field of political effort, and to substitute " direct action " through the strike and sabotage. Their philosophy was much like that of the French and Italian syndicalists, and their practical program was led by Heywood. In substance they repudiated the methods of political democracy and proposed the substitution of industrial democracy through direct action, non-political in nature.

These interpretations may be summarized as follows:

I. The doctrine of irresponsible industrial oligarchy.

II. The conservative theory of *laissez faire* and closely restricted government.

III. The liberal and progressive theory of stronger government, under more democratic control with a broader social program.

IV. The socialist program of socialization and democratization of industry as the function of the state, through political methods and forms — evolutionary socialism.

V. The trade union program of industrial democratization and social betterment through organized labor power, without independent political action.

VI. The theory of Anarchism, dogmatically opposing the state, *per se.*

VII. Syndicalism, despairing of political action, proposing communistic industrial organization instead of the state.

Of these the theories of irresponsible industrial Oligarchy, of Anarchism and Syndicalism were relatively weak, while of the remaining four the Liberal and Conservative theories were most widely held, with Socialism and Trade-unionism in powerful minorities. Toward the close of the period irresponsible Oligarchy and Anarchism declined as the other types of interpretation and leadership advanced; and the Conservative group occupied ground in the '70's and '80's, considered liberal, " laborite " or socialistic. It is always to be observed that party lines are frequently obscure, that class lines are criss-crossed and blurred, that the same person may indeed in various capacities entertain different theories, or different applications of the same doctrine.

These types of interpretations are given, not as ironclad and rigid groups of thought, for in the nature of the case the conditions were changing too swiftly to make fixed theories possible, but as general tendencies, which should make easier the analysis of the political ideas of this period.

CHAPTER III

ONE of the fundamental questions in a democracy is, who are the political people, and to what extent do they participate in public affairs? What is the theory of political eligibility, and in what ways do the eligible directly act upon the government?

The period since the Civil War has, broadly speaking, been characterized by an expansion of the electorate and by the construction of machinery for closer control over the acts and agencies of the government by the voter. In neither of these directions, however, has the line of ideas or of institutions been unbroken.

The question, who are the political people of the United States, has been answered in two ways. First the lines were expanded to include and later contracted to exclude many of the colored race. But on the other hand, the line of sex exclusion was wiped out in a large number of commonwealths. In the course of the legal and political controversy over these problems the political theory of suffrage has been a topic of widespread discussion.[1]

The question of democracy as between white and black first challenged the attention of the nation. There were three stages in this development. In the first, immediately

---

[1] Walter J. Shepard, "Theory of the Nature of Suffrage." *Am. Pol. Science Review,* Vol. VII, Supplement, 106.

following the Civil War the prevailing policy was to obliterate the color line in voting. In the second stage, the ballot was taken from the colored man in the South by various methods, in the main illegal, and in the face of vigorous protest. And in the third stage constitutional devices were constructed by means of which the colored vote in the South was practically eliminated, while the public interest in the question was less acute.

The theory of suffrage during the stormy time of Reconstruction was not separable from the war issues of which it was an integral part.[2] The argument that included the colored man in the electorate was based partly on the theory that suffrage is a natural right which all men are entitled to exercise; partly on the idea that the ballot was necessary in order that the colored man might protect himself in his civil rights; partly on the belief that this policy was necessary to maintain the Union; and partly on the hope that the dominant party would be the beneficiary of the colored vote.

The opposition to the extension of suffrage rested largely upon comparisons between the relative capacity of the white and black races and the conclusion that the negro could not intelligently exercise the franchise. Generally speaking, the rights of the state and those of the Union, party considerations, and the means of preserving the fruits of the war, were so hotly discussed that the theory of suffrage was rarely given thorough con-

[2] Dunning, W. A. " Essays on the Civil War and Reconstruction." Horace E. Flack, "The Adoption of the 14th Amendment." J. M. Matthews, "Legislative and Judicial History of the Fifteenth Amendment."

sideration. So confused was the situation that at one time after a protracted discussion the Senate voted to forbid any discrimination on account of race, color, nativity, property, education, or religious creed.[3] We ought, said Senator Sherman, to regard it as a fundamental principle of our government that all persons arriving at a certain age are entitled to equal rights.[4] Unless you show, said he, that you are willing to adopt a universal rule which tramples down their prejudices and the prejudices of other portions of the old States where they have not adopted probably the more advanced rules on this subject; unless you can show that you have dealt with this question in an enlightened spirit of statesmanship, you will be borne down by popular clamor. It will be said that this is a mere party expedient to accomplish party ends and not a great fundamental proposition upon which you should base your superstructure.

The chief champion of colored suffrage was the veteran Abolitionist, Senator Sumner, who flatly charged that the arguments against giving the colored man the ballot were the same as those against giving him freedom, and that they were made by the same persons and in the very same spirit. " There can be no States' rights against human rights," he declared. Alluding to the general argument against colored suffrage, the eloquent Senator exclaimed, " I have warred with Slavery too long not to be aroused when this old enemy shows its head under another *alias*. It was once Slavery, it is now Caste, and the same excuse

[3] "Congressional Globe," 3rd Sess., 40th Cong., p. 1040. The vote on the Wilson amendment was 31 to 27. The House refused to concur by a vote of 37 to 133 (p. 1226).
[4] "Congressional Globe," 3rd Sess. 40th Cong. p. 1039.

is assigned now as then. . . . The old champions reappear under other names and from other States, each crying out that under the national Constitution, notwithstanding its supplementary amendments a State may if it pleases deny political rights on account of race or color and thus establish that vilest institution, a Caste and an Oligarchy of the skin." [5]

Others, like Senator Willey, of West Virginia, rested the case on the consent of the government; on the principle that taxation without representation is tyranny; on the urgent necessity for guaranteeing civil rights; on justice to the negro; on the principles of human liberty; on the spirit of Christian civilization; on the belief that it was better both for white and black to improve the condition of the black man.[6]   A very common view of the case was that presented by Senator Morton, when he declared that " in this country there is no protection for political and civil rights outside of the ballot."

Eloquent protests against the amendment were made by Senators Hendricks, Bayard, Davis, Doolittle and others. Much of their discussion pugnaciously centered around the constitutional rights of the States in the federal Union, on which subject they could scarcely have ventured under the circumstances to hope for a majority.   But they did not fail to charge that the colored man was utterly incapable of intelligently exercising the suffrage.   " I do not believe," said Senator Hendricks, " that the negro race and the white race can mingle in the exercise of political power and bring good results to society. . . . I believe that it will bring strife and trouble to the coun-

[5] *Ibid.* 902.   [6] *Ibid.* 911.

try.[7] More violent was Senator Davis, who declared in the course of a debate: " Sir, there is not a negro in America who understands the principles of our government. There is not a negro living on the face of God's earth that can understand the principles of our government, and that is competent to take an intelligent or useful part in the administration of that government." [8] The race, he believed, was utterly incapable of self-government. The proposed amendment Senator Bayard said is intended to confer political power on an inferior race and if adopted will cause the antagonism of races to culminate in conflict where the two races exist in such numbers as to affect the social status of the community.[9]

The colored vote was cast in some states and was the controlling factor up to 1877, when the Federal troops were withdrawn from the Southern States. After that time the negro vote was largely eliminated, at first by various processes of force, fraud and intimidation, and later by formal amendment of State constitutions, after twenty years of struggle during which the carpet-bagger and the Ku-Klux-Klan had stirred the South and the whole nation to its depths.[10] In 1890 Mississippi began the process of constitutional limitation of the right to vote which has been carried on until the colored vote in the South has been rendered almost ineffective.[11] This result

[7] *Ibid.* 989.

[8] P. 995. Compare Senator Doolittle's protest, *Ibid.,* p. 1011.

[9] *Ibid,* Appendix. 169.

[10] A. B. Hart, " National Ideals," Ch. IV. J. A. Hamilton, " Negro Suffrage."

[11] South Carolina, 1895; Louisiana, 1898; Alabama, 1901; North Carolina and Virginia, 1902; Georgia, 1908.

has been brought about by means of educational requirements, property qualifications and the poll tax.   The so-called " grandfather clauses " were instituted and the whites excluded by other provisions were included by stipulating that the descendants of those who were voters in the year 1867 might be registered on the poll list.   The Congress of the United States, when strongly Republican, did not reduce Southern representation under the 15th Amendment.   At the same time, the Supreme Court permitted these constitutional restrictions to stand.[12]   The annexation of the Philippines raised the race question from an embarrassing angle.

The theory of the limitations on the colored vote has been stated with the utmost frankness by those who have stood sponsor for them.   Their defence was the necessity of maintaining the supremacy of the white race against colored rule.   The idea was repeatedly stated by political leaders on the platform, in constitutional conventions and in special treatises discussing the race problem, by Cable, Murphy, Page, Stone, and others.[13]   That the colored man is inferior and that his political domination would not be endured, were declared over and over again by Southern leaders.[14]   Mr. John W. Daniel said,

[12] Williams v. Mississippi, 170 U. S. 213; Giles v. Harris, 189 U. S. 475.   In a later case, however, the grandfather clause in Oklahoma was held to be unconstitutional. Guinn v. United States, 238 U. S. 347.

[13] " Debates Louisiana Constitutional Convention," 1901, p. 2937. See also *Alabama Convention Journal,* Address of John B. Knox, President, pp. 8-18. *Journal of Mississippi Convention,* Address of Judge Calhoon, President, pp. 9-11.

[14] See Geo. W. Cable, " The Negro Question " (1890), also the

" Whenever the Anglo Saxon is brought to confront the real thing and must submit to social degradation or the loss of liberty, they will accept tyranny rather than social degradation." The establishment of what was sometimes euphoneously termed, a "veiled protectorate" was strongly defended throughout the South. Mr. Murphy said, " White supremacy at this period in the development of the South is a necessity to the preservation of those conditions upon which the progress of the negro is itself dependent. Democracy, as the ignorant masses of our colored population rise to seize it, goes to pieces in their hands." Mr. Henry W. Grady declared that two races between whom a caste of race has set " an impassable gulf " are made equal in law and in political rights. " You cannot," said Senator Williams, " have any real liberty without real equality, and you cannot have real equality without real fraternity." " Side by side," said Mecklin, " with the written constitution, and its democratic principles has developed an unwritten constitution, the outgrowth of custom and tradition, and organically related to the actual facts of race differences and social conditions. This unwritten constitution is essentially white-man-democratic." [15] It antagonizes the principles of American democracy which presuppose " a social solidarity arising out of a common ethnic solidarity."

Among the more radical of the Vardaman type the

" Silent South," (1885). E. G. Murphy, " The Basis of Ascendancy " (1909). Alfred Stone, " Studies in the American Race Problem "; Thos. Nelson Page, " The Negro, the Southerner's Problem " (1904). Joseph Le Conte, " The Race Problem in the South," in " The Man and the State," p. 349 (1892).

[15] See J. M. Mecklin, " Democracy and Race Friction," p. 252.

sentiment in favor of negro inferiority was manifested not only in the movement for disfranchisement, but in the restriction of negro opportunity at every point where equality was approached.   This was evidenced not merely in the various laws providing for race distinctions,[16] but by determination to limit the further education of the negro; by toleration of "lynch law" on a considerable scale, and from time to time by the advocacy of a separation or segregation of the negro.[17]   John Temple Graves, for example, declared that "education spoils the laborer and makes him inevitably the aspirant for social and political equalities which will be forever denied him by the ruling race.   Industrial education will not win where mental education has failed."   Whether or not the colored man should be regarded as permanently inferior to the white and consequently accorded what might be termed a caste treatment, or whether opportunity for his development should be given, was freely discussed.   This latter policy was called opening the "door of hope."   The danger of holding the negro in permanent subjection was strongly emphasized by Murphy, among others, who asserted that there is no place in the South for a Helot class. He urged very strongly the danger not only to the negro but to the white as well of attempting to subjugate the

[16] Gilbert T. Stephenson, "Race Distinctions in American Law." J. E. Cutler, "Lynch Law," 1905.   "Legislation," said Justice Brown, "is powerless to eradicate racial instincts or to abolish distinctions based upon physical differences, and the attempt to do so can only result in accentuating the difficulties of the present situation." Plessy v. Ferguson, 163 U. S. 537 (1896).
[17] R. W. Schufeldt, "The Negro a Menace to American Civilization," 1907.   William H. Thomas, "The American Negro." (1901.)

colored man permanently. " To be long busied," said he, " with the task of holding a laborer by the throat is a confining and oppressive occupation — not to the laborer alone." [18]

At the same time, vigorous protests against the political subjugation of the negro were made, sometimes by the colored man himself and sometimes by his Northern defenders, in Congress and out.[19] Professor Royce, for example, considered the race prejudice of the white wholly unreasonable and merely a creation of the imagination. " Trained hatreds " he called them,[20] " race antipathies."

By the negro himself his case was frequently stated by such men as Kelley Miller (of Howard University), in " Race Adjustment " and DuBois in his touching " Souls of Black Folk." [21] DuBois in particular pressed with great eloquence the right of the negro to complete recognition in proportion to his real capacity. In modern industrial democracy, said he, disfranchisement is im-

[18] Upon the broader aspects of this whole question see J. A. Tillinghast, " The Negro in Africa and America," Publications American Economic Association, 1902. George W. Williams, " History of the Negro Race in America," 1883. George S. Merriam, " The Negro and the Nation." A. O. Stafford, " Negro Ideals." William G. Brown, " The Lower South." Atlanta University Publications. " Southern History and Politics," edited by J. W. Garner, 1914.

[19] See DuBois, " A Select Bibliography of the American Negro "; Library of Congress, " Select List of References on the Negro Question "; " Negro Year Book," 1914 — with excellent bibliography, 390–417. " The Negro Problem" by Booker T. Washington, DuBois and others. 1903.

[20] " Race Questions," p. 48 (1908). For more temperate studies of the negro see Howard W. Odum, " Social and Mental Traits of the Negro." 1910. John M. Mecklin, " Democracy and Race Friction," 1914; R. S. Baker, " Following the Color Line." 1908.

[21] See also DuBois and Washington, " The Negro in the South."

possible. In rapid succession, he pointed out, the negro lost the ballot, his civil rights, and his opportunity for education. We live, said he, " in a land whose freedom is to us a mockery and whose liberty is a lie." Industrial education and political disfranchisement of the negro, he charged, was an idea of Northern capitalism intended to make easier the economic exploitation of the South.[22]

The contrast between the leadership of Booker T. Washington and that of Frederick Douglass, the great champion of the negro slave, was pointed out by Miller. Douglass, he said, lived in the day of moral giants; Washington lives in the year of merchant princes. Contemporaries of Douglass emphasized the rights of man; those of Washington, his productive capacity. Douglass insisted upon rights; Washington insisted upon duty. Douglass' conduct was actuated by principle; Washington's by property.

The best known of colored leaders since the War was Booker T. Washington, whose unique life has been traced in his own volume, " Up From Slavery." [23] Washington's policy was to ignore, for the time being, political and

[22] DuBois said, "I sit with Shakespeare and he winces not. Across the color line I move arm in arm with Balzac and Dumas, where smiling men and welcoming women glide in gilded halls. From out the caves of evening that swing between the strong-limbed earth and the tracery of the stars I summon Aristotle and Aurelius and what soul I will, and they come all graciously with no scorn or condescension. So wed with truth I dwell above the Veil. Is this the life you grudge us, O knightly America? Is this the life you long to change into the dull red hideousness of Georgia? Are you so afraid lest peering from this high Pisgah between Phillistine and Amalekites we sight the Promised Land?"

[23] See life by Scott and Stone, 1916. The Hampton Bulletin and Atlanta University Publications contain much valuable material.

party considerations and fix attention upon securing a firm economic basis. By a proper training, he believed, the colored people might obtain a foundation upon which, when reached, they might rest securely and build safely. " The negro," he said, " will be accorded all the political rights which his ability, character and material possessions entitle him to, but help must come mainly from within." The duty of the negro was, he believed, to " deport himself modestly in regard to political claims, depending upon the slow but sure influences that proceed from the possession of property, intelligence and high character for the full recognition of his political rights." He affirmed his belief that the colored man should vote. But in the South, " we are confronted with peculiar conditions that justify the protection of the ballot in the states for a while at least, either by the educational test or property test, or by both combined; but whatever tests are required they should be made to apply with equal and exact justice to both races." His policy was never more clearly expressed than in his well known phrase: " In all things purely social as separate as the fingers; yet one as the hand in all things essential to mutual progress."

One of the striking features in the political theory and practice of this period was the extension of the suffrage across sex lines. The Fathers of the Republic had made no provision for votes for women. John Adams' wife, Abigail Adams, had once written him on the subject, but had received in reply a series of humorous objections.[24] Richard Henry Lee, however, favored woman's suffrage. The right to vote had been limited to men except in the

[24] Laura E. Richards, " Abigail Adams," p. 138.

State of New Jersey, where the Constitution makers of 1776 inadvertently omitted the word " male." [25]

Woman's notable part in the Civil War gave her a hearing, and immediately the demand for woman suffrage received extended consideration. First came the debate over the right to vote in the District of Columbia, then extended discussion in constitutional conventions such as those of New York, Michigan and Illinois.[26]   In 1878 an amendment to the United States Constitution was presented [26a] and for a generation the theory and practice of woman's suffrage has been debated in Washington. In the various memorials and petitions presented, in the speeches made on these occasions, and on the floor of both houses, may be seen the ebb and flow of the suffrage movement. In 1869, the women were given the ballot in Wyoming; in Washington, in 1883; in Colorado in 1893; in Utah and Idaho in 1896. A temporary lull in the movement was followed by a renewal of interest after the Progressive campaign of 1912, in which woman's suffrage

[25] Kirk H. Porter, " A History of Suffrage in the United States," Chapters 6 and 9. " The History of Woman Suffrage," four vols. edited by Susan B. Anthony and others. Ida Husted Harper, " History of the Movement for Woman Suffrage in the U. S." F. A. Cleveland, " Organized Democracy," Chap. XI. " The Woman Suffrage Year Book," 1917, bibliography, pp. 193–204. Earl Barnes, " Woman in Modern Society," 1912. An elaborate bibliography is given in Margaret Ladd Franklin's " The Case for Woman Suffrage," 1913.

[26] Horace Greeley, proposed a delegate Convention of women to offer suggestions as to subjects of interest to women. Mrs. Greeley, however, was one of the petitioners for suffrage.

[26a] After the decision against woman suffrage in Minor v. Happersett, 21 Wallace 112, in which it was held that the 14th Amendment did not confer suffrage upon women.

was a significant factor, and by 1914 twelve states had
adopted the principle of equal suffrage.   In the meantime
school suffrage and various forms of limited suffrage had
been adopted in about half the states.

The early theory of the case for suffrage was strongly
presented by Wendell Phillips in his striking address,
" Shall Women Have the Right to Vote," in 1851.   A
powerful statement was made by George William Curtis
in the New York Constitutional Convention in 1867.[27]
In the earlier years of this period particular emphasis was
laid by advocates of equal suffrage upon legal equality
and upon educational opportunity, and upon the right to
practice professions and to participate in public activities.
In the latter part of this period greater stress was placed
upon the economic, intellectual and cultural aspects of the
controversy.   Naturally in the later years more attention
was given to the practical workings of the equal suffrage
system where it had been put into actual operation.[28]

The suffrage argument followed at the outset certain
broad lines of approach.   The Revolutionary principle
that taxation without representation is tyranny was frequently revived.   Why, it was urged, should women tax-
payers be unable to express their opinion upon laws by
which their property may be taken while non-tax-paying
men were given the right to vote?   More immediately
effective, however, were the contentions regarding the legal

[27] " Orations and Addresses," I, 179–214; see also ' Fair Play for
Women," 1870, pp. 215–38. Compare the argument in Parliament,
1867, by John Stuart Mill.
[28] See Helen L. Sumner, " Equal Suffrage," discussing Colorado's
experience.

disabilities of women.   The common law theory of the *feme covert* did not accord to married women the right to hold personal property.   She could not enter into contracts, she could not undertake a suit at law, was not entitled to her own earnings, and in many other ways was not regarded as a legal person, and was seriously restricted in personal rights.[29]   These legal disabilities were coupled with the inability to vote, and were held to be the inevitable consequence of representation through others.

It was also believed that suffrage was a natural right and one of the inherent and inalienable privileges of human beings under the laws of nature.   This was the same theory that non-voters had employed in the first half of the century against those who clung to the idea that suffrage should be restricted to those who possessed taxable property, preferably real estate.   At this time it was said that all adult human beings are partners in the great enterprise of democracy, and all alike are entitled to share in political activity.   This theory had just been followed in the enfranchisement of the negro and was both familiar and forceful.   It was the argument that had rocked the country during the days of the long struggle for universal manhood suffrage and still carried with it a powerful appeal.[30]

With the rapid development of urban and industrial tendencies and the serious menace to the health and comfort of women and children, the considerations advanced in behalf of suffrage for women were somewhat altered

[29] Isidore Loeb, " The Legal Property Rights of Married Parties," 1900.   E. A. Hecker, " A Short History of Women's Rights," 1910. M. Ostrogorski, " Rights of Women," 1893.

[30] Merriam, " History of American Political Theories," Chap. V.

to meet the new conditions.[31] The need of legal protection of women in industry was strongly urged at the outset and in many states remedial legislations was obtained. With the entrance of large numbers of women into industry outside the home there came new situations imperatively requiring new types of protection. This factor had not been wholly neglected in earlier discussions, but was inevitably more strongly emphasized as larger and larger numbers of women left the home to take part in industrial activities. It is not without significance that the American Federation of Labor endorsed woman's suffrage in 1886.[32] It was now contended that the ballot was necessary in order to protect working women as well as working men, in regard to wages, hours, and working conditions, particularly in view of the fact that the unionizing or organizing of women was found to be more difficult than the same process among men. " Experience has fully proved," says Mrs. Stanton, " that sympathy as a civil agent is vague and powerless unless reenforced by effective power." All workers must possess the ballot in order to obtain legislation necessary for the adequate protection of women. Children, too, are included in the

[31] Dr. Azel Ames Jr. " Sex in Industry, A Plea for the Working Girl." 1875.

[32] Florence Kelley, " Some Ethical Gains Through Legislation "; Edith Abbott, " Women in Industry "; Carroll D. Wright, " Industrial Emancipation of Women "; Rheta Childe Dorr, " What Eight Million Women Want " (1910) ; William Hard, " The Women of Tomorrow," (1911) ; Helen Campbell, " Women Wage Earners," 1893. Abbott and Breckinridge, " The Wage Earning Woman and the State." (1912). Ida M. Tarbell, " The Business of Being a Woman." Correa Moylan Walsh, " Socialism and Feminism," 1917. Mary Roberts Coolidge, " Why Women Are So," 1912.

ranks of defenceless laborers whose rights women might protect.

The urgent needs of women were also indicated and emphasized as the problems of city development became more and more urgent.[33]   Most of the departments in an American city, it was said, can be traced to woman's traditional home activity, but in spite of this as soon as these affairs are turned over to the city they slip from woman's grasp.   It was pointed out that city government is to a considerable extent municipal housekeeping on a large scale and that in this process women are intensely and directly interested.   Food supply, water, sanitation, schools, play grounds, are of peculiar interest to women under the conditions of modern civil life.   Said Jane Addams: " If one could connect the old maternal anxieties, which are really the basis of family and tribal life, with the candidates who are seeking office, it would never be necessary to look about for other motive powers; and if to this we could add maternal concern for the safety and defence of the industrial worker, we should have an increasing code of protective legislation." [34]   In this way urbanism and industrialism are linked together in a defence of the cause of woman's suffrage.

This period also witnessed the closer examination of character and capacity of women as an evidence of qualification for participation in the elective processes.   With the general education of women, the intellectual possibili-

[33] See Jane Addams' " Newer Ideals of Peace." Mary Ritter Beard " Woman's Work in Municipalities." Helen Christine Bennett, "American Women in Civic Work." W. H. Allen, "Woman's Part in Government."
[34] Op. cit. p. 207.

ties of the feminine mind soon became evident, and the brilliant leadership of such women as Susan B. Anthony, Elizabeth Cady Stanton, Mrs. Catt, Jane Addams, and scores of others was in itself an argument of no mean power. The crude claims of sex equality early advanced by Victoria Woodhull [35] and others of her school were soon displaced by more scientific studies.[36] The intellectual traits of woman were more carefully scrutinized, and the specific value of her contribution to the joint cultural product of life more fully set forth.

Lester F. Ward, the eminent sociologist, early defended suffrage for women on broad biological grounds.[37] In his gynaecocentric theory [38] he maintained that the female sex was originally and is normally superior to the male; that the female is the more stable type; that control was temporarily wrenched away from the female, but that the steady and inevitable tendency is toward the domination of the female type. This idea, expressed in scientific terminology, has served as a basis for many who have adopted his position.

Mrs. Gilman elaborated the doctrine of feminine

[35] " Principles of Social Freedom," 1874.

[36] Mary Putnam Jacobi, " Common Sense Applied to Woman Suffrage," 1894; Helen B. Thompson, " The Mental Traits of Sex." W. I. Thomas, " Sex and Society," 1907; Theresa Schmid McMahon, " Women and Economic Evolution," 1912. Compare " Homo Sum " a brilliant argument by an English writer, Jane Ellen Harrison.

[37] " Dynamic Sociology," p. 648, The Subjection of Women; also " Psychic Factors in Civilization," Ch. 26.

[38] " Pure Sociology," Chap. 14 (1903); Compare W. W. Knight, " The Gynaecocentric Theory in the Light of Modern Biology." Leta Stetter Hollingsworth, " Variability as Related to Sex Differences in Achievement," in *American Journal of Sociology*, 1914, Vol. XIX, 510. XX, 335.

superiority in her sprightly volume "The Man-made World; Or our androcentric culture" (1907), dedicated to Ward. That one sex should have monopolized all human activities, called them man's work, and managed them as such is what is meant, she said, by the phrase, "androcentric culture." This man-made world she analyzed with great enthusiasm and acuteness. She pronounced force to be the natural governing agency of man, while love and common service are the maternal contribution. Destruction is the method of man; selection the way of woman. She contended that there had never been a democracy but merely an "andocracy," and further expressed the confident belief that all genuine economic democracy must rest upon a free womanhood. Here, in short, was a demand for something other than a traditional man-made world, a plea for legal, political and social equality in the broadest sense of the term. In this movement the contest for political equality becomes merely one of the elements in a far wider industrial and social struggle.[39]

Where women are like men they should have like liberty, and where they are different, the differences require representation, reasoned Dr. Jacobi.[40] The most important effect of suffrage is "psychological," the "consciousness of power for effective action." This has made men in free nations energetic, intelligent and powerful, and will react upon women in the same way. The ballot in short is necessary for the expression and development of woman's personality in a free world.

[39] See also Charlotte Perkins Gilman, "Woman and Economics." 1898. Elsie Clews Parsons, "The Old-fashioned Woman," 1913.

[40] Op. cit. 180.

But it may be urged that the government rests in last analysis upon force, and that this is in the possession of the masculine sex. To military functions and the maintenance of order by force, women are not adapted. This was characterized as the " Rob Roy argument." [41] And the reply was made " if women do not bear arms, neither do men bear children." " The man who exposes his life in battle can do no more than his mother did in the hour she bore him," said Dr. Jacobi. Further, the function of militarism tends to decline and disappear, while the function of maternity persists. Physical force as an agency is less and less employed, while the feminine qualities and traits are increasingly adapted to an industrial civilization, as distinguished from the militant type. Or from the point of view of physical force, if this is the test of suffrage, then men not of military age or capacity should be eliminated, while women capable of war-work, or possessing undoubted physical capacity for hard labor, should be included. Such a theory of suffrage, however, has never been put forth or applied, and if it were, would exclude many male voters and include many women.[42]

The woman's suffrage theory rested on a progressive, economic and cultural advance of women, raising the level of education, developing types of organization with recognized leaders, sharpening ambitions and ideals. Mrs. Catt once said that in 1800 the remonstrants were horrified at woman's learning geography; in 1810 at physiology; in 1820, geometry; in 1830 at college education;

[41] T. W. Higginson, "Common Sense about Women." 1882.
[42] See Jacobi, op. cit. Jane Addams, " The Long Road of Woman's Memory." 1916.

in 1840 at property rights for married women; in 1850 at speaking in public; in 1860 at freedom of organization; at 1870 at entrance into profession; in 1880 at school suffrage; in 1890 at holding of office; and in 1900 at the burden of voting.[43]

The demand for the ballot and political equality was of course only one phase of the feminist movement for improvement of the condition and opportunities of women.

The political struggle was perhaps the most dramatic, but back of it was the more quiet educational and economic progress.[44]   The ballot was an instrument of power, but also a symbol of social recognition, the evidence of emancipation.   With the changed intellectual and economic position of woman, came the quickened social consciousness, of which the political was a part.

At the beginning the suffrage movement was greeted with hilarity, with mingled amusement, surprise and contempt.   When a petition was presented to the Judiciary Committee of the New York Assembly in 1856, containing signatures of husband and wife, they reported that " they would recommend the parties to apply for a law authorizing them to change dresses, so that the husband may wear the petticoats and the wife the breeches, and thus indicate to their neighbors and the public the true relation in which they stood to each other." [45]   Much was made of the charge that suffrage advocates were merely notoriety seekers with an abnormal craving for publicity. Suffrage meetings were broken up at times, and the move-

[43] See Anthony, " History," IV, 392.

[44] Julia Jesse Taft, " The Woman Movement from the Point of View of Social Consciousness." 1915.

[45] Cited in Anthony, " History," I, 630.

ment proceeded only under the most serious practical difficulties. Economic and educational opportunities for women opened slowly.[46]

The body of theory opposed to woman's active participation in the affairs of the democracy did not develop as early as the philosophy of its advocates. No theory was needed, in fact — merely the preservation of a *status quo*. Custom, not reason, was the first as well as the last line of defence.[47] By far the best statements, however, were those contained in the debates of the various State constitutional conventions and in the discussions of amendment before Congress. A notable argument was that of Elihu Root in the New York Convention in 1894.

At first the objections to including women in the electorate centered around woman's " proper sphere." Those who opposed the extension of the ballot to women believed that God and nature had destined her to a non-political circle of activity from which she should not emerge. Scriptural citations from Adam's rib to St. Paul's command were piously employed to show that woman was

[46] S. Yundelson, " The Education and Professional Activities of Women," *Annals America Academy* XXV, 117.

[47] For statements of the case against woman's suffrage see — Pamphlets issued by the New York State Association Opposed to Woman Suffrage; Helen R. Johnson, "Woman and the Republic," 1897, Elizabeth McCracken, "The Women of America"; S. M. Buckley, "The Wrong and Peril of Woman's Suffrage (1909,"; Mr. and Mrs. John Martin, "Feminism"; Edward D. Cope, "The Relation of the Sexes to Government," 1888; James Weir, Jr., "The Effect of Female Suffrage on Posterity," in "The American Naturalist," 1895; Henry A. Stimson in "Bibliotheca Sacra," 1910, p. 335. Compare the much more complete argument of the English writer, Frederic Harrison, "Realities and Ideals."

divinely intended for a position of obedience and not for a position of co-operation or command.[48]   Religion was invoked against suffrage for women by Senator Freylin-huysen, who said, " The angel, it is true, appeared to Mary, but it is in the God-man that we are all alive." Some feared that the vote of woman would add to the power of the priest and Catholicism.

Great reliance was placed upon the argument touching the relation of government and force.   Women are unable to perform military duties, hence they should not undertake the task of government.   Although in a numerical majority, they would be unable to enforce their decrees if the male minority forcibly objected.   Physical power and responsibility ought not to be separated, and hence women should not exercise any other than an indirect influence in political affairs.   In 1866 Senator Williams said : " Sir, when the women of this country come to be sailors and soldiers ; when they come to navigate the ocean and follow the plow ; when they love to be jostled and crowded by all sorts of men in the thoroughfares of business ; when they love the smoke and dust of battle better than they love the enjoyments of home and family, then it will be time to talk of making the women voters ; but until then the question is not fairly before the country."   Others held that " in the settlement of our questions by force women are only in the way."   Said one : " Men may grant women anything but the right to rule them, but there they draw the line."

It was commonly held by the opponents of woman's

[48] Rev. J. D. Fulton, in " Woman As God Made Her," 1869, summons God, Nature and Common Sense against Woman Suffrage.

suffrage that the franchise is not a natural and inherent right, but a matter of fitness.   It is bestowed upon individuals by society as a matter of social expediency, and may not rightly be demanded by any one merely upon abstract grounds.   There can be no question of any deprivation of natural and inalienable rights of women.

It was further held that political interest is a prerequisite of suffrage, a necessary condition of entrance into the circle of the electorate; and it was believed by many that womankind was not commonly interested in and did not desire to have the ballot.   In Massachusetts in 1895 the question of woman's suffrage was submitted to women, who voted 22,204 for and 861 against.   The men's vote at the same time was 86,970 for and 186,115 against.   In the latter part of this period active organizations of women opposed to the grant of suffrage to their sex were formed, and these in many instances carried on vigorous campaigns.   The substantial political interest and capacity shown by enfranchised women and by other groups interested in public affairs in the later years made this line of reasoning less effective.   Both the friends and the foes of suffrage were stirring the political interest and awakening the political consciousness of women.

The chief objection to woman suffrage, from first to last, lay in the theory that natural sex differences have set out a separate sphere for woman, and that politics is not included within that sphere.   This was sometimes stated in the most florid language of compliment and chivalry, and again in terms of physical and psychical differences.   Sometimes it was " the hand that rocks the cradle rules the world " and again it was the elaborate

terminology borrowed from science.[49]   Now it was held
that woman's brain is smaller than that of man; her
emotions dominate her intellect, instinct replaces reason,
hysteria common sense.   Again it appears that the establishment of equal rights, will be " the first step toward
that abyss of immoral horrors so repugnant to our cultivated ethical tastes — the matriarchate.   Sunk as low as
this, civilized man will sink still lower — to the communal
Kachims of the Aleutian Islanders.[50]   Others believed that
women were incapacitated for voting because of various
psychological traits, as, for instance, idealism or emotionalism, both of which were regarded as dangerous elements.[51]   Emotionalism in undue proportions may un-
settle the equilibrium of states, while idealism may be
unwilling to deal with the practical difficulties which condition all human progress.   If the feminine element is
added to the electorate, the tendency will be a profound
modification of our national point of view and ultimately
our national policies.

To others, woman suffrage seemed, as in the earlier
days, to be tinged with radicalism, and in our day the pre-
cursor of socialism.[52]   Woman's vote is inconsistent with
republican government, and woman's suffrage has been

[49] Dr. W. A. Hammond, *North American Review,* 137, 137 (1883);
see also W. K. Brooks, "The Condition of Women from a Zoolog-
ical Point of View," in *Popular Science Monthly,* XV. 145, 347,
(1879).   An eloquent eulogy of "man" was given by Congressman
Bordle of New York, 1915.   63d Congress, 3d Session, p. 1457.

[50] James Weir, Jr., in "American Naturalist," 1895, XXIX, 815.

[51] F. H. Giddings, "Democracy and Empire," p. 214.

[52] See Caroline Corbin, "Woman's Rights in America," holding
that the remedy for our ills "does not lie in the direction of woman
suffrage nor any other socialistic doctrine."

allied with despotism, monarchy and ecclesiastical oppression, on the one hand, and with license and misrule on the other.[53] " The need of America," it was said, is not an increased quantity, but an improved quality of the vote.[54] Doubtless the radical tendencies of some of the earlier advocates of woman's rights and the support generally given to suffrage by liberal groups tended to create and continue this oppression.

Others argued in general that few of the economic or political evils complained of could be cured by the ballot.[55] They urged that as far as women were concerned they might be more effective without the ballot than with it; that as far as there was political interest and capacity among women, it might be most effectively applied through the exercise of the gentle art of feminine persuasion, historically standardized in its methodology. In this way the social prestige of the American woman would be preserved, while the political life of the nation need not lose the keen interest of such women as are specially adapted to governmental work. They contended that wages and working conditions of women could not be materially affected by the ballot, but depend primarily upon other than political causes; that legal equality was rapidly being attained and in some cases more than equality where special historical privileges were retained; that legislation for the protection of children was not de-

[53] See Helen K. Johnson, "Woman and the Republic," 1897, p. 321.

[54] N. Y. State Assn. Opposed to Woman Suffrage, 1894. Compare Gail Hamilton, "Woman's Wrongs," 1868.

[55] See extended argument of Henry A. Stimson, "Bibliotheca Sacra," 1910, pp. 335-346.

pendent upon the votes of women. In short, they emphasized the great importance of public opinion in the creation and enforcement of law, disparaged the efficiency of political action, and held that the political world was not a sphere in which woman might be as effective as she would be elsewhere.

Further, it was often said that the participation in political struggle will not only be the least helpful action, but it may also deprive women of the secure field of extra-political influence which they now possess. As political competitors the compliance by courtesy will be lost. The deference accorded the sex will be difficult to preserve in the new atmosphere of partisan activity,[56] and at the same time the distinctly feminine influence will be seriously impaired. Woman will be unsexed, some said, and in time become a different creature. With her will go the home and the historical traditions that center around it. Domestic harmony may be destroyed and grave evils spring up as a result of domestic neglect on the one hand, or political disagreements on the other.

Briefly stated, the underlying idea of this group was that the right to vote rests upon political interest, experience, and capacity; and that the feminine sex, measured by these standards falls short of the mark, and should be excluded from the electorate; that their active exercise of political power would be harmful to the state as a whole and to the sex; that they are already adequately represented through the family and that their indirect

[56] Helen K. Johnson, *op. cit.,* p. 284, "In order to be preserved in bodily, mental and spiritual freedom, woman must yield with grace to the hand that serves her."

influence through persuasion is more valuable to the community than their direct political action.

The general tendency of the argument was toward broader consideration of the place of woman in the life of the community. With the wider education of women in elementary and higher schools, with the entrance of women into industry outside the home on a large scale, the character of the whole discussion naturally shifted from the earlier basis over to the broader field of feminism. As woman's educational, economic and political interests and power became more evident, the line of theoretical objection to woman's suffrage gradually receded and inertia rather than argument remained to be overcome. Universal education and economic independence soon did their work, and under their combined pressure the theoretical position rapidly collapsed.

During this period there were those who believed ability to read and write to be an essential prerequisite to participation in the electoral processes of democracy. They contended that no one should be allowed to pass upon candidates or measures who could not read the language of his country, or of some country.[57] They insisted that illiterates must be strictly excluded from the electorate, and that the decision of all political questions must be reserved to those who possessed the ability to read.

In some states educational qualifications were required of voters. A number of these instances are found in the

[57] G. H. Haynes, " Educational Qualifications for the Suffrage in the United States," P. S. Q. XIII, 495 (1898). J. B. Phillips, "Educational Qualifications of Voters," University of Colorado Studies, III. No. 2, 1906.

Southern States, where this test was designed to disfranchise the negro, just as the ante-bellum restrictions had been aimed at the immigrant.[58]   But similar restrictions were imposed in certain New England States [59] and in some of the Western States.   In the territorial possessions of Hawaii and the Philippines, ability to read and write was made a qualification for voting, although in the Philippines this qualification was made an alternative to the ownership of property.   On the whole, the conclusion was reached that literacy was not an accurate test of character or of qualifications to act as an elector; and this conclusion was reflected in the constitutional law of the time.[60]

From time to time it was suggested that suffrage be limited by the imposition of property qualifications of some sort.   Appalling spectacles of political corruption frequently induced this feeling and sometimes led to specific suggestions.   A notable instance of this was the recommendation of the Tilden Commission in 1875. This body, including William M. Evarts, E. L. Godkin, James C. Carter and Simon Sterne, recommended a property qualification for local voting where taxes and expenditures were involved.[61]   In the early part of this period there was a strong tendency on the part of property

[58] See Debates in N. Y. Constitutional Convention, 1915, pp. 290 ff. See Speech of Wagner in defence of the immigrant, p. 2923.

[59] See Porter, *op. cit.,* Ch. 9.

[60] See Holcombe, " State Government," p. 150.

[61] Report of the Tilden Commission in " Municipal Affairs," III. 434.

owners in cities to favor the exclusion of non-tax payers from the suffrage; but this feeling did not find political expression. Much later Albert Kales in "Unpopular Government" (1914) advocated special property qualifications for the upper houses of legislatures. These theories of the electorate of tax payers were not adopted however. On the contrary, the few remaining property qualifications for office holding were removed and the tax-paying barriers were leveled. Even poll tax requirements were generally either removed or fell into disuse, except in the South.

The development of the theory of suffrage may be summarized in this way. The sex barrier was shattered if not wholly broken, while the race line was redrawn in the South. Educational and property tests made little progress, except when employed as a means of reducing the colored vote. The successful entrance of women into the fields of education and industry gave their demands a solidly increasing strength, while the difficulty of the colored man in striking a firm foundation either in education or in industry made it a hard struggle for him to maintain his political or even his legal equality. There was little systematic discussion of the theory upon which persons should be admitted to or excused from participation in the affairs of the state. There was some consideration of suffrage and natural rights and some attention to capacity as the basis of right; but in the main the tendency was to avoid a general and consistent theory. Looking at the three earlier barriers to completed democratic suffrage, namely, class, race and sex, it is clear that the class limitation was only feebly represented, that of race fell and rose, while that of sex was first slowly and then swiftly removed.

Assuming that it is determined who are the active citizens of the state, the next question is: What is the scope of individual participation in the government? How and where shall he touch the state directly?

The direct action of the voters in the affairs of the government was both widened and narrowed in this period. The tendency to increase the number of elective offices by transfer from the appointive list began during the Jacksonian era and was intensified as the work of the government expanded. But in this period the movement was decisively checked. Additional officers in the state and local government were sometimes made elective during the early part of this period, but later the practice declined. In the state government, the increase in elective officers approached a standstill during the end of the period, while in many municipalities the number was positive reduced, with the exception of provision for elective boards of education. In the Federal field, the number of elective officers was increased by the Constitutional Amendment providing for popular election of Senators. The demand for popular election of Federal judges, however, made no headway. On the whole the tendency was decidedly toward reducing the number of elective officials, particularly toward the end of this period.

The political idea underlying this new tendency, which came to be called the " short ballot " movement, was expounded and illustrated by many publicists.[62]   To them

[62] See Chas. A. Beard, " The Ballot's Burden," P. S. Q. 24, 589;

it seemed that democratic control is diminished rather than increased by the necessity of choosing a large number of officials. They maintained that the voter was confused by a long list of offices, with the duties of many of which he was entirely unfamiliar, and that he tended to fall back upon the party label, instead of exercising an independent judgment; that his actual control over his agents was less and not greater. " Elaborate your government," said Woodrow Wilson.[63] " Place every officer upon his dear little statute; make it necessary for him to be voted for, and you will not have a democratic government." Elections, said Childs, the active sponsor of the short ballot movement, must be interesting. Each elective office must be visible. " Hide and Seek Politics " must be ended. Power and responsibility must be made to stand out clearly. The principle of " conspicuous responsibility " of officers must be brought into play, in order that intelligent choice may be made; and in order that democracy may be made genuinely effective. Increasing the number of elective offices does not add to the extent of popular control, but on the contrary renders it weaker.

In municipal governments, this principle was generally recognized, but in the state field the change in fundamental theory was far less marked. One of the most notable statements of the short ballot idea was made

Richard S. Childs, " Short Ballot Principles "; Edna D. Bullock. " Short Ballot," 1915; " Special Libraries, Select List of Reference on the Short Ballot," 1911; " Equity Series," 15, 156–61 (1913). Debates in Ohio and New York Constitutional Conventions, 1912, 1915. Arthur George Sedgwick, " The Democratic Mistake," 1912.

[63] See *North Am. Rev.*, Vol. 191, 585.

by Senator Root, Chairman of the New York Constitutional Convention in 1915.[64]   The Senator emphasized in the clearest terms the confusion arising from divided responsibility in state government and the importance of the unification of authority.

On the other hand no little opposition developed to this new principle.   Many believed that the reduction of the number of elective officers was equivalent to the diminution of the power of the average voter; that every office removed from popular election was an office removed from popular control.[65]   Vigorous protests were made against what was conceived to be an effort to deprive the citizen of his fundamental rights.   Why not get the autocratic idea at once and be done with it, it was said.   " Do not the people know enough to govern themselves and elect their officers? "   " I hope I shall never see the strong right arm of the people withered and atrophied by the laziness that shrinks from exercising duties and bearing governmental responsibilities," said the Attorney-General of Ohio.[66]

It was charged that the movement was aristocratic in its origin and purposes, and was inspired by those unfriendly to democratic government.   It is advocated by those who are willing to sacrifice democracy to " efficiency."   It is fostered by Wall Street, and favored by the political bosses.   " Beware," said one, " when you hear the lords

[64] See " Record," pp. 3387 ff.

[65] See " Proceedings of Ohio Constitutional Convention," 1912.

[66] See speech of Atty. General Timothy S. Hogan, 1913, reprinted by National Short Ballot Organization; " Record of New York Constitutional Convention," 1915; pg. 3239. The Short Ballot Amendment was defeated in Ohio in 1912.

of invisible government denouncing invisible government." It was looked upon as an entering wedge, intended in the end to restrict the voters' control over their own affairs.[67]

On the other hand, the direct primary added the nominating process to the party electors' tasks, substituting direct choice of candidates for the selection of delegates to the conventions.[68] In this way the party voter was given a much wider field of activity than before. In the same group of duties must also be included the election of party committeemen representing the executive side of the party organization.

From another point of view the functions of the elector were enlarged by the devices known as the initiative, referendum and recall.[69] These extensions of democratic control over legislative policy and the personnel of officialdom were most widely adopted in cities, particularly in conjunction with the commission form of government; but they were also taken up by many of the states. By 1917, twenty-one states had adopted some form of the state-wide initiative, referendum or recall, while twenty-two others had adopted some form of these institutions either for all or for certain cities. In fact, there were only four

[67] The plan "came from a heart that in its inmost core hates self-government, and that seeks for opportunity to limit and control it." Brackett in New York Constitutional Convention, 1915, 3303.

[68] This topic will be more fully discussed in Ch. VIII.

[69] See E. P. Oberholtzer, "The Referendum"; Munro, "The Initiative, Referendum and Recall," 1912; Beard and Schultz, "Documents on the State-Wide Initiative, Referendum and Recall," 1912; Munro, "Bibliography of Municipal Government," pp. 48-60. A. N. Holcombe, "State Government in the U. S." Ch. 13; Debates in Congress and in Constitutional Conventions.

states remaining, Delaware, Rhode Island, Indiana and Vermont, which had made no provision for any of these new plans.

The referendum was first used in adopting constitutions or amendments, then for bond issues, public utility company franchises, city charters and liquor laws; then, together with the initiative, it was employed on a larger scale for all problems, with certain exceptions, both in the local and state fields. The political philosophy of the referendum will be discussed in connection with the development of American thought regarding representative government.

The recall was applied most largely to cities, but also to states.[70] In many instances it did not apply to judges, even where otherwise in use. The recall was designed as a check upon unrepresentative officials. Its advocates believed that only through such machinery could the recalcitrant officer be held to a decent respect for the opinions of his constituents. The underlying theory of the recall was that this device made possible a closer check on the agencies of government than under the system of fixed tenure of office. Hereditary tenure, life term, long term, short term, and finally indefinite terms are stages in the evolution of public control of all public servants, it was said. Where the processes of the criminal law and of impeachment fail, and where the pressure of public opinion is insufficient to avoid serious betrayal of public trust, the possibility of recalling the official was believed to be desirable. It was contended, in fact, that the possi-

[70] See F. T. Barnett, "Operation of the Initiative, Referendum and Recall in Oregon"; E. P. Oberholtzer, "The Referendum."

bility of the recall generally made its use unnecessary; that the recall was, in the language of Woodrow Wilson, " the gun behind the door."

In municipal affairs relatively little opposition was made to the adoption of the recall, especially when coupled with the commission form of government, in which individual officers were given wider powers than heretofore. It was there presented as an offset to consolidation of power in the commission. But when applied to states, there was much more serious discussion, and particularly with reference to judges. The chief consideration advanced against the recall was that it would tend to suppress initiative and independence in public office; to produce a timid and servile type of public agent; and that practically it would increase the difficulty of obtaining competent men for public positions by adding to the expense of elections and creating uncertainty of tenure. In general the theoretical consideration of the recall was a part of the discussion regarding the initiative and referendum and the representative system of government in its broadest terms, as well as of the bitter controversy over the degree and extent of public control over the courts.

On the whole, the theoretical and practical tendencies regarding popular participation in the work of government were conflicting. The basis of the democracy was broadened by extending the circle over the line of sex, and first broadened and then narrowed along the line of color. The electors' duties were diminished by the reduction of the number of elective offices, and increased somewhat by the development of the direct primary, together with the initiative, referendum and recall. Aside from the race question, the tendency was toward broadening the electorate and increasing direct popular control over the acts and agencies of government. The spirit and motive in these institutional changes, apart from the race limitation, was fundamentally democratic, but there was not a general consensus of opinion as to the theoretical basis of suffrage, or the theoretical limits of the electors' direct participation in the democracy.

CHAPTER IV

LEGISLATIVE AND EXECUTIVE POWERS OF GOVERNMENT

DURING this period, generally speaking, the legislative bodies continued the decline begun during the first half of the 19th century. In the individual states confidence in the representative bodies was shattered by repeated exposures of the most flagrant corruption of their members. Now it was the "black horse cavalry" of New York, and again it was the "jackpotters" of Illinois. Now it was the influence of railways, now of insurance companies, now of liquor interests, now of several special interests in combination. Subservience to the control of the political machine, failure to respond to the evident will of the community, frequent displays of incompetence and inefficiency all tended in the same direction, namely, toward the weakening of public confidence in the representative capacity of the law-making bodies in the several states.[1] There were, of course, always notable exceptions to this particularly under progressive Governors from Tilden of New York to Johnson of California.

The state legislatures, already much limited, were further restricted by the additional prohibitions of special legislation in the new constitutions and by the increasing

[1] "Distrust of State Legislatures — The Cause — The Remedy, in Governor's Conference Proceedings," 1913, pp. 214 ff. Paul S. Reinsch, "American Legislatures."

length and detail of the constitutions themselves.[2] At the same time, in many instances a popular check was established in the form of the referendum as a popular veto on the acts of law makers, while the initiative was often added as a spur to their activity. In only a few instances was any attempt made to broaden the scope of the legislatures' power. Sundry, scattering proposals were made for the application of commission government to the state or the substitution of a single chambered legislature for a bicameral, but no effective support was found for either of them.

In the national government the period opened with the complete supremacy of Congress over the unpopular President Johnson, culminating in the failure to impeach him by only one vote. During this time the legislative body unquestionably was closer to the sentiment of the nation than was the executive. But the congressional scandals of the '70's, notably that of the Credit Mobilier, shattered public confidence in the impartiality of that body.[3] Later with the appearance on the field of stronger and more vigorous rulers, such as Cleveland, Roosevelt and Wilson, this temporary predominance passed away and Congress receded into the background. The Senate in particular during this time lost much of its public influence because of the frequent corruption observed in the indirect election of its members, and the widespread feel-

[2] Charles C. Binney, " Restrictions Upon Local and Special Legislation in State Constitutions," 1894.

[3] " Report of Committee on Credit Mobilier," 3rd Session. 42nd Congress, 1872–3; Senator Hoar's speech Mch. 6, 1876, on extent of corruption, cited by Rhodes, *op. cit.,* VII, 193.

ing that the senators were subservient to the wishes of property and privilege rather than the mass of the community. At one time, indeed, the Senate was termed " the millionaire's club " because of the considerable number of wealthy men in that body. The demand for direct election of United States Senators was presented as a remedy for this situation, and after twenty years' battle was finally achieved. The persistent opposition of the senators to the constitutional amendment providing for their direct election, only added fuel to the flames of popular indignation. The final passage and ratification of this amendment making the senators directly responsible to the voters of their states, was designed to re-establish the upper house in public esteem and confidence.

The power of the Speaker of the House, great even in the days of Henry Clay, was developed during this period, but this great authority came to be linked with reactionary tendencies, and occasioned a great popular protest which finally found expression in the overthrow of the speaker, if not of the system.

On the whole, it cannot be said that the legislative branch of the Federal government materially improved its strategic position. The executive tended constantly and steadily, whenever in strong hands, to overshadow and direct it. The appeal of the President of the United States over the head of the legislature to the people, was a simple and effective procedure, and was not infrequently employed, especially in the régime of Roosevelt. The general tendency of the time was for the rôle of leadership to pass from the legislative body to the executive.

Strangely enough, in the cities alone did the legislative

branch of the government hold its own. During the years immediately following the Civil War the city council reached its lowest point in incompetence and boss-rule. The sordid stories of betrayal of public trust echoed from one coast to the other. So serious and exasperating were the conditions, that the public mind was finally ready for the most drastic measures. The old bicameral councils were abolished in almost all instances, provision was made for the election of the council at large, the initiative referendum and recall were widely adopted, and finally, in a great number of cities, the so-called " commission government " was installed. Under this system a small legislative body, usually of five members, elected at large, was made the responsible governing body of the municipality. It is true that in some instances, the commission possessed both legislative and executive powers, but the strong tendency was toward legislative and supervisory functions, rather than administrative. The appearance of the city manager plan is in point here. In this way the revival of the legislative body was brought about in many of the American cities. In many others, however, the municipal legislature was wholly overshadowed by the executive, and even its financial powers were seriously curtailed as in New York and Boston, and in many of the larger cities the executive was more trusted than the legislative branch of the government.

During this time, there may be seen the beginnings of a constructive legislative policy, in the form of more scientific methods of legislation. In relation to the enormous amount of current legislation in the United States, there had been relatively little reliable information on which to base laws and relatively little attention was given to precision in the form of the law. This frequent carelessness as to facts, and indifference as to form of law constantly weakened the legislative prestige and incidentally tended to enhance the power of the courts. During this period there began a determined effort to provide a more effective basis for legislation. This took the institutional shape of the legislative reference bureau, an organization for the purpose of systematically securing comprehensive information and so analyzing and digesting it as to make the facts available for the purposes of the law makers. A beginning was made with the "Legislative Bulletin" of New York State. The movement achieved a notable success in Wisconsin under the leadership of McCarthy.[4] The idea spread rapidly to other states and was also incorporated in the policy of many cities. Many systematized efforts were made by the various branches of the Federal government, where however administrative initiative and technique were more noticeable, until it may fairly be said without too great optimism that a much more solid basis of information was placed under the acts of the various law-making bodies.

Notable assistance was also rendered to legislative bodies by the appointment of special commissions of various kinds for investigating and reporting upon specific topics, as, for example, the subjects of taxation, industrial and social legislation and education. Many inquiries were of indifferent value, some were outright " junkets,"

[4] See C. H. McCarthy, "The Wisconsin Idea"; Frederick Howe, "Wisconsin, An Experiment in Democracy."

but many of them furnished a solid basis for constructive legislation. In the absence of expert administrative initiative, much was accomplished toward enlightening the electorate and the law-maker, and also toward drafting of statutes.

Furthermore, progress was made in the development of definite canons of legislation. Ernst Freund, in his " Standards of American Legislation," undertook to outline a constructive policy. Basing his conclusions upon a study of legal history in the United States, and comparisons of the methods employed in foreign countries, Freund outlined certain principles of legislation. These were grouped under two main heads: " Correlation " and " Standardization." Under " Standardization " he included conformity to scientific laws, standardization of juristic data, definite method in reaching determinations, and stability of policy. He recommended as specific aids to legislation, the preparation of bills by special commissions, the delegation of power to administrative commissions, the organization of drafting bureaus and the formulation of so-called " standing clauses." [5] Here is seen the beginning of legislative technique, aiming at greater deliberateness in the process of law-making, and greater accuracy in the expression of the legislator's will. While it cannot be said that legislation, broadly speaking, was placed upon a solid foundation, either in material or in method, yet it is clear that the existence of a problem was realized and a start was made toward the solution. If the way was not found, there was at least a realization

[5] See Chap. 7, on constructive features. Cf. Chester Lloyd Jones, " Statute Law Making," 1912.

that the way was lost and an effort was made to find a trail.

It may be fairly said, then, that during this period the legislative body as compared with the other branches of the government did not gain in power or prestige. With the exception of commissions established in numerous cities, the legislative branch of the government was rarely the chief beneficiary of the people's confidence. Frequent revelations of bribery, of boss control, of influence by special interests, of ignorance, incompetence and carelessness, made it difficult for public opinion to lean heavily upon the legislature.

Yet with all these sweeping qualifications, the broad fact must not be ignored that never was there a larger quantity of legislation placed upon the statute books at any period in history than during the last fifty years of American political life. Notwithstanding the suspicion of the law maker, there was a widespread confidence in the desirability and efficacy of law, and a general willingness to embark upon the interesting enterprise of law making. If Americans had lost faith in legislators they still retained their trust in laws. Individual citizens, and countless committees of citizens, leagues, associations and societies of all types investigated, agitated and drafted bills, organized lobbies, and vigorously pursued their several propagandas of law. And the law makers, often uninformed, frequently reluctant, always overworked, yielded alternately to the pressure of overwhelming public demand and to the lure of irresistible personal or political gain. Public opinion, the real governing power, would not be denied, and regardless of personnel, of parties, factions, machines, bosses, interests, the great flood went its way.

A notable development of the machinery of government was the change from the indirect election of United States Senators by state legislatures to direct choice by the state electorate.[6]   President Andrew Johnson strongly advocated this change in 1868, but for obvious reasons his recommendation passed by with little recognition.   In the seventies and eighties, however, a steadily increasing demand was made for direct election of senators,[7] and in 1893 a constitutional amendment for this purpose passed the house of representatives by a two-thirds vote.   It was not until 1913, however, that the amendment was finally adopted by the senate.   By that time practically two-thirds of the states had declared their preference for the change, and a constitutional amendment or convention was imminent.   Furthermore, in various states, led by Oregon, advisory popular votes were rapidly coming into use, and tending to render the legislative act merely a ratification of popular vote.   It was clear that the end of indirect election was in sight.

The advocates of direct election of senators pointed to the frequent deadlocks in state legislatures over the choice of United States Senators, and the importance of freeing the legislatures from the demoralization and delay caused by the selection of these officers; to the influence of party bosses in the choice of senators; and the scandalous cor-

[6] See A. P. C. Griffin, "List of References on the Popular Election of Senators," Library of Congress, 1904; George H. Haynes, "The Election of Senators," Appx. 3, p. 277.

[7] See Prohibition Party Platform, 1876; Union Labor Party, in 1888; People's Party, in 1892.

ruption accompanying senatorial elections in many instances.[8] They charged that the senate had deteriorated from its earlier standards and had become a rendezvous for the rich; that it failed to interpret the democratic sentiment of the nation; and that it reflected the interests and opinions of the few as against the many. Unquestionably, the greatest force in the argument for the direct election of senators came from the general conviction that the senate was too far removed from popular control, and was too closely affiliated with political machines and special interests to represent effectively the democratic national sentiment. This feeling appeared in the very earliest arguments for direct election and continued throughout a struggle which extended over a quarter of a century.

The defense of the original method of electing senators was adroitly conducted by Senator Hoar and others of his colleagues, including Senators Chandler, Edmonds, Root, and Depew. They believed that direct election, by throwing into sharper relief the contrast between the vote of the small states and that of the larger ones, would ultimately destroy the equal representation of the states in the senate and upset the federal equilibrium. They feared that the conservative influence of the senate would be weakened and perhaps ended if senators were made responsible directly to the voters of their states,— that

[8] A history of direct election of senators and a statement of arguments for and against is given in Haynes', *op. cit.* Haynes classified the members of the United States Senate in 1906, as follows: Representing Statesmanship, 17; Rank and File, 23; Wealth, 14; Political Manipulation, 16; Accident, 2; Past Services, 3; Unclassified, 15.

the senate would echo the passions of the people rather
than reflect their sober second thought.   For a hundred
years, said Senator Hoar, " Senators, while they have resisted popular passions of the hour, have lead, represented,
guided, obeyed and made effective the deliberate will of
a free people."   The most valuable features of the constitution, it was believed, were the indirect election of
the senate and the indirect choice of the supreme court.
The direct, immediate, hasty action of any mass of individuals on earth, it was said, " is the pathway to ruin
and not to safety."   It was freely predicted that the next
step would be the direct election of the president and of
federal judges, " by the brute force of numbers."   Senators, furthermore, strongly opposed any fundamental
change in the constitution.   If there is social unrest, said
they, then that fact itself is a reason why no change should
be made while the public is in that frame of mind.[9]
But the distinguished character of the senators and the
eloquence of the argument, did not prevail.   They only
dammed the stream, until the mass-weight of long delayed
public demand broke through the wall.

The theory of democratic representation itself was
widely discussed during this time.   The two most important phases of discussion were proportional representation and direct legislation.

The proportional representation movement began immediately after the close of the War, and continued inter-
mittently throughout the entire period.[10]   The contem-

[9] See Sen. Root, " The Direct Election of U. S. Senators," 1911,
" Addresses," 257-83.
[10] See " Report from the Select Committee on Representative Re-

porary English movement attracted much attention in America and the writings of John Stuart Mill,[11] who sponsored proportional representation in England, and of Thomas Hare were widely read here.[12] At first a number of cities adopted some form of limited or cumulative vote.[13] Illinois was the most conspicuous example, in the constitution of 1870. In 1872, the New York legislature passed a bill for the cumulative vote for the election of aldermen in New York city, which was vetoed by the Governor. Later a limited vote plan was adopted, but subsequently abandoned. In Pennsylvania the limited vote was employed in the city of Philadelphia under the constitution of 1874.

In the '90's the theory of proportional representation was revived and a new movement begun. The Proportional Representation League was organized in that year and an energetic campaign begun throughout the country. After a time the tendency died down, and was then reawakened in connection with the reorganization of city government. Recently a number of municipalities have

---

form." U. S. Senate, March 2, 1869, Appendix, 3rd. Sess. 40th Cong. p. 268.

[11] "Considerations on Representative Government," 1861.

[12] Election of Representatives, Parliamentary and Municipal, 1859. For a history of this movement see John R. Commons, "Proportional Representation," 1st Ed. 1896, Chap. X. Also John H. Humphreys, "Proportional Representation."

[13] Thomas Gilpin, "On The Representation of Minorities of Electors to Act with the Majority in Elected Assemblies," 1844; Simon Sterne, "On Representative Government," 1871; Salem Dutcher, "Minority or Proportional Representation," 1872; C. K. Buckalew, "Proportional Representation," 1872; Thomas D. Ingram, "Representative Government," 1884. See also the files of "Equity."

adopted some one of the several forms of proportional representation or preferential voting as a part of a city charter.

The argument in favor of the new system was based partly on the abuses arising from political gerrymanders of districts, and partly on the broader theory that representation of other than territorial groups is desirable. It was important, it was said, to represent not merely geographic areas but certain groups or classes of voters having certain views in common. Such a process will tend to bring together in the law-making body more truly typical elements than purely territorial districts. It would tend to assemble the direct representatives of various interests and open the way for the comparison and legislative compromise of views.[14]

Further, it was maintained that proportional representation would enlarge the voting power of the elector by giving him a wider range of choice, particularly in those systems where first and second choice are permitted. It would enable a citizen, so the theory ran, to use his vote as in a convention, where the selection was not made on the first ballot. It would further tend to avoid elections by a minority only.

There was no sharply formulated body of objections to proportional representation. The early experiments with cumulative voting had not proven successful, and although the new principle was widely different the various systems were likely to be roughly lumped together by the

[14] The whole subject was discussed in the House of Representatives, June 24, 1870: also Dec. 12–14, 1871; also in various state constitutional conventions of this period.

voter.[15]   Generally speaking, the theory prevailed that territorial or geographical suffrage on the district basis is preferable to any other type of what were sometimes called " fancy franchises."   In the urban communities, where the system of ward politics had aroused very general distrust of local representation, there was a warm welcome for a new plan: but election at large was the alternative adopted.   There was not much argument against the proportional system.   The public attitude might be more properly characterized as that of indifference toward it.   Long accustomed to the territorial system, it was not to be expected that there would be any sudden change in the political theory of representation.

The battle over direct legislation aroused much wider and deeper interest.   During the earlier part of this period, little thought was given to this topic.   The referendum had been applied to state constitutions during the Jacksonian period, and the submisssion of the organic law to the popular vote had become a settled principle with only isolated exceptions.[16]   The referendum was quietly applied to city charters, to municipal franchises, to bond issues, and to the regulation of the liquor traffic — all without any general stir of public interest.   But in the latter part of the period the referendum was proposed as a measure of more general application.[17]   In addition the initiative was suggested; and both institutions were advocated on a state-wide or more rarely a nation-wide scale. The relation of the initiative and referendum (usually

---

[15] See Blaine F. Moore, " Cumulative Voting in Illinois."
[16] Ellis P. Oberholzer, " The Referendum."
[17] See *Equity* of July, 1917.

both) to representative government was called in question and a discussion was opened on a scale which quickly became nation-wide — a battle center in state constitution making and a tilting point for Roosevelt, Bryan, La Follette, Wilson, Lodge and Root. The political theory of these new weapons for democracy has been and still is an object of discussion in the course of which the fundamentals of government have been drawn into consideration.

The case for the referendum rested largely upon the generally acknowledged corruption of many legislative bodies, upon their responsiveness to machine and corporate suggestions, their frequent unresponsiveness to the public will, and upon the belief that this supplementary machinery was necessary to secure really representative legislation.[18] To some extent these devices rested upon the belief in the efficacy and ability to direct legislation as such. But greatest emphasis was placed upon the widespread corruption of legislative bodies, of which there was abundant proof, as in New York, Ohio, Illinois, and on the disclosures regarding a nation-wide system of legislative debauchery. A " jackpot " legislature, controlled by a common bribery fund, became a familiar term, although it cannot be concluded that such practices are new in the history of American legislation.[19] The control of legis-

[18] The Initiative and Referendum was sustained by the Supreme Court in Oregon vs. Pacific States Telephone & Telegraph Co., 53 Ore. 162; Kiernan vs. City of Portland, 112 Pac. 402. A good statement of the popular argument is found in the proceedings of the Michigan Constitutional Convention of 1908, pp. 546–82, and the Ohio Convention of 1912.

[19] Paul S. Reinsch, " American Legislatures and Legislative Methods," 1907, Chap. VIII, on " The Perversion of Legislative Action."

lative bodies by political machines and bosses in many instances by bi-partisan machines and bosses, made popular control over representatives more difficult than ever. The far-reaching influence of special business interests in securing grants and privileges or in blocking the demands for public regulation — as in the case of railroads, public utilities, and liquor interests — were deeply influential in arousing the public distrust of legislative bodies. Organization of the whole political-commercial system in the lobby, or the " Third House," as it was often called, was an active influence that frequently controlled legislation.

The advocates of direct legislation characterized this situation as the " break-down of representative government," and urged the referendum as a check upon corrupt or hasty legislation and the initiative as a spur to action where inertia prevailed. The frequent necessity of organizing vigilance committees of citizens to prevent legislation adverse to the public interest, aroused the deepest public concern, as on the other hand did the necessity of elaborate and repeated demonstrations and demands to obtain much desired legislation in the public interest. Woodrow Wilson said : " The most ardent and successful advocates of the initiative and referendum regard them as a sobering means of obtaining genuine representative action on the part of the legislative bodies. They do not mean to set anything aside. They mean to restore and re-invigorate, rather." Elsewhere he characterized these weapons as the gun behind the door, not to be frequently employed, probably, but useful in times of emergency.[20]

[20] See Munro, " The Initiative, Referendum and Recall," p. 88; Beard and Schultz, " Initiative and Referendum and Recall "; Ohio

Wilcox said: " The referendum is offered as a remedy, a specific for legislative corruption." [21]

It may be said, then, that the general theory of the advocates of the referendum was that of a popular veto on the acts of the lawmakers and an appeal over the legislature to the electorate in cases of legislative obstruction. There were those who advocated direct legislation in preference to indirect law-making by representative bodies, but on the whole their part in the general movement was inconsiderable. Broadly speaking the political idea underlying the demand for these new devices was that the legislative process required the aid of a popular veto and a popular spur.

That these measures would lead to the oppression of the minority by the majority they did not believe or concede. On the contrary, they contended that the popular vote was likely to be more conservative in action than the legislature.[22] In any event the ultimate reliance must be on the character of the American people, and upon their attitude toward life, liberty and property. And this institution, it was contended, is fundamentally conservative and wholly unlikely to lead to hasty steps. On the other hand, it was urged that it would tend to prevent an intrenched minority from protecting a special privilege or preventing action by the majority in the general interest. Those who are opposed to legislation " to enforce trusteeship "

Constitutional Convention Proceedings, 1912, Argument of Roosevelt, pp. 378–87.

[21] "Government by all the People." Nathan Cree, "Direct Legislation," 1892. J. W. Sullivan, "Direct Legislation," 1893.

[22] Wilcox, *op. cit.*, 67.

in the use of capital " will naturally be against them." In other words, the only minorities adversely affected would be those who held special privileges inimical to the general interest.

During the early years of this period the new plans for enlarging democratic control were ignored or lightly dismissed as radical, populistic or socialistic measures requiring no serious attention. With the opening of a new century, the rise of the Progressive movement and the elevation of these problems to the plane of national party issues, much more thought was given to the fundamental questions involved. Some of the theories advanced in opposition were inextricably involved with general tendencies of democratic government, of representation, and of the proper function of government. Others bore more directly upon the detailed workings of the specific plans suggested.[23]

Direct legislation, it was held, involves the serious weakening of representative government, and its further degradation. It will tend to make membership in legislative bodies unattractive and undesirable, and will ultimately make our law-making bodies less useful than they are now. The destruction of representative government

[23] W. H. Taft, "Popular Government," 1913. Elihu Root, "Experiments in Government." Nicholas Murray Butler, "Why Should We Change Our Form of Government?"; Henry Cabot Lodge, "The Constitution and Its Makers," 1911. F. N. Judson, "The Judiciary and the People." Proceedings of Ohio Constitutional Convention, speech of Senator Burton, pp. 748–54. "The Initiative and Referendum," published by the National Economic League, 1912, contains arguments against the initiative and referendum by Senator Sutherland, Gov. O'Neall and others.

began, said Butler, when we reduced the representative to a mere delegate, under the lash of party system. " When we began to instruct a representative as to what he is to do when elected. . . . When we reduced the representative from the high, splendid and dignified status of a real representative chosen by his constituency to give it his experience, his brains, his conscience and his best service, and made him a mere registering machine for the opinion of the moment, whatever it might happen to be." The adoption of the new measures proposed will tend to carry this process still further, and reduce the representative body to a still lower status.[24]

Further, the mass of the people should not be burdened with the decision of questions which should come before the skilled law-makers for their extended consideration. They cannot be expected to devote the necessary time and attention to the close study of the difficult and complicated issues presented for their action. Nor is it desirable or necessary under a democratic form of government that this task should be undertaken by the entire community. On the contrary, representative government is the product of a long evolutionary process of specialization in the political world, somewhat akin to the division of labor in industry. It is better that attention should be fixed upon the relatively few but important measures of more general importance. There is danger, too, that there may be hasty and immature legislation which will not promote any genuine public interest. In brief, the whole process of deliberative legislation will be broken down, and the advance of national democracy indefinitely delayed.

Further it was strongly urged that these measures

[24] *Op. cit.*

would destroy the protection of the minority under our system of government, and open the way for the tyranny of the majority. We want, said Senator Root, to protect the minority, but this cannot be continued and that right " cannot be maintained except by jealously preserving at all times, and under all circumstances, the rule of principle which is eternal over the will of majorities which shift and pass away." [25] The characteristic feature of the American governments, said he, is that all aim to preserve rights by limiting power. " This system of limitations must be preserved if our governmental system is to continue." Slavish subordination of a representative, however, to temporary popular passion against his better judgment is a serious evil. In short, the initiative and referendum tend to destroy or at least to render ineffective the governmental protection given the minority against the majority and tend to make possible serious encroachments upon property rights.

Some of the objections made were directed to the purposes for which the measures under consideration might be employed. From this viewpoint they were condemned as socialistic in tendency and even in intention. Thus Butler declared that there was now no way by which a socialistic state could be reached under our system of government except by political revolution; but he feared that this might be brought about by means of the initiative and referendum. Direct legislation might be employed for class purposes, to promote the interests of one group at the expense of another, and of the poor at the expense of the rich. Property interests, it was felt,

[25] *Op. cit.,* p. 73.

would not be adequately secured except through the more deliberate processes of legislative action. The purposes of the new school, said Mr. Taft, include the power to " change or qualify the right of property so as more nearly to equalize property conditions." It was believed that the popular vote would be essentially radical and that conservative measures should not be expected under a régime where direct legislation was freely employed or was possible.

A typical theory was that of Lowell who held that under certain conditions a referendum possessed distinct value. "That direct popular action upon laws," said he, "when wisely and scientifically applied will prove highly useful in certain conditions of society we may well believe without expecting to usher in the millennium." [26] But in general these devices are undesirable, and in the main the chief reliance for law-making must be placed on the regularly elected representatives of the state.

These arguments were closely interwoven with the theoretical discussion of the recall, and particularly with the recall of judges and of judicial decisions, but for the purposes of analysis these topics are temporarily separated here. The political philosophy and the practical policy both of liberal and conservative were parts of the differing interpretations of democracy which were characteristic of the time.

The outstanding features in the development of institutions and the theory of the executive branch of the government were:

[26] A. Lawrence Lowell, " Public Opinion and Popular Government," 1913, p. 233.

(1) The strengthening of the prestige of the executive and the development of the idea of executive leadership and initiative.

(2) The development of a new tendency toward expertness and efficiency in democratic administration.

(3) The tendency toward administrative consolidation and centralization.[27]

A striking feature of this time was the development of the idea of executive initiative and leadership. This was not, it is true, new to American politics since the days of Andrew Jackson and Abraham Lincoln. In the early constitutions, the executive had been weakly constructed and in the first generation of our history the leadership had rested largely in congress and in the legislative bodies; while in the next period it might be said that leadership was divided between the executive and legislative bodies of the government, from local to national. But in the last period and particularly toward its close the executive tended to dominate the law making branch of the government. Many factors contributed to this result. Among these were the continued unpopularity of the legislative bodies, the gradual consolidation of executive power, the development of a permanent and expert administrative corps, the demand of the people for vigorous and effective leadership against strong special groups, the general familiarity with powerful executive types and forms in

[27] J. H. Finley and J. F. Sanderson, "The American Executive and Executive Methods"; John A. Fairlie, "National Administration," Chap. I and II; Mathews, "Principles of American State Administration"; Holcombe, "State Government."

social and industrial life. President Roosevelt began to speak of " my policies," Woodrow Wilson, a candidate for Governor of New Jersey, declared his intention of assuming the responsibility for State affairs if elected. If this was " unconstitutional," he expected to be an " unconstitutional governor."

This tendency was most strikingly evident in municipalities where the new theory took the form of a demand for what came to be called a " municipal dictator." Beginning with the Brooklyn charter in 1882 and expressed more fully in the New York charter in 1897, many cities moved toward an executive with large powers. The theory was that political power should be centralized, as in the case of the boss, but that the leader should be elected and responsible. It has been seen that the growth of the American city government tended to thrust the municipal dictator aside in favor of a commission, but down to the present time the executive in the larger cities, such as New York, Boston, Philadelphia and Chicago, remains as a dominating or as an equal factor in the government. On the other hand, the creation of the city manager as an expert administrator under the supervision of a commission was not designed to establish executive political leadership, but on the contrary was intended to divorce politics from administration, to leave the legislative body supreme in political affairs with an efficient executive tool for carrying out whatever it was decided to do.

In school government the same tendency toward the development of executive power appeared. At first the school trustees, an elective body, were supreme in school policy and administration, but as time went on these officers were in many instances made appointive, and the superintendent emerged with certain independent or coordinate authority. He was often given by statute a definite term of office, rights to certain independent powers in the appointment of teachers and choice of curriculum, and in short, was set up against the board as a coordinate authority. In some cases, but not frequently, the superintendent was made elective.

In the states, the Governor tended to play an important rôle. His appointive power was very materially increased as new offices, boards and commissions were created from year to year. A few were made elective and some were placed under the merit system, but in the main the control was vested in the Governor. Where he did not already possess the veto power, as in Ohio and Rhode Island, it was conferred upon him, and the strength of his veto was also somewhat accentuated as new state constitutions were formed. He announced a legislative program, and upon the general acceptance of this and his skill in obtaining its enactment by the legislature depended in large measure his popularity. The formulation, enactment and execution of the legislative policy was a criterion by which the Governor came to be judged as weak or strong. In proposals for the establishment of an executive budget, a system in which the initiative in appropriation is taken by the Governor, lies a further recognition of the desire to focus leadership in the state.[28] This was of prime significance, because the appropriating power had been

[28] See New York Bureau of Municipal Research Bulletins, 69, 70, 73; Responsible Government; Budget Legislation in Two States; and Three Proposed Constitutional Amendments, 1916.

historically the chief prerogative of the parliamentary body. With the executive budget it was definitely planned to take from the law-makers to a large extent control over the expenditure of public funds. The various plans for the reorganization of state government, such as those of Croly and U'Ren, emphasized the importance of giving to the Governor more distinct recognition of his position as a political leader. In some of these plans the Governor was given authority to initiate proposals for legislation and on the failure of the legislature to approve them, to submit the projects directly to the voters.

In the Federal field the same underlying tendencies were at work. President Johnson was completely overwhelmed by Congress, and for a considerable time the legislative branch of the government under the " elder statesmen's " guidance was stronger than the executive, but with the presidency of Cleveland, McKinley, Roosevelt [29] and Wilson, the scales were tipped the other way. The demand for direct election of senators and the attack on the powers of the speaker tended to weaken the law-making branch of the government. It came to be recognized as a proper function of the president to outline a legislative policy, to use all lawful means to obtain legislative enactment of his program, and finally, to supervise its actual administration. The energetic executives did not shrink from this task, but on the contrary constantly enlarged the scope of their activities. It became the political fashion to speak of " administration policies,"

[29] In " New Nationalism " he regarded the executive power as the steward of the public welfare.

although theoretically the policy of the government was determined by the legislature, while the executive administered policies that has been determined upon. The President employed not only the weapons of party leadership, but also the effective public appeal to the nation as a whole. In this capacity, if he struck a popular chord, he was irresistible; while if he failed, the result was attributed not to a mistaken view of governmental relations, but to the weakness of the individual who made the effort.[30]

It is, of course, dangerous to place too great stress upon the personal power or prestige enjoyed by any particular executive, for nothing is more evident than that this tide ebbs and flows. Jackson was followed by Van Buren, Lincoln by Johnson, Roosevelt by Taft. Yet, viewing the situation broadly, it is fair to say that there was during this period a distinct development of the theory and practice of presidential leadership.

The president came to possess the double attributes of a Prime Minister, who is leader of the legislative body and also of an independent executive who is not responsible to the legislative body. Executive expansion was contested by the leaders of Congress, by the party bosses, by any selfish interest affected, and in addition to this encountered the inevitable inertia of long-standing custom. From time to time as the flood subsided, Congress and the party leaders resumed their earlier position of ascend-

[30] See Benjamin Harrison, "This Country of Ours"; Grover Cleveland, "Presidential Problems"; Theodore Roosevelt, "Autobiography"; William H. Taft, "Presidential Problems"; "Our Chief Magistrate"; Woodrow Wilson, "Constitutional Government," Ch. 3.

ancy, yet with relatively little effect upon the tidal movement.

The executive branch of the government was further strengthened by the fact that the spoils system was challenged in this period by the merit system. Along with the institution of this new plan went the recognition of the importance of the expert in government. The reign of " King Andrew " Jackson had definitely ended popular hostility to the executive branch of the government as such, but at the same time the spoils system of which Jackson was the champion had taken away from the executive the chief means by which an intelligent and sustained initiative could be maintained, namely, a relatively permanent and experienced corps of administrators associated with the executive.

During this period the spoils system was subjected to violent attack, beginning at the close of the War. This was carried on so successfully that by 1883 a national Civil Service Act was placed upon the statute books. The essential principle of this measure was the substitution of administrative qualification instead of party service as a guiding principle. Inadequate in its scope and often imperfectly administered, the measure was extended in area and more rigidly applied as time went on. In the states relatively little progress was made in this direction, in counties almost none, but in the cities a material advance was made in the last half of this period. The most striking feature in the whole movement was not the comprehensiveness of the laws, or the completeness of their enforcement, which left much to be desired, but the appearance of the new political idea supplanting the historic doctrine, " to the victors belong the spoils."

During the period now under discussion, it came to be generally conceded that there is no inherent incompatability between democracy and efficiency.[31] Under the relatively simple conditions of Jackson's time, the loss from unskilled service was not so great or so apparent. The growing burdens of government, and the increasingly specialized technique of administration forced upon the public the recognition of the absolute necessity of trained public servants. At the same time universal public education, and the absence of class distinctions in the governmental service, opened the door to the whole democracy. With more limited facilities for general education, the effect of the merit system might have been to limit public employment, in large measure, to the class in the community whose economic situation was such as to make education possible. The American system of schools, organized upon a democratic basis, insured the democratic character of the public service against the dangers of aristocratic rule and bureaucracy. Under these circumstances the idea of expert and permanent administration spread rapidly, starting with a small group of active exponents and finding its way throughout the entire society. This feature was most conspicuous in municipal government, and least evident in the rural political agencies, but the expert idea was everywhere recognized and began to be everywhere evident.

[31] See W. H. Allen, " Efficient Democracy "; A. L. Lowell, " Public Opinion."

In the latter part of this period the merit system, which at first concerned itself largely with examination for entrance into office, and with methods for separation from service, was intensified and further developed by the idea of efficiency in the broader sense of the term. The work of classification of official positions and their standard-ization was undertaken in many cities and to some extent in states and the federal government. Efficiency in the conduct of administrative work of every description was extensively instituted, and solid advances were made toward the betterment of the executive service. In the earlier period investigations and inquiries had generally centered around the criminal phases of official conduct, pointing toward the grand jury and the criminal court. But between the customary character of many of the offences and the rigid technicalities of the law there were many failures to secure conviction; and the chief value of such inquiries was educational rather than punitive. They succeeded in dramatically exhibiting to the public the inner workings of the political system, and finally in fastening a social stigma upon the practices toward which the community had been somewhat complaisant. But the terrors of the criminal law were not at all adequate to remedy the situation, and there began a series of efforts to improve the efficiency of the service by careful analysis of its workings and constructive suggestions looking to-ward reorganization.

In cities like New York and Boston and Chicago, mu-nicipal research work was undertaken; in the various states commissions on economy and efficiency began to

appear with notable frequency.[32]   In some cases the work
of these bodies was largely ignored, while in other instances many recommendations were put into practical
effect.

It is not the purpose of the present inquiry to give a
detailed description of these undertakings or to appraise
their value; but it is important to note the gradual development from the spoils idea to the merit system, and the
advance from the more or less formal and mechanical
beginnings of the merit system to the more systematic and
scientific methods and results of the broader efficiency
movement.   The significant fact is that American political
thought began to recognize the urgent necessity of organizing administrative machinery in such a manner as to
make possible the permanent retention of skilled public
servants, who while amenable to public control, were at
the same time effective instruments in the hands of the
democracy.   This change of political attitude is of prime
importance in any analysis of American political thought
and institutions.

Another important phase of administrative development
was seen in the advance of the idea of consolidation and
centralization.   By the middle of the century public administration, outside the Federal government, had reached
the low water mark of decentralization in the United
States.   Both in cities and in states the utmost confusion
prevailed within the administrative ranks.   Many independent officers, boards, and commissions had been freely

[32] See G. S. Weber, "Organized Efforts for the Improvement
of Methods of Administration in the U. S." (1919).

created and left without any central responsible guidance. During the latter half of the century, however, there was a conspicuous tendency to consolidate these scattered administrative agencies, under the governor in the state, and under the mayor in the municipality. In the cities this movement was most rapid, but it was also evident within the commonwealths as well.[33]

The powers of appointment, removal and direction were gradually transferred to the Governor, or the Mayor, and in some cases to the president of a county board. In this way a much more compact form of executive was gradually built up. In the national government decentralization had never been established, and it was the national principle of consolidation that was adopted and applied in the states and cities. Many administrative officials were still left outside the control of the central executive, notably treasurers and comptrollers, but in the main the steady tendency was in the direction of consolidation.

In many states there was also a movement toward central supervision over local administration which still further strengthened the executive.[34] This was particularly noticeable in the fields of public sanitation, education, finance, charities and corrections, although by no means confined to these activities. In fact, as functions of government developed, it was not uncommon for the new activity to be taken over in whole or in part by the

[33] See New York State Library Bulletins on Legislation and Reviews of State Legislation.

[34] Columbia University Studies in History, Economics and Public Law; VIII, 2, 4; IX, 3; XVI, 3; XVII, 4. Mathews, " Principles of American State Administration."

state government. This was notably true in the " good roads " movement. Opposition to this tendency developed, but on the whole was ineffective except in cases where state administrative supervision touched the enforcement of liquor legislation or entered the province of industrial disputes, as in the case of state constabulary. In most instances, however, there was acquiescence in the new policy indicating the general current of thought toward a closer integration of administration. Local self-government did not lose its charm, but slowly it came to be recognized that there was both economy and democracy in providing a central clearing house for local activities, and in the maintenance of certain minimum standards of local efficiency by some large political area.

Another striking feature of the period was the growth of administrative bodies with sub-legislative powers of various descriptions. Notable illustrations of this development were seen in the public utilities commission, in various local sanitary authorities, and in the national immigration and revenue bureaus. This advance was a double gain for the administration, for on the one hand it took from the legislative body a sub-legislative power and from the court a certain field of judicial determination.[35] The slow processes of piece meal legislation, ad-

[35] Frank J. Goodnow, " Principles of the Administrative Law of the U. S."; T. B. Powell, " The Principle of the Separation of Powers," 1913; " Administrative Exercise of the Police Power," *Harvard Law Rev.*, 24, 268; John B. Cheadle, " Delegation of Legislative Function," 27 *Yale Law Journal*, 892; J. B. Winslow, " A Legislative Indictment of the Courts," *Harvard Law Review*, Vol. 29, p. 395; Goodnow, F. J., " Private Rights and Administrative Discretion," Am. Bar Assn., 1916.

ministrative custom, and judicial decision, gradually rounded out a field of Administration, with power to prescribe a wide variety of rules affecting not only public officials but private persons as well. A study of the nature, extent and limitations of this power, and of the legal and administrative principles developed is not a part of this discussion, but it constitutes a notable development in the general advance of the executive power.

There appeared the beginning of a science of administration, and of administrative law. The practices, principles, rules, of law and administration were gradually brought together and shaped into coherent form. In this field Goodnow [36] was most active, for a generation inspiring and developing the study of the principles governing administration, and endeavoring to place it upon a scientific, or at least upon a legal basis .

Out of all this institutional change and public discussion there emerged, then, a new type of executive in the American theory and practice. An administration, expert and permanent, consolidated and centralized, endowed with the opportunity of party and public leadership, vested, after a fashion, with residuary powers of prerogative to do what the law omitted to authorize elsewhere. In short, executive leadership, which appeared hateful to the democracy in the days when it threw off the yoke of monarchy, powerful administration, which it had held in terror as a part of the institution of kingship, and later under suspicion as a part of an aristocratic system — these took their place again on a democratic basis in the institutions and ideas of the people.

[36] "Comparative Administrative Law," 1893. See Ch. X.

Some efforts were made to obtain stricter popular control over the newly endowed executives. The process of impeachment had become, as it was characterized, a "rusty blunderbuss." In place of it there was established, principally in local governments, although to some extent in the states, a new institution known as the recall. Under this arrangement the tenure of the executive might be terminated at any time, in the pleasure of the electorate. Only occasional use was made of this, even in the cities, but it was held to be a useful contrivance where the executive could not be kept in check by the force of public opinion.[37]

The new development of the executive stood in close relation to the current theories and practice in social and industrial life. The boss in cities and states was the first to gather in his hands the scattered threads of political authority, and to assume the rôle of dictator in the city, county or state. In his central position he united the powers of government otherwise difficult to coordinate, and held in his hands not only administrative but legislative and even judicial control as well. He established a strict party merit system and developed the technique of organization efficiency. It was an easy transition to establish a responsible elective boss endowed with similar powers, but recognized as a responsible part of the framework of the government. The principle of " conspicuous responsibility " was substituted for that of the boss, who was certainly conspicuous enough, but was not readily held responsible. Likewise in the industrial field, the centralization of executive power was very marked. Not

[37] Oberholtzer, *op. cit.*

only were there large corporations and combinations of corporations with wide power, but in them there were powerful figures in whose hands vast authority was placed. The railroad kings, the trust magnates, the industrial barons, were conspicuous examples of highly centralized executive authority and of conspicuous industrial leadership. At the same time, in the domain of organized labor striking figures appeared who were also possessed of far-reaching authority hitherto unknown in the history of the country. Men like Gompers were powerful and dominant factors, matching the captains of industry. Centralization was the order of the day in politics and industry as in society. The political development was a part of the general movement. The boss, the industrial magnate, the labor leader and the centralized political executive were all a piece of the same cloth. The times were not favorable to checks and restraints upon action, but rather to the close concentration of power and leadership equipped for instant and energetic action on a great scale.

The earlier idea of the separation of governmental powers and balance of powers as an indispensable prerequisite of democracy and liberty were vigorously attacked, both in constitutions, in systematic thought and in general sentiment during this period.[38] The three-fold separation and balance of power collapsed completely in the cities adopting the commission form of government, and

[38] William Bondy, "The Separation of Government Powers," Ch. V; Thomas Reed Powell, "The Separation of Powers," 1913; A. R. Ellingwood, "Departmental Cooperation in State Government."

in general less emphasis was placed upon the importance of the separation. The theory long entertained that liberty could not be preserved without vesting the separate powers of government in separate organs of government, and balancing these organs against each other, was challenged in many quarters. It was also strongly defended, not only by the inertia of long established habit of thought, but by systematic arguments in its favor. Goodnow was among the most conspicuous of those who assailed the older idea.[39]

He advanced the theory that there are in reality only two powers of government; one the formulation of the will of the state, which he called " politics," and the other the execution of the predetermined will of the state, which he characterized as " administration." Under " politics " is included constitution-making, the ordinary legislative activities, the selection of governmental officers, the action of the courts to the extent that law is really made, the activities of political parties and the general supervision of the execution of the will of the state. Under " administration " would be set the ordinary activities of executive bodies and the bulk of the work of the courts in the administration of justice. Goodnow maintained that this division was fundamental in nature, and logically superior to the earlier three-fold classification. Using this as a basis, he drew a line between political officials who are properly elective and the administrative

[39] Frank J. Goodnow, " Politics and Administration"; see also J. A. Smith, "The Spirit of American Government"; A. N. Holcombe, " State Government"; Herbert Croly, " The Promise of American Life," and " Progressive Democracy."

officials, who are properly appointive. " Politics " should supervise and control " administration," but should not extend this control farther than is necessary for the main purpose.

The check and balance theory was characterized by a distinguished authority in politics as the " Whig theory of political dynamics "— a doctrine of physical balances and equilibriums corresponding to the physical theory of the universe developed during the 18th century.[40] He and others emphasized the organic nature of political relations as against the purely mechanical conception. They urged the necessity of viewing the government as a whole, rather than dividing it into separate parts and trusting to the natural activity of those separate organs for the custody of democracy and liberty. We must think, they urged, less of checks and balances and more of coordinated power; less of separation of functions, and more of the synthesis of action.

Indeed, the conclusion was widely reached that the check and balance system instead of supporting liberty, endangered it; that instead of serving as a barrier against tyranny, it became the bulwark of special privilege and interests lurking in its complications. " Hide and seek politics," as it was termed, is favorable to the political machine and special privilege which undertake to override the will of the democracy. It was frequently asserted and widely believed that unless some method could be found of simplifying the form of government, it would be impossible for a democracy to succeed. " Conspicuous responsibility," by which was meant the organization within

[40] Woodrow Wilson, "Constitutional Government," Ch. 8.

the government of responsible and powerful leadership, took the place in democratic thought of the purely mechanical idea of arbitrary checks and balances. What was known as the " short ballot " movement was only a part of a larger drift toward more perfect organization of political leadership designed to make more directly and certainly effective the opinion of the community.

On the other hand, there was not only the inertia of institutions, but some systematic defence of the check and balance doctrine. Woolsey [41] early defended the balance of power as a political theory, although emphasizing as Hamilton had done in the Federalist, the importance of interrelation and interdependence. The courts used the language of the balance of powers, in their decisions, although somewhat modifying the severity and rigidity of the classification. Cooley in his " Constitutional Limitations " set forth the legal doctrine with great emphasis. [42]

The constitutional provisions of all the states and of the United States remained unchanged in this respect, preserving the three-fold separation of powers and the formal balance between them. In the cities to be sure, the legislative and executive branches of the government were frequently united, but generally speaking the earlier system survived both in constitutions and courts. Public opinion, political parties, the unwritten constitution slowly translated the doctrine from a principle of liberty to a rule of political convenience — to a separation of agencies on the principle of the division of labor, yet with leadership and authority tending to centralize in the executive

[41] " Political Science II," Ch. 9 (1877).
[42] T. M. Cooley, 1st ed. of work, 1868,

branch of the government.   As far as the relation between
legislative and executive branches of government are
concerned, it could scarcely be said to be a general opinion
that liberty depended on their rigid separation and skillful
balance.

A notable effort was made during this period to provide
by constitutional amendment for more intimate relation
between the legislative and executive branches of the national government by allowing Cabinet members to have
seats in Congress.   But though supported by eminent authority, this proposal did not prevail.

On the whole, it may be said that during this time the
doctrine of checks and balances, as between governmental
organizations, was weakened, and that the theory of the
responsibility to the electorate tended to replace it; that
popular distrust of the legislative branch of the government grew, but on the other hand popular confidence in
the executive increased, as seen notably in the development of executive leadership, in the weakening of the
spoils system, and in the strengthening of technical administration.[43]

[43] The consideration of the relation of the courts to these branches
of government will be found in the following chapter.

CHAPTER V

THE COURTS AND JUSTICE

THE relation of legal justice to democracy is one of the significant problems of popular government. Alexander Hamilton contended, in the *Federalist,* that since the judiciary had neither " force " nor " will," but only the " power of judgment," it could never be formidable. Nevertheless, it is notable there have been sharp conflicts on fundamental questions of justice at various times between the courts and the greatest leaders of our democracy — Thomas Jefferson, Andrew Jackson, Abraham Lincoln and Theodore Roosevelt. The function of the judge is at best a difficult one, seeking amid complicated social, political, economic, ethical and cultural facts a principle of justice which will be recognized by his profession and by the community.[1] To fuse the past and the present in a juristic rule of action useful for the future is a work of the very greatest gravity — one of the highest triumphs of human intelligence in the field of social relations. Much more difficult is this process in a period of rapidly changing economic facts and social ideals. Working under the powerful pressure of unscrupulous political and economic interests ; in a period of active law-making by the community, and more than all, in a period when the

[1] " The truth is," said Justice Holmes, " that the law is always approaching and never reaching consistency. It will become entirely consistent only when it ceases to grow."

economic, social and class origins and implications of law
and justice are scrutinized and challenged as never before,
the task of legal logic, of penetrating insight, of balanced
judgment, of invention of formulas of democratic justice, is more, than commonly heavy.

Certainly no study of American political thought would
be complete without an analysis of the fundamental tendencies of judicial organization and action at the points
where the judicial system touches our political development most closely.   This task is particularly important
where legal and political ideas are as closely interwoven
as in the United States.   It is true that the undertaking
is rendered more difficult by the absence of an adequate
history of American law, which thus far exists only in
fragmentary form.   But the important position of the
legal profession in the actual conduct of governmental
affairs, the legalistic character of much of our political
thought, and the commanding position of the courts in
American political life, makes some discussion of certain
fundamentals indispensable.[2]   Some day the full story of

[2] See "Two Centuries' Growth of American Law" (1701-1901)
by members of the Faculty of Yale Law School, 1901; T. M. Cooley
and others, "The Constitutional History of the U. S. as Seen in
the Development of American Law," 1889; John F. Dillon, "Laws and
Jurisprudence of England and America," 1894; Simon E. Baldwin,
"American Judiciary," 1905; Oliver Wendell Holmes, "The Common Law," 1881; Charles Warren, "A History of the American
Bar" (1911); "Centennial History," Harvard Law School, 1817-
1917; Holcombe, "State Government in the United States"; Sir
Frederick Pollock, "The Genius of the Common Law," 1912; J. B.
Ames, "Lectures on Legal History," 1913. The early development
of American law is discussed by Paul S. Reinsch in "English Com-
mon Law in the Early American Colonies."

American law in its development as a part of our social history will be told.

That lawyers have played a leading rôle in American public life has been generally conceded by close observers. Burgess once characterized the government of the United States as the "aristocracy of the robe," and warned the bar and the bench of their grave responsibility for leadership in the affairs of state.[3]   Judge Brewer said: "Sneer at it as any one may, complain of it as any one will, no one can look at American society as it is to-day — and has been during the century of national existence — without perceiving that the recognized, persistent and universal leader in social and political affairs has been the gentleman of the green bag."[4]   The presence of large numbers of lawyers in legislative and administrative positions and in posts of party leadership has very materially affected the formulation of American political thought,[5] although in the latter period the lawyer was often obliged to struggle for the ascendancy even within the gates of the temple of justice against the "practical views" of the party boss and the industrial magnate.[6]

[3] "Political Science," II, 365.

[4] American Bar Association, 1895–443. See also Haynes, "Representation in State Legislatures"; John R. Dos Passos, "The American Lawyer," 1907; Julius H. Cohen, "The Law, Business or Profession," 1916, with bibliography, pp. 395–398. Compare James Bryce, "The Influence of National Character and Historical Environment on the Development of the Common Law," American Bar Association, 1907, pp. 444–462.

[5] In 1894 Judge Dillon estimated that of 3122 U. S. Senators, 2068 were lawyers; of 11,889 members of the House, 5832, of governors, 578 of 987 (total of 1157, but information available regarding 978).

[6] Woodrow Wilson, "The Legal Education of Undergraduates,"

At the outset the judges were chosen by the Legislature or the Governor.   There was no particular evidence either of confidence in or fear of courts as such, although there was opposition to lawyers and the common law.   Soon after the establishment of the Republic, however, the judges began to make their influence felt, and then a sharp controversy arose regarding the proper position of the court in a democracy.   Neither the vigorous assaults of Thomas Jefferson nor the bold defiance of the Supreme Court by Andrew Jackson, nor the onslaughts on the courts in the various states were sufficient to stay their steadily advancing authority.   Chief Justice Marshall effected an alliance with the growing spirit of nationalism and employed his skillful legal logic to develop and expand the powers of the federal government as against the authority of the separate states.   In this he was preeminently successful and greatly enhanced the power and prestige of the courts.   In individual states the judges also obtained the power to declare void the acts of the legislature and secured the position of general defender of the Constitution.   Justice Gibson rendered a famous dissenting opinion contrary to the right of the court to overrule state law, but this was overriden and the contrary doctrine everywhere prevailed.[7]   Attempts in different states to prevent what were termed the " encroachments " of the judiciary were successful in isolated cases.[8]

American Bar Association, 1894, p. 439; "The Lawyer and the Community," American Bar Association, 1910, pp. 419-39. Much important information on the personnel of the American Bar is given in W. D. Lewis' "Great American Lawyers."

[7] Eakin v. Raub, 1825, 12 Sergeant & Rawle, 330.

[8] W. W. Willoughby, "The Supreme Court," 1890; W. Car-

Toward the end of the period the Dred Scott decision, undoing the historic Missouri Compromise and operating in the interests of the slave-holders, did not improve the position of the judiciary. On the contrary, it served to evoke the most vigorous protest throughout the North, where the chief critic of the Supreme Court was Abraham Lincoln, who opposed the Dred Scott decision in set terms, and defended his position with great force and ability.

By the end of this period, then, the courts had gained their independence from the legislature and the veto power over legislative acts. They had lost power through the substitution of short terms for life tenure, and through their direct responsibility to the electorate in the states. They had gained through the acquiescence of the public in the theory that courts were the special guardians of rights guaranteed by the Constitution and through the courts' obvious sympathy with nationalism.

During the war it was inevitable that the judiciary should receive a set-back in the emergencies of military conflict. When President Lincoln suspended the writ of habeas corpus in Maryland, the Supreme Court of the United States undertook to intervene, but the officer of the court was checked by the bayonet. Nor did the wavering conduct of the court in the later legal tender cases add to its prestige as an interpreter of unchanging law.[9] Nor did the partisan position taken by the Supreme

penter, "Judicial Tenure in the U. S." 1918; H. L. Carson, "History of the Supreme Court of the U. S." (1902).

[9] Legal Tender cases, 1870. 12 Wall, 457. See George Bancroft, "A Plea for the Constitution of the United States of America Wounded in the House of its Guardians," 1886; Richard C. McMurtrie, "Plea for the Supreme Court," 1886; Brinton Coxe, "Es-

Court judges in the Hayes-Tilden election contest, when every one of the Justices appointed to serve upon the non-partisan electoral commission voted in strict harmony with his party affiliations, improve its general position.

After the War, attention centered around the rapidly developing industrial situation with its new forms and forces. The 14th Amendment, intended primarily for the protection of the civil rights of the colored man, was called in question on a much larger scale than was planned originally, and in far different connections, where corporate and property rights were involved. The clauses prohibiting states to deprive any person of life, liberty or property without due process of law and forbidding denial to any person of equal protection of the law, enabled the court to exercise a far-reaching jurisdiction. This power was freely exercised, not only by the federal courts but by those of various commonwealths.   In the epoch-making Granger cases (1876) the Court laid a broad foundation for regulation of " business affected with a public interest "— a milestone in the advance of social policy in the United States.

The attitude of the Supreme Court toward the income tax clearly operated in the economic interest of the few, and it was sharply criticised, not only by publicists, but by leading economists of the type of Seligman.   After nearly twenty years of effort, the Constitution of the United States was so amended as to authorize specifically the application of an income tax.   The Anti-Trust Law of 1890 was sustained, but the rule of reason developed

say on Judicial Power and Unconstitutional Legislation," 1893 (posthumously published).

in the Standard Oil and Tobacco cases left the public mind
in a dazed condition as to the real significance of the
act.[10]

In dealing with the problems of monopoly and competition and of organized labor and capital, the courts encountered stormy seas, and on the whole did not master
the situation. The novel and free use of the court's veto,
the strict application of ancient rules to new situations,
entirely alienated the confidence of labor, and resulted in
the widespread loss of popular trust in juristic ability to
administer even-handed justice in an admittedly difficult
situation. Of the three classes of cases, those affecting
the prohibition of monopoly, the regulation of industry,
the position of organized labor, the court left the public
in doubt as to the first, perplexed as to the second, and
aroused the united opposition of organized labor as to
the third. On the other hand, the development of the
" police power " by a process of judicial reasoning, and
the liberal tendencies developed in many quarters during
the last decade, tended to create confidence in the juristic
capacity to frame rules and canons, adapted to modern
conditions.

On the whole, the Judiciary, like the Legislative branch
of the government, tended to lose in relation to the Executive as the interpreter of democratic consciousness. The
carelessness and corruption of legislative bodies tended to
strengthen the position of the Court in relation to that
body, but the legislative bodies were more easily reached
and readily reversed their decisions without loss of dignity

[10] Trans-Missouri Case, 166 U. S. 290 (1897) ; Standard Oil Case,
221, U. S. 1 (1911).

or decorum. The fortieth general assembly might undo
the work of the thirty-ninth, not only without hair-split-
ting or mumbling apology, but with frank recognition of
a changing situation — with joy over their conversion.
If, as a shrewd political observer says, "The Supreme
Court follows the elections returns," the legislative bodies
can follow more quickly; and with no loss of dignity.
The Court can never seem to run — it must always walk,
ponderously, and with due regard for the burden of
precedents.[11]   The righteous indignation and swift action of the just judge with a flaming heart and cool brain
has sometimes won the admiration and confidence of a
community; but the combination is difficult.

During the last half century our legal system was developed under the troubled influence of the new forces
that have so profoundly affected the mode of thought and
life in America.   The jurists were confronted with the
difficult problems of readjustment to the new and swiftly
changing situations created by urbanism, industrialism
and spoils politics.   The law met with many shocks
during this time.   It came in contact with frontier conditions where primitive justice reappeared in the shape of
Vigilantes.   It fell across the sharp race conflicts between
black and white and white and yellow.   It met the inertia
of the local community.   It felt the weakness of administrative provisions for law enforcement.   It was touched
by the blight of criminal and spoils politics, particularly
in the great cities.   It was entangled in the warfare be-

---

[11] "Legal truth," says Wurzel (Juridical Thinking, p. 418), "is
bound to appear strictly logical in form even where in the nature
of things it cannot really be so."

tween economic monopoly and free competition on one side and the struggle between union and employer on the other.[12] And it was strained by the difficulties of securing fair litigation between the poor and the rich, when poverty and wealth stood side by side before it.

Our jurisprudence was spared the force required to upturn the deep-rooted inertia of the past encountered in many other countries, but on the other hand it was obliged to struggle for stable legal principles in a shifting society where gigantic economic forces but little understood were working at amazing speed in the midst of unformed political tendencies and institutions. The lawyer and the judge must deal with the political boss and the trust and union magnate, and the law itself must meet the sharp challenge given by the economic interpretation of history to its own standards of justice. Only the most brilliant strategy and tactics executed with the greatest energy and skill would have been able to master this situation and develop through juristic divination, legal logic and clear-cut legal formulas the principles and the procedure so nicely adapted to all the new situations as to satisfy the community sense of justice. As the result of this situation, both the spirit and the form of the legal system became a storm center of public discussion, which went down to the foundations of law and justice, particularly during the last quarter of the century.

Roughly speaking the first half of the period under discussion was characterized by the dominance of complaisance and conservatism as to organization and political

[12] See Sir Frederick Pollock in "The Genius of the Common Law," Ch. VII on "Perils of the Market-Place."

theory, while during the second part of the period there began a pronounced tendency toward sharp criticism of the technical organization of the court and of the underlying philosophy upon which its decisions were based. At the same time there began a constructive movement for judicial reform not unlike in its general spirit — although, of course, wholly different in its immediate methods and purposes — that of Bentham in England during the first quarter of the 19th century. At the very time when the *status quo* in the world of judges and jurisprudence seemed most firmly established, the revolution against its form and spirit was taking definite shape in the popular mind, in the ranks of the bar, in the schools of law, and in the innermost circles of the very highest courts. The central point of theoretical interest during this period was the relation of the judiciary to the determination of questions of public policy.

The prevailing theory of the relation of the courts to the machinery of government was somewhat as follows: The Constitution of the state or the nation, as the case may be, has guaranteed certain fundamental protections to persons and property as against the government. Constitutions have further divided the powers of government into three distinct branches. If the legislative or executive department overrides these constitutional rights of individuals, it then becomes the function of the court to declare such attempt void and to refuse to carry it into effect. The courts have been made the special guardians of the fundamental guarantees of the Constitution, and have been given the right and duty of protecting them against all other parts of the government, whenever in the opinion of the court they have been transgressed. This, it was said, was one of the peculiar and distinguishing features of the American system of government, and one by which it may be differentiated from all other governments, even those which are constitutional and democratic. This doctrine was clearly stated by many eminent jurists and by various courts of the states of the United States. The distinguished publicist Burgess said, "It is then the consciousness of the American people that law must rest upon justice and reason, that the constitution is a more ultimate formulation of the fundamental principles of justice and reason than mere legislative acts, and that the judiciary is a better interpreter of those fundamental principles than the legislature." [13]   "I do not hesitate," said Burgess, "to call the governmental system of the United States the aristocracy of the robe and I do not hesitate to pronounce this the truest aristocracy for the purposes of government which the world has yet produced." [14]

Judge Dillon declared "If we are not struck with judicial blindness, we cannot fail to see that what is now to be feared and guarded against is the despotism of the many — of the majority." [15] Of the opposite theory Judge Dillon said, "It is the doctrine of absolutism, pure

[13] "Political Science," II, p. 365.

[14] "The Court," said Evarts, in the New York Constitutional Convention of 1867, "is the representative of the justice of the State, and not of its power. . . . The judge is not to declare the will of the sovereignty, whether that sovereignty reside in a crowned king, in an aristocracy, or in the unnumbered and unnamed mass of the people." III, 2367.

[15] "Laws and Jurisprudence of England and America," p. 204, quoting 114 U. S. 291.

simple and naked, and of communism which is its twin
. . . the double progeny of the same evil birth." [16]   It
was believed that the great advantage arising under this
plan was that it afforded fundamental rights of private
property and of personal rights, a degree of security which
they could not possibly obtain elsewhere or otherwise under republican government; that it prevented hasty and
unwise legislation of a type to which democracy not so
safe-guarded would be only too prone; that it made possible the protection of the minority against the majority.

It had long been held that the courts might negative
legislative acts regarded by them as unconstitutional.   At
first the tendency was to declare acts void because of
conflict with natural law or justice, for violation of the
principles of the social compact, for contravening the
fundamental limitations laid down by Locke.[17]   In
Trevett v. Weeden (1786),[17a] the Court argued that the
Legislature could not alter the fundamental laws of the
State, and in support of their contention quoted Locke
and Vattell.   In Bowman v. Middleton,[17b] the Judges held

[16] Compare Woodrow Wilson, "Constitutional Government,"
Chap. VI; A. L. Lowell, "Essays on Government"; Hadley, "Freedom and Responsibility," p. 23.

[17] Two Treatises on Government, Sec. 135–140 (1689). Locke's
four limitations were that the legislative body cannot "be ab-
solutely arbitrary over the lives and fortunes of the people"; must
rule "by promulgated standing laws and known authorized judges";
"cannot take from any man any part of his property without his
own consent"; "cannot transfer the power of making laws."
A. C. McLaughlin, "The Courts, the Constitution, and Parties," Ch.
I; E. S. Corwin, "The Doctrine of Judicial Review."

[17a] Chandler's Criminal Trials, 269.

[17b] I Bay (S. C.) 252.

the "plaintiff could claim no title under the act in question, as it was against common right as well as against Magna Charta . . . that the act was therefore *ipso facto* void." In Calder v. Bull (1798), (3 Dall 386), Justice Chase said, "that there are acts which the federal or state legislatures cannot do without exceeding their authority. There are certain vital principles in our free republican governments which will determine and overrule an apparent and flagrant abuse of legislative power; as to authorize manifest injustice by positive law, or to take away that security for personal liberty or private property for the protection whereof the government was established. An act of the Legislature (for I cannot call it a law) contrary to the great first principles of the social compact cannot be considered a rightful exercise of legislative authority." [18] But later the theory upon which this power rested was that the higher law of the Constitution is superior to the subordinate law of the Legislature created by the Constitution. This has been named the doctrine of "paramount law." [19]

Under the sharp stress of new industrial conditions,

[18] In Vanhorne's Lessee v. Dorrance, 2 Dall, 304-1795, natural rights and the letter of the Constitution were combined in the court's argument.

[19] Marbury v. Madison, 1 Cranch 137, 1803. A clear statement of the early theory of limited authority is found in 1853, in Sharpless v. The Mayor of Philadelphia, 21 Pa. St. 147, in which the Court said: "The judges can be imagined to be as corrupt and as wicked as legislators. What is worse still, the judges are almost entirely irresponsible, and heretofore they have been altogether so, while the members of the legislature who would do the imaginary things referred to 'would be scourged into retirement by their indignant masters.'"

the power of the courts was invoked in repeated instances to invalidate laws expressing a social policy of the community. Among such acts were those affecting the hours and conditions of labor and the so-called employers' liability acts. In addition to these came the use of the injunction in industrial disputes and a long series of cases involving picketing, boycotting and unionizing.[20]

Now appears the more highly developed theory that laws may be negatived for reasons explicitly or implicitly, involving differences of social policy. In Loan Association v. Topeka, 1874, the court said: " There are limitations on such power (i. e. of Government) which grow *out of the essential nature of all free governments*, implied reservations of individual rights without which the social compact could not exist, and which are respected by all governments entitled to the name. . . . This is not legislation. It is a decree under legislative forms." [21]

It is true that in the Granger cases in 1876 (Munn v. Ill. 94 U. S. 113) the Court developed the advanced doctrine that the state may regulate business " affected with a public interest " in spite of the vigorous dissenting opinion of Justice Field. But from this time forward the doctrine of inherent limitations upon legislative power was developed and applied in new and varying forms of " public purpose," " freedom of contract," " economic liberty," " due process of law."

[20] Commons and Andrews, in "History of Labor in the U. S.," 2, p. 501 ff. Report of the Industrial Relations Commission, Vol. I, 38 (1915).

[21] 20 Wall. 655. See also Toledo v. Jacksonville, 67 Ill. 37 — 1873; In re Jacobs, 98 N. Y., 1885; Godcharles v. Wigeman, 113 Pa. 431 — 1886; Millett v. People, 117 Ill. 294.

The doctrine of " liberty " was invoked by the Court against various forms of social legislation. When the Pennsylvania Legislature undertook to prohibit the payment of certain workers in store orders instead of cash, the Supreme Court of that state held that the coordinate branch of the government was transgressing the limits of its power and infringing on certain inherent rights. The acts of the legislature are an infringement alike of the right of the employer and the employee. More than this, " it is an insulting attempt to put the laborer under a legislative tutelage which is not only degrading to his manhood but subversive of his rights as a citizen of the United States."

When the New York Legislature attempted to restrain the manufacture of cigars in tenement houses, the court held that this was the natural right of a cigar maker guaranteed to him under the Constitution and not to be taken away by the law-making body. Mr. Peter Jacobs, defended by the brilliant Wiliam M. Evarts,[22] was held to be threatened in his liberties, and was accordingly given protection from the law, as against the legislature, which the court said " arbitrarily deprives him of his property and of some portion of his personal liberty." " Liberty in its broad sense," said the judges, " as understood in this country means the right, not only of freedom from actual servitude, imprisonment or restraint, but the right of one to use his faculties in all lawful ways, to live and work where he will, to earn his livelihood in any lawful calling and to pursue any lawful trade or avocation." " If such legislation can be sanctioned," said the court,

[22] " The Arguments and Speeches of W. M. Evarts."

" we are not far removed from the time when governmental prefects supervised the building of houses, the rearing of cattle, the sowing of seed and the reaping of grain, and governmental ordinances regulated the movements and labor of artisans, the rate of wages, the price of food, the diet and clothing of the people, and *a large range of other affairs long since in all civilized lands regarded as outside of governmental functions."* [23]

The Colorado Legislature passed an eight-hour law applicable to the smelting industry, but this, too, was held an interference with the inalienable right of labor.[24]   If we are to follow the logic of the legislature, said the court, it would be lawful to compel men to work 14 to 16 hours a day to keep them from drunkenness and idleness. It might be required that no man weighing less than 120 pounds work in a stone quarry; that only those with good eyesight engage in watchmaking; that those suffering from a sluggish liver be forbidden to follow sedentary occupations; that the sale and quality of garments, that the quantity and quality of food and beverages might be regulated, and conceivably a minimum wage for the support of the workers might be established by law — all of which the judges believed were illustrations of impossible and undesirable situations.

In Illinois, the " truck act " was likewise held void, as an interference with liberty of contract.[25]   The Court believed that the workers must be protected in their rights, even against any presumed social stigma.   " Those

[23] In re Jacobs 98 N. Y. 98, 1885, Cf. Roosevelt's Autobiography.
[24] In re Morgan, 26 Colo. 415, 1899.
[25] Frorer v. People, 141 Ill. 171 (1892).

who are entitled to exercise the elective franchise are deemed equals before the law, and it is not advisable to arbitrarily brand by statute one class of them, without reference to and wholly irrespective of their actual good or bad behavior, as too unscrupulous and the other class as too imbecile or timid and weak to exercise that freedom in contracting which is allowed to all others." In a similar case in West Virginia [26] the Justice said: " The property which every man has in his own labor, as it is the original foundation of all other property, so it is the most sacred and inviolable. The patrimony of the poor man lies in the strength and dexterity of his own hands, and to hinder him from employing these in what manner he may think proper, without injury to his neighbor, is a plain violation of this most sacred property." In a long series of cases arising under laws regulating the hours and conditions of labor, the natural liberty of contract was held to be assailed by the law-makers and therefore placed under the protection of the Court.[27]

In Lochner v. New York (198 U. S. 45, 1905) the Court held void a law limiting the hours of certain workers, saying: " It is unfortunately true that labor, even in any department, may possibly carry with it the seeds of unhealthiness. But are we all on that account at the mercy of legislative majorities? The act is not a legitimate exercise of police power, but a meddlesome interference with the rights of individuals." In another case

[26] State v. Goodwill, 33 W. Va. 179 (1889).

[27] See Wilcutt & Sons Co. v. Driscoll, 200 Mass. 110, in which the doctrine of probable and natural " expectancy" was developed. Also Adair v. U. S., 208 U. S. 161 (1908).

(Ives v. South Buffalo Railroad Company, 201 N. Y. 271, 1911) said the Court: " In a government like ours theories of public good or necessity, are often so plausible or sound as to command popular approval; but courts are not permitted to forget that *the law* is the only chart by which the ship of state is to be guided."

It was said that the power of the court is the only practical safeguard against the unrestrained will of the people. In other words, this power of the court was regarded as the corner-stone of liberty — the basis upon which our Constitution is raised. Whether the judges thought that the decisions of the courts as to fundamental rights were final interpretations both of justice and of policy was not always made clear. In many instances it seemed that they so looked upon their verdict, forgetting even the processes of constitutional amendment. Thus Goodnow says: [28] " The courts of the United States have really taken the position *that there is no due process of law by which the individual may be deprived of these absolute, substantive, inherent natural rights.*" The Court held in substance that there are certain rights of persons and property outside the field of government: that the courts must not only maintain the forms of procedure in the protection of these rights, as in the case of " due process," but that the old content of these rights, without regard to social changes, must be maintained.

It is not difficult to trace the economic and social theory underlying juristic logic in many instances. In the income tax case, for example, Justice Field said: " The present assault upon capital is but the beginning. It will

[28] " Principles," p. 267.

be but the stepping stone to others larger and more sweeping, until our political contests will become a war of the poor against the rich; a war constantly growing in intensity and bitterness." " If," said the Court, in the workmen's compensation case in New York, " such economic and sociological arguments as are here advanced in support of the statute can be allowed to subvert the fundamental idea of property, then there is no private right entirely safe, because there is no limitation upon the absolute discretion of the legislature and the guarantes of the Constitution are a mere waste of words." [29] In the famous tenement house case of New York the Court said, in negativing the act: " What possible relation can cigar making in any building have to the health of the general public? " The court could not see how a cigar-maker " is to be improved in his health or his morals by forcing him from his home and its hallowed associations and beneficent influence." [30] Judge Jackson said, in his famous injunction opinion: [31] " I do not recognize the right of laborers to conspire together to compel employes who are not dissatisfied with their work in the mines to lay down their picks and shovels and to quit their work without just or proper reason therefor, merely to gratify a professional set of agitators, organizers and walking delegates who roam all over the country as agents for some combination, who are vampires, that live and fatten on the honest labor of the coal miners

[29] Compare Horace Stern, " An Examination of Justice Field's Work in Constitutional Law," in " Great American Lawyers." Miscellaneous writings of Joseph P. Bradley, 1902.
[30] 98 N. Y. 114.
[31] U. S. v. Haggerty, 116 Fed. 510 — (1902).

of the country, and who are busybodies, creating dissatisfaction amongst a class of people who are quiet, well disposed, and who do not want to be disturbed by the unceasing agitation of this class of people." [32]

On the other hand, the court had developed a notable doctrine of the right of public regulation over business affected with a public interest in the Granger cases, and had sustained the Interstate Commerce Act and the Sherman Anti-Trust Law. The Granger cases stand as a landmark in the development of the power of governmental regulation. The Court here held that property is " clothed with a public interest when used in a manner to make it of public consequence and affect the community at large. When, therefore, one devotes his property to a use in which the public has an interest, he in effect grants to the public an interest in that use, and must submit to be controlled by the public for the common good, to the extent of the interest he has thus created." " For protection against abuses by legislatures the people must resort to the polls, not to the courts." Furthermore, the court had built up through a long series of decisions the doctrine which came to be known as the " police power " under which a great variety of legislative acts otherwise unconstitutional were neatly sustained.[33] This

[32] See also the still more emphatic utterances in 116 Fed. 520. But see Francis M. Burdick, " Is Law the Expression of Class Selfishness? " Harvard Law Review, 25-349. On the other hand, see Hadley, " Undercurrents in American Politics," Chap. II.

[33] See Ernest Freund, " The Police Power" (1904). Also, " Standards of American Legislation," 1917. Also article on " Police Power " in McLaughlin and Hart " Cyclopædia of American Government."

power was never carefully outlined, but was held to be a general authority to protect the health, safety, morals, comfort and convenience of the community. It was defined by Freund as " the power which has for its immediate object the futherance of a public welfare through restraint and compulsion exercised over private rights." It was invoked in the regulation of public utility corporations to justify control over their rates and service, and used in a wide variety of measures touching public safety, morals and order, labor legislation, the protection of women and children, and the regulation of various public callings.

Particularly in the field of public morals were the decisions of the courts favorable to vigorous legislative action. Laws prohibiting the sale of intoxicating liquors were usually sustained, but this principle had been established before the Civil War.[34] Other classes of laws affecting the public morals, public safety and public health were frequently approved by the courts who found at these points that " personal liberty " must yield to the " public interest." The police power afforded a convenient way of escape from a rigid and otherwise inelastic system, and made possible a long series of laws otherwise under the ban. It furnished a safety valve for needed legislation which might otherwise have been delayed. It opened a way toward progressive social policies which for a time seemed to be effectively barred except by the difficult processes of constitutional amendment or through the slow changes in the personnel or opinions of the judges. In cases where the economic relations between labor and

[34] Freund, "Standards," p. 197.

capital were not directly involved, the police power was
on the whole very freely invoked to prevent interference
with legislative programs.[35]   That a clear line of political
theory was followed no one contended.   On the contrary,
the court declined to define the police power sharply
and left the free development of the doctrine to be pieced
out case by case as occasion arose.

At the same time there were distinct developments of
the power of public bodies to carry on specific types of
enterprise.   In the famous case of Loan Association v.
Topeka (20 Wall. 655) the Supreme Court had held that
the city of Topeka, Kansas, could not issue bonds in aid
of the King Bridge Company.[36]   The Massachusetts
Supreme Court held, in 1892, in an advisory opinion,[37]
that it lay beyond the power of the municipality to enter
into the fuel business.   It had also been held unconstitutional to appropriate money for the purpose of purchasing
seed grain for farmers,[38] or to issue bonds for reimburse-
ment of inhabitants of a burned-over district in Massachusetts;[39] or again, to provide funds for a municipal
plumbing store (1897).[40]   In the later cases, however,
a much more liberal attitude was assumed.   This was

[35] For example, Jacobson v. Mass (1905), 197 U. S. 11, sustaining a vaccination law, and McCray v. U. S., 195 U. S. 27
(1904), sustaining the anti-oleomargarine law.

[36] See *Yale Law Journal*, Vol. 27, p. 824, Note on Municipal
Fuel Yards.

[37] Opinion of the Judges, 155 Mass. 598; again, in 1903, 182
Mass. 605.

[38] State v. Osawakee, 14 Kans. 418 (1875).

[39] Lowe v. Boston, 111 Mass. 454 (1873).

[40] Keen v. Waycross, 101 Ga. 588.

notably true in the famous Portland case,[41] where the Supreme Court of Maine held that the city might sell fuel to its citizens without contravening the fundamentals of government.[42]

The conservative spirit of the law was not frequently formulated in strictly systematic fashion. Indeed, it was less in need of formal statement, for it stood upon the philosophy of precedent involved in the recognized doctrine of *stare decisis*. In case after case, however, the conservative theory was assumed and applied by the courts in dealing with specific issues as they were presented in litigation.[43] Fundamentally the legal system rested upon the English common law as a basis for for-

[41] Laughlin v. Portland, 111 Maine 486 (1914); Jones v. City of Portland, 210 U. S. 217 (1917). See also the Homestead Commission case, Opinion of the Justices, 211 Mass. 624 (1912).

[42] Mr. Pound has also indicated various points at which the private law has been greatly socialized, enumerating seven specific instances:

(1st) In regard to limitations on the property and so-called anti-social exercise of rights;

(2nd) Regarding limitations on freedom of contract;

(3rd) Limitations on the *jus disponendi;*

(4th) Limitations on the power of the creditor or injured party to exact satisfaction;

(5th) The imposition of liability without fault, particularly in the form of responsibility for agencies employed;

(6th) The change of *res commune* and *res nullius* into *res publicae;*

(7th) Insistence upon the interest of society in dependent members of the household. See *Harvard Law Review,* Vol. 27, p. 195. Compare Ely's "Property and Contract."

[43] See cases cited by Pound, *passim;* and Freund, "Standards of American Legislation."

mulation and decisions.   But the courts tended to regard
the common law as a closed book, as a classical body of
legal principles of continuing application without much
regard to the changes in social and economic conditions.
What Sir Frederick Pollock called " the genius of the
common law " was not always clearly in evidence, although apparent from time to time in individual instances.
The toughness of the texture of the common law rested
upon an English characteristic which the famous commentator Bagehot called an " illogical moderation "— a
fine touch and a discriminating sense in determining the
general spirit and tendencies of the time and weaving
them skilfully into the fabric of the law.   The extreme
rapidity with which economic conditions were changing
made the application of such a principle difficult at best
— particularly when these changes radically altered the
ways of life and the relation of class to class as in the
last half century.

The underlying political principle of the conservative
theory was that of *laissez faire*.   " The characteristics of
the early common law were essentially individualistic in
nature," says Freund.   The law, said he, favored property and the possessor, was based upon the ideas and
principles of the propertied middle class as against the
non-propertied, and developed prior to the times of the
working class movement.   In addition to this, the original tendency, our courts generally adopted the *laissez
faire* theory of economics current in the early part of the
19th century.   To this they added, as time went on, the
doctrines of the English sociologist Herbert Spencer,
who endeavored to translate the doctrines of natural

law and the Manchester school of economics into the current language of natural science. The essence of this philosophy was that the burden of proof rests strongly upon any effort to expand the functions of the government in any direction. This theory was stated in the decisions of the courts and became particularly clear whenever the law touched on the questions requiring a readjustment of judicial standards to meet new conditions of labor and production. Notable illustrations of this were seen in their attitude toward the liability of employers to employes in case of accident under new working conditions, and particularly in the position toward social legislation designed to ameliorate abuses arising in the course of the new working conditions, as the limitation of the hours of labor,[44] the definition and limitation of nature of "public purpose," and in other cases involving readjustment of the law to new industrial and urban conditions. Where industrial relations were concerned, liberty of contract, individual rights, freedom, equality, justice were construed upon the fundamental hypothesis of the desirability of a minimum governmental interference with the affairs of individuals. The assumption constantly in evidence was that the individual best knew his own interest and that the state should not interfere with his conduct unless in a very grave emergency and an emergency of the type already indicated under the classical common law. But this did not hold true where moral considerations were involved.

A systematic statement of the prevailing legal philosophy was that made by James C. Carter, a leader of the

[44] See Freund, *op. cit.* for abundant illustrations of this attitude.

American bar in his day,[45] in " Law and its Origin,
Growth and Function." [46]   This volume presents a picture of a type of political theory, widely prevailing in
juristic circles.   Carter held that law is a rule of social
conduct growing out of human experience, a result of
custom and growth — evolution, in the modern terminology.   These rules are found or discovered by the judges
on inquiry and are applied to specific cases as occasion
required.   They cannot be created; they are preexisting,
awaiting discovery and application.   " Society," said
Carter, " cannot at will change its customs.   Indeed, it
cannot will to change them." [47]   Reform can be brought
about only through unreflective custom, or through individuals, and " by a change and improvement in their
thoughts."   It follows then that the legal system should
be left to the judges in the course of litigation, the court
discovering any applying the fixed rules of justice growing out of historically created situations.

His guiding principle of widest application was taken
from the Spencerian adaptation of the Manchester school
of economics, namely: " The sole function both of law
and legislation is to secure to each individual the utmost
liberty which he can enjoy consistently with the preservation of the like liberty to all others." [48]   Or, applying
the idea more closely to the courts: " The sole function of
the judicial power is to preserve the peace of society and
leave its members to work out their own happiness and

[45] See Lewis, " Great American Lawyers."
[46] Published posthumously, 1907.
[47] P. 320.
[48] P. 337.

that of their fellows by a free exercise of their own powers." [49]

Broadly speaking, then, the fundamental political theory of the court was that of a minimum interference with persons and property, as a general social policy. Where public opinion was strongly and continuously expressed, as in regard to public utilities or trusts, the court was inclined toward a liberal view: or in cases where a principle classifiable under morality was concerned, the judicial attitude was also favorable to state action. The " police power " was the great formula to compass social legislation otherwise inadmissable.

In the latter part of this period, there arose a storm of protest against the attitude of the courts, and there was a vigorous effort to limit the discretion of the judges in various ways. The decision of the court in the Income Tax case, in negativing measures of social legislation, the free use of the injunction in industrial disputes, and other decisions of a like character, aroused intense and prolonged indignation in many quarters. At first the protests were characterized more by their fury than by their keenness or intelligence, but gradually the opposition focused more closely upon the issues, and at the close of this period many distinguished jurists united in condemning the action and policy of the court. Indeed, the most distinguished of these were members of the Supreme Court of the United States, who in their various

[49] P. 323: Cf. Harlan F. Stone, "Law and Its Administration," 1915, p. 44. J. E. Keeler, *Yale Law Journal*, V. 14, " Survival of the Theory of Natural Rights in Judicial Decisions." Morris R. Cohen, " Jus Naturale Redivivum." *Phil. Rev.* 25, 761.

dissenting opinions stated the ground for objection most clearly. The list of those who protested included a long series of publicists, from Bryan to La Follette and Roosevelt, and publicists of the type of Goodnow, Pound and Freund. They held that the courts were applying 18th century theories of economics and social policy to new and changed conditions; that they were departing from the original principle that only in cases where there was a clear transgression of a constitutional restriction should there be any effort to negative the act by the court.[50]

It is significant that the conservative tendency had no sooner reached its full formulation in court decisions and in systematic statement than a liberal movement appeared in the field of jurisprudence. The popular criticisms of the courts and of the legal system began in the '90's to take on a scientific character. The social point of view and the methods of social science began to find application to legal problems. An early warning was that given by Prof. Thayer, who called attention to the activity of the courts in declaring laws unconstitutional. " The courts," said he, " must not step into the shoes of the law maker." [51]   Under no system can the power of the courts

[50] G. G. Groat, "Attitude of American Courts in Labor Cases," p. 389; B. F. Moore, " The Supreme Court and Unconstitutional Legislation "; Charles G. Haines, " The American Doctrine of Judicial Supremacy "; Henry R. Seager, " The Attitude of American Courts Toward Restrictive Labor Laws," *Political Science Quarterly*, 19, 589; J. B. Thayer, " Legal Essays," 1908; Frank Parsons, " Legal Doctrine and Social Progress," 1911; Laidler, H. W., " Boycotts and the Labor Struggle," 1914, bibl. p. 473.

[51] Jas. Bradley Thayer, "Legal Essays," containing, " The Origin and Scope of the American Doctrine of Constitutional Law," 1893.

go far to save the people from ruin. Our protection lies elsewhere." " The tendency," said he, " of a common and easy resort to this great function now lamentably too common is to dwarf the political capacity of the people and to deaden its sense of moral responsibility." [52] Our doctrines of constitutional law, he held, had tended to drive out questions of justice and right, and to fill the minds of the law-makers with thoughts of mere legality — of what the Constitution allows rather than of what is right. He believed that the safe and permanent road of reform was to impress upon our people a far stronger sense than they have of the great range of possible mischief that our system must work upon the Legislature, and of the clear limits of judicial power, so that responsibility may be brought sharply home where it belongs.[53]

Formidable opposition to the general theory of the court appeared within the ranks of the judges themselves. In this movement, Judge Holmes, believing that " one may criticise what one reveres," was the most conspicuous figure. In his " Common Law " published in 1881, he had already analyzed with great keenness the nature of legal logic. " The life of the law," said he, " has not been logic; it has been experience. . . . The very considerations which judges most rarely mention, and always with an apology, are the secret root from which the law draws all the juices of life. I mean, of course, the consideration of what is expedient for the community

[52] Thayer's " Marshall," pp. 103–110.

[53] Compare the standard doctrine in Cooley's classical work on " Constitutional Limitations " (1874), Chap. 7, on " Declaring Statutes Unconstitutional."

concerned." [54]   The principles developed in the course of litigation are, he maintained, " in fact and at bottom the result of more or less definitely understood views of public policy.   Most generally, to be sure, under our practice and traditions, the unconscious result of instinctive preference and inarticulate convictions, but none the less traceable to views of public policy in the last analysis." [55]

Later, he had said, "I think that the judges themselves have failed adequately to recognize their duty of weighing considerations of social advantage."   Alluding to the fear of socialism here and in England, he went on to say: " I think that something similar has led people who no longer hope to control the legislatures to look to the courts as expounders of the Constitutions, and that in some courts new principles have been discovered outside the bodies of those instruments, which may be generalized into acceptance of the economic doctrines which prevailed about fifty years ago, and a wholesale prohibition of what a tribunal of lawyers does not think about right.   I cannot but believe that if the training of lawyers led them habitually to consider more definitely and explicitly the social advantages on which the rule they lay down must be justified, they sometimes would hesitate where now they are confident, and see that really they were taking sides upon debatable and often burning questions."

As a member of the Supreme Court of the United

[54] Pg. 35.
[55] " The Path of the Law," in *Harvard Law Review,* 10, 457, 1897; Felix Frankfurter, " Constitutional Opinions of Justice Holmes," *Ibid.,* 29, 683 (1916).

States a number of his dissenting opinions cut squarely across the logic of the majority and challenged openly the validity of their basic principles. In the bakeshop case the distinguished Justice said: " This case is decided upon an economic theory which a large part of the country does not entertain. . . . The 14th Amendment does not enact Mr. Herbert Spencer's " Social Statics." . . . A constitution is not intended to embody a particular economic theory, whether of paternalism and the organic relation of the citizen to the state or of *laissez faire*."

Equally notable was the opinion of Judge Winslow, of Wisconsin, in which he upheld the Workman's Compensation Act of that State.[56] " When an 18th century constitution forms the charter of liberty of a 20th century government, must its general provisions be construed and interpreted by the 18th century mind, in the light of 18th century conditions and ideals? Clearly not. This were to command the race to halt in its progress, to stretch the state upon a veritable bed of Procrustes. Where there is no express command, or prohibition, but only general language or policy to be considered, the conditions prevailing at the time of its adoption must have their due weight; but the changed social, economic and governmental conditions and ideals of the time, as

[56] Borgnis v. Falk Company, 147 Wis. 327 (1911). In the Standard Oil case, Justice Harlan, dissenting, said: " The courts have nothing to do with the wisdom or policy of an act of Congress. Their duty is to ascertain the will of Congress and, if the statute embodying the expression of that will is constitutional, the courts must respect it. They have no function to declare a public policy nor to amend legislative enactments."

well as the problems which the changes have produced, must also logically enter into the consideration and become influential factors in the settlement of problems of construction and interpretation."

A direct attack not always careful in its choice of facts and narrower in its range, yet reflecting a broad democratic sentiment, was made by the radical, labor and socialistic groups. They openly charged both judicial corruption and class prejudice, resulting in the betrayal of the interests of the many into the hands of the few. They did not hesitate to denounce in unsparing terms the personnel, the procedure, the spirit and the practical results of legalism as developed during the last quarter of a century.[57]

The specific abuses enumerated were the nullification of laws upon technical grounds, the discrimination against the poor in favor of the rich, the failure to protect workers in their constitutional rights, the failure to protect workers against non-payment of wages and overcharges, the unwarranted extension of the use of the injunction in labor disputes, the exclusion of workers from juries, the charges of fictitious crimes and requirement of excessive bail, the unwarranted suspension of the right to the writ of *habeas corpus*.

[57] See Gilbert Roe, "Our Judicial Oligarchy"; Gustavus Myers, "History of the Supreme Court." The most authoritative formulation of this position was found in the Report of the Industrial Relations Commission (1915), Vol. I, pp. 38-61. See also the testimony and special reports of J. Wallace Bryan, on Trade Union Law; Edwin E. Witte, Injunctions in Labor Disputes; Redmond S. Brennan and Patrick F. Gill, The Inferior Courts and Police of Paterson, N. J.

That this scathing indictment of the court was widely accepted as just there can be little question. A comparison of classes would seem to show the chief distrust of courts in the ranks of labor, the chief confidence among the employers, and the middle class alternating, first on one side or the other, as the particular issues affected or influenced them.

In a significant work not much noticed, Myers undertook to show the class bias of the courts in rendering their decisions. They are " the able servitors of the ruling economic forces." Specific instances of corruption and collusion are alleged, with cases of close corporate connections. General emphasis is laid on " class consciousness," however, rather than on personal corruption.[58]

Particularly it was urged that the use of the terms " due process of law " and " freedom of contract " for the purpose of negativing legislative acts was carried far beyond reasonable bounds. " Into the general clauses of the constitution they had read," says Freund, " a purpose of fixing economic policies which, however firmly rooted in habits of thought and structure of society, are by their very nature unfit to be identified with the relatively immutable concepts of due process." [59]   The attempt of the

[58] " History of the Supreme Court," 1912.
[59] Cf. Ely's " Economic Theory and Labor Legislation," also the notable study on " Property and Contract " (1914), particularly Pt. II, Chaps. 4 and 9, and Appendix IV. Cf. Felix Frankfurter, "Hours of Labor and Realism in Constitutional Law," *H. L. R.* 29, 353 (1916). Morris R. Cohen, " Process of Judicial Legislation," *Am. Law Rev.* 48, p. 161. Goodnow, " Principles of Constitutional Government," Ch. 21; " The American Conception of Liberty and Government "; Groat, *Op. cit.* 389.

courts to check modern social legislation by constitutional principles, he says, can only be properly estimated if we recognize the exercise of "a political and not a strictly judicial function." He indicates, however, that the courts have been aided by the shortcomings of legislators; that a check was demanded by the conservative sense of the community; and that on the whole our main reliance for the protection of individual rights must be found " in the continued exercise of the judicial prerogative."

A specific criticism was made by Freund in the domain of constitutional law.[60]   Constitutional decisions, he believed, must not be regarded scientifically as based on the canons of jurisprudence, but as " in the main issues of power and policy." [61]   The decisions of the courts in these cases are almost wholly lacking in constructive spirit or attainment.   They are almost entirely negative in their animus and effect.   From the point of view of legal science it would be difficult to conceive of anything more unsatisfactory.[62] No rule " has been formulated in such a manner as to embarrass an honorable retreat, and if an inconvenient precedent is encountered there is little hesitation in overruling it." [63]   Decisions favoring so-called " inherent limitations " are among the most loosely reasoned.   Indeed, " the greatest defects of the decisions from a legal standpoint constitute their saving grace." [64]

[60] " Standards of American Legislation " (1917).
[61] P. 130.
[62] P. 211.
[63] P. 211.
[64] See his keen analysis of the treatment of " due process of law " by the Courts.

The evolutionary theory of political society was the clue to the new development of the legal attitude taken by Goodnow.[65] He pointed out that the early theory of law rested upon the doctrine of the social contract which in turn rested upon the conception that society was static rather than dynamic. With the general acceptance of the evolutionary theory, it becomes evident that " a static society is all but impossible," and that legal theory must now reckon with the assumption of a continuous process of change in social and economic conditions accompanied by a continuous adjustment of law to the new situations — upon a pragmatic rather than an absolute basis. *Stare Decisis,* the rule of precedent, taken as a fundamental, he believed to be unworkable. We must abandon the theory that " our constitutions postulate a fixed and unchangeable political system and a rigid and inflexible rule of private right " and adopt a theory that will permit of " continuous and uninterrupted development."

In comprehensive fashion Roscoe Pound challenged the traditional legal philosophy.[66] In the United States

[65] Frank J. Goodnow, " Social Reform and the Constitution " (1911) ; " Principles of Constitutional Government " (1916).

[66] " The Scope and Purpose of Sociological Jurisprudence," *Harvard Law Review,* 24, 591 ; 25, 140, 449 (1911) ; See also, among other writings: " Mechanical Jurisprudence," *Columbia Law Review* VIII, 605 (1908) ; " Political and Economic Interpretations of Jurisprudence," *Am. Pol. Sc. Rev.,* VII, 94; " Courts and Legislation," Ibid, VII, 36; " Law in Books and Law in Action," *Am. Law Rev.* 44, 12; " Puritanism and the Common Law, Ibid, 45, 811; " The End of Law," *Harvard Law Review,* 27, 195, 605; " A Feudal Principle in Modern Law," *Int. Journal Ethics,* XXV; " Limits of Effective Legal Action," Ibid, XXVII, 150. " Juristic Problems of

the basis of deduction is the classical common law of the 17th, 18th and first half of the 19th century. The leading conceptions of our traditional case law have come to be regarded as fundamental concepts of legal science. This has led to a rigid and unyielding type of law, inadequate to the demands of modern social and industrial life — to what he terms "mechanical jurisprudence." Thus it happens that the common law for the first time is not on the popular side, and also that the law is not on the side of scientific development and tendencies. The courts do not have the facts of the present. "They have but one case before them to be decided upon the principles of the past, the equities of the one situation, and the prejudices which the individualism of common law institutional writers, the dogmas learned in a college course in economics, and habitual association with the business and professional classes, must inevitably produce.[67]

Pound assailed the juristic system with vigor and acumen, with legal logic, social and economic philosophy, and the citation of an imposing array of cases. Specific inquiry was made into the bearing of mechanical jurisprudence upon social legislation. Judicial decisions upon liberty of contract were scrutinized, and attributed to the individualistic and narrowly juristic doctrines of the state and of law, to the training of lawyers and judges in the 18th century law, economics and politics.

Reviewing the various schools of jurisprudence, Pound

National Progress," *Am. Journal Soc.,* XXII, 721; "The Law and the Law of Change," *U. of Pa. Law Rev.,* 1917, 659, 748.
    [67] H. L. R. XXI, 403.

finds that the "analytical" is useful for purposes of reform in certain situations, but neglects the social processes of which the law is a part. From the historical jurisprudence much good may be derived, particularly in the study of the immediate past, but attention too long fixed on the past may result in insufficient attention to the living present. The "philosophical" jurisprudence he regards as likely to develop into a dogmatic system of principles and formulas, which may lack a real and positive content. In the last century it was sterile, although now reviving into fruitfulness again. Genuine sociological jurisprudence takes as its point of departure the "social interest," and endeavors to formulate rules of law, on the basis of full consideration of social facts and forces, and the social bearings of the proposed canon of conduct.

His interpretation of the "sociological" however, rejects the "positive type, which seeks mechanical social laws, as uncontrollable by human will or the operations of the planets. He will have none of "social physics." Nor does he concede the doctrine of the "economic interpretation" of history. Law is not an inevitable result, the unconscious interpretation of dormant social forces by judge or legislator. "The conscious endeavor to adhere to the ideal and the necessity of working with the materials afforded by the received tradition and in the manner prescribed by the traditional mode of reasoning" are often a forceful check on class interests. Tradition, professional criticism, the logical demands of an accepted system, are all factors in determining the rule finally adopted by the judge.

Pound holds to the distinctions between " legislation " and " law," and maintains that the " will " element in law is less significant than the " reason " element, while the traditional element plays a large part both in the actual law and in legal history. A complete theory of law must reckon with all the complicated factors, past and present, traditional and rational, the complex social, economic forces, real and idealistic, which must be interpreted in a rule or principle.

Neglected fields in jurisprudence are the study of the social effects of legal institutions and doctrines, the sociological-legal preparation for legislation, the methods of law enforcement, the study of sociological-legal history, the reasonable and just solutions of individual causes, and in general making " effort more effective in achieving the purposes of law."

He proposed a pragmatic, sociological legal science. " The sociological movement in jurisprudence is a movement for pragmatism as a philosophy of law; for the adjustment of principles and doctrines to the human conditions they are to govern rather than to assumed first principles; for putting the human factor in the central place and relegating logic to its true position as an instrument." [68]

Following the German jurist, Ihring, Pound holds that law must recognize the priority of social interests, just as individual interests have been critically worked out, as in the case of property and contracts. We must start from the premise that " individual interests are to be secured by law because and to the extent that they are

[68] " Mechanical Jurisprudence," op. cit.

" social interests." Furthermore, the law must develop a scientific method of acquiring pertinent facts. The court must in a manner become a bureau of social justice. In short, the great problem of law is that of socialization.[69] To define " social justice " is to define " social interests," to study the means of securing these social interests by new methods, to study the social effects of legal institutions and legal doctrines, to compel law making and legal interpretation upon the basis of social facts to which the law must apply.

In brief, the characteristics of sociological jurisprudence are that it looks more to the working of the law than to its abstract content. It regards law as a social institution capable of improvement by human effort. It lays stress on social purposes rather than on legal sanction or penalties. It considers legal precepts as aids to justice rather than as inflexible formulas.

There appear the beginnings of a new development in jurisprudence. In this the study of the logic of the law, of legal history, of social and economic forces, of sociology, in the broad sense of the term are essential factors.[70]

[69] With Pound compare earlier types such as: W. G. Miller, "Philosophy of Law," 1884; E. L. Campbell, "The Science of Law," 1887; W. T. Hughes, "Datum Posts of Jurisprudence," 1907; W. S. Pattee, "The Essential Nature of Law," 1909; E. B. Kinkead, "Jurisprudence Law and Ethics," 1905; Hannis Taylor, "Science of Jurisprudence," 1908.

[70] M. M. Bigelow, "Centralization and the Law," 1906. John Chapman Gray, "The Nature and Sources of the Law," 1909. Morris R. Cohen, "Legal Theories and Social Science," New York Bar Association (1915), p. 177. Recent Philosophical Legal Literature in French, German and Italian (1912–14), *International Journal of Ethics*, 26, 538. See also "Business Jurisprudence," in *Har.*

The study of law is broadened by a much wider acquaintance with the best results of other juristic systems, and by more complete preparation and equipment for the measurement of social forces. A notable study was that of Wigmore on the " Principles of Judicial Proof." [71] The translations and publications of the Association of American Law Schools are illustrative of a broadening tendency in the study of the law, and the prefaces are as significant as the translations, for they show the wide degree of interest in bench and bar. The Modern Criminal Science Series, the Modern Legal Philosophy Series and the Continental Legal History Series are indicative of renewed interest in the broader problems of jurisprudence.

A broad view of the whole legal situation was given by Keedy, in a remarkable study of " The Decline of Traditionalism and Individualism." [72] Acute criticisms were made of the logic of the law, and of the quality of judicial reasoning by many incisive minds.[73] Wigmore indicated that judicial decisions are characterized by lack

Law Rev., 28, 135. Edw. H. Adler, Labor, Capital and Business at Common Law, *Ibid.*, 29, 241.

[71] 1913, See bibliography, pp. 1173-74: The Psychology of Testimony, *Ill. Law Rev.*, 3, 399 (1909): G. F. Arnold, Psychology Applied to Legal Evidence (1906).

[72] *U. of Pa. Law Rev.*, 65, 764 (1917): Compare R. L. Fowler, " The New Philosophies of Law," *Harvard Law Rev.*, 27, 718, declaring the new legal philosophies are " philosophies of socialism."

[73] John. H. Wigmore, The Qualities of Current Judicial Decisions, *Ill. Law Review*, 9, 529 (1915); W. N. Hohfeld, Fundamental Legal Conceptions as Applied in Judicial Reasoning, *Yale Law Journal*, 16, 23, 26, 710 (1917); T. R. Powell, Logic and Rhetoric of Constitutional Law in *Journal of Phil. Psych., etc.* Collective Bargaining before the Supreme Court, *P. S. Q.*, 33, 396. W. W. Cook, Privileges

of acquaintance with legal science, unfamiliarity with controlling precedents, over-emphasis on technique, undue servitude to precedent, and to some extent show the marks of political, class and economic influence.

One of the most striking developments in legal science was in the field of legal pedagogy where the case method was discovered and applied by Christopher Columbus Langdell in 1871.[74] The basis of this method was the belief that law is a science; that the number of fundamental legal doctrines is less than is generally supposed; that the mastery of these and the ability to apply them with constant facility and certainty to the ever tangled skein of human affairs constitutes the true lawyer; and finally that these principles may best be learned from the study of cases rather than from formal texts.

Yet these developments are not characteristic of the period as a whole, but are the phenomena of its close. Nor were they characteristic of the law, but must be looked upon as symptomatic. On the whole, legal and judicial statistics, legal history, the comparative study of jurisprudence, juristic psychology, were of relatively slight significance in the progress of American law. It

of Labor Unions in the Struggle for Life, 27 *Yale Law Journal,* 779.

[74] A Selection of Cases on the Law of Contracts, 1871. See Josef Redlich's report on "The Common Law and the Case Method in American University Law Schools," 1914, for Carnegie Foundation for the Advancement of Teaching. Of particular interest "The Improvement of Legal Scholarship and the Promotion of Legal Research" (p. 48), and "The True Significance of Langdell's Invention." Compare the interesting discussion in the American Bar Association, 1894, in which Woodrow Wilson, Wigmore, Baldwin, Keener and others took part.

was only at the very close of this half century that attention began to turn toward the historical, comparative, and philosophical types of study that had been familiar on the continent for a generation and in England on a less comprehensive scale and with less attention to the philosophy of law for about the same length of time.   On the whole, the period was marked by a type of legalism,[75] divorced from the study of economic, political and social science to which the law is intimately related.   It was not realized that the jurist is something of a political and social philosopher and that the depth and breadth of his philosophical equipment will condition the juristic product, that law and political, economic and social science are inseparable.

[75] Berolzheimer, "Die Kulturstufen der Rechts und Wirtschaftsphilosophie." Cohen; Recent Philosophical Legal Literature in French, German and Italian, *Int. Journal Ethics,* 26, 528.   E. Barker, "Political Thought in England": Chap. VI.   The Lawyers.

CHAPTER VI

THE tenure of judges remained practically unchanged during this period.[1]   Attempts were made to change from elective to appointive systems, or *vice versa,* but without material alteration.   The term of judges was, however, notably extended.   New York in 1876 increased the judicial term from eight to fourteen years;[2] Pennsylvania in 1873 from eight to twenty-one years.   Eight states increased the term of judges from an average of four to seven years to an average of eight to fifteen years. The impeachment process was very rarely employed, although used at the close of the period of the famous case of Judge Archbold.

Aroused by a quarter of a century of decisions in many cases unfavorable to social legislation, vigorous attempts were made to curb the power of the court.   The control of the judges by the democracy became a topic of widespread and bitter controversy in the course of which many significant changes were proposed.   Most of these involved closer responsibility of the judges to the electorate.

---

[1] William Carpenter, "Judicial Tenure in the U. S."

[2] Dorman B. Eaton's, "Should Judges Be Elected" (1873), and the Transactions of the Commonwealth Club of California (1914), Vol. IX No. 5 on election of Judges are illustrations of the sporadic discussion running through this period.

The specific remedies suggested most widely included the recall of judges, the recall of judicial decisions, the requirement that legislative acts should not be declared invalid except by an unusual majority of the court, the complete abolition of the right to negative laws, popular election of judges, modifications in the organization and procedure of the courts.[3]

In the States of Michigan, Idaho, Colorado, Arizona, Nevada, Washington, Oregon and California the recall of judges was adopted, and in Colorado the recall of judicial decisions.   In Ohio the new constitution provided that acts of the legislature could not be held unconstitutional except by a vote of five of the seven judges.   In many of the States proposals for change in tenure were made, and in all of them there was animated discussion over the basis of judicial office-holding.   If judges are the custodians of the constitutions, then who shall watch the courts, was the question raised in the minds of many. If the law-interpreting body is wrong and the legislature is right, then what is the remedy?

It was freely charged that the courts were obstructing necessary social and economic legislation; that they were using the economic theories of generations past to block the adoption of new policies designed to meet new indus-

[3] See Gilbert Roe, "Our Judicial Oligarchy"; W. L. Ransom, "Majority Rule"; Theodore Roosevelt, Proceedings of the Ohio Constitutional Convention, 1912, p. 378; Hiram Johnson, Ibid., p. 544; William Jennings Bryan, Speeches, p. 663; Albert M. Kales, The Recall of Judicial Decisions, Illinois State Bar Association, 1912, p. 203; Judge R. M. Wanamaker, Illinois State Bar Association, 1912, p. 179; Judge Walter Clark, Address, April 27, 1906; and January 27, 1914; W. F. Dodd, The Recall and the Political Responsibility of Judges, *Mich. Law Review,* Vol. 10, p. 7 (1911). *An. Am. Acad.,* Sept., 1912.

trial conditions. It was contended that the power of the judiciary was being employed to protect property against persons and defeat regulative measures in the interest of the many as against the privileged position of the few. It was pointed out that under the American system originally the judicial veto had been only sparingly employed, either to protect the nation against the states or to maintain the independence of the judiciary. In many quarters it was openly maintained, as it was widely believed, that the courts had become the guardians of wealth and privilege against the legitimate demands of the mass of the people. Even where the judges were personally honest, it was said that their class prejudices had led to decisions against the commonwealth, or that their devotion to precedent made their reasoning processes inadequate to solve modern problems. The conclusion was drawn that if the judges were made amenable to recall, or if their decisions in particular cases might be reversed by popular vote, the interests of the public would be more adequately protected. There was difference of opinion as to method, but agreement in principle.

This idea was most authoritatively stated by Roosevelt in his Ohio speech. His position, in brief, was that if the legislature and the court disagree regarding the interpretation of the constitution upon a question of policy under the police power the electors should arbitrate between them. If the legislature of a state limits the hours of labor for women, believing it constitutional, and the court holds that such action is unconstitutional, then the people shall decide whether the proposed law is or is not within the scope of constitutional power. If the court held that a Workmen's Compensation Act is unconstitutional, while the legislature believed that such an act is valid, then the question of the validity of the law should be determined by popular vote. If some such measure is not adopted, we shall be the victims of " perfunctory legalism " and there will continue to be " monstrous perversion of the constitution into an instrument for the perpetuation of social and industrial wrong and for the oppression of the weak and helpless." [4]   The power to interpret is the power to establish, and if the people are not to be allowed finally to interpret the fundamental law, ours is not a popular government.

Ordinarily the process of constitutional amendment would be applied at this point, and the necessary adjustment made. This has frequently been done in the last quarter of a century, as in the case of the California amendment to make direct primaries constitutional; of Idaho, in the effort to legalize an eight-hour law; and of New York, in the case of the Workman's Compensation Act. Yet it was contended that this process was slow and difficult, and that the extraordinary majorities required for constitutional amendments gave the minority an unwarranted ability to block the genuine judgment of the majority. Ransom, however, maintained that the vote on a specific question, such as the constitutionality of an eight-hour day for women, would be more conservative in its tendency than a general amendment covering a wide

[4] Ohio Constitutional Convention, 1912, 386. See also " The New Nationalism," 231.   D. F. Wilcox, " Government by All the People," Chap. 19. Duncan Clark, " The Progressive Movement " (1913), Chap. 13.

variety of cases; and that it was therefore superior to the constitutional amendment.

Governor Johnson defended the recall against its assailants. " The recall," said he, " will make no weak judge weaker and it will make no strong judge less strong. It menaces just one kind of judge, and that is the corrupt judge, and he ought to be menaced by something." [5] That the just judge would be intimidated by the " mob " he did not believe. " He mounts the bench," said the Governor, " and in a week sitting there he is metamorphosed in that brief period — and he looks snarlingly behind him and he sees the mob and the rabble — the same mob and rabble that put him on the bench, the same mob and rabble to which he appealed when he wanted to gratify his ambition; the same mob and rabble that elevated him at his own behest and to which in the first flush of success he was so duly grateful. But suddenly it has become a mob and rabble."

The argument for the recall rested in part upon the failure of the earlier provision for removal of judges by the impeachment process or on joint address of the Legislature. That procedure had practically ceased to function, and the long-term judge was not amenable to public control by any governmental process. It was held that if his opinions failed to reflect the mature opinion of the community there was no ready means of redress, in view of the difficulty of obtaining a constitutional amendment, against the will of an entrenched minority holding some special privilege.

Wilcox denied that the judicial recall would result in

[5] Ohio Constitutional Convention, 1912, p. 547.

the oppression of the minority. " We must not confuse,"
said he, " majorities of men and majorities of dollars." [6]
Judges can have no just claim to be shielded when " ob-
durately applying the obsolete but unrepealed injustice of
the past." The courts must put aside their " policy determining " functions or submit to the same type of control as other departments of government. The truth is the
judiciary is now generally recognized to be " the bulwark
of the vested interests, of property rights, so-called."
Following Hadley, of Yale, he declared that the new balance of power is between the forces of property on the one
hand and the forces of democracy on the other, with the
judiciary as arbiter. The " independence " of the courts
is mainly independence from the people — and the case
is made worse by judicial incompetence. Not only do the
courts stand as " the bulwark of special interests and spin
red tape that binds the poor to their poverty," but they
are a part of the political patronage system of the time,
dispensing favors in receiverships and trusteeships. Lawyers practicing before these very judges fear to speak
the truth widely known in the profession. The chief
danger in the recall, he predicted, is not that it would be
misused to degrade the courts and make the judges pup-
pets, but that it might not prove effective as a remedy
because the people are essentially conservative. Yet it is
more important that they exercise this power themselves
than that it be imposed upon them by the " arbitrary restraints " of an " inflexible institution."

There was during the latter part of the period a demand

[6] *Op. cit.*, p. 222.

for the abolition of the judicial power to declare laws unconstitutional. This was the official demand of the Socialist Party, and met with some support in various quarters. The court's power was held to be a usurpation not intended by the Fathers of the Republic; and by others it was maintained that the Constitution makers were fearful of democracy, and deliberately devised the mechanism as a means of protecting the propertied class. In either event, the opposition to the judicial veto was based upon modern social and economic conditions, and the belief that the exercise of such authority was undemocratic in spirit and tendency; that it operated solely or chiefly in the interest of property and privilege, and that it served no useful purpose in the democracy.[7] In general this was the theory both of Socialism and of organized labor, and of many scattered persons in various groups.

The doctrine of judicial review generally prevailed, however, and was the generally accepted principle, although conditioned upon its fundamentally democratic exercise. More accurately speaking, a small and compact group sustained the doctrine of judicial review for personal or class reasons, covering property interests, such as might be affected, for example, by an Income Tax case; another group included jurists because of traditional influence, and from the belief that law in general is a finished court product, while legislation is a crude contriv-

[7] Allan L. Benson, "Usurped Power of the Courts." "Our Dishonest Constitution." William Trickett, "The Great Usurpation," *Am. Law Review,* 40, 356.

ance; while a far larger group upheld the power on broader grounds of the general expediency of a judicial review of legislature action.

Theoretical and practical opposition to the new measures was decidedly vigorous and determined. President Taft vetoed the act admitting Arizona to the Union in 1911, on the ground that the constitution of the state contained a provision for the recall of judges.[8] In the campaign of 1912 this was one of the leading issues under discussion. The American Bar Association in 1911 adopted a resolution condemning the recall of judges and of judicial decisions, and appointed a committee to carry on a campaign against it.[9]

President Taft and Senator Root were particularly energetic in their criticism of the proposed plans. They held that the recall of judges would place weak and wavering men on the bench, and drive away vigorous and independent characters. The judges would become timid and time-serving. The tendency would be to substitute for " the fearless and independent judge a spineless, flabby, cowardly judge, a reed shaken by every wind." " I do not hesitate to say," said Mr. Taft, speaking of the judicial recall, " that it lays the ax at the root of the tree of

[8] Geo. W. Wickersham, " The Changing Order," 1914. Ch. 12-13. Fred J. Stimson, " The American Constitution," 1908. J. Hampden Dougherty, " Power of Federal Judiciary over Legislation," 1912.

[9] See Proceedings of American Bar Association in 1911, and the years following. Also Proceedings of many of the States, notably New York's Report of Committee upon the Duty of Courts to Refuse to Execute Statutes in Contradiction of the Fundamental Law (1915), pp. 230-365; (1916), pp. 163-220, a striking and typical document.

well-ordered freedom, and subjects the guarantees of life, liberty and property without remedy to the fitful impulse of a temporary majority of an electorate."

" It would," said Senator Root, " strike at the very foundation of our system of government. It is imperative that we protect individuals against the democratic absolutism of the majority." If changes in the Constitution are necessary, then amendments ought to be proposed and passed in an orderly fashion. Dr. Butler believed that the judges are not properly the servants of the people but " of the law." If the recall is adopted, tyranny and injustice are sure to follow. The recall, in short, " is the most monstrous perversion of republican institutions and of the principles of true democracy that has yet been proposed anywhere or by anybody." [10]

In his presidential address before the American Bar Association in 1911 Ferrar referred to the new " Homeric Thersites " who " sets the hydra-headed Demos on the throne of justice." [11] The recall means absolute democ-

---

[10] Senator Sutherland said, " It is the old contest between idealism and stubborn matter-of-fact reality. It is the story of the philosopher's stone over again — the dream of transmuting all the metals into gold — the hunt for the master key that will open all locks, however different in size and shape — the problem of fitting square pegs into the round hole, the puzzle of how to eat one's cake and have it — the search for the chimera of perpetual motion — the quest for the mythical pot of gold at the foot of the rainbow — and all the other impossible undertakings which have vexed men's souls and turned their brains and filled the lunatic asylums since mankind divided into those who see facts and those who see visions." (62nd Cong. 1st Sess. 2802.) See also " Martin W. Littleton," p. 1501.

[11] P. 232. See Augustus P. Gardner, The Recall of Judges and Judicial Decisions. W. D. Guthrie, Criticism of the Courts, in " Magna Charta," p. 130. R. G. Brown, Recall of Judges, Minn. Bar

racy, says he. It signifies the right of the changing majority of the people to rule without any limitation or restraint whatever upon their power. For three hundred years, said a committee of the American Bar Association, the courts have protected the mass of the people against the pressure of the few. " Is it any reproach upon the courts," they asked, " that they have extended the same protection to the rich and powerful when assailed by popular prejudice? " [11a]

The objections to the recall of judges were most substantially stated in President Taft's veto of the resolution admitting Arizona as a State in 1911.[12] In this famous message the President declared that the recall would permit the oppression of the minority by the majority. A popular government, he said, is not a government of a majority by a majority for a majority of the people. It is a government of the whole people by the majority of the whole people under such rules and checks as will secure a wise, just and beneficent government for all the people. It is the function of a constitution to check the hasty action of the majority and thus secure respect for the otherwise unprotected rights of the minority. The power and duty of enforcing these constitutional provisions falls to the judiciary who are not popular representatives. In order to fill their office properly

Assn., 1911. Senator H. C. Lodge, The Constitution and Its Makers, before the State Literary and Historical Association of North Carolina, November 28, 1911. F. J. Stimson, Certain Retrogressive Policies of the Progressive Party, *Am. Pol. Sc. Rev.*, VII, 149. Harlan F. Stone, "Law and Its Administration," p. 48.

[11a] 1912, p. 583.

[12] 62nd Cong. 1st Sess., p. 3964.

judges must be independent, deciding every question that comes before them according to law and justice, and without regard to popular majorities. The recall, however, would subject the judges to " momentary gusts of popular passion." Under these conditions of legal terrorism the character of the judges would deteriorate to that of " trimmers and time-servers," and independent judicial action would be a thing of the past.

That the judge is out of touch with the movement toward wider democracy he did not concede. On the contrary, he thought that " the cases in which his judgment might be affected by his political, economic or social views are infrequent." Individual instances there may be, but they are not many, and do not call for radical action. Usually, he thought, it will be found that the courts respond " to sober popular opinion as it changes to meet the exigency of social, political and economic changes."

Woodrow Wilson also opposed the recall of judges, contending that judges are not law-makers but are administrators. Their duty is not to determine what law should be, but to determine what the law is. Their independence, their sense of dignity, and freedom is of the first consequence to the stability of the state. To apply to them the principle of the recall is to set up the idea that determinations of what the law is must respond to popular passion and not to popular judgment.

Evidently a prime cause of difficulty lay in the transfer of judicial lawmaking from the field of every-day judge-made law to the much larger domain of broad questions of public policy. The inner core of the law and the fiber

of legal justice are always made by the slow and sometimes almost imperceptible processes of application and
adjustment of the old law to new conditions.   In this
field, undoubtedly, traditional philosophy, traditional
point of view, class bias and conservatism play their part
along with legal logic and common sense.   But in the slow
processes by which fundamental standards of justice are
shaped, the unreasoned tendencies often pass but little
noticed, and in the long run the evolutionary product may
be claimed as a triumph of juristic reason.   But the application of this process of making law, somewhat esoteric
and oracular in its nature, to the burning questions of
public debate in our land, was much more difficult, and
aroused an opposition unmistakably different from that
of the malcontent.   That the legislative bodies did not
always inspire public confidence and that their measures
were sometimes hastily and imperfectly drafted helped
the courts in the task of declaring many laws invalid.
But even this argument lost its weight as public opinion
was more and more clearly formulated and its demands
more and more urgently pressed.   The general desire for
certain fundamental constitutional laws differing from the
ordinary law also came to the aid of the courts as the
special guardian of the higher law.   But as it became evident that constitutions could be amended only with very
great difficulty — difficulty so great, indeed, as to make
an easy defence for privilege attacked by law — public
opinion was aroused against what seemed to be final decisions on fundamental questions of public policy.   It
was not to be expected that the democracy would quietly
accept the government of the minority through control of

courts and constitutional interpretation. There were many ways forward: through more direct control over judges or their decisions; more flexible modes of constitutional amendment; readier response to public opinion by constitution-amending authorities; more liberal interpretation by courts, and more discreet use of their judicial negative.

During the last half century, American political thought has turned toward the practical difficulties arising from the organization of our legal system. The first controversy was over codification of the law, and began shortly after the War. This may be said to date from the original code drafted for the State of New York by David Dudley Field, in 1865, down to the abandonment of the plan in 1887. By the middle of the century the legislatures had begun to take a hand in the moulding of the law which had gone on for some time without much interference on their part. They began to enact the common law into statute here and there, changing it somewhat from time to time, and also altering the procedure as they went. Field attempted to produce a complete state code, containing the entire law of the commonwealth in written and enacted form. His contention was that such law would be made more accessible, simpler and more intelligible both to the lawyer and the layman. He aimed at a systematization of the law after the general fashion of the codification championed by Bentham.[13] The Field code was never adopted in New York, but was taken up in part by the State of California subsequently. Over the

[13] See report of Committee of Mass. Legislature, headed by Story (1836), American Jurist, XVII, 17–93.

desirability of codification an animated controversy arose
in which the demand for legislative crystallization of the
law in statutory form and the counter demand for a free
hand for the courts in the moulding of the law were
strongly presented.

The great leader of the opposition to codification was
James C. Carter [14] of the New York bar. Indeed, the
whole controversy dramatically resolved itself into a
duel between two legal giants, who fought for nearly a
quarter of a century like feudal barons over the domain
of the law — Field, one time attorney for Jay Cooke and
Tammany Hall, and Carter, a leading corporation lawyer
of New York. Carter's argument against placing the law
in statutory form turned partly upon a specific and destructive criticism of Field's effort, but more broadly
speaking upon the undesirability and impossibility of bet-
tering the law by legislative enactment at that time. He
preferred the gradual development of the judicial system
at the hands of the courts to the systematic treatment at
the hands of the legislature, as proposed by Field and
those of his school. A clearer issue would doubtless have
been drawn upon the question of a national code, but this
was not possible under the Constitution as it stood, and
was therefore excluded from the discussion.

The opposition to systematic codification prevailed in
general, although in not all of the states and in many
more partial revisions and digests were made from time to
time as the convenience of the law-makers or the demand
of public sentiment dictated. What Sir Henry Maine

[14] Proposed Codification of our Common Law (1883). The Province of Written and Unwritten Law (1890).

termed " tacit codification,"— that is, by text writers and judges — went on at a rapid rate. However, the nominal victory rested with those who championed a progressive development from case to case through the courts as against those who demanded a new code of law from the representatives in the form of the legislatures of the states. It was a victory for the conservative as against the radical theory of the making of the law in the states; for the unconscious as against the conscious process of developing the general legal system of the country; for the court as against the legislature as an interpreter of community ideals of justice.

As the end of the century approached, the attack on judicial ills become more and more energetic. Critical analyses and constructive proposals came thick and fast. Judicial organization and procedure became topics of widespread discussion, not only among the members of the bar, but among the members of the community in general. With the technical details of this great process we are not here intimately concerned, but the broad features and the underlying principles of the movement are of great significance in any appraisal of the tendencies of American political thought.

The critics of the system were recruited from many quarters. Business was far from satisfied with the delays and uncertainties of the law's procedure; labor was in anything but a peaceful frame of mind in contemplation of the court's activities; scientific students of the system were sharp in their criticisms; members of the bar were not quick to defend the system, while the average citizen was mystified by the eccentricities of what was called the law.   Neither Mr. Gompers nor Mr. Taft could approve the law's delays, and while Senator Root and Col. Roosevelt differed widely regarding the recall of judicial decisions, they were united in believing that reform of judicial procedure was an imperative necessity.

As early as 1885, David Dudley Field and John F. Dillon, being a sub-committee of the American Bar Association, " to consider delay and uncertainty in judicial administration," presented a memorable report on the situation as they found it.[15]   " A single word," the committee said, " expresses the present condition of the law — chaos.   Every lawsuit is an adventure more or less into this chaos."   But notwithstanding this terrific indictment of the law, no concerted and effective movement followed. Later, notable critiques of the legal system were made by Mr. Taft in 1895,[16] by the National Economic League in 1911,[17] by the Industrial Relations Commission in 1915, and by many others.[18]

Senator Root, in a famous address before the American Bar Association in 1914, declared: " The general result, however, is that in all litigations in these jurisdictions we have a vast multitude of minute, detailed, technical rules that must be followed — traps to catch the unwary, barbed wire entanglements; barriers which the subtle and adroit

[15] Transactions, American Bar Assn., 1885, pp. 323–449.

[16] Recent Criticism of the Federal Judiciary, American Bar Association, 1895. See also, " Administration of Criminal Law " in " Present-day Problems," p. 333 (1905).

[17] See John H. Wigmore, " The Problems of To-day," Congress of Arts and Sciences, Vol. 2, p. 350. For a general discussion of these problems see J. M. Mathews, " Principles of American State Administration," Ch. 15–17.   Arthur N. Holcomb, " State Government in the United States," Ch. 11.

practitioner can interpose to hinder the pursuit of justice.
. . . While the law is enforced, justice waits. . . . In
such a game the poor stand little chance against the rich,
or the honest against the unscrupulous." [19]

The defects in the practical administration of justice
were broadly sketched by the National Economic League.
The general difficulties enumerated were those arising
from the development of industrial and urban centers, the
shifting of ideas as to the nature and purpose of law, and
the great increase of litigation under modern conditions.
Local causes were found in the tenure, mode of choice,
and personnel of the bench, in the education and organization of the bar, and in bad legislative technique. Inefficiency in litigation was attributed to defective organization of the courts, want of proper organization of the
administrative side of tribunals, and to procedural weaknesses, to the concurrent jurisdiction of state and federal
courts, to local partisanship, and various other causes of
local operation. Further specific defects enumerated
were: detailed legislation regarding procedure; emphasis
on procedural rights as against substantive rights; " record worship "; preservation of sharp formal issues; over-
emphasis on procedural form; piece-meal disposition of
cases; excessive number of trials and re-trials; too great
freedom of the jury from the guidance of the court.

There were also included: the special problems of
metropolitan cities; the lack of adequate provision for
petty causes; the survival of legal institutions designed
to obstruct the process of debt collection in pioneer
communities. The causes of inefficiency in the enforce-

[19] Addresses, p. 493.

ment of law were found in lack of coordination between
law and administration; in the break-down of the common law policy of individual initiative; in the increased
burden of law in the modern community; in the diver-
gence of class interests; in the failure of popular interest
in justice; while additional local causes were seen in the
diversity of interest in different parts of the state and in
the contact of criminal law and politics.

The remedies proposed in this notable review of the
legal field were the proper training of the legal profession;
improved methods in the election of judges; the grant to
courts of greater power over rules of procedure; improvement of legislative law-making, and a thorough study of
the new problems of industrial and urban societies.

During the last decade and indeed since the report of
the Bar Association Committee in 1885, energetic efforts
have been made to reorganize the courts and to modernize
procedure, but thus far without revolutionary results.
The general type of judicial organization has not been
rapidly altered, while the modes of procedure have been
changed here and there in several states.   In urban communities, where under the sharp pressure of new conditions the effects of the old system were earliest apparent,
more successful attempts have been made in introducing
newer methods.

In the reform of criminal procedure, much less rapid
progress was made.   Mr. Taft declared, " I grieve for
my country to say that the administration of the criminal law in all the states of the Union (there may be one
or two exceptions) is a disgrace to our civilization."
Processes originally designed to protect the individual

against arbitrary interference with his liberty were deeply imbedded in the life of the community. And even when it became evident that these historic guarantees were being habitually and effectively employed by professional criminals against society, a change in the direction of modified procedure came very slowly.[20] The frequent absurdities and inconvenience of criminal procedure became intolerable, however, and a strong demand was made for such revision as would make possible the adequate protection of society. Then the grand jury, the petit jury, the coroner, the form of indictment, the liberty of appeal, the nature and use of the record, delays in trial, were all subjected to keen critical analysis and later to diligent reconstruction. While in a number of States significant changes were made, on the whole progress in this direction was extremely slow. Conservatism in the attitude of bench and bar and politics in the practical workings of the system combined to render rapid changes extremely difficult.[21] Notable proposals have been made by the American Judicature Society

[20] See report of Chicago City Council Crime Committee (1915), of which the writer was chairman.

[21] Law enforcement is a topic that would well repay intensive inquiry which is not attempted here. From remote times the English legal system has had a way of quietly ignoring law and allowing it to lapse into disuse, without formal repeal. In America there has been added to this the decentralization of our law-enforcing machinery, which has often been equivalent to local option law enforcement, the common unwillingness to create strong administrative agencies for any purpose, the laxness in the legislative technique of drafting, the passage of hortatory legislation, lynch law and other features. The history and tendencies of this phase of our political evolution is an interesting study which is not undertaken here.

for the reorganization of local courts, but thus far these
have not been carried out.

In the administration of punitive justice significant
changes have been made, in which the names of William
Penn and Edward Livingstone, and in later days of
Wines and Henderson are widely known. The absence
of class interest and of professional prejudice and the
presence of a strong humanitarian sentiment prevailing
from an early period in American history, made progress
in this direction less difficult. No attempt will be made
here to cover this large and important field.

During the last half century, the great problem of the
court was the adjustment of the law to meet the new
urban and industrial conditions, to keep pace with the
evolution of new social and governmental policies adequate to the new forces and facts of American life by
means of new legal technique. In this admittedly delicate
and difficult task there was a general feeling that the
courts were not cordially or successfully cooperating, but
that, on the contrary, a narrow position was frequently
taken, and that the text of the law and the letter of the
Constitution, were so construed as to make difficult the
adoption of a vigorous social policy. There was a very
general belief that the court did not fully represent the prevailing sentiment of the time, or voice the inner ideal
feelings of the nation; but that through its legalism, its
literalism, its formalism it was holding the balance of
power in favor of the few rather than of the many. This
was relatively easy in view of the peculiar circumstances
of the case, for to hold — as the court frequently did —
to a policy of non-interference, while one of the parties

was in possession, was equivalent to deciding in favor of
that party.   When the court held that legislative measures
of social policy, such as the Workman's Compensation
Act [22] or the limitation of the hours of labor, were unconstitutional, they ruled in favor of the privilege affected.
Likewise in the development of the power of the court
through the use of the injunction in labor disputes, a
broad principle of interpretation was followed, to the advantage of the propertied class.   But in the construction
of the rights of labor precisely the opposite principle of
narrow, strict and technical construction was adopted.
Under a democratic system of government the organ or
agency that most clearly reflects the judgment and will
of the community is most powerful.   To lose touch with
this community life is like cutting off the current of
power.   This is what happened to the American courts,
to the extent that they failed to rise to a far-seeing interpretation of the law in relation to social and economic
conditions.[23]

The half century's development of political thought
regarding the judicial branch of the American political
system may be summarized as follows.   The organization and procedure of the judiciary have undergone rela-

[22] The "fellow servant" doctrine, says Pollock is "a sad example
of the wrong way to use fiction." Op. cit. p. 104.

[23] Edouard Lambert, in "Codes and Cases," says: "Judicial law
is naturally conservative and trails but slowly after the changes in
usage and the mutations in our economic life. By the mere fact that
it must wherever possible hide its innovations under the cover of
interpretations it arrives generally only by tortuous and indirect
ways at a goal which the legislature may gain directly, and consequently much more slowly."

tively little change, although during the last quarter of a century constructive criticism has developed comprehensive plans for systematic reorganization. Notable changes have been made in the sphere of punitive justice, however, where humanitarian and sociological influences have effected broad advances through legislation rather than through judicial interpretation and adaptation.

Looking at the responsibility of the courts to the democracy, it appears that during the whole of this period the courts have employed their power in opposition to many policies of social legislation. During the first part of the period this process was not clearly understood, but in time the character of the court's action became clearly evident. When this occurred there arose a vigorous protest which took the shape of various demands for closer responsibility of the judges to the people either by way of the " recall of judges," or the " recall of judicial decisions," and of other demands for a broader spirit in interpretation of the law. Few changes were made, however, in the structure of the courts, although many modifications were made toward the close of this period in the spirit and temper of their decisions.

The underlying spirit of the law was conservative. This was true not merely in the sense that all institutions are conservative, that is that they lag behind the ideal conceptions of right in changing social and economic conditions. Conservatism in this case was reenforced by the doctrine of the sanctity of precedent, by the tendency to regard the common law as a closed book, by the unconscious individualism of the common law, and the conscious Manchesterian-Spencerian theory of govern-

mental non-interference. One of the evidences of this
was the overthrow of the codification movement, although
the federal factor in the situation was not inconsiderable.
Then came the tendency displayed in the construction of
industrial questions arising between the many and the
few, toward the preservation of the old status, which was
of course equivalent to the decision in favor of the few.

Toward the end of the period came " sociological jurisprudence " challenging the earlier "mechanical jurisprudence. In reality both were sociological after a
fashion, but one held the sociology of Spencer pointing
to non-interference on the part of the government as a
basic principle, and the other was the social type, leading
to the consideration of social interests as paramount in
public and private law. The distinction between these
tendencies was not wholly one of method, as close analysis
will show. More sharply characteristic was the difference in the degree of democratic spirit found running
through them. Justice, it has been said, is an affair of
the heart as well as the head; it is not wholly made up
of legal logic and analogy; economic interests and
political ideals and standards are not and cannot be
ignored; and any system of jurisprudence whether
mechanical, historical, evolutionary, sociological, analytical, philosophical, eclectic or otherwise, must be influenced largely in last analysis by sympathies, interests
and ideas represented. The significant feature of the new
jurisprudence was the modification of the earlier method
through the closer consideration of the living social, economic and political facts, and the inspiration of the social
spirit and the social point of view.

Down to the end of this period the earlier forms continued in the main, but vital forces were clearly moving toward comprehensive change in the organization, procedure, technique and spirit of the law. Revolutions in public law are not uncommon, but in private law the processes of evolutionary change are much more frequently encountered. It is these slow moving developments that were occurring in the American judicial system. Unquestionably the narrower type of legalism tended to lose its hold on the bench, the bar and the mind of the public and a broader spirit of social justice to take its place. Toward this goal the personnel of the bench, the ethics and education of the bar, the movements toward reorganization and modification of procedure, the sweeping changes in punitive justice, the swift rise of sociological jurisprudence, the slowly rising movement toward scientific research in jurisprudence, the drift toward the broader social point of view were tending. If the courts lag behind the community's ideals, at least they follow its general direction and are closing up the gap. The new ideals of social justice, of right, of liberty and equality, springing from the new social conditions, move forward with a massive power offsetting their reluctant pace. Democratic and social gains finding their way through slow and painful processes into the inner fibre of the juristic principle and rule will be dislodged with equal difficulty.

But the making of public law upon broad questions of public policy can never be the function of the judicial system in an alert democracy that knows its mind and its way, and the effort to do so embarrasses the judiciary in the work of constructing the inner core of private law. Just as in public administration there are many important internal problems of organization and adjustment which normally are developed and decided within the administration, itself amenable to democratic supervision and control, so in judicial administration there is an inner field where juristic logic shapes the rules of justice; but also amenable to democratic supervision and control. Yet if the bureaucracy actually attempts to govern, or the judicial administration to rule, challenging or evading democratic control, or seeming to do so, there is conflict, and democratic control will be demonstrated even at the temporary cost of reduced efficiency in judicial or other administration. A democracy will recognize its limitations in passing upon expert administration in law or elsewhere, but it will demand and obtain allegiance; and it will act more rationally when this is conceded. No doors will be closed to it, by any other lock than its own rational restraint. The genuine faculty of juristic divination and creation — the quality of the great and just judge — is nowhere more highly venerated than in a democracy like ours; but nowhere is there a firmer determination that the public judgment shall utter the last word of decision on broad questions of social policy.

CHAPTER VII

DEMOCRACY AND CONSTITUTIONAL CHANGE

ONE of the important features of this period was the development of the theory of constitutionalism in the broader sense of the term. The Federal Constitution was a skilful compromise between conflicting interests and principles by means of which national existence was made possible. It represented an accommodation of jangling local and general interests through which the nation became a practical reality. The state and federal constitutions signalized the development of a written document in which certain " natural rights " of men were declared and guaranteed, a plan of government outlined, and provision made in most cases for continuous change. These constitutions were striking illustrations,— the most imposing thus far in the history of democracy,— of voluntary conscious law-making, deliberate outlining of systems of political order and progress. They were victorious over " traditionalism," were forward looking and experimental in their tendency. The orthodox constitution of that day was the mass of customs, traditions and laws which the feudal-absolutist régime had accumulated, or at best was the piece-meal product of English evolution. The ruling group of that time looked with horror upon a Constitutional Convention deliberately framing the outlines of fundamental law for the community. The most skilled representatives of reaction, such as Burke, De Maistre, Von Haller, levelled their fire at the " paper constitution," the " artificial " government, at the absurdity of supposing that any body of men could create political constitutions of any type, democratic or otherwise. De Maistre compared would-be constitution makers to the ambitious designers and builders of the Tower of Babel, and predicted a like outcome for the unholy experiment.[1] In comparison with current theory, the Fathers were not only liberal, but revolutionary in their methods and aims. In the movement from " status to contract," from unconscious custom to deliberate rational choice and selection of ways and means of governing the community, the Revolutionary state constitutions and the Federal Constitution were epoch-making.[1a]

Given the constitutions, there came the question of their progressive adaptation to changing conditions. But the logic of interpretation was not the logic of their origin. Born in the spirit of revolution, they were applied under the influence of *stare decisis;* prophetic in outlook they were applied in terms of precedent.

In the course of time, through the activities of such nationalists as Marshall and Webster, the Federal Constitution became an effective instrument against the particularism of the several states. It was made so by the deft process of judicial interpretation, and by the close-drawn legal analogies from private law. The na-

[1] See Dunning, " History of Political Theories," Vol. III.
[1a] See Merriam, " History of American Political Theories," Ch. 2–3.

tionalistic arguments, both of Marshall on the bench and
of Webster in the Senate, were based upon the letter of
the law and close analysis of the text of the document,
upon an interpretation of specific words and phrases.
The textual analyses of the Constitution came to be
identified with the national cause and with the interests
of progressive national development.   Legalism in the
narrower sense and literalism came to be the standard
methods of interpretation.   The constitution was not conceived by either party to the contest as a living, growing
document, as an evidence of the nation's development,
capable of growth with the growth of the nation, but
rather as a contract, a fixed and determined thing in the
nature of a finality.   Both North and South stood constitutionally upon the *status quo*.   Indeed, the Constitution came to take on something of the quality of the
common law, originating in time immemorial, and not
subject to change except by interpretation and application,
in which case theoretically the law itself was not changed.
In the hands of lawyers accustomed to the careful use of
legal logic this process was not a difficult one.   In short,
although the Constitution was in fact the greatest example
of conscious voluntary law-making that the world had yet
seen, it tended to become in effect an unchangeable, permanent and established Precedent, to be differentiated but
not disputed, to be interpreted but not to be altered, to be
discussed as a fixed feature of political organization and
not as a flexible measure of national life and growth.
Jefferson had said that he did not consider the Constitution as the Ark of the Covenant, as " something to be too
sacred to be touched," but this is what the Constitution

actually became in the course of legalistic interpretation. For two generations the Constitution remained un-amended, and finally came to be considered an end in itself instead of a means, a thing in itself, rather than an in-strument designed for a purpose, a terminus rather than a starting point.[2]

During the Civil War this attitude was fundamentally changed. What if democracy must choose between its life and the Constitution? The answer was that the na-tion's existence was paramount to any interpretation of the written document. In the agonies of the great struggle, perplexing constitutional problems were not solved by the refinements of legal analysis, but by the stern necessities of national life. When, for example, the Court undertook to prevent the suspension of the writ of habeas corpus, it was quietly but firmly brushed aside until the guns had ceased firing. Lincoln declared that, " Measures otherwise unconstitutional might become law-ful by becoming indispensable to the preservation of the Constitution through the preservation of the Nation." [3] He would cut off a limb of the Constitution, he said, in order to save the life of the nation. He would not permit the Constitution to interfere with the purpose for which the Constitution was framed, namely, the establishment and maintenance of a democratic nation.

Evidence of the same spirit is given by the statement of Fisher that " if *the* Union and *the* Government cannot be saved out of this terrible shock of war constitutionally, *a*

[2] H. V. Ames, " Proposed Amendments to the Constitution of the U. S."

[3] Works, II, 508.

Union and *a* Government must be saved unconstitutionally." [4]   Men began to point out that there is an unwritten constitution as well as a written constitution.   Jameson, for example, distinguished constitutions as " organic growths " from constitutions which are " instruments of evidence."   " Organic " constitutions are the product of various social and political forces.   The others are attempts to " express in technical language some particular constitution." [5]   Some distinguished between the constitution of a nation and the constitution of a government, one resting on " the genius, the character, the habits, customs and wants of the people," and the other upon a particular legal formulation. [6]

Of even greater significance was the later theory of Hurd, [7] who maintained that sovereignty does not at all depend on the constitution and the law, but itself makes constitutions and laws.   It is idle to seek in the Constitution an answer to the question whether the States or the United States is sovereign, because in the nature of the case the Constitution is not the creator, but the creation of power.   Sovereignty is a matter of fact rather than of law, and it is to the facts back of the Constitution, not to its text, that we must look for an authentic interpretation of the question of supreme power.   If the United States was not legally and technically a nation, then, they reasoned, it ought to be one.   It was destined to be a

[4] Sydney Fisher, " The Trial of the Constitution," p. 199 (1862).

[5] J. A. Jameson, Constitutional Conventions, Sec. 63 (1866).

[6] O. E. Brownson, " The American Republic," Chap. VII (1866). Compare Elisha Mulford, " The Nation," Chap. IX (1870).

[7] John C. Hurd, " The Theory of our National Existence " (1881) ; " The Union State " (1890).

nation, and political facts must yield to the social and political forces which have decreed the existence of the nation. And in this spirit the constitutional document must be interpreted. At the same time radical changes were made in the text of the Constitution itself. The 13th, 14th and 15th Amendments, passed in rapid succession, materially altered the scope of the United States Constitution. This was particularly true of the 14th Amendment, with its significant provisions regarding the protection of civil liberty.

After the War, however, the old spirit quietly returned, and took up the practical application of the wide powers given in the 14th Amendment. The authority there granted to protect civil liberty was an expression of the war spirit and was given primarily for the purpose of protecting the colored man in his new-found freedom. Practically, however, the race question was soon thrown into the background, while the industrial struggle over corporations and property rights became the subject of intensive and extensive interpretation. The 14th Amendment was born in the struggle over slavery, but it lived as a principle of action during the great struggles of modern industrialism. In this process of interpreting "equal protection" of the laws, "due process" of law, "liberty," and "property," the old textual methods and the technical spirit were revived and reintroduced. Living touch with the shifting and changing of social and economic conditions was often lost. Then once more the doctrine of literalism prevailed, as before the Civil War. No further amendments to the Constitution were made for forty years, until it seemed that the Constitution had become practically unamendable.   From 1870 until 1912, a period of unparalleled growth and change, the formal Constitution remained unchanged.   At the same time the earlier doctrine of the Constitution as a finality, a precedent, an unchangeable instrument, temporarily ousted by the War, and the somewhat violent adoption of the 13th, 14th and 15th Amendments, was once more enthroned as a working principle.

The expression of a constitutional theory widely entertained was voiced by the distinguished jurist, E. J. Phelps, in his Presidential address before the American Bar Association in 1879.   On that occasion, he urged that constitutional questions be taken from the realm of general discussion and placed under the exclusive jurisdiction of the bar.   Lawyers, he believed, should unite in " setting their feet upon and their hands against all efforts to transgress the true limits of the Constitution or to make it at all the subject of political discussion."   The Constitution, he said, should not be " hawked about the country, debated in the newspapers, discussed from the stump, elucidated by pot-house politicians and dunghill editors, scholars in the science of government who have never found leisure for the grace of English grammar or the embellishment of correct spelling." [8]

It was not long, however, before proposals for greater flexibility in the national Constitution were made from various quarters.   Burgess pointed out the danger to national development from the possibility of veto by a small group of states, containing three million population (1880), and urged that the way to amendment be made

[8] Proceedings, p. 190.

wider and easier.[9] If a minority can block the mature and deliberate will of the majority, then there is danger of violence and revolution. War should not be the only way of changing the Constitution. In a notable proposal he urged that amendments should be made by Congress in joint session by a majority vote of two successive Congresses, and ratification by the legislatures of the commonwealths acting in joint assembly by majority vote. The vote of each legislature should have the same weight in the count as that of the state in the Presidential election and an absolute majority of all the votes should be necessary for final ratification. " There is," said he, " a growing feeling among our jurists and publicists that in the interpretation of the Constitution we are not to be strictly held by the intentions of its framers, especially since the whole fabric of our state has been so changed by the results of rebellion and civil war. They are beginning to feel — and rightly, too — that present conditions, relations and requirements should be the chief consideration, and that when the language of the Constitution will bear it, these should determine the interpretation." [10]

In the individual states, the principle of restricted interpretation also developed, but the state constitutions were more easily amendable. The boundary lines between constitutional and statutory law were largely broken down. Constitutions of such length and detail had been adopted, containing so many provisions ordinarily statutory in character, that it became difficult to distinguish the organic law from the statutory law.

[9] " Political Science," Vol. I, 142 ff.
[10] *Op. cit.,* p. 152.

" Constitutionalism " in the state, therefore, never reached a degree of development comparable to that of constitutionalism in the nation. There had never been in the state the same tradition of inflexibility which from time to time grew up around the national document. Frequent amendments were made in the various commonwealths, either by constitutional convention or by revision from time to time.[11] The referendum principle in the adoption of state constitutions had been put in force prior to the Civil War, and in the latter part of this period a number of commonwealths adopted the initiative in the amendment of such constitutions. Under this system it was possible to amend the organic law of a state without recourse to the Legislature, thus increasing the flexibility of the fundamental law of the state.

On the other hand, the doctrine of the flexibiltiy of the Constitution developed as a part of the general democratic movement. " There is," said Judge Amidon, " a very general understanding that formal amendment is impossible." [12] The declaration of the unconstitutionality of the income tax law in 1894 led after a long struggle to the amendment of the Constitution, making the income tax constitutional. The demand for direct election of Senators precipitated another long struggle. Other

[11] See Jameson, " The Constitutional Convention "; Holcombe, " State Government in the United States," p. 92; W. F. Dodd, " Revision and Amendment of State Constitutions "; Mathews, " Principles of State Administration "; Roger S. Hoar, " Constitutional Conventions."

[12] American Bar Assn., 1907, p. 468. " A changeless constitution becomes the protector not only of vested rights but of vested wrongs."

amendments pressed hard for consideration and for passage until the desirability and the necessity for constitutional change came to be widely evident.

Lowell discussed the " fetichism " of Constitution worship and indicated that it must in time give way.[13] Woodrow Wilson asserted that " the Federal Government was not by intention a democratic government. In plan and structure it had been meant to check the sweep and power of popular majorities." [14] Smith, in a notable essay, likewise contended that the Constitution was adopted in a spirit of reaction and that its makers deliberately made it difficult to amend, because of their fear of democracy. Constitutional provisions designed to obstruct government are an anomaly in popular government, and they must eventually yield to the demand for more democratic provisions.[15] Beard [16] discussed in detail the economic basis of the Constitution, and drew from it a confirmation of Wilson's doctrine of the '90's.

The Progressive Party in its platform of 1912 placed flexibility of the Constitution in the forefront as one of the necessary means of social and political betterment. Mr. La Follette, Mr. Roosevelt and many others of the nation's political leaders defended the necessity of easier methods of effecting fundamental change in the foundation law. They contended that the Constitution was an

[13] A. L. Lowell, " Essays on Government," p. 126 (1889).

[14] " Division and Reunion," p. 12 (1893), quoted by Smith.

[15] J. Allen Smith, " The Spirit of American Government " (1907), Chap. 3-4.

[16] Charles A. Beard, " Economic Interpretation of the Constitution." Compare H. C. Lodge, " The Constitution and Its Makers " (1911).

instrument of national growth and progress and must be
modified not only by the decisions of the courts, but from
time to time as the needs of the people demanded.   They
insisted that the national life could not be held within the
limits of an unchanging written document, but must be
free to develop and expand with the changing needs of
the new time.   Senator La Follette, in particular, proposed a specific plan of constitutional amendment.   He
would permit submission of an amendment by vote of
both houses of Congress, or the initiative of one-fourth
of the States; and ratification by a majority vote, in a
majority of the states.   This gateway amending process
he regarded as fundamental in the attempt to meet new
social and industrial conditions by constitutional change.

Goodnow called attention to the static character of the
constitutional system, and the danger arising from over-
rigid law.   A modern program of social reform is blocked
by constitutional restrictions and " Few can refrain from
asking the question why Americans alone of all peoples
should be denied the possibility of political and social
change." [17]   Either changes in the mode of formal
amendment or in the spirit of interpretation are essential,
if the nation's way toward free development is to be kept
open.

Croly [18] asserted that the Constitution had become over-
rigid and in this respect unadapted to the conditions of

[17] " Social Reform and the Constitution," p. 333.   C. G. Tiedemann,
" The Unwritten Constitution of the United States " (1890).   Com-
pare Andrew C. McLaughlin, "A Written Constitution in Some of
Its Historical Aspects," *Mich. Law Rev.*, V (1907); H. P. Judson,
" The Essential Elements of a Written Constitution," 1911.

[18] " Progressive Democracy."

modern life. The "monarchy of the Constitution," or the "monarchy of the Word," are terms employed to indicate the supremacy of legalism in the domain of constitutional amendment and interpretation. Admitting the educational advantages of the system, the combination of "democracy and moralistic legalism" was on the whole narrowing in its tendencies. Divergences in social ideals and concepts of justice, constantly appeared and rendered the task of operation a painful and difficult one. The existing method calls for "amendment by unanimous consent" or constitutional interpretation "under the immediate direction of a group of benevolent guardians." A nation blessed with common sense will adopt more democratic measures for keeping its "Law" adapted to its needs.

Toward the close of the period when it seemed that the Constitution could not be amended, the demand for the preservation of the document in its textual integrity became more insistent, for it then seemed that the Constitution would afford a protection for property rights in a degree and in a form otherwise unattainable. Thus the rigid Constitution was defended by Butler, who believed that certain fundamental guarantees were embodied in the written law and that these should under no circumstances be changed. We must build, he thought, upon foundations that are not subject to continual revision and reconstruction.[19] In the same spirit Mr. Root and others declared against any effort toward hasty change.

[19] "Why Should We Change our Form of Government?" p. 29. William D. Guthrie, "Magna Charta," pp. 42–86, on Constitutional Morality. William Howard Taft, op. cit.

Great stress was placed upon the importance of a fundamental, permanent law, as a barrier against passionate and violent action on the part of the majority, and especially as a protection for personal rights and private property. Self-restraint, said Senator Root, is a necessary quality in all human conduct, but even more important where men are acting in mass than as individuals, because masses are more difficult to control than individuals. " The makers of our Constitution," said he, " wise and earnest students of history and of life, discerned the great truth that self-restraint is the supreme necessity and the supreme virtue of a democracy." Long and slow processes of change are desirable in order that new proposals may be fully analyzed and weighed and finally adopted or rejected only after mature deliberation. The doctrine of the force of precedent, the literal text of the Constitution, the emphasis of legal logic as against the current social and industrial conditions, all contributed to the same result, namely, the development of a " constitutionalism " akin on a larger scale to the " legalism " found in the field of private law. The elements of growth, development, adaptation, progressive unfolding of the national spirit in the organic law, were excluded in great part, particularly in the early years of this period.[20]

[20] Compare Bryce, " The very considerations which have made odious to some American reformers those restrictions on popular powers behind which the great Corporations and Trusts (and capitalistic interests generally) have intrenched themselves, had led not a few in England to apply the same restrictions as inevitable safeguards to property. . . . In other words, the establishment in Brittain of the status of rigid Constitution has begun to be advocated, and advocated by the persons least inclined to trust Democracy." " Constitutions," p. 82.

There were several ways in which constitutional change might be made. Alterations in the formal process of amendment were possible. The pressure of public opinion upon legislative bodies might become more quickly effective. The judicial interpretation of constitutions might be broadened and liberalized. All of these ways were followed, particularly during the latter part of this period. In the cities charter-making was usually submitted to a popular vote: in the states easier methods of amendment were adopted, of which the most notable was the amendment by constitutional initiative and referendum, as in Oregon. Again there was a readier response to public opinion on the part of legislative bodies. As the voices of protest increased, the 16th and 17th Amendments were submitted and ratified, in the national field, and many amendments were proposed in the several states. Constitutional Conventions were called in states like Michigan, Ohio, New York, Massachusetts and other significant urban and industrial centers.[21] In many cases amendments were passed for the purpose of meeting constitutional objections raised by the courts. A notable case of this sort was the California amendment, authorizing the establishment of a direct nominating system after three adverse court decisions on laws passed by the Legislature. Finally the judicial attitude toward constitutional interpretation was somewhat modified during this period under the pressure of public opinion and with

[21] See Dodd, op. cit. Ch. V, on the working of the Constitutional Referendum, and Appendix, pp. 295-344 for detailed list (1899-1908). On the theory of the powers of Constitutional Conventions see Dodd, op. cit. J. A. Jameson, "The Constitutional Convention" (1866).

the aid of technical information.   A famous case was the reversal by the Illinois Supreme Court of its early attitude holding the limitation of the hours of woman's labor to be unconstitutional.

There thus developed conflicting theories regarding the flexibility of the organic law in a democracy, the conservative clinging to a rigid and relatively unchangeable system, while the liberal advocated the theory of relatively easy translation of the public will into fundamental law. Yet it has been pointed out that the differences in theory are not wholly logical in origin and aim, but correspond in many cases to differences in economic attitude.   Hadley said that industrial property right is more fully protected in the Constitution of the United States than anywhere else in the world.   Clauses originally inserted to prevent sectional strife were used to " strengthen vested rights as a whole against the possibility of legislative or executive interference." [22]   Consequently the fixed constitution together with the judicial power to hold ordinary legislation unconstitutional, afforded an unusually ample protection, which a flexible system might not retain.   The conflict of interests overshadowed the more ultimate question of the principles of constitution-making in a democracy, and there was little broad discussion of the relative merits of rigid and flexible constitutions, such as Bryce has outlined in his " Essays on History and Jurisprudence."

Yet in spite of the confusion many changes are distinctly evident in the general theory of the organic law of

[22] Arthur Twining Hadley, " Undercurrents in American Politics," p. 41 (1915).

the democracy. There is less emphasis on the bill of rights, which was the chief factor of the Revolutionary State Constitution. There was less reliance on the three-fold system of checks and balances as the citadel of human liberty. There was feverish argument over provisions for amendment which in a number of the Revolutionary constitutions were omitted altogether. There was less reliance upon narrow textual interpretation of constitutional documents, and more of a disposition to test new policies by the standards of social utility. Goodnow's discussion of social reform and the constitution seemed to represent the general trend of political theory toward a readier adaptation of the fundamental law to changing social and economic conditions.

In the first great interpretation of the Federal Constitution, made in the *Federalist,* solemn warning was given against endeavoring to secure liberty by constitutional restraints alone. All such precautions are mere paper barriers.[23] The guarantee of free institutions lies in the " general genius of the government." " Particular provisions, though not altogether useless, have far less virtue and efficacy than are commonly attributed to them." [24] It is in the spirit and temper of the people, rather than in the written word, that confidence must be placed.

[23] No. 47.
[24] No. 83.

CHAPTER VIII

THE UNIT OF DEMOCRATIC ORGANIZATION

THE territorial basis of the state is a perennial problem of politics. The city state, the national state, the world state have appeared from time to time as the local habitats of authority. There has always been an intimate relation between land and patriotism, for " native land " comes to mean more than soil, including an interwoven group of economic, social, racial, cultural, religious and emotional associations and interests. Especially in democratic countries has the question of the area best adapted to most successful operation of government been a subject of frequent speculation. Can democracy succeed over a wide area with great population, or must it be limited to a restricted area and a relatively few people? Must the government be close to the people in the territorial and physical sense in order to preserve its democratic sympathies? To what extent may authority be delegated and centralized without severing that relation between people and government on which the cooperative enterprise of democracy depends?

Down to the time of the Civil War, the centers of political activity and interest had been the state and the nation, rivals in the contest for supremacy which finally resulted in armed conflict. State sovereignty and nationalism had absorbed the attention of jurists and philosophers. Back of this struggle lay an intense interest and devotion to the units and agencies of rural government, which had played so large and vital a part in the early days of the colonies and of the Republic.

During this later period the nation and the city were the centers of greatest activity. Whether we consider the problem from the practical, the juristic or the theoretical point of view, these two organs of government drew to themselves the eyes of public interest. In the background were the rural governments, the state and the undeveloped problems of internationalism.

In the earlier period of our history, universal emphasis was placed upon the functions of the local governments — in this case, rural governments.[1] The New England town meeting in particular was an active and powerful factor in government. Thomas Jefferson, while President, said: " I felt the foundations of the government shaken under my feet by the New England township." In the course of time, however, interest in the rural local government lagged, as the pressing problems of the nation and the city clamored for adjustment.

For three quarters of a century the overshadowing topic of political thought had been the relations between state and nation. Behind the legal and political controversy was the rivalry between free and slave labor systems.

[1] See John A. Fairlie, "Local Government in Counties, Towns and Villages"; John W. Burgess, The American Commonwealth, *Pol. Sc. Quart.,* I, p. 9; Simon Patten, Decay of State and Local Governments, *An. Am. Acad.,* I, 26; Alfred L. Reed, "The Territorial Basis of Government under the State Constitutions" (1911) ; H. S. Gilbertson, "The County, The Dark Continent of American Politics"; Francis Lieber, "Civil Liberty and Self-Government" (1853).

With the close of the Civil War this struggle was ended, and the legal and industrial chapter closed. No further doubt remained regarding the supremacy of the nation over the state. The doctrine of state sovereignty was abandoned, although restated in final form by such talented leaders of the "Lost Cause" as Davis [2] and Stephens.[3] This period was marked by the steady advance of nationalizing tendencies. The common property of the nation was developed into additional states, and new territory added in 1898. Business overleaped local boundaries and became nation-wide. State lines did not coincide with industrial areas. Likewise labor and education were nationalized. There was, it is true, frequent discussion of the constitutional position of the state in public law, and the significance of its constitutional position. But the silent force of events was stronger than words. As the state had been used as a defence for the institution of slavery, now it often became a means of opposition to railway control and subsequently to corporate regulation, to the imposition of the income tax, to the regulation of child labor, to the control of the liquor traffic, to the grant of suffrage to women, until the state began to suffer severely in popular thought as the " twilight zone " of causes seeking refuge from popular control. There was no evidence of a desire to abandon the dual system of government, but there was much unmistakable sentiment in favor of limiting the state to local

[2] Jefferson Davis, " The Rise and Fall of the Confederate Government."

[3] A. H. Stephens, " A Constitutional View of the Late War between the States " (1867). See Merriam, " American Political Theories," Chap. 7.

functions and of giving to the national government powers commensurate with the far wider scope of national affairs.

During this period of economic and social reconstruction the political idealism of America centered increasingly around the national government. Following the Civil War there was a saturnalia of political corruption in Federal affairs unexampled in our history. But there came a change. The Federal government was the first to adopt the merit system in 1883. It attracted aggressive leaders of the type of Cleveland, Roosevelt and Wilson, who stood for national ideals as few leaders in state or urban life. In the meantime there came a flood of corruption and a flood of light on the conditions of states and cities, and while great deeds were wrought there, yet on the whole during the latter part of the period the leadership was national rather than local. The political faith of the people turned toward the outstanding national personalities and programs which seemed to interpret more adequately their hopes.

The people turned instinctively toward the nation as the most vigorous and effective expanding of the ideals of its political life. Contests over the railways, the tariff, the trusts, currency, conservation, and foreign affairs were fought principally, although by no means exclusively, upon the national stage and scale. Both commercial and political thought tended to be national in character and scope, leaping over the boundaries of states. The great fear of centralized power which had characterized our early history and the jealousy of the nation fostered by the " States' Rights " school was gone.

The nation came to be looked upon as the appropriate agency for the solution of most of the urgent problems of the time.   Under the 14th Amendment, the national government was called upon not merely to protect the civil rights of the negro, but to adjudicate a wide range of economic and social problems.   The nation was asked to regulate the railroad and the trust; to prevent child labor; to encourage and subsidize agriculture; to ease the farmer's burden by establishing rural credits; to conserve our national resources; to stimulate industry through sweeping impositions of tariffs and bounties; to solve the industrial problem through corporate regulation.   The nation was called upon to grant votes to women, to prohibit the sale of intoxicating liquors; to provide a national commercial code, and even a national criminal code.   The power of taxation, the post office, and the power given inter-state commerce were invoked as agencies for extension of the practical authority of the national government.

Various types of national agencies were involved in this nationalizing process.   The federal courts under the 14th Amendment brought under their jurisdiction the protection of persons and property in a wide variety of cases, and the weight of the federal decisions was very great. The courts reached out into a broad field of legislation which constantly tended to increase the relative importance of the national government.   At the same time the administrative agencies of the federal government steadily amplified the number of points of contact with the citizens of the states, particularly in connection with the work of the Departments of the Interior, Agriculture, Com-

merce and Labor.[4] In short, the national influence was
a steady and penetrating force making its way through
the life of the States.

During and immediately after the War, there was developed a theory of the organic character of the nation
as distinguished from the earlier idea of the nation as a
legal entity created by means of contract. Men came to
believe that the nation grew and was not merely made by
the legal creation of contractual rights and obligations.
It was early pointed out by Lieber that there is a wide
difference between " people " and a " nation." " People "
signifies merely the " aggregate of the inhabitants of a
territory without any additional idea." [5] " Nation," on
the other hand, implies a homogeneous population inhabit-
ing a coherent territory, a population having a common
language, literature, institutions and being an organic unit.
Jamison,[6] Hurd,[7] Mulford,[8] Brownson,[9] Woolsey,[10]
Draper [11] and others reasoned to the same effect — that
the nation was an organic product, the result of an evolutionary process. The Supreme Court held that " The
union of the States was never a purely artificial and arbitrary relation. . . . It began among the Colonies and
grew out of common origin, mutual sympathies, kindred
principles, similar interests, and geographical relations." [12]

[4] John A. Fairlie, " National Administration."
[5] Miscellaneous Writings, II, 128.
[6] " The Constitutional Convention " (1866).
[7] " The Theory of our National Existence " (1881).
[8] " The Nation " (1870).
[9] " The American Republic " (1866).
[10] " Political Science " (1877).
[11] " Thoughts on the Future Civil Polity of the U. S." (1865).
[12] 7 Wall. 725.

Philosophical formulations of the new nationalism were made by many writers. Of these, however, there were two distinct types. One was the statement of the principle of national supremacy, emerging from the war struggle. The other was a doctrine of nationalism in relation to social reform. Burgess preached an exalted doctrine of the national state and its world mission. In his doctrine the national state is the most mature product of political history, political science and practical politics. It solves the problem of international relations, avoiding world empire; it solves the relation of sovereignty to liberty. It solves the problem of the relation of central to local government, in that it rests upon the principle of self-government in both domains. "Where uniformity is necessary it must exist, but where uniformity is not necessary variety is to reign in order that through it a deeper and truer harmony may be discovered." On the other hand, the state or "commonwealth," as he constantly termed it, was dropping behind in the race for political supremacy. "The commonwealth government" he argued, "is now but a sort of middle instance — too large for local government, too small for general, but is beginning to be regarded as a meddlesome intruder in both spheres — a tool of the strongest interest and the oppressor of the individual." [13] The Supreme Court he sharply criticized for the refusal to place civil liberty under federal protection, in the Slaughter House cases,[14]

[13] See his remarkable discussion on "The American Commonwealth," in *Political Science Quarterly,* Vol. I (1886).
[14] 16 Wall. 36 (1873).

and its failure to embody the national spirit and will in national jurisprudence.

A generation later, Croly celebrated the alliance between the principles of nationalism and the principles of democracy — the democracy of Jefferson, which was unnational, and the nationalism of Hamilton, which was undemocratic. Here he found a formula for the progressive solution of political and social problems.[15] It is the way in which the " promise of American life " is to be realized, the type form for the political civilization of the future. The failure of states to function he attributed partly to defective internal organization and partly to lack of an adequate program recognizing the real scope of the states' powers. Local and educational reforms, for example, are proper subjects for state activity, while commerce and industry have so far outgrown state laws as to be beyond effective state control. The state in a majority of cases has no meaning at all as a center of economic organization and direction, since business is related to the national system, or centers around the municipality.

Goodnow in an incisive study of the legal possibilities and limitations of social reform, pointed to the nation as the road to advance upon. If we were framing a scheme of national government, he said, our own experience and that of other countries would undobutedly lead us to accord to the national government greater powers than are now possessed under the Constitution as now interpreted and applied. Even now the federal power steadily ex-

[15] " The Promise of American Life " (1900). " Progressive Democracy " (1914).

pands and the process is resented only by those whose interest is to escape control.[16]   Col. Roosevelt, in his " New Nationalism " (1910) glorified the nation as the great instrument of social and political progress, and preached the gospel of a vigorous national policy directed toward democratic ends.   The New Nationalism puts the national need before sectional or personal advantage.   It is impatient of the confusion that results from local legislatures attempting to treat national issues as local issues. He did not ask for " overcentralization," but for a spirit of nationalism in common affairs.[17]   There must be no neutral ground " to serve as a refuge for law breakers, and especially for law breakers of great wealth, who can hire the vulpine cunning which will teach them how to avoid both jurisdictions."

After the War the State was, of course, no longer even a claimant of sovereign power.   The states' rights tradition was not much more cultivated in the South than in the North.   If one invoked the state against the income tax the other appealed to it against child labor legislation. After the Spanish War, nationalism was as strong in the South as anywhere else, if not stronger, as a result of its large native population.   Twelve new states were added to the Union during this time.   They did not have the historical traditions of the original colonies and they had no part in the long struggle over States' Rights and Secession.   They had a local interest, opinion and pride, yet it was not, on the whole, that of a State, but more likely to be that of a section or region — in these cases, the

[16] " Social Reform and the Constitution," p. 14.
[17] *Op. cit.,* 27–28.

West, or the Southwest, with dominant agricultural or mining interests.

Strong sectional interests survived, but these were represented by territorial groups, as the South, the East, the Central States, the South West, the Coast. These units often reflected political and economic views, as in the case of the currency question, railroad regulation, democratic and social reform. The state line did not accurately measure and localize industry, whether in the form of capital or labor, nor was it a measure of education, or religion, or party.[18] With the return of the Democratic party to power, in 1885, there was little evidence of the survival of state interests, as such, although the balance of sectional interests was somewhat altered by Wilson's election in 1912.

In quantity of legislation, the American state during the period under consideration has probably never been surpassed in the history of law-making. Literally thousands of laws were enacted every year.[19] Many of these were purely local and special in nature, but many of them were general in character, and covered a wide range of human activities. But their law-making was often caught between the fires of national questions, which they could not adequately control, and local affairs which they might better have left to the localities.

Of great significance was the fact that there sprang

[18] H. J. Ford, The Influence of State Politics in Expanding Federal Power, Proceedings of American Political Science Association, V, 53; also Sen. Root, Addresses, 363 (1906); somewhat modified in 1909, p. 375.

[19] In 1906–1907, for example, the number of laws passed by the various state legislatures was 16,064, of which 7,672 were indexed in

up a movement in favor of uniformity of state legislation and that the bulk of the states appointed commissioners for this purpose.[20]   The principal motive was to obtain agreement, if possible, in dealing with the law governing business relations throughout the country.   It was keenly felt that the perplexing variations in the law and procedure of many states were hampering and burdensome, and that some coordinating body was necessary.   Yet even in this field, effective concurrent legislation was made very difficult by divergent judicial interpretation and application, and a national business code came to be looked upon in many quarters with complaisance.   The situation was such that whether states were aggressively active or remained passively inactive, the nationalizing tendencies pointed toward the need of a larger unit of control than the individual state.

Some fundamental changes were made in the suffrage and in direct legislation, and toward the end of this period there were numerous suggestions for the complete reorganization of state government.   But none of them took root.   The People's Power League of Oregon, under the inspiration of the ingenious Mr. U'Ren, worked out a plan based upon the theory of executive leadership, but this was rejected by the voters.   The commission government proposal of Governor Hodges, of Kansas, was not favorably received.[21]   Neither Mr. Croly's interesting

the *New York State Library Bulletins* on state legislation of that year.

[20] See Proceedings of Commissioners on Uniform Legislation, since 1892.

[21] See Holcombe, " State Government in the U. S.," Chap. XIV; also Mathews, " Principles of American State Administration."

suggestions for state reorganization nor the official proposal of the Socialists met with a wide response.[22]

The states did not fully realize their possibilities either in internal organization or social and industrial policy. There were, of course, notable exceptions, as in Wisconsin under the leadership of La Follette, and California, under Johnson, yet these leaders gravitated to Washington as a more fruitful field for progressive legislation.

Possibly the best presentation of the importance of the state in our system of government was made by Wilson.[23] He urged the importance of the state as an experiment station in which new plans might be tried. " Every commonwealth," he declared, " has been a nursery of new strength; and out of these nurseries have come men and communities which no other process could have produced. Self-government has here had its richest harvest." If our system of states had not come to us " by historical necessity, I think it would have been worth while to invent it." Local affairs are not uniform, and cannot be made so by compulsion of law. What we seek is co-operation, but not the strait-jacket. Variety will not impair energy, if there is genuine cooperation.[24]

Our states have not been created: they have sprung up of themselves, irresponsible, " self-originated, self-constituted, self-confident, self-sustaining, veritable communities demanding only recognition." The remedy lies, not merely in changing the division of powers between state

[22] See Conference of Governors, 1908.

[23] Governors' Conference Proceedings (1910), pp. 42–54.

[24] See also " An Old Master and Other Essays," 1893; " Constitutional Government," Ch. VII.

and nation, along lines of actual alteration of interest, but in reorganization of the state from within.   Instead of upsetting an ancient system, we should " revitalize it by reorganization."   " Centralization is not vitalization," said he, and the atrophy of the parts will result in the atrophy of the whole.

The urban population which in 1870 was 20.9 per cent. of the population, had reached 46 per cent. in 1910.   In many of the industrial states, the urban population grew to much more than half of the total.   The problems of municipal organization and activity were so urgent that they called for continuous attention along the whole line, from the individual elector to the Supreme Court of the United States.   The economic and social importance of the urban center was very largely increased, and the new situations presented new questions of the greatest complexity.   Organized corruption on a large scale developed in the larger cities, soon after the Civil War.   The type first revealed was that seen in the machinations of Boss Tweed, and similar " gangs " in various other cities. Simultaneously there began organized efforts for municipal betterment, commonly called " reform."   This contest over the form, function and personnel of city government continued for almost half a century; and the din of the struggle still echoes throughout the land.

The rural democracy of earlier days was familiar to Americans, but the difficulties of rapidly growing urban communities presented a new set of difficulties, for which we were unprepared.   Jefferson once said: " When they (the American people) get piled upon one another as in Europe, they will become corrupt as in Europe."   These troubles were intensified on the one hand by the heterogeneity of the population which made that "common understanding" upon which all democratic governments rest, more difficult to attain quickly; and on the other by forms of governments which made prompt and effective action difficult even when there was a consensus of opinion; and not least of all, by the bitter struggles in the industrial world, so frequently finding a battleground in cities.

The city was a new type of social aggregate, differing in form and function from the old. It was a social and industrial unit, with distinct interests and problems of its own, arising from its local conditions. The political boundaries coincided in the main with those of the local aggregate, with suburban exceptions. The city was a local business center, a local social center, a local grouping quite different in community of interest from the state or the county. Issues and problems appeared, of primary interest to the local community, and of only secondary and minor importance to the state or nation. There was vitality and vigor in the city, and there was vivid life and color. However bad or good it was, the quality of the city was not atrophy or decline, but the recalcitrance of unruly struggling life forces, challenging control.

It is not within the scope of this discussion to consider the varied and interesting legal and political problems of our cities, but merely to direct attention to the characteristic political ideas underlying and appearing in the effort to adapt the old municipality to the new conditions of its modern life. These typical ideas are: the growth of the sentiment for local autonomy; the tendency toward the abandonment of the doctrine of checks and balances; the rapid extension of the functions of government.

A definite doctrine of municipal autonomy developed during this period. This idea came to be called " municipal home rule," and its essence was the theory that the city should govern itself in affairs primarily local in nature.[25] As millions of people came crowding together upon very limited areas, the collective problems of a safe and convenient life became greater. Far broader authority was required to meet the desperately urgent problems of housing, sanitation, public safety, public utilities, police and public welfare. At the same time there was urgent need for reorganization and readjustment of forms of government, originally designed for rural communities, but largely inapplicable under urban conditions. Out of these sharp local needs there were formulated local doctrines and demands for autonomy. A municipal conciousness and interest sprang up, and a new theory of the position of the city in the larger life of the state and nation.

This local demand was given recognition in the form of broader grants of local powers in many states either by constitutional amendment or by statutory enactment, or by broader judicial interpretation of local powers.[26] In the earlier period these grants were limited to a few states,[27] but later the number was very greatly increased.

[25] H. L. McBain, " Law and Practice of Municipal Home Rule " (1916).

[26] See W. B. Munro, " Government of American Cities," Chap. 3.

[27] In addition to Missouri and California, Washington, 1889;

Missouri in 1875 and California in 1879 were the first states to grant municipal home rule of a limited type in constitutional form, but later the advance of the movement was more rapid. At the close of this period some thirteen states had been given " home rule " by constitutional amendment. Where no constitutional changes were made, statutory enactments enlarging the powers of municipalities were the staple of every session of every legislature.

The new doctrine was that the city ought to be given local powers adequate to its local needs. The false position of the municipality is one of the chief causes, it was said, but not the only cause of the defects of city government. The legislature, it was conceded, should have theoretically large powers over cities, but the legislative policy should be such as to permit of the development of a large sphere of municipal action in which the cities may move free from legislative interference. This position was illustrated by many striking cases in the local history of particular states.

Freedom and responsibility, said Howe, are essential to life and growth. " We have placed our cities in strait-jackets and then expected them to develop strength and character. We have deprived them of self-government and then wondered why self-government was a failure." Give the city adequate power to deal with local questions, and there will arise a spirit of " local patriotism which would raise the American city from its present

Minnesota, 1896; Michigan, 1908; Colorado, 1902; Oregon, 1906; Oklahoma, 1907; Arizona, Nebraska, Ohio, Texas, in 1912; Maryland in 1915.

decadence to a position of splendid achievement." [28]
Goodnow, however, took a position unfriendly to the development of local autonomy for cities. " City populations," said he, " if permitted to develop free of state
control, evince an almost irresistible tendency to establish oligarchical and despotic governments." [29] Whether
or not larger powers should be given a city, depends on
the political capacity of the particular population in
question. That this view was widely taken throughout
the United States, particularly in the rural sections, there
can be little doubt.

There was widespread distrust of urban populations,
and a desire to curb their political activities both inside
and outside the city limits.[30] Concrete evidence of this
is given by serious restrictions placed upon the representation of cities in New York, Pennsylvania, Michigan,
Missouri, as well as the older systems which came to dis-
criminate against the New England cities,[31] and by the
reluctance with which municipalities were given additional powers of government. Specific statements of this
sentiment are found in the debates over state constitu-

[28] Frederick Howe, " The City, the Hope of Democracy," p. 163
(1905). Oswald Ryan, " Municipal Freedom," Chap. 9 (1915).
L. S. Rowe, " Problems of City Government." D. F. Wilcox, " The
American City "; Frank Parsons, " The City for the People," Chap.
3; Beard, " American City Government," Chap. 2; Horace E. Dem-
ing, " Government of American Cities." See on this general topic;
Munro, " Bibliography of Municipal Government."

[29] " Municipal Government," p. 378 (1909). Also Chap. 3 on " The
Character of City Populations."

[30] New York Con. Convention, 1915 Home Rule debate. California Con. Conv. 1878.

[31] G. H. Haynes, " Representation in State Legislatures."

tions from that of California in 1878 to New York in
1915.

The feeling was intensified by the fear on the part of
certain property interests in the cities of the radical tendencies of urban populations, and thus an opposition from
within the walls of the city was raised against the grant of
wider powers to the municipality. Furthermore, the
larger units of transportation, of water supply, and sew-
age disposal, of park areas, in some cases made more
difficult the definition of local government areas.

The struggles of the city for political readjustment
further led to the abandonment of the doctrine of checks
and balances, in municipal government. At the outset
the form of American city government had been simple.
It consisted of an elective council, which chose the mayor
and any other administrative officials. Imitation of the
Federal system brought about the adoption of the
bicameral legislature, and of the independently elected
mayor. Later came other elective officials and boards.
After the War, there began a process of reconstruction.
The double-chambered council was generally abolished,
the powers of the various elected officials were concentrated in the mayor, and finally in the commission government the powers of mayor and council were united
in a single body. This involved the rejection of the historic political theory of checks and balances, under which
the upper house of the legislature was presumed to check
the lower, or vice versa, and the executive to watch over
both of them. Of this there was no concealment, but on
the contrary, the fullest discussion. Many of the evils
of municipal management, beginning with the Tweed

régime, were directly attributed to the complexity of the checking system, and its failure to permit definite location either of power or of responsibility. It was openly stated that the purpose of the new type of government was to concentrate power in clearly responsible hands. This course was presented as an alternative to the forms of "boss rule" and mal-administration so familiar to American cities.[32]

At the same time the concentrated form of government was usually accompanied by new devices for popular control in the form of the initiative, referendum and recall. These were presumed to supply the check and balance destroyed under the new plan of consolidation, substituting direct responsibility to the electors for the mechanical adjustment abandoned. These plans were adopted in most of the new charters with which cities were generally experimenting, but were most commonly encountered in the western and central sections of the United States.

The cities, under the pressure of the industrial and social conditions developed symptoms, diseases and remedies earlier than elsewhere, and often became centers of progressive social programs. In dealing with the unregulated, competitive public utility the municipalities made notable progress toward regulation, and were ready for experiments with public ownership and operation. Housing and sanitary problems received an impetus from the city. Budget and financial systems were more readily adopted than in state or nation, and the same was true

[32] See Munro, "Government of American Cities," Ch. 12; H. Bruere, "The New City Government."

of merit and efficiency systems, where the cities led the way. In local judicial administration significant advances were made in procedure, in the prevention of crime and reclamation of criminals, in the application of modern psychology to jurisprudence. In the organization of recreation and the development of the democratic community center the cities made notable progress. If they furnished hideous examples of systematized corruption and crime, they also displayed readiness in the construction and systematization of social measures, many of which were not only useful for the locality alone but models for other agents of government. The urban community specialized both in evil and in virtue: or more accurately, the modern industrial and social tendencies developed most rapidly in urban centers, and their strength and weakness was there most sharply accentuated; the lights and shadows of modern life were there most clearly painted.

The American city was the storm center of powerful forces, economic, social and political. Its rapid increase in population, the heterogeneity of its people, the sharply emerging class distinctions, the power of organized labor and the formidable concentrations of capital, the violent outbursts of radicalism, and the alternately subtle and brutal tactics of reaction, the sinister power of the boss, and the counter-organization of militant " reform " — all these made the city a center of genuine political interest and activity. While the United States had been chiefly a rural democracy, it now became partly urban and partly rural, with all the changes involved in such a fundamental transition.

Summarizing this movement, it appears that the period opened with the abandonment of the doctrine of state sovereignty which had few defenders in expressed theory or general sentiment. The nation became the generally accepted center of political interest and action through which public opinion was to find expression — nation-wide democratic opinion working through the politically organized nation. Both state and local government tended to recede into the background of thought and action, although custom and tradition, as well as forms of law, still afforded them wide scope for activity. Localism did not lose its hold upon public thought, but it declined from its position as claimant to the throne of public interest and political supremacy. Its strength was the strength of inertia; vast, it is true, but not like the earlier strength of vigorous and aggressive action. The earlier identification of centralization with tyranny died down, although decentralization still remained one of the most striking characteristics of American theoretical institutions. Yet the tide was turning the other way. The urban centers alone showed signs of vivid consciousness, and despite their large scale corruption and inefficiency the cohesive force of their common interest had made them vigorous organs of political thought and action which found expression in a political theory of urban autonomy and a constitutional demand for home rule; in vigorous reconstruction of their local governments; and in the beginnings of a social and political policy.

None of these positions was by any means uncontested. But they emerged slowly as great landmarks in the evolution of American political ideas. Nationalism fully established became more confident and aggressive in its attitude. Its rival, the state, had been definitely overcome and subordinated. The city was a vigorous but not a dangerous competitor.

CHAPTER IX

INTERNATIONALISM — PACIFISM — MILITARISM

INTERNATIONAL relations did not occupy a large space in the political thinking of the early part of the period. For a long time the deep wounds of the Civil War were slowly healing, and the bones of nationality were knitting. A great western territory was being occupied and settled. For a generation the interests of America were largely domestic. But as the free lands of the nation were almost exhausted, as the balance of foreign trade began to turn in our favor in 1896, and as the expanding tendencies of commerce began to press against our territorial boundaries, the international organization entered the background of the American mind.

With the Spanish War a new era began. The United States came into the military possession of Spanish lands in the East; and the whole problem of imperialism and colonization was thrust upon us. Sharp differences of theory and policy at once appeared. On one hand arose the opinion that no territory should be held by the United States without the agreement of its people. The doctrine of the "consent of the governed" was applied to the Philippine Islands and the conclusion drawn that no such territory could rightfully be retained, inasmuch as the population was unwilling to accept American control. To hold the people in subjection would be not only a violation of the rights of man abroad, but would in the end demoralize democracy at home by introducing ideas and practices incompatible with democratic principles.[1] Such a step would be the first approach toward a broader policy of imperialistic expansion in the course of which free government would be lost. Overseas possessions will require a larger navy and a more formidable army. These in turn are likely to provoke other wars and wider conquests.

" I warn the American people," said the veteran statesman Schurz, " that a democracy cannot so deny its faith as to the vital conditions of its being. It cannot long play the king over subject populations without creating within itself ways of thinking and habits of action most dangerous to its own vitality — most dangerous especially to those classes of society which are least powerful in the assertion and the most helpless in defence of their rights." With great force and eloquence these considerations were presented, and they reflected the political ideas of a large group of Americans who believed that safety for democracy lay in isolation from all other and particularly from all European powers.

On the other hand, the policy of overseas expansion was vigorously defended by statesmen and philosophers, and took deep root in public opinion. The consent of the

[1] W. J. Bryan, " Speeches," II, 17 — 1900; David Starr Jordan, " Imperial Democracy," 1901; Charles Francis Adams, " Imperialism," 1898; Carl Schurz, " American Imperialism," 1899; " Life of Thos. B. Reed," by Samuel W. McCall, p. 252; Louis F. Post, " Ethics of Democracy," Chap. VI; Congressional Record gives debates, especially on ratification of peace treaty and on government of Philippines. Sen. Hoar was the leading opponent of imperialism.

government, it was urged, is conditioned upon capacity for political action. If a population is not capable of democratic self-government, then they must be subjected to a process of political education, until such time as they can govern themselves. They must be held as wards of the government, until they reach political maturity. This condition will be hastened by education, industrial training and tentative advances toward complete self-government. In any event, the alternative is not that of consent or no consent, but of " democratic education," or subjection under Japanese or German auspices. Nor was there failure to point out that American trade interests would be expanded, and the national welfare promoted. Commerce follows the flag, it was said.

Inevitably there arose out of this controversy over a particular territory the broader question of democracy's position in the family of nations — a problem of deepening interest from this time forward. The world-old question of the unit of democratic organization and the relation of democracy so organized to other nations reached and touched America. Notable was the prophecy of Giddings:[2] " Is it not a foregone conclusion that the United States having been brought, as England many years ago was brought, face to face with this problem in its practical form will make precisely the choice that England made; and that it will resolutely give its attention to the task of doing its share in that attempt to bring tropical regions under efficient government and a sound industrial organization, which is the only ultimate possibility to be thought of by humane and far-seeing men? "

[2] " Democracy and Empire," p. 285.

The annexation view prevailed, but with the understanding that as soon as the Philippines were ready for self-government (in the judgment of the United States) they should be given independence. The Supreme Court reluctantly sustained the principle of the Congressional acts for the government of the newly acquired territory.[3]

Yet the Philippine question was only an incident in the international relationships of the United States, and the broader problem of the relation of one democracy under modern conditions to the other states of the world, rapidly became urgent.[4] The Monroe Doctrine was developed and applied, and diplomats of the type of John Hay intelligently competed with European states in the outlines of a national policy, particularly in the Orient. The nation was drifting out on the international sea.

The acquisition of overseas dependencies floated the nation gently into the swift current which was certain to lead to the mingling of international waters. Doctrines of international duty and mission were developed and widely, although not universally, accepted. America slowly awakened to international consciousness and the sense of international rights and duties; began to think and act internationally. Whether as imperialist or pacifist in tendency; whether to bring to the world peace or a sword; whether inspired by selfish motives of gain or altruistic sentiments of humanity was not so significant in the general growth of American thought as the

[3] De Lima v. Bidwell, 181 U. S. 1.
[4] Roland G. Usher, "Pan-Americanism," 1915; "The Challenge of the Future," 1916. John H. Latane, "America as a World Power."

fundamental fact that the international instinct and interest awoke, and that internationalism won its way against the historic traditions of " splendid isolation."

From the beginning of the Republic, the military function of the state has been minimized. Even in the Colonial days, the Quakers made opposition to war an article of their religious creed, and consistently refused military service from the earliest days. William Penn prepared a universal peace project in 1693 in the form of an essay on the present and future peace of Europe. The Friends were continuously active in opposition to war, and their influence is seen throughout the whole pacifist movement from William Penn to Jane Addams.[5]

Opposition to a standing army was one of the cardinal principles during the Revolution, and the maintenance of such an establishment was one of the popular charges against the British government. Any large permanent military establishment was regarded as a menace to the liberties of the people, inconsistent with the genius of a free people. The Jeffersonian Democracy opposed any extensive development either of military or of naval power, and made this policy a part of their political program. Furthermore, the supremacy of the civil over the military power was generally regarded as one of the fundamentals of a free government. Notwithstanding the wars of 1812 and 1845 and the prominence and popularity of Andrew Jackson, leader of the Democracy which

[5] On the general history of the peace and war movement see: Krehbiel, " Nationalism, War and Society," 1916; Hirst, F. W., " Library of Peace and War," 1907; Fried, " Handbuch der Friedensbewegung," 1911–13; Edwin D. Mead, " The Literature of the Peace Movement."

bore his name, a very strong anti-war sentiment developed in the United States prior to the Civil War.

The American Peace Society was founded in 1828 for purposes of propaganda against militarism, after a number of state societies had been established. Many of the Abolitionists were non-resistants in principle, and were against the use of force by government whether for external or internal purposes. Men of the type of Dr. Channing,[7] Charles Sumner,[8] Ladd,[9] Quincy, Emerson and others were unceasing in their attacks upon the evils of war. They analyzed the causes and consequences of national strife in elaborate arguments, impressively arrayed. The property losses of war were set down and totalled, the atrocities of battle and the hardships of the soldier's life were pictured in detail, the conflict between brute force and the standards of Christianity was fully expounded, plans for international conciliation and arbitration were considered and types of international government were discussed. Ladd developed with strong support from Sumner the idea of a Congress of Nations with a High Court of Judicature.[10]

The geographical isolation of the United States from the other powers of the world, the imperfect means of communication and transportation, the traditional fear of a standing army and in fact of any strong government as a menace to liberty — all these factors combined to

[7] Discourses on War.

[8] " The True Grandeur of Nations," 1845.

[9] Essay on War. See also Jonathan Dymond, " An Inquiry into the Accordancy of War with the Principles of Christianity," 1834.

[10] See William Ladd, " An Essay on a Congress of Nations." 1840.

render easy the development of a peace philosophy and policy.   In the Northern states and among those opposed to slavery this sentiment was particularly strong, while in the South the pacifist doctrines were less cordially received.   In the Mexican War, this contrast was particularly noticeable.   The Civil War rudely broke the continuity of organized opposition to the use of military force.   A great army was placed in the field to preserve the Union and to destroy slavery; and another to serve the opposite purpose.   The anti-war movement as a philosophy came to a sharp halt.   There was bitter and continued criticism of the conduct of the war, but even the Garrisonian Abolitionists tacitly if not openly accorded their approval to the military movement.

During the last half-century, the anti-militarist movement revived and went forward with renewed impetus. The echoes of the Civil War soon died away.   The mighty military establishment built up during the great struggle over the cause of the Union was quickly dismantled.   The army melted away; officers and soldiers mingled in civil life; and the war spirit soon disappeared, not to emerge for a generation.   During this time the United States still continued to be isolated politically from European states, although constantly brought nearer by improvements in means of transportation and by international trade.   Various forces combined to facilitate the pacifist movement.   The swift growth of industrialism tended to drive into the background the militaristic tendencies of men, and labor became increasingly jealous of the use of military force in industrial conflicts. At the same time the settlement of the far-reaching terri-

tory to the west and the industrial reorganization of the
south afforded an outlet to the expansive tendencies of
the nation.   The period of peace was again interrupted
by the Spanish War of 1898, but this was of such brief
duration that it did not deeply affect the general movement against war.

The leaders of all groups united in a peace philosophy
and program which went forward almost without opposition from any influential element in the nation.   Mr.
Bryan and Mr. Root, Mr. Taft and Mr. Debs and Mr.
Carnegie, the Federation of Labor and the Bankers' Association, the churches, the parties, the schools, the statesmen, representatives of all sections and classes were
united in their devotion to a thorough-going peace program.[11]

The American Peace Society continued its efforts begun in 1828; the American Association for International
Conciliation was organized in 1906; the American Society
for the Judicial Settlement of International Disputes in
1910; the World Peace Foundation and the Carnegie Endowment in the same year; and the Church Peace Union
in 1913.   There was active participation in the Inter-
Parliamentary Union.   The United States vigorously assisted in the Hague Conferences.[12]   Under Presidents
Taft and Wilson the formation of arbitration treaties was

[11] See Publications of National Peace Congress: Lake Mohonk
Conferences on International Arbitration, 1895–; The World Peace
Foundation, 1910–; American Assn. for International Conciliation,
1906–; Carnegie Endowment for International Peace, 1910–.

[12] See Instructions to the American Delegates to the Hague Peace
Conferences and their Official Reports (Carnegie Endowment for
International Peace, 1916).

actively and successfully pursued as a distinct policy of the nation. The military function of the government was reduced to the lowest terms. Just before the Spanish War, the standing army of the United States was less than 75,000 in a population of as many millions, while the state militia had been brought down to the minimum in numbers, equipment and efficiency.

The peace philosophy during this time was elaborately developed by many statesmen and scholars. In general, however, the type of argument shifted away from that advanced in the earlier period of our history. Emphasis was placed upon factors which had hitherto been largely neglected. Considerations taken from biology, psychology, economics, ethnology, sanitation, industrialism and internationalism were now made parts of the case against war. In the latter part of this period, the influence of the European crusade against militarism was felt in many quarters here. The scientific arguments advanced by Bloch,[13] Angell,[14] Spencer,[15] Novicow,[16] and above all the moving appeals of Count Tolstoi, the great Russian apostle of peace, were felt throughout the land.[17] The counter attacks made by the European apostles of militarism had little vogue; and indeed were

[13] "The Future of War."
[14] "The Great Illusion."
[15] Political Institutions.
[16] "War and Its Alleged Benefits."
[17] "War and Peace," 1889. Compare Liebknecht, "Militarism," 1907. The literary side of the war problem was reflected in Stephen Crane's "Red Badge of Courage," 1896; Mary Johnston, "Cease Firing," 1912; Ednah Aiken, "The Hate Breeders," 1916. With these compare Zola's "The Downfall," 1898; Zangwill's "The War God," 1911; Bertha von Suttner's "Ground Arms," 1894.

scarcely known except among the small circle of special-
ists in social science and certain of the army group.
Nietzsche,[18] Treitschke,[19] and Bernhardi,[20] with their
practical application of the Darwinian theory to group
struggles among the nations, passed practically unno-
ticed.[21] They were not seriously considered either by the
mass of the people or even by the few who were familiar
with the general tenor of these war-like speculations.

The new anti-war argument rested upon many diverse
bases. David Starr Jordan, the biologist, undertook a
biological demonstration of the deteriorating effect of
war upon the human race.[22] Rome declined, he contended, because the old Roman stock was exterminated
in the course of the long protracted wars waged by that
nation. " No race of men or animals," he said, " has
improved save through selection of the best for parentage,
while war makes sacrifices of its most desirable parents."
The destructive effects of war upon race stock he undertook to demonstrate in detail statistically and scientifically. Attention was directed to the large war losses
arising from defective sanitation in war times. Specific
losses from disease were brought into clearer relief than
before, and the general laxity of conditions accompanying the military process.

[18] " The Will to Power."
[19] " Politik."
[20] " Germany and the Next War."
[21] See also Cramb, J. A., " Germany v. England," 1914; " Origin
and Destiny of Imperial Britain and Nineteenth Century Europe,"
1915.
[22] " War and the Breed," 1915; " The Human Harvest," 1906;
" War and Waste," 1900; " War's Aftermath," 1914; Vernon L.
Kellog, " Beyond War," 1912.

The new pacificism was entitled " inductive or practical " in contrast to the early type termed " deductive " or " idealist." Its scope covered a challenge of the economic benefits of war; an elaboration of the biological losses from war; an analysis of the dangers from competitive armament; an analysis of certain weaknesses of nationalism; and elaborate projects for the reconstruction of society.

Jane Addams, profound student of urbanism, industrialism and feminism, pointed out the ethical disadvantages of the war idea and system.[23] In modern industrial civilization the earlier war virtues have no real place. New types of courage and patriotism must be developed to meet these new conditions. " It is the military idea, resting content as it does with the passive results of order and discipline which confesses a totally inadequate conception of the value and power of human life." " Great constructive plans and humanized interests," she continued, " have captured our hopes and we are finding that war is an implement too clumsy and barbaric to subserve our purpose."

At the same time the eminent psychologist, William James,[24] developed the necessity of providing what he called the " moral equivalent of war." The military

[23] " Newer Ideals of Peace," 1907. Ch. VIII; compare Lucia Ames Meade, " Swords and Plowshares " 1912; Chas. W. Eliot, " The Road Toward Peace," 1915.

[24] " Moral Equivalent of War." Compare Henry Rutgers Marshall, " War and the Ideal of Peace," 1915; Beals, " The Higher Soldiership," 1912; A. B. Hart, " School Books and International Prejudices," 1911; George M. Stratton, " Syllabus of Lectures on " The Psychology of the War Spirit," 1915.

virtues of " intrepidity, contempt of softness, surrender of private interest, obedience to command " must still continue as the enduring cement of states. " It is only a question of blowing on the spark until the whole population gets incandescent, and on the ruins of the old morals of military honor, a stable system of morals, of civic honor, builds itself up." As a substitute for military conscription he urged the drafting of all youth to form for several years an " army enlisted against nature "; to contend with the " sour and hard foundations of his higher life." He would draft them "to coal and iron mines, to freight trains, to fishing fleets in December, to dishwashing, to clothes washing, and window washing, to road-building and tunnel making, to foundries and stoke-holes, and to the frames of the sky-scraper."

The earlier calculation of the enormous cost of war by destruction of property and suspension of productive labor was further developed by inquiry into the underlying economic causes of conflict between nations.[25] The influence of trade jealousy, desire for commercial expansion and business opportunity, for exploitation of new territory, the far-reaching influence of commercialism as a factor in inviting conflict, were closely examined. Sometimes this was the work of the Socialists who interpreted all war in terms of the capitalistic class selfishness and desire to use the machinery of the state for commer-

[25] George R. Kirkpatrick, " War? What For?" 1910; George E. Roberts, " Economic Effects of the War," 1915; Henry C. Emery, " Some Economic Aspects of War," 1914; Mass. Comm. on the Cost of Living, " Waste of Militarism," 1910; Alvin S. Johnson, " Commerce and War," 1915.

cial purposes; and again in less partisan fashion by students of the problem interested only in the analysis of the fundamental causes of national strife.[26]

Likewise the racial characteristics set down in the earlier days under the general head " prejudice " were more closely examined, with a view to ascertaining their fundamental nature, their causes, and the means of lessening, if possible, their force or reconciling their common existence. The roots of race antipathy and the deep sentiments of cosmopolitan human sympathy, an understanding of the elemental race forces and forms were sought as the key to the mystery of war. Jane Addams declared that " The advocates of Peace would find the appeal both to Pity and Prudence totally unnecessary could they utilize the cosmopolitan interests in human affairs with the resultant sympathy that is developing among all the nations of the earth." A comprehensive inquiry was made or begun into all the varied and complex elements out of which warfare springs.

The united opposition to the development of the war function of the government undertook in the broadest way the construction of the machinery for the prevention of international conflicts. This goal had not been ignored in the days of Sumner, but now the abandoned project was taken up with the greatest zeal and energy. A systematic attempt was made to lay the foundations of a permanent peace tribunal — a parliament of man, of the type prefigured by the Hague Tribunal.[27] Butler

[26] See the elaborate plans outlined by the Carnegie Endowment for International Peace, summarized in the annual year books.

[27] Raymond L. Bridgman, " World Organization "; " The First

discussed the elements of the "international mind"[28] in philosophical style. The socialist groups considered the future possibilities of international labor organization. The political scientists inquired into the various types of international unions as possible points of vantage from which a permanent association might ultimately be formed.[29] Lippman recognized that peace is not merely negative idea, but involves positive and constructive action. He would not leave the world to "harder men." Pacifists, he remarks, "may be good monks and perhaps they will be saved by faith. They will not be saved by works. For they are leaving mankind in the lurch." He presented in pursuance of his theory a tentative outline of international organization whose chief task would be the administration of the backward states,— a prime cause of modern warfare.

Under the leadership of President Taft an earnest effort was made to provide for international arbitration, as a means of ensuring peace; and in spite of much opposition this program was steadily advancing. Mr. Bryan had likewise committed himself to this policy and had rendered effective service in the cause. Mr. Carnegie endowed the Peace Foundation and constructed the Peace Temple at The Hague. The overwhelming tendency of America was to favor all means of reducing the horrors of war, limiting armaments, arbitration of disputes, and ultimate elimination of war among civilized nations. It

Book of World Law," 1911; David Jayne Hill, "World Organization," 1911; B. F. Trueblood, "The Federation of the World," 1899.
[28] "The International Mind," 1912.
[29] Paul S. Reinsch, "Public International Unions," 1911.

was confidently hoped that the international *duellum*
would follow the personal duel to oblivion.

A searching study of the underlying causes of war
and the necessary bases of peace was made by Veblen.[30]
He first projected an analysis of national patriotism, the
origin of which he found in the necessity for group action
in the earlier stages of growth and the survival of which
he found to be at cross purposes with modern life. The
civilised scheme is cosmopolitan in character " both in
its cultural requirements and in its economic structure."
Modern culture cannot be held within the frontiers of
any one state, " except at the cost of insufferable crip-
pling and retardation." Modern culture is the " culture
of Christendom at large, not the culture of one and another nation in severalty, within the confines of Christendom." [31]

The chief obstacles to peace he found in the imperialistic ambitions and dynastic organization of Germany
and Japan. There is no neutral course between uncon-
ditional surrender to these powers and their practical
elimination. As constructive steps he proposed a " policy
of avoidance " of offense and occasion for annoyance,
" peace by neglect." In this the chief moves are the
" neutralization " of citizenship and the " neutralization "
of trade relations.[32] Nations, he believed, are " held up
in their quest for peace chiefly by an accumulation of
institutional apparatus that has outstayed its usefulness."

[30] " An Inquiry into the Nature of Peace and the Terms of its
Perpetuation," 1917.
[31] Cf. E. V. Robinson, " War and Economics in History and
Theory," in *P. S. Q.*, 15, 581.
[32] Chaps. V–VI.

This machinery must be internationalized by neutralizing merchant shipping, maritime trade, commercial transactions, and the "personal and pecuniary" rights of citizens abroad — citizenship in the broadest sense of the term. There might be loss under such a régime to dynastic or business enterprise, but not to the common man. Veblen's proposal then was not the construction of any new machinery, but the gradual abandonment of the old or that part of it from which the chief national or international irritations arise.

The policy of the national government was definitely directed toward the ultimate elimination of the military activities of the state, or toward any present step that seemed to lead in that direction. It is not to be assumed, however, that there was entire agreement among all the various types of peace advocates. There were anarchists who were against all coercion as such whether external or internal; there were socialists who were against wars as capitalistic enterprises and some who were against all wars; there were non-resistants who were for peace at any price; there were those who were willing to uphold righteous or defensive wars as against unrighteous or unjust wars; there were those who coupled in principle and in policy preparedness and peace propaganda. Even the apparently solid peace movement had deep differences beneath its placid surface. There were those who were willing to fight for peace and those who were in a mood for non-resistance under all circumstances. But the peace philosophy as such passed current with little question of its real value in exchange. All classes were theoretically in favor of the abstract desirability of eliminating war.

There was no military group to defend militarism, and no party or philosophy supporting it as in Germany.   It was difficult to obtain the necessary public interest to secure an adequate appropriation for the most rudimentary type of national defence.

Yet throughout this period war was not without its quiet defenders, and its outspoken apologists.   One of the most important military works of the century, and probably the most significant of all in regard to naval affairs, was that of Captain Mahan on " The Influence of Sea Power upon History " [33] (1890).   This penetrating study of the significance and value of the control of sea routes was read with interest everywhere, and is said to have furnished the immediate impulse to the development of the German sea policy.   Capt. Mahan also took up the defence of war against those who denounced this part of the work of government as an unmixed evil.[34] We must not lose sight of the fact, that " all organized force is in a degree war, and that upon organized force the world has so far progressed and still progresses." There are economies in war of a fundamental nature. Just as it is cheaper to build dykes than to suffer a flood; as it is cheaper to maintain police than to tolerate anarchy; so war is to be preferred to the chaos of unorgan-

[33] " Influence of Sea Power upon the French Revolution and Empire," 1892; " The Life of Nelson," 1900; " The Interest of America in Sea Power," 1897; " The Lessons of the War with Spain," 1899; " The Problems of Asia," 1900; " Retrospect and Prospect," 1902; " Types of Naval Officers," 1901; " Interest of America in International Conditions," 1900; " Armaments and Arbitration," 1912; " Sea Power and the War of 1812," 1905.

[34] " Some Neglected Aspects of War," 1899; " Armaments and Arbitration," 1912.

ized conflict between the blind and leaderless forces that always are found in the world somewhere or other in some form or other. War is an admittedly crude means of preserving world order, yet at the present stage of the world's progress cannot be abandoned with safety by any state. Nor can compulsory arbitration prove effective against the impulse to war, unless the heart, the desire for peace is there.[35]

Sumner also declared that war possesses an educative value of no little importance in the evolution of society. War provides a rude and imperfect selection of the most aggressive types of the race.[36] It allows the elimination or subordination of the unfit. Giddings believed the brotherhood of man must be brought about by " blood and iron," as much as by " thought and love." [37]

Capt. Homer Lea in " The Valor of Ignorance," 1909, and " The Day of the Saxon," 1912, also staunchly upheld the doctrine that war is inevitable and that militarism is therefore indispensable. Arbitration and disarmament are futile expedients, based on ignorance or indifference regarding the fundamental laws of nature. War cannot end until human characteristics are so altered that " complete socialism and harmonious anarchy prevail." In the meantime all the influences of industrialism, commercialism, feminism and political quackery are to be resisted and overcome.

Colonel Roosevelt emphasized the importance of mili-

[35] See his address before the Church Congress of Providence, R. I., 1900, on " War from the Christian Standpoint."

[36] " War and Other Essays," 1911.

[37] See " Democracy and Empire," p. 343.

tary and particularly of naval preparation throughout his public career. He opposed the negotiation of peace treaties providing for the submission of all questions to arbitration, including under that head " national honor." After the outbreak of the Great War, he undertook a vigorous campaign for preparedness. This was not based upon a defence of war, however, but upon the danger and folly of national indifference to the imminent dangers arising from foreign military aggression. In this he was supported by many other publicists and by a strong body of public opinion.[38]

The outstanding features of this period were the disbanding of the world's greatest military force; the enthusiastic pursuit of a peace policy; the vigorous policy of arbitration and international agreement; the adoption of a colonial policy; the gradual drift into the sea of world politics.

Nationalism and peace policies were the characteristic marks of the period, while Imperialism appeared apologetically, and the international point of view was just beginning to appear. Labor and Capital both looked closely toward internationalism, but the democracy as a whole was indifferent and unprepared.

[38] " Fear God and Take Your Own Part " (1916), Message to Congress, Dec., 1906; Hudson Maxim, " Defenceless America," 1916; R. Stockton, " Peace Insurance," 1915; R. M. Johnston, " Arms and the Race," 1915; Emory Upton, " Military Policy of the U. S.," 1907.

CHAPTER X

ONE of the most striking features of American democratic development is the party system.[1] " There is a sense," says a distinguished commentator, " in which our parties may be said to have been our real body politic." [2] No feature of American politics attracted more attention during this period than the compact organization and the widespread activities of the political parties. They were a unique product of our political life — phenomena that loomed up prominently on the national landscape — political formations that were difficult for democracy to explain. In general the growth of the party followed the broad lines of the times. As business and labor developed their organizations, so the party developed its machinery. As business developed the corporation and the magnate, and as labor developed the union and the leader, so the party system developed its machines and its boss. As business developed its super-corporation and labor developed the super-union, so the party shaped the super-machine.

[1] H. J. Ford, "The Rise and Growth of American Politics "; J. A. Woodburn, "Political Parties and Party Problems "; Jesse Macy, " Party Organization "; William M. Sloane, " Party Government in the United States "; P. O. Ray, " Political Parties and Practical Politics "; Ostrogorski, " Democracy and the Organization of Political Parties "; James Bryce, " The American Commonwealth."

[2] Woodrow Wilson, "Constitutional Government," p. 218.

Its rich resources of men and money, the perfection of its elaborate mechanism, the far-reaching character of its organization, made the party a formidable instrument and a powerful political factor, aside from its primary purposes and ideals. So the party came to be a part of the government, often more important than the nominal rulers themselves. When Senator Root, an excellent authority on this subject, said that for many years under Senator Platt the real government of New York was at 49 Broadway, he uttered a truth of more than local application. In every section of the country and at all times in this period the extra-legal and unofficial agency known as the party to a very large extent took the place of the official agency known as the government. Designed as a means for quicker and easier formulation of public opinion, the party in many cases became an end in itself rather than a means; and in the strength of its mechanism often forgot the purpose of its existence.

In the main the two-party system continued, although there were many minor groups which sometimes rivalled or alarmed the majority parties. The most successful machine or boss was often able to control both parties and thus to create a single " bi-partisan system " in which party hostilities became relatively tame. Thus particularly in local affairs the bi-party system often became a practical unity of command. In the national field, the boss and the machine and bi-partisanship were less fully developed in their organization and less confident in their activities.

One of the most conspicuous features of the early part of this period was the struggle over the " spoils " system, and the political ideas developing out of that controversy. This system was originated in the Jacksonian era. In 1820 the preliminary step was taken in the passage of the famous Crawford law, which limited the term of most appointive federal officials to four years. In President Jackson's first message to Congress the idea that public office should be used as a party reward was boldly avowed. He held, first, that experience is not very important for a public servant, and, secondly, that long tenure of office is actually detrimental to good public service. " There are perhaps few men," said Jackson, " who can for any great length of time enjoy office or power without being more or less under the influence of feelings unfavorable to the discharge of their public duties." The Executive also informed the Congress, " That the duties of all public officials are, or at least admit of being made so plain and simple that men of intelligence may readily qualify themselves for their performance. And I cannot but believe that more is lost by long continuance in office than is generally to be gained by their experience." Such was the doctrine of rotation in office, as announced by the President of the United States in 1829.

The spoils theory was bitterly opposed by Webster, Calhoun and others, but their vigorous and eloquent protests were in vain.[3] The system of using administrative positions as rewards for partisan service was fully and completely established. The use of such offices to build

[3] Webster declared: " The existence of parties in popular government is not to be avoided, and if they are formed on constitutional questions, or in regard to great measures of public policy, and do not run to excessive lengths, it may be admitted that on the whole they do no great harm. But the patronage of office, the power of

up a party became an accepted principle of the political code. Unfortunately, the system was established just before the time when the work of the government began to expand at a rapid rate, and the number of official positions to increase proportionately. In the great period of expansion and development following the War, the original spoils system had extended far beyond any bounds intended or even imagined by its founders. If the political leaders in the '30's who entrenched the spoils idea could have looked beyond the simple conditions of their day and foreseen the great growth of cities, the expansion of the functions of government, the increasingly technical nature of public employment, they might have hesitated to place the administration of public affairs upon a partisan basis. The spoils principle spread like disease through the body politic. The idea that public office is the perquisite of the dominant party was easily interpreted to mean that all the powers of office were likewise legitimate spoils of the party in power. The spoilsmen's eyes were opened to the dazzling possibilities of political control as a means of securing wealth and power. The growth of cities and the expansion of industry offered one of the most fertile fields of political exploitation ever spread before the eyes of political adventurers. Franchises and crime in cities, taxes in counties and other local governments, legislation and public institutions in the states, customs, excises, public lands, tariff, railroad and corporation legislation in the federal government;

bestowing place and emoluments, create parties not upon any principle or upon any measure, but upon the single ground of personal interest," Congressional Debates, Vol. XI, 459.

with public works, contracts and public funds in city, country, state and federal government alike were added to the spoils which at first had included only the " jobs."

The enormous expenditure of the Federal Government during the Civil War, the rise of the public utility about the mid-century, the utter inadequacy of our system of taxation under the new urban and industrial conditions, the control of the individual states over commercial and criminal law in the absence of a national code, were temptations to which the spoilsmen readily succumbed.   So insidious is the spoils idea that it spread from appointment to office to favoritism in official function, and from favoritism across the boundary line to fraud and crime.   The expansion of the public service came at a time when the spoils doctrine had just been firmly fixed in the political practice of the American party.   New offices became additional assets of the dominant party, and the total number of party employes, and the total " wage fund " at the disposal of the party were enlarged.   This unfortunate coincidence of the establishment of the spoils system and the increase of political positions cannot be too strongly emphasized.[4]

In the generation following the Civil War, a new idea appeared in the field and contested for the mastery with

[4] Wm. D. Foulke, "Fighting the Spoilsmen"; Samuel P. Orth, "The Boss and the Machine," 1919; George S. Bernard, "Civil Service Reform Versus the Spoils System," 1885; L. G. Long, "Parties and Patronage in the U. S."; E. P. Wheeler, "Sixty Years of American Life," Chs. XII, XIII on Municipal Reform; E. L. Godkin, "Problems of Modern Democracy," Ch. 4 on Criminal Politics, 1896.

the well-intrenched spoils system.[5]   At the end of the period the newcomer was victorious in theory, although by no means supreme in practice.   The new idea was commonly called by the unpromising name of " Civil Service Reform."   Its essential principle was that administrative positions should be filled and removals made on the basis of fitness for public service rather than for party service.   The leader in this movement was George William Curtis, who was assisted by such men as Dorman B. Eaton, E. L. Godkin, Horace White, Carl Schurz and others.[6]   Their theory was that the corruption and inefficiency then evident on a scandalous scale arose from the application of the spoils principle.   They believed that this tendency unchecked would be ruinous to the public service and that democracy could not succeed in the long run unless it could obtain and hold the service of competent administrators.   It was not difficult for them to indicate glaring instances of waste and extravagance under the spoils system and this was done with great clearness and persistence over a long period of time, in the face of public apathy and bitter party hostility.[7]   Little by little, however, both public opinion and party leaders themselves began to demand action.   The assassination of President Garfield in 1881 by a disappointed

[5] Dorman B. Eaton, " Civil Service in Great Britain," 1880; F. W. Whitridge, " The Four Years' Term or Rotation in Office," 1883.

[6] " Orations and Addresses," Vol. II; the best discussion of this general movement is found in Carl Fish, " Civil Service and the Patronage," 1903.

[7] See Jenckes, Report, 1868, 40th Congress, 2nd Session, II. H. R. 47 — an impressive 220-page document. Of special interest is the questionnaire on p. 17.

office-seeker was a tragic lesson which was not without its weight in obtaining the passage of the Civil Service Law in 1883. In the states and cities similar legislation reluctantly followed, as well as supplementary federal orders and acts.[8] The field of public employment is still far from being covered by the merit system, but public opinion is unquestionably hostile to the spoils method and theory, however tolerant toward frequent lapses in practice.

By no one was the case so effectively stated as by Curtis, who for a quarter of a century fought an unceasing, unyielding and often thankless battle for the merit system. His addresses and activities are an impressive monument of his life and work. Curtis' argument was that the oligarchy known as the " machine " usurped the power of the people and placed " bosses " in power in place of the true party " leaders." Instead of men who led " by molding and guiding the popular intelligence, by the sympathy of common conviction, by resistless argument and burning appeal," they substituted party managers " whose opinions, if they have any, upon great public questions, they cannot or do not express, and if they could express, nobody would care to hear; huge contractors of votes, traders and hucksters in place and pelf. And while this system makes personal servility the basis of political success, and while it demands instantaneous and unquestioning party allegiance, it does not hesitate to betray the party by bargaining with the enemy."

[8] Holcombe, " State Government," p. 338. This long struggle may be traced in the publications of the National Civil Service Reform League, particularly in " Good Government."

For this, he held, there are two remedies. First, that of independency, and second, that of removing patronage from the control of the machine.

The defense of the old spoils system was not expressed in systematic form, although not without strenuous defenders. The advocates of the old régime attacked the proposed plan, criticising its artificiality and mechanical tendencies, pointing out that adequate appointments are not always made by means of competitive examinations; declaring its rigidity unsuitable to the flexible requirements of public service. It was also contended that party service is legitimately rewarded by public position; that the burdensome routine work of the party must be carried on continuously; that volunteers cannot be counted upon; that funds for the payment of party workers cannot be readily raised; and hence the only alternative is to reward the party soldiers with public employment.

But the chief popular consideration urged in defense of the spoils system was the appeal to the fear of aristocracy, bureaucracy or monarchy. The cry was raised that democracy was in danger of overthrow, if the proposed qualifications for office were permanently set up. The most dire predictions of the undemocratic result of such a new principle were made in Congress and elsewhere, and the changes were rung over and over again upon the inevitable monarchical tendencies of such a system as was proposed. Thus Congressman Woolbridge declared that the civil service was no more corrupt than business, and maintained that the new system was fundamentally undemocratic and was merely borrowed from England. The only real safety device was that the " stables should be occasionally cleaned " by a change of parties.[9] Typical of these arguments was the speech of Congressman Charles H. Grosvenor, who for long years fought to cripple the Civil Service Law by reducing the appropriation for its enforcement.[10] The Congressman contended that the new system created a special class apart from the common people. He charged that the " civil service trust " was the greatest and most dangerous one in the country; he predicted that the next step would be the establishment of a general system of civil pensions; he ridiculed the questions asked of applicants by examiners and singled out the various infelicities in the practical operation of the system.

Doubtless the brilliant Wendell Phillips reflected a certain sentiment when he declared against civil service reform in his Harvard Phi Beta Kappa address.[11] He stated that the new system contravened the " fundamental plan of our institutions and contemplates a coterie of men held long in office largely independent of the people — a miniature aristocracy filled with a dangerous *esprit de corps.*" He proposed that each district choose its own postmaster and custom house officer, believing that the " responsibility of choice would quicken the political interest of the communities." [12]

Notwithstanding the entrenched position of the spoils system and its vigorous defense by the powerful party

[9] 39th Cong., 2nd Sess., p. 1034.

[10] 55th Cong., 1st Sess. Appendix, pp. 419–45. See also debates in the 47th Cong., 2nd Sess. on Civil Service.

[11] Speeches, Vol. II, p. 363, note, 1871.

[12] The Democratic platform of 1896 denounced life tenure of office, and indirectly the merit system.

machines, both the principle and the practice were gradually forced back, and the other doctrine took their place in public opinion, in democratic philosophy and in public administration. The democracy concluded that the principal argument of the political machine regarding the aristocratic or bureaucratic tendencies of the proposed plan was not sound; that the spoils system, whatever its origin, was continued for the purpose of serving personal, factional or party interest before the primary interests of the public were considered; and that democracy was entitled to have capable public servants in order to carry out its will. In the long contest between party service and public service as a basis for administration the victory rested with public service.

Another striking change in political thought was seen in the tendency to regulate and recognize legally the political organizations which began as voluntary associations. At the outset the party was unknown to the law. Little by little party processes were drawn into the circle of legislation and finally many important phases of party procedure were regulated by law. This striking development of party recognition and regulation is characteristic of the last third of a century.

The regulation of elections began at an early date, and at first included such measures as registration and some form of written or printed ballots. After the War the number of registration laws was increased, especially in the cities where the neighborhood check on voting was not as effective as in the rural districts. Later the whole process of elections was placed under minute supervision by the Australian ballot system.[13] This took away from the parties the duty of furnishing ballots for voters, provided for secret voting, and set up elaborate machinery to prevent intimidation, bribery, fraud, and other irregularities at elections. At the same time, parties were finally defined and recognized in the law. Numerous objections were offered, both on theoretical and practical grounds, but in the main the sentiment in favor of strict regulation was overwhelming. Gov. Hill of New York, in his famous veto of the Australian ballot law, in 1889, denounced the measure " as a disfranchisement of the people, as a surrender of the inherent right under our free institutions." But the able reply of Louis F. Post demolished these objections.[13a] A strong factor in creating general sentiment was also John H. Wigmore's " The Australian Ballot," published in 1889.[14] The constitutionality of these acts was challenged, but they were uniformly sustained by the courts as regulations necessary to protect the purity of the ballot and the freedom of elections.[15] What would earlier have been regarded as unwarranted interference in the private affairs of voluntary associations was accepted by the courts and by the community as a reasonable regulation in defense of the machinery of democracy.

A common check upon the representative tendencies of

[13] E. C. Evans, "A History of the Australian Ballot System in the United States."

[13a] " Election Reform (Pamphlet)," 1899.

[14] See also " Constitutionality of Australian Ballot Laws," *American Law Review*, 23, p. 719.

[15] Evans *op. cit.* Chap. 6.

the party organization was refusal to support the party ticket. The Liberal Republican movement of the '70's, and the Mugwump movement of the '80's, were the most conspicuous early forms of this dissatisfaction. The greatest personality in this field was Carl Schurz, whose dashing independent career was one of the political features of his day.[16]

The defense of independency in party affairs was strongly presented by Lowell.[17] Parties, he thought, lacked adequate principles of action. If, he said, " in a free country, government by the party be a necessary expedient, it is also a necessary evil, and evil chiefly in this, that it enables men, nay, even forces them to postpone interests of prime import and consequence to secondary and ephemeral, often to personal interests, but not only so, but to confound one for the other." If you ask them, said he, " Have you any principles? " the answer would be — like Parley to Captain Standard —" Five hundred." Yet if the politicians must look after the parties, then there must be somebody to look after the politicians, somebody to ask disagreeable questions and to utter inevitable truths; somebody to make sure not only what but whom the candidate will represent. The old parties cannot be reformed from within, therefore there should be " a neutral body not large enough to form a party by itself, nay, which would lose its power for good if it attempted to form such a party, and yet large enough to moderate between both." Of the formation of such a group he

[16] See, the " Reminiscences " of Carl Schurz.
[17] James Russell Lowell, " The Independent in Politics," 1881; " Literary and Political Addresses," Vol. VI, p. 190.

thought he read the signs in his day, and he looked forward hopefully to its ultimate influence on practical political affairs.

The nominating processes were left undisturbed by the government for nearly one hundred years. The frequent occurrence, however, of fraud, corruption and violence in the selection of party candidates led to a general and insistent demand for interference by the State.[18] Serious discussion of the need of party reform or regulation began in the '60's and '70's. McMillan, in his " Elective Franchise," in 1880 advocated the direct primary, as did others following him.[19] Beginning with the California and New York acts of 1866, the regulations covered only the most flagrant forms of fraud and force, and they were usually optional in character. Later, however, they became compulsory, state-wide and comprehensive in their scope. After the adoption of the Australian ballot law, the tendency was to apply to the nominating process all of the detailed precautions and safeguards provided for the conduct of an election. Overlapping the regulation of the election of delegates to conventions came the demand for the direct choice of candidates, commonly known as the direct primary movement. Starting simultaneously with the regulated convention movement, it made little headway for a generation. It was renewed and revived, however, in the late '90's, at which time the most conspicuous advocate of the primary reform was

[18] Merriam, " Primary Elections " (1909).
[19] Dorman B. Eaton, " The Independent Movement in New York," 1880; G. W. Lawton, " The American Caucus System," 1885; Albert Stickney, " Democratic Government," 1885.

Robert M. La Follette, who made a powerful presentation of the evils of the convention plan and a convincing appeal for the new system.[20]   In the closing years of the 19th century and in the first decade of the 20th, the direct nominating method swept like wildfire over the whole country, until at the end of this period it was generally recognized as the accepted method of selecting state and local officials, and was further applied to Congressional elections and in many instances to Presidential nominations.   At the close of this period, the direct primary was supported by Hughes, Roosevelt, Wilson, and other powerful party leaders throughout the country.[21]

This revolution of the attitude of the public toward political party organizations was brought about largely as the result of widespread distrust of the party machine and the boss, and the feeling that the helplessness of the people was in great measure due to the intricacies and complications of the nominating methods.   Additional impetus was given to the popular movement by the belief that the party machinery itself was being employed by special industrial interests to promote their private welfare rather than the general good of the community. There was also involved in the movement a feeling that the people should participate more widely in the choice of their officials, and that the old nominating methods interfered with popular choice.[22]   But the chief factor

[20] "The Menace of the Machine," Univ. Chicago Record, 1897.

[21] See Proceedings of Conference of Governors 1910, p. 117, ff. for extended discussion.

[22] As early as 1880 Curtis declared that of 60,000 Republicans in New York City 50,000 had no voice in the primaries. *Op. cit.,* Vol. II, p. 151.

after all was the prevailing sentiment that the party government had somehow become unrepresentative, and that more direct control over its machinery was necessary in order to bring it back to its original purposes.

A vigorous protest was made against this movement, but in the main the arguments were summarily overridden.[23] It was emphatically asserted by party managers that the direct primary would disrupt the party and put an end to the party system; that it would result in increased expenditures and indifferent results; that it would impose still heavier burdens upon the electorate; that it would destroy the essential elements of compromise and concession appearing in ordinary political conventions; that an inferior class of candidates would be named; and that it involved fundamentally an impracticable and undesirable extension of the power of the individual voter.

Mr. Ford believed that the direct primary would decrease the degree of popular control. " Its pretence of giving power to the people is a mockery," he declared. The new method will not in any effective way alter the political system under which bosses and machines inevitably control. Among the effects of the direct primary are " graft, irresponsibility, and a tendency toward och-

[23] See W. H. Taft, " Popular Government," Chap. V.; H. J. Ford, " The Direct Primary " in *North American Review,* Vol. 190, p. 1 (1909) ; Report of the Joint Committee of the Senate and Assembly of the State of New York, appointed to investigate primary election laws of this and other states, 1910; Report of Connecticut Commission on laws relating to direct primaries and corrupt practices at elections, 1907; National Conference on practical reform of primary elections, N. Y., 1898; C. E. Fanning, Selected Articles on Direct Primaries, 4th Ed., 1918.

locracy." I have yet to find an instance," said he, " in which the direct primary has actually tended to promote good government, and it is only by some dire confusion of thought that good men can advocate such a pernicious nostrum."

In the field of public regulation there was included not only party legislation but also party administration, not only the nominations made by the party, but the party organization and management.[24] Elaborate provisions were made covering the election and powers of party officials and committees, including their number and terms and the definition of their rights and duties, often in some detail. The methods of choosing the local State and national committeemen were fixed by statute, and indeed, the whole organization was legalized and regulated as if it were a part of the government. This movement rested upon the same fundamental conviction that in the absence of well-defined rules and regulations the party machine and boss were not sufficiently responsive to the will of the party and that by the agency of legal regulation they might be rendered more amenable to mass control.

In large cities especially the party organization had sometimes become an institution similar to a private club, and entrance to it depended on the consent of those in authority. Black-balling, blue-penciling, and black-listing were practices not infrequently encountered. " Sluggers " and " bouncers " were not uncommon in party meetings. Much more alarming was the general lack of

[24] See Jesse Macy, " Party Organization"; Merriam, " State Central Committees," in *P. S. Q.*, 19, 224.

information as to when, where and how the processes of party government were carried on, and how to take effective part in them. It was in the hope of democratizing this process that the aid of the law was invoked and that the great voluntary associations in the shape of parties were subjected to minute regulations.

Yet these measures did not pass without challenge. On the contrary they aroused the bitterest opposition from the old system. On the legal side, a determined but hopeless protest was made against regulation of party affairs by law. The " natural rights of parties," were strongly urged. To sustain legislation regulating the business of political parties, it was said, would " stretch the arm of the criminal law to an unwarranted extent over the citizen, in derogation of the constitutional right of citizens to assemble for their common good." [25] Said the appellants in one case: " What would your honor think of an act of the Legislature which undertook to provide for and regulate the election of the officers of a religious denomination in the State?" In a notable dissenting opinion, Justice Cullen, of New York, said: " The right of the electors to organize and associate themselves for the purpose of choosing public officers, is as absolute and beyond legislative control as their right to associate for the purpose of business or social intercourse or recreation."

In spite of these arguments and protests, the people, the legislatures and the courts took a different view. The controlling theory was that the affairs of political parties are matters of fundamental concern, and that their form

[25] Merriam *op. cit.*, Ch. 6.

and method may be regulated whenever the public interest requires. The courts held in express terms that
the political party under our conditions has practically
become an integral part of the government, and that its
due regulation is as much a matter of public policy as the
ordering of any other part of the framework of the body
politic.

The strong appeal for the liberty of association made
by the opponents to primary regulation was overruled,
and the courts held in almost unbroken series of decisions
that the regulation of the primary process was entirely
within the scope of legislative authority. In some instances the courts connected the right of primary regulation with the regulation of the ballot provided under
the Australian ballot law. In other cases, however, this
narrow and technical ground was abandoned and the
court placed the right to regulate squarely upon the
broad principle of public interest in the political party
as an integral part of the government.

Not only was this true, but the courts sustained the
most sweeping legislation regulating the organization
of the political party, determining the framework of its
committees, their membership, terms, modes of election
and duties. This field had hitherto been regarded as entirely within the discretion of the political party, but under the new conditions was included within the range of
primary laws. This action was sustained by the courts in
the broadest terms when the question was brought before
them for adjudication.[26]

[26] See Goodnow, " Politics and Administration," Ch. 9. A notable
case was People v. Dem. General Committee, 58 N. E. 124.

Beginning in 1890, the idea that party activity should be regulated in the interest of the democracy was further expressed in legislation. In various States " corrupt practices " acts were passed.[27] At first these laws were practically ignored, but after the election of 1904 the movement was revived and additional steps were taken both by the State and by the national government. The Federal law of 1907 paved the way and that of 1911 was of special importance. The purpose of these regulations was to provide for publicity in regard to campaign receipts and expenditures, to forbid certain types of expenditure altogether, and in many cases to impose a limit on the amount of expenditure incurred. In some instances attempts were made to provide for the payment of part of the expense of elections by the public, and in the case of Colorado, in 1909, by an outright appropriation of State funds.[28] These laws were copied at the beginning from the English act of 1883 regarding the use of money in elections, although the later American laws were much different from the English originals.[29] The basis of these acts was the general belief that parties and candidates were being controlled or unduly influenced by corrupt use of money, whether in the

[27] G. L. Fox, " Corrupt Practices and Election Laws in the U. S. since 1890"; Proceedings Am. Pol. Sc. Assn. (1905); Holcombe, " State Government," p. 221 *et seq.;* H. J. Ford, *op. cit.,* Chap. 24; Henry J. Peterson, " Corrupt Practices Legislation in Iowa."

[28] See Message of President Roosevelt, Dec. 3, 1907; Proceedings of Conference of Governors, 1913; Gov. Baldwin's paper on State Assumption of Nomination and Election Expenses, p. 137, and discussion thereon.

[29] E. A. Jelf, " Corrupt and Illegal Practices Prevention Acts."

hands of individuals or of corporations.[30]   Defects in the scope of these laws and great gaps in the machinery for enforcement, as well as inherent difficulties in reaching the root of this situation by law, greatly minimized their practical effect.   Yet they served to indicate clearly the advancing line of public control over party activities and the general anxiety to protect the democratic processes of political life by publicity of action and by prohibition of notorious abuses.[31]

The remarkable development of the machine and the boss, and the workings and significance of the party system stimulated a considerable current of political speculation during this period.   Various attempts were made to interpret and explain the meaning of the party system in American political life, and to make clear its relations to democracy.   At first the surprising developments were interpreted in terms of the moral obliquity of the boss and the machine, accompanied by appeals to the criminal law and the conscience of the culprits; or in terms of the political indifference of the voter, accompanied by exhortations designed to stimulate the lagging political interest and activity of the citizen.   Often the party evils were charged to the urban communities, to the immigrant peoples, or to almost any new feature in social life. But in time the theories of the party were more and more fundamental in their analysis, and constantly tended to explain the party in other than personal terms.

[30] See Ivin's " Machine Politics and Money in Elections in New York City," 1887.

[31] G. W. Birge, " The Free Pass and Bribery System," 1905.   Hudson C. Tanner, " The Lobby and Public Men," 1888.

There first appeared an interpretation attributing these new and unwelcome political phenomena to defects in the election machinery, making democratic and constitutional processes in the party difficult if not impossible. This culminated in demands for political " reforms " of various kinds, such as registration laws, the Australian ballot, and the primary laws in their various forms. There was also an interpretation in terms of the structure of the government, finding the clue to the situation in the decentralization of the government, and the consequent development of the political party as a necessary co-ordinating power. There was a further interpretation in terms of social forces finding the explanation of the party in the inter-relation between business and politics; or in the inter-relation between classes.

On the whole, however, the scientific study of political parties left much to be desired, in practical description, analysis and interpretation. It was some time after the machine and the boss had become active that any careful attempt was made to survey and appraise the function of the political party in a democracy.[32] Like the corporations in the industrial world, the " machines " in the political world were forms of organization whose movements were wholly bewildering to the community in general. The purpose and scope of reasonable organizations in both fields, their historical development, their social causes, consequences, and significance were

[32] Compare Robert Michels, " Political Parties " (translated); Ratzenhofer, " Wesen und Zweck der Politik," discussed in A. W. Small's, " General Sociology," Ch. 22, illustrating group struggle in its party aspects; Graham Wallas, " Human Nature in Politics."

slowly realized. De Tocqueville was the first careful student of America's parties and politics, and he had no successor until James Bryce wrote his " American Commonwealth " in 1888. This was an epochmaking study and was followed (1902) by the elaborate work of Mosei Ostrogorski, of Polish Jewish-Russian origin, on " Democracy and the Organization of Political Parties." It was only in the twentieth century that studies like those of Lowell, Macy, Wilson, Woodburn, Goodnow, Ford, Brooks, Ray and others began to stir the soil of the party field.

Roughly speaking, it may be said that during the early part of this period the first named explanations in personal terms were the more common, while during the latter part of the period the tendency was to place greater emphasis upon the structural and the social elements in the situation. As the analysis of the different factors became sharper, the thoughtful observer was more and more inclined to seek a clue in the deeper forces of industrial and social life, and in the fundamental features of the structure of government.

What was commonly called party " reform " may be said to have covered the following stages: There was, first, reaction against graft, bribery, " boodle," the prostitution of the public service to spoilsmen, the incredible activities of criminal politics which scarcely found theoretical defence and which could not be openly supported even by their most favored beneficiaries. Then there was a reaction against the evidently imperfect forms and methods of ascertaining the public will in primaries and elections. Then there came a movement against decentralization in government as the cause of governmental corruption and inefficiency. This was expressed in the demand for the short ballot, for " conspicuous responsibility " and for a general tightening of the loose screws in the machinery of the government. And finally, there came a movement based on the theory that the present party situation is the outcome of an alliance between certain industrial and political forces — between the centralized power of the " trust " on the one hand and of the " machine " upon the other. In this phase of the movement there was developed a program of further democratization of the government on the one hand, and the development of a broader program of governmental activity on the other.

One of the most thoughtful interpretations of the party system was that of Goodnow, a tireless student of public administration, who explained the position of the party in terms of the structure of the government.[33] Because of the three-fold separation of powers and the general decentralization of the organs of political authority, says Goodnow, it has not been possible for any central controlling agency to develop within the government itself. But some central authority is necessary. Hence, the political party has assumed the function of coordinating the several powers and duties of the regular government and of acting as the responsible agent. " It has been impossible," says Goodnow, " for the necessary control of politics over administration to develop within the formal governmental system on account of the independent position assigned by constitutional law to execu-

[33] " Politics and Administration."

tive and administrative officers.   The control has therefore developed in the party system." An extra governmental, superior or controlling agency has been created in the form of the political party.   For this reason the party in our system of government is more powerfully developed than elsewhere.   In short, the party is in a sense the government.   On this basis he explains the permanence of the party, the intense party loyalty developed, the payment for party work out of the public treasury and the mingling of national parties in local affairs.   By the same logic, he holds on the other hand that the institution of a system in which responsibility and power are sharply defined within the government would tend to relieve the party of many of its burdens and eliminate some of the worst abuses found in the present system.   Organization of political leadership and responsibility inside the government will tend, he believes, to reduce the necessity for a highly organized leadership outside the formal government.

" The political system," said Wilson, " is a system of checks and balances, embodied in the Constitution." " The Whig dynamics," he termed it.[34]   We have undertaken the task of " framing the functions of government by outside parties."   And this is the explanation of the modern party.   By this process a degree of political unity and coherence has been obtained.   The party has furthermore been a very useful nationalizing influence, creating national opinions and judgments as over against

[34] " Constitutional Government," Chap. 8 on Party Government in the United States; Croly, " Progressive Democracy," Ch. 16, on Executive vs. Partisan Responsibility.

local interests and preferences. But as the work of nationalization is more nearly perfected, changes become necessary. The thing that has served us so well might now master us if we left it irresponsible. The question is, therefore, whether we are ready to make our legislatures and executives our real bodies politic instead of the parties.

Roosevelt assailed the spoils system and the indifference of good citizens; and, notably in the campaign of 1912, depicted the " Invisible Government," composed of the party machines and special privilege. Roosevelt distinguished between the boss and the leader in this way: A leader leads the people; a boss drives the people. The leader gets his hold by open appeal to the reason and conscience of his followers; the boss keeps his hold by manipulation, by intrigue, by secret and furtive appeals to many phases of self-interest, and sometimes to every base phase of self-interest. Strong and genuine party leadership is needed to replace the leadership of the boss working through the spoils system for special interests.[35]

Croly [36] discussed the party in terms of governmental structure, although with more attention to social and economic forces than in the case of Goodnow. The party system, reasoned Croly, endeavors to do for the people what they should do themselves. " It seeks to interpose two authoritative partisan organizations between the people and their government. . . . It demands and obtains for a party an amount of loyal service and personal sacrifice which a public-spirited democrat should lavish only on the state." The paradox of our political life is

[35] Autobiography, p. 164.   [36] *Op. cit.*

that the individual can be effective only as a member of a party, while within the party he must make larger sacrifices than he should ever be called upon to offer. The organization of executive leadership within the government will help to solve this problem, but it cannot be expected to go all the way. If established, it must be accompanied by the executive initiative and the recall in order that the power of the executive may be genuine and that popular control over the leader may be really effective.

Senator Root expressed the opinion that we have created double governments. The real governing power is without legal responsibility and is practically free from statutory and legal restrictions.[37] " What is," he asks, " the government of this state? The government of the constitution? Oh, no; not half the time, nor half way."

" For I don't remember how many years Mr. Conkling was the supreme ruler in this State; the governor did not count; the legislatures did not count; comptrollers and secretaries of state and what not did not count. It was what Mr. Conkling said; and in a great outburst of public rage he was pulled down. Then Mr. Platt ruled the State; for nigh upon twenty years he ruled it. And the capitol was not here, it was at 49 Broadway."

" The ruler of the State during the greater part of the forty years of my acquaintance with the state government, has not been any man authorized by the constitution or by the law; and, sir, there is throughout the length and breadth of the State a deep and sullen and long

[37] " Addresses," p. 20. " The Function of Political Parties as Agencies of the Governing Body," p. 191–4.

continued resentment at being governed thus by men not of the people's choosing."

" That system," he continued, " finds its opportunity in the division of powers, in a six headed executive."

Senator Depew once said: " The Capitol has been this corner ('The Amen Corner' in the Fifth Avenue Hotel). I know Governors who thought they did things from the Executive Chamber, but they were done from the Amen Corner. I know Speakers who are looked to for the make-up of committees from the lower house of the Legislature. They said they would consult the members of their families in the rural regions, and I have found that the families they consulted were Senator Platt in the Amen Corner." [38]

Another group of interpretations was made in terms of political and industrial relationship. Conspicuous here were LaFollette, Bryan, Wilson, Roosevelt, and writers of the type of Steffens,[39] Veblen,[40] Chapman,[41] Croly. This doctrine attributed the power of the machine and the boss in the cities and elsewhere, to an alliance between the party ruler and those who sought or held industrial privileges of various kinds. Concentrated industrial power allying itself with concentrated political power in an offensive and defensive alliance, was seen as the fundamental cause of this new development in

[38] " Autobiography of Thomas C. Platt," 494. See also New York Bureau of Municipal Research, " The Constitution and Government of New York. An Appraisal," 1915.

[39] "Struggle for Self Government," 1906; "The Shame of the Cities."

[40] " Theory of Business Enterprise," 1904.

[41] " Causes and Consequences," 1899; " Practical Agitation," 1907.

democracy. This was variously characterized as the alliance of big business with big politics, as the "invisible government," and as the government of the political democracy by an industrial aristocracy.

As railroad, insurance, and local public utility investigations made more and more evident the alliance of politics and industrial privilege, the public analysis of the situation more and more inclined toward an examination of the underlying causes of the distressing symptoms of political disorder. The "Invisible Government" in which the twin powers are the political boss and the industrial magnate popularly summarized a very general theory of party pathology. The evils of the industrial system and the evils of the political situation were linked together, as joint product and joint cause, with joint need of modification and reorganization.

It is not to be concluded, however, that the connection between business and politics dated from the 20th century. In the campaigns of the '70's, '80's and '90's these relations were pointed out by the various insurgent groups and parties, and constantly throughout the great struggle for railway control,[42] in the anti-monopoly movement, and in the free silver controversy. The early utterances of Henry Ward Beecher, of Wendell Phillips, of Sen. Cushman K. Davis, indicated in unmistakable language their appreciation of the relation between political corruption and industrial exploitation. It was a Congressional committee that reported in 1873: "It is notorious in many state legislatures that these influences (gigantic corporations) are often controlling, so that in

[42] Haynes, "Third Party Movements."

effect they become the ruling power of the State." Yet as the corporation on the one hand, and the machine on the other were more fully developed, the frequent institutional combination between them was more and more perfected and was more widely noted, and their interrelationship as a basis of a party theory more widely accepted.

Significant interpretations of the local boss system were made by Steffens among others. Conceding certain merits in the institution, he sharply characterized the system however as " an organization of social treason," and the boss as " the chief traitor." [43] He uses his qualities of natural leadership to betray his people into the hands of the special selfish interests with whom he is allied. Analyzing the situation in " The Dying Boss " he says: " They have power, the people have, and they have needs, great common needs, and they have great common wealth. . . . And having thus organized and taken over all this power and property and this beautiful faith, you do not protect their rights and their property. . . . You sell them out. . . . They buy the people's leaders, and the disloyalty of the political boss is the key to the whole thing." [44]

From the point of view of the socialist, the root of the

[43] Lincoln Steffens, " The Dying Boss," *McClure's Magazine,* 43, 79 (1914). Apology for Graft, *Am. Mag.,* 66,120, 1908. Henry George, Jr., " The Menace of Privilege "; Jane Addams, " Why the Ward Boss Rules," *Outlook,* Apr. 2, '98, also " Democracy and Social Ethics "; M. K. Simkhowitch, " The City Worker's World in America," 1917, Ch. 9. Grace Abbot, " The Immigrant and the Community," 1917, Ch. 10. " The Immigrant in Politics."

[44] Lincoln Steffens, *McClure's Magazine,* 43, 79 (1914).

boss system is found in the capitalistic organization of industrial society.   To him the spoils system is merely the means by which the small group of capitalists control the political as well as the industrial activities of the mass of the people; and work their will while keeping within the forms of democratic government.   That this mockery must continue is inevitable until the capitalistic system is destroyed and a socialistic organization of industry is substituted in its place,[45] is his contention.

The interpretation of the party system as a unifying and educational agency was made by Macy and others.[46] They dwelt upon the value of political organization as an instrument for breaking down the barriers of section, as well as of religion and race, and creating a common Americanism in a way attempted or accomplished by no other agency.   They did not contend that the party had been completely successful in this movement, but indicated the great practical value of the service rendered in the assimilating process.[47]

Another view was taken by McLaughlin,[48] who held that the political party is chiefly an agency for electing men to office.   "We should not be far wrong," says McLaughlin, "if we should declare that there are two or

[45] Ghent, W. J.   "Our Benevolent Feudalism"; Compare Michels, "Political Parties."

[46] Jesse Macy, "Political Parties," also "Party Organization and Machinery"; W. M. Sloan, "Party Government."

[47] Significant studies are those of the British thinkers: David G. Ritchie, "Studies in Political and Social Ethics," pp. 66–107; James Bryce, "Hindrances to Good Citizenship."

[48] Andrew C. McLaughlin, "The Courts, the Constitutions and Parties," Chs. II and III.

more great armies in existence, each controlled by a select few whose main ambition is victory, and the objects of the people's desire are attained by the organizations accepting a principle as a means of winning success." The element of the issue or principle in party organization in existence he reduces to a minimum. Its activities rest " largely on tradition, on party name, on personal pride, and sometimes on a dominating principle." Its chief function is to put men into office, and this is the chief duty of its leaders. A principle will be abandoned for a victory. He agreed also that the party serves as a coordinating agency.

Likewise Lowell regards the parties primarily as " brokers " of ideas, policies, candidates. This is primarily an age of advertising and brokerage, and the party leaders serve the useful purpose of purveyors of political ideas and agents. These they present and advertise, looking for acceptance and approval which spells political success. Lowell plead for the more specific and concrete study of party forces and personalities as a preliminary to their clearer interpretation.[48a]

Few attempts were made at systematic defense or explanation of the machine and the boss. Their strength did not depend upon philosophy, literature or the written law. It rested upon the ability of a few selfish and powerful men willing to exploit an unorganized community at any cost, and upon widespread indifference and apathy, dependent on powerful economic and social forces. Yet it is clear that so widespread a system did not endure for so long a time without some general explanation or

[48a] " Public Opinion and Popular Government."

justification on the part of its defenders and participants.[49]

Brooks in his important study enumerates four types
of defence. These are, first, that political "corruption
makes business good," second, that corruption may be
offset by the high efficiency of those who engage in it;
third, that it saves us from mob rule; fourth, that corruption is part of an evolutionary process on the whole beneficent.[50] These types he examines and illustrates in some
detail, concluding that the first and the second are commonly held while the latter are still only slightly supported. But none of these is tenable, he held. Primarily abuses exist because they are immediately profitable
to certain persons who are unscrupulous enough to profit
by manipulation.

Brooks concluded that on the whole our current political
morality is not inferior to our business and social morality. The great unsolved problem is the general improvement of social and business ethics on which political
evils rest. Unless this is done no real progress can be
made.[51]

Only occasionally does the system find theoretical justification. Ford maintained that the rule of the bosses
and party machines, though a poor exchange for demo-

[49] See M. H. Simkhovitch, "Friendship and Politics," *Pol. Sc.
Quarterly,* 17, 189; William L. Riordon, "Plunkitt of Tammany
Hall," Chap. I; "Honest Graft and Dishonest Graft"; R. C. Brooks,
"Corruption in American Politics and Life"; G. Myers, "The Se-
cret of Tammany's Success," *Forum,* Vol. 31, p. 188; Josiah Flynt,
"The Tammany Commandment," *McClure's Magazine,* Vol. 17, p. 543.

[50] *Op. cit.,* p. 4.

[51] *Op. cit.,* p. 75.

cratic government, was on the whole better than any
substitute available in the present condition of American
politics.[52]   He believed that the party system was necessary in order to give the actually dominant classes political power which they did not normally possess.   That
without such a governing agency there would be disorder, violence and possible chaos.   Just as mediæval
feudalism held the masses together until the modern nation
was formed, so the party feudalism performs a like service in establishing " connections of interest among the
masses of the people."

An elaborate and formal defence of the spoils system
was made by D. G. Thompson, in a volume entitled
" Politics in a Democracy," published in 1893.   This interesting philosophy of Tammany Hall and the spoils
system generally contains a full statement of a theory
of the machine.   The fundamental premise of Thompson
is that a " governing syndicate " is necessary in most
cities until such time as people are able to govern themselves without a political superior.   " It is commercial
in principle and not necessarily vicious.   At all events
it is a natural and readily explicable product of evolution."   Tammany Hall is a governing syndicate which
undertakes the rule of New York for the benefit of the
people, and roughly represents the public will.   At the
head of the syndicate is the leader, commonly called the
" boss."   The merit of the boss consists " in his knowl-

[52] Compare Brooks Adams, " The Theory of Social Revolutions,"
1913, Ch. I, declaring that the present system " serves to hold society
together in a transition stage of political evolution.   It is not the betrayal of democracy, but the " diplomatic treatment of ochlocracy."

edge of conditions and quickness in apprehending a
change in them, and in his knowledge of and ability to
control men." He holds his position not by election,
but by common consent. His tenure depends upon success. He leads because " he is quick to rise to the top
of the wave that propels him forward."

But though Tammany is ruled in an autocratic way,
its fundamental sympathies are democratic. Its success
is due to its adherence to national democracy, to good
municipal administration, and to the development of a
net-work of social activities. Tammany can be defeated
only by another syndicate with the same general type of
organization. But for this purpose the so-called " better element " is inadequate. They are unreliable; they
are too independent; there are too few who have a real
interest; and on the whole they are a minority of the
community. Tammany affords a discipline over the
" lower classes "; which is most admirable for the public
interest. " It is far better in every way," says Thompson, " for the city, that half educated, illiterate and newly
naturalized voters should be held, if they can be, under
the influence and sway of a strong, well compacted and
centralized organization; that they be taught an allegiance to it, and learn to obey the behests of its com-
manders."

The opposition to Tammany arises from race prejudice; from religious antagonism; from the resentment
of paternalism against the plain people. Tammany is
fundamentally democratic and stands out against the
aristocracy of social position and of intellect and wealth.
Of its opponents, he says, " Even in the office of hogreeve,

they would prefer that a Ralph Waldo Emerson should serve, rather than a Patrick O'Flaherty." If there is evil in Tammany, it is due largely to the activities of those who publicly denounce it, that is to say, to business interests. " The truth of the matter is that the business community is primarily and chiefly responsible for political corruption of all sorts, and particularly with interference with legislation for private ends." The general popular indifference is due to a tendency toward self rule, toward the industrialism which Spencer discusses and which Thompson approves. The chief need, after all, is not a reform of the party, or the government, but improvement of the individual sense of responsibility and duty.

While the underlying idea was seldom so frankly and clearly stated as by Thompson, there is little doubt that this doctrine was fairly representative of the ideas of those who directly employed and profited by the methods of the professional spoilsman. The system was tolerated and silently justified and supported by those who were its beneficiaries for reasons not much different from those set forth in the writings of the apologist for Tammany Hall.[53] Charles Norman Fay [54] gives a frank defence of corruption, quoting a well known citizen as follows: " I have no more hesitation in buying —— than in buying a pound of beef. We are serving a great public need, on the whole cheaply and well. Buying these rascals is a part of the cost of service which the people put on us.

[53] Job Hedges, "Common Sense in Politics"; Clarkson, "The Politician and the Pharisee," *N. A. R.,* 152–613 (1891); Brander Matthews, "The American of the Future" (1910), Ch. 13.

[54] " Big Business and Government," Chap. 28, 1912.

Well, they pay the bill." Senator Root said, "Good men, good citizens, honest law-abiding men, justified themselves in the directorates of these railroads and other public service corporations in spending the money of the corporations to elect Senators and Assemblymen who would protect them against strike bills." [55]

More cynical than any of these apologies was the famous dictum of Senator Ingalls: "The purification of politics is an iridescent dream. Government is force. Politics is a battle for supremacy. Parties are the armies. The decalogue and the golden rule have no place in a political campaign. . . . The commander who lost a battle through the activity of his moral nature would be the derision and jest of history. This modern cant about the corruption of politics is fatiguing in the extreme."

The development of political thought regarding the political party as an agency of democratic government may be summarized briefly in this way. At first, the extensive organization and far-reaching power of the party were scarcely perceived at all. Then came the dawning consciousness of the existence of a powerful organization often dominating the parties and the community, particularly under urban and industrial conditions. Then came a series of desperate efforts to destroy the "machine" and the "ring" by appeals to the democratic instinct of the voters. Then followed a long series of statutory attempts to regulate and restrain the party "machine," to democratize and constitutionalize it. The underlying theory of this movement was that the power

[55] Addresses, p. 188.

of the party system was due principally to the laxity of the law. Then public attention turned toward the problem of political leadership in a democracy, and the idea arose that the organization of "conspicuous responsibility" within the government itself might eliminate some of the worst evils by providing a rallying point for public interest and action. At about the same time there appeared interpretations of the party in terms of the relation between government and industry in which the party system was depicted as a by-product of the political-economic system. Common to all these theories was the tendency to look upon the party as an organic part of the government — as an integral section of a governmental arrangement. The boss, the machine, the bi-partisan ring, were severely censured, but party organization and leadership itself came to be considered a part of the democratic process, and not merely as the voluntary activity of private persons.

As the party grew up alongside of the government, so there sprang up inside of or beside the party various types of unofficial organizations. The earliest feature of this movement was the growth of Independency. The Liberal Republican movement of the '70's; the Mugwump movement of the '80's, and the "anti-machine" and "insurgent" movements of the last twenty years were illustrations of unofficial activity within the party itself. Much of this sentiment in the early period clustered around the Grange and the Knights of Labor. These efforts offset the tendency toward an unswerving type of party allegiance, checking this development sometimes by protest and sometimes by counter organization.

A further phenomenon, indicating the growth of unofficial government, is seen in the development of great
numbers of volunteer political organizations undertaking
the function of instructing, advising, exhorting, men-
acing, obstructing and assisting the government and the
electorate. In some instances they too became the government to all intents and purposes. These groups
sprang up as the result of the scandalous abuses in city
government, and often took the shape of vigilance committees or emergency organizations, to re-establish the
popular control over the government. The committee
formed in New York City in the Tweed days was one
of the first and most conspicuous examples of this, and
the municipal history of almost every city affords some
illustration of citizen uprisings. These organizations,
while often merely ephemeral, often tended to establish
themselves as institutions. There came into existence a
long series of societies, clubs, leagues, aside from the
established commercial, agricultural, labor, fraternal and
other similar societies, carrying on a continuous work
of criticism and construction in political affairs. Occasionally they took the shape of municipal parties, but
more commonly not. The Citizens' Union, the Bureau
of Municipal Research in New York City, and the Municipal Voters' League in Chicago are conspicuous illustrations of this type of citizens' organizations.

Nor were they confined to cities alone. On the contrary, state and national organizations flourished. They
might be conservative, liberal or radical. They might
be directly concerned with the structure of government
or with some proposed function of government. They

might be directed toward structural changes in governmental machinery, as the short ballot, proportional representation of some type, initiative and referendum, public ownership, defence of "constitutional government"; with questions of administrative efficiency, with the qualifications of candidates, with social reforms in such fields as the protection of children and women, penology, recreation, education. Of these groups the number was very large and frequently there were not only organizations, but counter organizations also.

In the frequent absence of effective political leadership, or of administrative initiative, these associations played an active and often a very important rôle in public affairs, and were a significant part of the political society. Although outside the government and outside the parties, they often formulated and expressed public opinion in platforms and elections more clearly than the government or the parties themselves. They differed from the unpaid public servants acting in various public capacities in that they held no technically responsible position in government; nevertheless they were from time to time more powerful. They did not often apply lynch law personally, as did the Vigilantes occasionally, although this was threatened sometimes,— as when ropes were dangled over the heads of the law makers of Chicago,— but they often brought such pressure to bear as to compel action. They were at one end of the field, while the invisible government of the boss and the magnate were at the other. Much of the current legislation came from this group, and much of the demand for effective administration; much of the vital public discussion by which public opinion is shaped and made. They often did the work of parties and of parliamentary bodies; and sometimes that of administration.[56]

While the government was being centralized and while the party system was being regulated and officialized, the unofficial voluntary organizations were springing up in other and less official types of association and action. On the whole, public opinion favored these extra legal agencies more than it did the government. Political leadership developed slowly within the government, while vital currents of confidence flowed through the regular party and the insurgent or independent reserves outside the party. Organizations of capital, organizations of labor, party organizations and the unofficial citizens' organizations all grew more rapidly in power than did the formal government itself. If we consider in this connection the expansion of the electorate in the development of direct legislation, the process of the development of popular government is still more striking. American thought, while it was political in tendency, was somewhat indirectly political, distrustful of officialism and inclined to lean upon the extra legal agencies. The boss, the machine, the invisible government, the party, the insurgents, the reformers, all made their machinery and developed

[56] W. H. Tolman, "Municipal Reform Movements"; T. C. Devlin, "Municipal Reform in the United States"; W. B. Munro, "The Government of American Cities," Ch. 14; Theodore Roosevelt, "The Strenuous Life," pp. 41–62; F. A. Cleveland, "Organized Democracy," Chap. 8–9; Gustavus Meyers, "History of the Great American Fortunes," Vol. I, p. 236; Roscoe Conkling, "Life and Letters," gives his famous attack on George Wm. Curtis in 1877, p. 538.

their power with rapidity startling in comparison to that of the government. Rigidity and stiffness of formal government, and flexibility and adaptability in informal government, were the characteristic features of the time. Outside the hard lines of constitutional and formal government, the political thought and enterprise of the day seized with great avidity the new forces of the new time, sometimes for public and sometimes for private ends, and shaped them into a many-hued variety of forms, unknown to tradition, unforeseen by the Fathers and unwelcome sometimes even to their own creators. These new types were not the result of conscious calculation. They were the instinctive product of political interest and activity finding expression wherever it found an open way leading to political result. The appreciation of these extra-legal, quasi-governmental, semi-political forces and factors is fundamental to an understanding of the development of American institutions and the progress of American thought during the last half century.

On the whole, the significant features of the period were the protest against the "machine," and its tendency to sacrifice the end to the means; the determined effort to insure democratic party control by restriction of patronage and control of nominating methods; the transition to party interpretation in terms of governmental structure, and of economic and social relations; increasing attention to the theory and practice of leadership in a democracy, and toward the intimate relation between political and social causes and effects.

CHAPTER XI

GOVERNMENT AND LIBERTY

THE early Fathers looked theoretically upon all government with suspicion. They believed that the less government the more liberty, the more government the less liberty. The Colonies wished to be left alone by Great Britain. Later, the individual states wished to be left alone by the national government. The local divisions of the state, in many instances, wished to be left free to develop undisturbed by the commonwealth; and citizens generally wished to be let alone by the government, feeling that only in this way could their individual liberty be preserved. They were not greatly interested in cooperative or collective action, either as individuals, as states, or as a nation. Their political theory, their public law, their national policy, all were based upon a philosophy of isolation.

During the next generation the earlier individualism was intensified by the frontier conditions under which American life expanded and developed. The philosophy of the pioneer was the philosophy of self-reliance. Individuals were thrown back upon themselves under the conditions of settlement in new countries. In many instances men were miles from their nearest neighbor, left to wrestle with nature, little aided by government or society. Indeed, there was as simple a government under frontier conditions as it is possible to conceive on a civilized basis. There was almost a total absence of any official or governing class. There was little organized military activity. In short, the frontier conditions were fundamentally favorable to the advancement of the individualistic idea.

Theoretically individualism was reflected in the writings of Emerson, Thoreau and the group in New England known as the " transcendentalists," who at the same time, however, were humanitarians, not averse to communal action. Many collectivist experiments were made during this period.

The discussion of liberty during this period centered around the institution of slavery. This was assailed by the abolitionists and the anti-slavery group as an unwarranted invasion of the individual right of the slave. Anti-slavery and the rankest forms of individualism went hand in hand during this period, shading over into religious or utopian socialism. William Lloyd Garrison, leader of the radical wing of the Abolitionists, was an advocate of non-resistance and " no government "— a member of the sect called the " Come-Outers," who " came out " of society, and the State, and the church, separating themselves from these institutions, as far as it was possible to do so. The slavery controversy, however, cut squarely across the track of humanitarianism, and for a generation economic and social problems were subordinated to the abolition struggle, to the conduct of the war, and to the difficulties of reconstruction and reorganization.

During the last half of the century the question of the limits of governmental activity was raised in many concrete ways. The transformation of conditions wrought by urban and industrial tendencies profoundly modified the facts of life and influenced its philosophy. Under the new conditions it was inevitable that new rules of conduct should be shaped to meet the new surroundings and relations. Regulations adapted to rural and agricultural conditions were often ill-fitted to urban industrial centers, while the changes in industrial organization vitally affected the form of legal and political relations. The competitive process was radically changed, and the rule of the early régime must be modified to meet the new situations. Inevitably in the transition state, there were conflicting doctrines as to what the government should do, and how far it should go in the regulation of the social and industrial process. Monopoly soon challenged competition in industry, and the new conditions required new interpretations. Specific controversies involved questions of law and political philosophy which compelled close inquiry into the analysis of the proper work of the government. On the one hand the concentration of capital in large corporations, and in still larger holding companies, raised the question as to the legal power and political duty of the government toward these new combinations. On the other hand the concentration of labor in well organized and powerful unions raised another set of questions regarding the right to organize, the " collective bargaining " process, strikes, picketing, blacklisting, boycotting, the " closed shop " and other problems collateral to the concentration of labor power.

Again, the progress of social legislation involved the consideration of fundamental questions of political theory. To what extent should the State regulate working and living conditions of men, women, and children, how far modify the traditional relations between " master " and " men," how far intervene in the industrial process for the protection of society.

Again, in connection with the problem of governmental ownership of public utilities in cities, and of railroads and natural resources by the Federal government, the whole question of the proper function of the State was clearly raised. Industrial theories of competition against consolidation, of the small and competing business against the large monopoly business called for and were answered by divergent political theories of State activity or non-interference.

In the same way the governmental policy of tariff, of subsidies to railways and merchant marine, of taxation for public purposes, of the regulation of the liquor traffic, all involved to some extent the consideration of the fundamental purpose for which the State exists and the limits which should be imposed upon its action. Likewise the use of the taxing power of the government raised the legal and theoretical questions as to what constitutes a " public purpose."

The theory of the activity appropriate to the State underwent a material change toward the last half of the 19th century. Several distinct phases of this movement appeared, among them the following:

1st. The continuation of the earlier individualistic theory and its application to new industrial conditions;

2nd. The development of a social-political theory best represented by the doctrine of " social politics " and the legal theory of the " police power " ;

3rd. The development of the general theory of State socialism ;

4th. The development of the doctrines of anarchism, and syndicalism.

The individualistic theory developed during this period was largely a re-statement of the earlier doctrines applied with little change to new conditions. Strong emphasis was laid on the value of individual enterprise, the importance of individual initiative, upon the significance of self-reliance and responsibility as factors in the growth of the community. It was asserted that these were the typical qualities upon which American prosperity had been based, and upon which American energy and enterprise fed. The settlement of a vast new territory, the development of the lines of communication and transportation, the organization of manufacturing and mining, and the growth of industry in general were attributed to this individualism. Thus broadly stated, the theory was the generally accepted doctrine of the period. In the earlier part of this epoch these qualities were generally imputed to the population as a whole, but toward the end the tendency was to attribute the chief values of individualism to the industrial leaders, or, as they were called, " captains of industry." To their inventive and creative power were due, in great part, it was said, the industrial gains of the period. The conclusion was drawn, that the individual should be as little as possible restrained by the law; that the State should pursue, ex-

cept in cases of extreme urgency, a policy of non-interference with the development of individual conduct, and
the individual person or corporation should be left un-
trammeled by irksome restrictions of a paternal government.

Non-interference became the slogan of many interests
obviously anxious to avoid governmental regulations.
Railroads threatened with regulation, corporations held
in check by public measures, certain industries resisting
sanitary and social regulation, raised the banner of
laissez-faire. They asked for a free hand in the conduct
of their enterprises, and they generalized their conclusions into a law of minimum governmental control.

In its earliest stages, this theory was a re-statement
of the economic doctrine of the " natural laws " of industry under which economic processes are most safely directed, and was hostile to governmental interference with
these processes of natural law.   Political economists were
often quoted in support of a policy of *laissez faire,* but
their frequent insistence upon the application of the principle in the form of free trade reduced their marginal
utility.   Thus the well known economist David A. Wells
held that " the reformation of the individual is something
more important than the reformation of society." [1]
" The destruction of the poor is their poverty, and they
stand in their own light."   Conditions, not legislation,
may reduce the hours of workingmen.   " A shorter day,"
said he, " is an absurdity because it will reduce production
and hence wages.   One day's rest in seven is a curious
provision."   There are evils in the existing equality of

[1] " Recent Economic Changes," 1889, p. 431.

wealth, but there will be still greater evils if there is nothing but equality.

These ideas were expressed in systematic form by various thinkers and writers. Sumner,[2] for a generation the most conspicuous opponent of State activity, declared that the United States stands for individualism and personal liberty. All political questions, said he, are "struggles of interests for larger margins of the product of industry." The decision of these contests might better be left to free contract than to governmental adjudication. "Which may we better trust," he said, "the play of free social forces or legislative and administrative interference?" Again, he says: "The truth is that the social order is fixed by laws of nature precisely analogous to those of the physical order. The most that man can do is by his ignorance and conceit to mar the operation of the social laws." Sumner proclaimed that the evils of society are due in great measure "to the dogmatism and self-interest of statesmen, philosophers and ecclesiastics, who in the past time have done just what the socialists now want to do." He grouped together as institutions, liberty, equality before the law, responsibility, individualism, monogamy, and private property. He assailed all socialistic "projects for curing poverty by making those who have share with those who have not,"[3] and decried the attention given to "nasty, shiftless, criminal, whining, crawling and good for noth-

[2] William Graham Sumner, "What Social Classes Owe to Each Other," 1883; "The Forgotten Man," 1887; "The Challenge of Facts," 1914.

[3] T. N. Carver, "Essays in Social Justice," 1915.

ing people." Sumner impartially denounced protection, fiat money, humanitarianism and trade unionism.

Vigorous assertions of the doctrine of non-interference were made by industrial organizations, notably the American Association of Manufacturers. In their constitution of 1904, one of the declared objects was " the maintenance of individualism." " We stand," said Mr. Emery, " upon the theory of principles in which the individual is the unit of authority, the unit of power and the unit of growth." [4] " The owners of factories," said Mr. Post, " have the absolute right to the management of their properties and must maintain such rights against any mob of bandits and law-breakers." [5] " The workingman," said Mr. Post, " carries some boards to the building and a horse hauls some more. Which ' creates ' and to which should the building partly belong? Both work and both execute, but neither originates nor creates any wealth whatever. Both are paid an agreed, understood and full equivalent for their services; — the horse his oats, hay and water, and the workman his money." In general they denounced all movements in the direction of Socialism, but were not opposed to railroad regulation or to a national tariff commission.[6] They sharply criticized Seth Low, Samuel Gompers, and the National Civic Federation defending what they called " diversified industry " as against " socialized industry," in which there is a great massing together of capital, as in the larger industries reaching or approaching monopoly form. To-

[4] Proceedings, 1905, p. 205.
[5] Ibid., p. 284.
[6] See Kirby, Ibid., 1913, p. 72, on Conservatives and Radicals.

ward the end of the period, however, an effort was made for the adoption of a new plan, including a constructive legislation program.[7]

The particular right they believed to be menaced was that of "industrial liberty," and the center of the controversy was the "right to work." The right of an employee to work "where he pleased, when he pleased and for what he pleased" was held to be fundamental,[8] and must be protected at all hazards by the law of the land.[9]

A striking statement of the general position of the Association was that given in the following extract from the proceedings of 1913.

"But when they have proof of constantly recurring murder, arson, destruction, intimidation, assaults, organized conspiracies for crime, and nefarious plots equal to the Russian Nihilists; when we see inherent rights of American laboring men blasted by the cruelties of a defiant labor trust; when we witness our boasted constitutional precepts repudiated, human life endangered or crushed, unconscionable compacts to exclude men from labor unless unionized, tagged and labeled like so many cords of wood; when we observe dynamite, nitro-glycerin and the torch demolishing property and shattering lives; cruelties administered by all kinds of ingenious and iniquitous methods; when we see legitimate industry cunningly boycotted, and subtle schemes devised to defeat the sale of manufactured products except under rules of

[7] Proceedings, 1914, p. 193.
[8] *Ibid.*, 1905, p. 206.
[9] *Ibid.*, 1913, p. 68.

union czardom; when, I say, we observe this panorama of innumerable criminal acts, done shamelessly in the name of unionized labor, then, I declare, with personal conviction, that it is high time that language commensurate to describe such atrocities, be employed to bring to our realization and to our citizenship the frightful conditions that menace our lives, our liberty, our property and our inheritances."

In the New York Constitutional Convention of 1915 William Barnes, as a delegate, presented an amendment to the constitution forbidding the legislature " to establish a wage for service to be paid any employee by a private employer." [10] In presenting this amendment the philosopher-boss discussed the ideal of equality, as he termed it, and general trend toward the " Prussian principle." The concept of the democratic state, said Barnes, where equality is the basis of all law, is in direct antagonism to the autocratic state where every one is made subject to what is declared to be the collective interest. He denounced the general policies of social legislation and the tyranny of collectivism. These measures are not an " antidote to socialism," but tend to prepare the mind for it and make the final triumph of socialism easier and sooner. " The oppression of the crowd, crowd interest, crowd demand for mediocrity, might even lead the human race back to the protoplasm from whence it emerged."

In the course of an animated discussion upon the Barnes principle, Judge Clearwater stated still more emphatically the doctrine of old-time individualism. The

[10] Proceedings, p. 1802.

distinguished jurist declared that immigration into the United States since 1880 had been distinctly bad. We were building up, said the judge, a class of " proletarians," who would undermine the principles of government and industry upon which our nation was built. " By proletarian," he said, " I mean the man who has no property, who has not the industry, frugality and self-denial to accumulate property; a man who will breed children and who will throw himself without scruple or reserve upon a community for support. That is the proletarian, and that is the proletarian class, that is growing up in our seaboard states, and in no city greater than in this imperial city of New York." [11]

As against the collectivist tendencies evident in legislation, he appealed to the earlier ideals of American life. Over against social justice he set up frugality, honesty, simplicity, the desire for more education, the desire to accumulate property, the desire to lay aside something for old age.[12]

Butler believed that the remedy for modern ills is not to be found in political action. There are, " only two deepseated influential enemies of human happiness and human order — ignorance and selfishness." [13] For these he prescribed as sovereign remedies the specifics of education and morality. Through these fundamental agencies, rather than through changes in the form of government

[11] P. 1833.
[12] See page 1834, for a full statement of Judge Clearwater's doctrine of the earlier American ideal. In this connection notice the vigorous replies made by Wickersham and Schurman.
[13] " Why Should We Change our Form of Government?"

or in the extension of the activities of government, can permanent improvements be made. Senator Root voiced the same conviction when he said that " the problem of human betterment is not a problem of revolution. It is simply and solely a matter of individual self betterment." " If," said the Senator, " men's standards of action be raised, if their citizenship be really sincere and vital, then society is already reformed and nothing else remains to be done." At the same time any interference with individual liberty by the government should be most closely watched and restrained, because the habit of undue interference destroys that independence of character in its citizens, without which no free government can endure.

The venerable Burgess,[14] founder of the School of Political Science in Columbia University, declared that the new " school of sociologists and political economists, seeks to accomplish by governmental force what should be left to influence, religion, conscience, charity and honor." We are attempting the " substitution of the club of the policeman for the crozier of the priest, the supervision of education, morals and philanthropy by administrative ordinance." We are threatened by Cæsarism, " the rule of the one by popular acclaim, the apotheosis of government and the universal decline of the consciousness of and the true desire for true liberty."

The most compact statement of the later theory of limited state activity is made by a group of thinkers including Taft, Butler, Root, Lodge, Gary and others [15] in a recent

---

[14] " The Reconciliation of Government with Liberty," 1915, p. 380.
[15] See Beale's edition of Spencer's " Man vs. the State," containing Mr. Root's preface to " The New Toryism"; Sen. Lodge, " The

edition of Herbert Spencer's famous attack upon state activities.   Here are found in concise form the doctrines of conservative leaders upon the vexed problem of the extent of governmental enterprise and action.

Significant was the activity of the National Civic Federation, which undertook the reconciliation of the strained relations between labor and capital and which recognized the need of publicity and of public regulation upon a far larger scale than heretofore.[16]   They reflected the higher Conservatism to which it seemed desirable to pre-- serve the large scale system of production, but to modify relations between employer and employe in many significant particulars.

Practical types of these men were Seth Low and Mark Hanna, who recognized the value both of the corporation and of labor organizations and were willing to modify their individualism to a degree.[17]   Andrew Carnegie also held strongly to individualism, but recognized the value of the labor union and the significant evolution-

Coming Slavery"; E. H. Gary, "Over-Legislation"; Augustus P. Gardner, "From Freedom to Bondage"; Nicholas M. Butler, "The Great Political Superstition"; David Jayne Hill, "The Man vs. the State"; Harlan F. Stone, "The Sins of Legislators"; Chas. W. Eliot, "Specialized Administration"; W. H. Taft, "The Duty of the State."   Compare L. A. Coolidge, "An Old Fashioned Senator" (O. H. Platt of Connecticut), Ch. 32; James O. Fagan, "The Autobiography of an Individualist."

[16] Ida M. Tarbell, "New Ideals in Business," 1917.

[17] Mark Hanna, "Socialism and Labor Unions," *National Magazine*, 1903; Croly's "Life of Mark Hanna,"; compare Henry Clews, "The Wall Street Point of View," 1900; John D. Rockefeller, "Random Reminiscences of Men and Events," 1909; John Moody, "The Masters of Capital."

ary tendency of the times.[18] Only through exceptional individuals as leaders, says Carnegie, has man been able to ascend. " It is the leaders who do the new things that count, and all these have been individualistic to a degree, beyond ordinary men, and worked in perfect freedom." [19] Where he differed from the Socialist, he said, was regarding the " advisability of any violent change from individualism." The steel magnate expressed a belief in evolution rather than in revolution, in gradual and conservative change rather than in rash innovation, and predicted that the next stage in evolution would be the joint stock ownership of large scale enterprises by combinations of capitalists, managers and workingmen. No one knows the future of communism, but we can see clearly the approach toward joint share-holding and joint management of industry, said he.[20]

The necessity of material modification of earlier standards of *laissez faire* is recognized by many defenders of conservatism. Senator Root clearly realized that we have " just begun to appreciate the transformation in industrial and social conditions wrought by the inventions and discoveries of the past century." He recognized that the power of organization has materially changed the practical effect of the system of free contract, that the interdependence of modern life has deprived the indi-

[18] Andrew Carnegie, "Problems of To-day," 1908; *North Am. Rev.*, 1889, on "Wealth," 148, 653; see also "Triumphant Democracy," 1887; "The Gospel of Wealth," 1900; "The Empire of Business," 1902.

[19] " Problems," 174.

[20] *Ibid.*, 77. Carnegie favored progressive inheritance taxes up to at least one half.

vidual of his power of self-protection, and has opened new avenues by which fatal injuries may be inflicted upon his rights, his property, his health, his liberty of action, his life itself. Old customs and old rules must disappear and new formulas and principles must be worked out. There will be new forms through which the law will continue to render its accustomed service to society. The danger is that the reaction will be too violent, he fears, and that the useful limits of State interference will be transgressed, that interests or prejudices will take the place of even-handed justice.[21]

It will be observed that these discussions of individualism do not rest heavily upon the philosophical foundations of the 18th century individualism. The state of nature, natural rights, the social contact, the staple of the early theory, have little place in these conclusions, and in fact are distinctly repudiated by many. It was not the philosophy of Locke that was followed, but rather the theory of the classical economists and the sociological theory of Herbert Spencer, whose famous treatise on Social Statics is much more in evidence than the 17th and 18th century doctrines of natural law.

In this connection it is interesting to note that when Spencer visited America in 1882 he lamented the excesses to which competition had gone, and was willing to concede that there was need for governmental interference.[22] Referring to the doings of " railway autocrats, not only when overriding the rights of share-holders, but

[21] Addresses, p. 519 ff. (1916).
[22] "Life and Letters of John Fiske," II, 248. Spencer's Essays, Vol. III, 471 ff.

in dominating over courts of justice and state governments," he said that the American people were losing their freedom. As to the doctrine of *laissez faire,* " I have contended that in its special sphere, the maintenance of equitable relations among citizens, governmental action should be extended and elaborated."

In short, the individualism of this period might more accurately be characterized as an industrial and social individualism, in contrast with the political individualism of the earlier times. The individualism of the Fathers was based upon a belief that strong government is identical with absolutism; that the more powerful the state, the weaker the individual. The later type of individualism rested upon the supposition that industry and trade flourish in proportion as they are left alone by the government and particularly that the captain of industry must not be prevented from following his natural bent: — in short, upon a fear that governmental interference meant the repression of industrial activity. The individualism of the Fathers grew out of the fear of political absolutism. The individualism of the last half century grew out of the fear of business depression or repression. The individualism of the Fathers was based upon an ideal of liberty: the later form upon an ideal of industrial production.

It is not to be presumed, however, that the current philosophy was wholly individualistic. The interference of the state in the establishment of the protective tariff was not unwelcome. On the contrary, governmental action was vigorously demanded. Many of the economists during this period, notable among them Sumner, contended for " free trade," but the dominant statesmen, the ruling political party, and the business interests in general, were closely identified with a program of tariff legislation and subsidies for the up-building of American industries. Nor was it regarded as socialism for the government to grant large tracts of land to railroads as bonuses for the construction of new lines, or to guarantee or to pay their bonds. Nor were subsidies for the stimulation of a merchant marine regarded as contrary to the principles of *laissez faire*.

Likewise in dealing with large combinations of capital in the form of trusts, the principle of individual industrial competition was not uniformly defended. It was commonly held that municipal and other public utilities should be governed by the principle of monopoly; and that competition was impracticable and undesirable in this field. It was commonly held that " pooling " was necessary and desirable, and that governmental interference with the consolidation of railroads was unwarranted. In opposition to proposed legislation in restraint of corporations, it was frequently asserted that the principles of individual competition had broken down, and that of large combinations or monopolies must necessarily take its place.

Far-reaching modifications of the individualistic idea appeared during the last half century, and particularly during the last quarter of the century. The growth of great cities, the development of the trust and the labor union, the increasing fund of scientific knowledge regarding social conditions, all tended to force a readjustment of the position of lines of thought. Evidence of this is found on every hand: — in the platforms of political parties, in the legislation of the States and of the nation, and to a limited extent in the decisions of the courts, and in the formulation of systematic doctrines.[23]

At the close of the Civil War began the great struggle for railway control, which shook the foundations of state and national politics for a generation. It is true that the currency problem raised the question of governmental control over the nation's money, and consequently the question of the proper sphere of government. But the contest over the regulation of railroad rates and service was much sharper, and as far as public opinion went, more successful. The verdict was soon reached that the extraordinary situation demanded extraordinary remedies, and that governmental supervision of railway enterprise was necessary and justifiable in the common interest. To this conclusion, of course, the fact that the government had granted lands and given bonuses to the railroads materially contributed. The theory of the right to public regulation of business affected with a public interest was finally given recognition in the famous Granger Cases in 1876, and later, in the creation of the Interstate Commerce Commission in 1887, after a Congressional struggle extending over twenty years. In the latter part of the period public attention was directed to the enforcement and administration of the act, and latterly toward the subject of governmental ownership of the railway system.

Overlapping the struggle for railway control came the

[23] See Jeremiah Jenks, "Governmental Action for Social Welfare, 1910."

broader question of corporate activity. How far should the state interfere with the process of competition, as seen in the development of modern business? What is unreasonable or reasonable combination? What are the limits of fair competition? What is just as between competitors in business and what is just as between employer and employe? The many and complicated phases of this problem precipitated a long and violent discussion over industrial facts and over the underlying theory of government. When the interests of a jobber or consumer clashed with the manufacturer the issue was one thing. When the small business clashed with the big business, it was another. When the employe clashed with the employer it was still another. Thus the small business man would fight the railroads' high rates, or the trust's inteference with competition, but also the union's demands for higher wages or shorter hours. That the system of unrestricted competition had broken down was generally conceded, but the type of public restraint and the degree of public control were subjects of nation-wide thought and discussion. In the urban problem, in the regulation of public utilities, in the shaping of new policies of social hygiene, in the regulation of professions, the differences were less sharply expressed. But in the regulation of industrial relations as between businesses, and as between employer and employe, the most widely divergent views appeared.

Outside the field of industrial controversy there is striking evidence of a quietly developing social policy. The marks of this become increasingly clear during the last quarter of a century, and particularly during the last decade. Throughout the legislation of this time runs the doctrine, expressed or unexpressed, of the greater need for collective action. In city government, for example, a social policy appeared in the activities of the health and building departments for the protection of the community from unsafe and unsanitary conditions. Moving in the same general direction were the park systems, playgrounds, recreation facilities, neighborhood or social centers, the far-reaching developments of public education; and the establishment of various departments of " public welfare."

When the establishment of Central Park was first proposed in New York City, and for many years thereafter, the plan encountered the most vigorous opposition. The park was denounced as an aristocratic institution borrowed from the practice of the nobility abroad. Seven years after the establishment of the Park, the New York *Herald* said: " It is all folly to expect in this country to have parks like those in old, aristocratic countries. When we open a public park Sam will air himself in it. He will take his friends from Church Street or elsewhere. He will knock down any better dressed man who remonstrates with him. He will talk and sing and fill his share of a bench, and flirt with the nursery maids in his own coarse way. Now, we ask, what chance have William B. Astor and Edward Everett against this fellow citizen of theirs? Can they and he enjoy the same place? " [24]

Unquestionably a striking evidence of a community policy has been the development of city planning schemes.

[24] Cited by F. L. Olmsted in " Journal of Social Science," III, p. 28.

In New York, Chicago, Boston, Philadelphia, and practically all the large centers of the country, "city plans" and zoning systems have been outlined, either by voluntary associations or by public act. These plans involve comprehensive study of the needs of each local community with respect to arrangements of streets, parks and public places, transportation, housing and recreation facilities. In short, they constitute an attempt on the part of the city to regulate and control its own growth and development. While most of these plans have thus far been only imperfectly executed, they show a distinct tendency toward conscious social control through governmental agencies. They are indications that the community is disposed to study itself, to analyze the social, industrial and living conditions of men and women and to apply such remedies as the situation may indicate. Most of these advances have not been made as a result of formulated theory, but of necessity and dictated by distressing conditions.[25]

In the field of state government, the most notable advance toward a social-political policy has been made in the field of labor legislation. The statutes of the commonwealths are filled with provisions concerning employers' liability and workmen's compensation, detailed factory and workshop regulations, child labor protections. limitation of hours of labor for women, and in certain trades for men, and in some instances a minimum wage.

[25] Dr. Eliot attempts to distinguish between Collectivism and Socialism in "The Conflict Between Industrialism and Collectivism in a Democracy" (1910). "Collectivism has no general theory on that subject (ownership of all means of production) and in practice is simply opportunist in regard to it." Pg. 2.

While these statutes are in no sense and no place complete, yet they constitute a striking advance toward a collective policy. They appear to be forerunners of a general comprehensive plan of social legislation. They are significant not simply because of what they actually embody, but of what they seem to foreshadow in the way of future accomplishment. This is particularly true of such acts as contemplate or provide for the minimum wage, civil pensions for public employes, and workmen's compensation.

In taxation is seen another significant development of democratic control. Of particular interest here is the evolution of the income tax and of the inheritance tax, both of which made their way against overwhelming difficulties, but were finally firmly established in democratic theory and in law.[26] The " public purpose " of taxation was likewise materially broadened, and also the use of the right of eminent domain. The area of the special assessment was broadened both by legislative and by judicial interpretation.

In the federal field notable legislation has been enacted regarding hours of labor, safety appliances, workmen's compensation, and still more conspicuously in the regulation of child labor. Furthermore, the far-reaching policy of the federal government in regard to internal improvements, protective tariff, and the wholesale distribution of the public domain, may all be classified under the broad term of social politics. Fostering manu-

[26] Seligman, "Essays on Taxation"; Max West, "The Inheritance Tax"; Victor Rosewater, "Special Assessments"; John Lewis, "A Treatise on the Law of Eminent Domain."

factures by governmental action, settling a vast territory by practically free grants of public land, stimulating and developing industry and agriculture by governmental grant and bonus, financial assistance to railroads, are all evidences of State expansion on a huge scale. The opposition to tariff and internal improvements was not based on individualistic grounds, but largely on the constitutional principle of states' rights, or the economic theory of free trade, or of practical abuses in the system.

The conservation policy of the United States government stands upon the same basis. In this case there is a consciously designed plan for preserving the natural resources of the country. This rested partly upon the desire to avoid evident waste of assets, and partly upon desire to prevent control by special as opposed to general interests. The broad policy of preserving and protecting the nation's water power, timber, minerals, and other similar resources, is an illustration on a large scale of drift away from opposition to state interference.[27]

Analyses of the function of the government were made by a number of systematic thinkers. Among them was Woolsey,[28] who divided the duties of the government under four heads, namely, the redress of wrongs, prevention of wrongs, care of the outward welfare of citizens in such affairs as industry, health and highways; and finally, duties in regard to spiritual matters. In all

[27] See Merriam: "Outlook for Social Politics in the United States," in *American Journal of Sociology*, 18, 676. Charles R. Henderson, "The Social Spirit in America," 1901.

[28] "Political Science," Part II, Ch. IV, 1877.

cases he believed that the burden of proof rested upon those who proposed any additional activity of the State.

A striking instance of the rapidity of the change in political theory is seen in a copy of Woolsey's "Political Science" given to the University of Chicago by the late Dr. Henderson, one of the most earnest advocates in his later years of an active social program on the part of the government. In his discussion of the sphere and ends of the state, Woolsey had said, "It may enforce moral observances, may protect, and even institute religious worship, and may provide for the wants of the needy and distressed." On the margin, under date of January 1, 1878, Dr. Henderson had written: "I protest." But under date of 1894 he had written, "I am not so much under Mr. Spencer's influence now." At the end of his life there was no more active and successful advocate of state action to relieve the wants of the needy and distressed than was Henderson.

A significant step was taken in 1883, when Ward attacked the widely current doctrine of Spencer [29] and his American disciple Sumner. Ward emphasized the importance of psychic forces in evolution and what he termed the "efficacy of effort" as a cardinal principle of progress. He sharply criticized the Spencerian individualism, urging the superiority of artificial and "teleological" purposes over the "natural" or genetic. He asserted the supremacy of the principle of cooperation over that of competition, and declared in flat contradiction

[29] "Dynamic Sociology, 1883; "The Psychic Factors of Civilization," 1893; "Pure Sociology," 1903; "Applied Sociology," 1906.

to Spencer that "individual freedom can come only through social regulation."

In 1886 the newly formed American Economic Association declared in its preliminary statement: [30]   "We regard the state as an educational and ethical agency whose positive aid is an indispensable condition of human progress.   While we recognize the necessity of individual initiative in industrial life, we hold that the doctrine of *laissez faire* is unsafe in politics and unsound in morals, and that it suggests an inadequate explanation of the relations between the state and the citizens." [31]   As finally adopted, this statement read: "We regard the state as an agency whose positive assistance is one of the indispensable conditions of progress." [32]

In 1887 Gen. Walker, the leading economist of his day,[33] referred to "those of us who discerned the coming of the storm and removed ourselves and our effects from the lower ground of an uncompromising individualism to positions somewhat more elevated and seemingly secure." [34]   It must be noted, however, that in criticizing Mr. Bellamy's "Looking Backward" this position seemed to be somewhat modified.   He there declared that "perfect competition . . . would result in absolute justice." [35] The fact is, he said, "many persons are careless to the

[30] Publications of American Economic Association, Vol. I, p. 6.

[31] See Lewis H. Haney, "History of Economic Thought," 1911.

[32] "Proceedings I," p. 35.

[33] See the enlightening remarks of Prof. H. C. Adams, Johnston, White, Seligman, Clark and others.

[34] "Discussions on Economics and Statistics," I, 344.

[35] *Atlantic Monthly* 65, p. 248, 1890.   "Mr. Bellamy and the New Nationalist Party."

point of absolute dishonesty in charging upon the organization of society things which are the proper effects of the constitution of nature on the one hand, or of human wilfulness on the other."

About the same time James, who seemed to represent the general view, said, " We do not regard [the state] as a merely negative factor the influence of which is most happy when it is smallest, but we recognize that some of the most necessary functions of a civilized society can be performed only by the state, and some others most efficiently by the state; that the state, in a word, is a permanent category of economic life and not merely a temporary crutch which may be cast away when society becomes more perfect.[36]

A significant analysis was made of the function of the state by H. C. Adams, in his study of the " Relation of the State to Industrial Activity," in 1887. His fundamental position was that neither the English idea of the individual as supreme nor the German theory of the state as supreme was the correct view. Both state activity and individual activity are in reality functions of *society* — " the living and growing organism, the ultimate thing disclosed by an analysis of human relations." The point of view in the discussions of the sphere and duty of government, therefore, should be that of society rather than that of the individual or the state.

Dunbar denied that the common interpretations of the English classical and political economy were correct, and held that neither Adam Smith nor his successors had ever

[36] Publications American Economic Association, Vol. I, p. 26.

occupied a position of unreasonable hostility to state activity.[37]   He flatly contradicted any theory that *laissez faire* was a "part of the logical structure of the old economic doctrine."

Wilson in his "State" laid down the general principle that the state should do nothing which was "equally possible under equitable conditions to optional associations."[38]   He distinguished between what he termed "interference" on the part of the state, and "regulation," the latter involving an equalization of conditions in all branches of endeavor.   The limit of such activity, he believed, was that of "necessary cooperation," the point at which such enforced cooperation becomes a convenience rather than an imperative necessity.   This line may be difficult to trace, but nevertheless must be drawn.[39]

W. W. Willoughby[40] analysed the governmental function into activities relating to the life of the state and the preservation of internal order, activities relating to the preservation of human liberty, and activities relating to the general welfare.   From another point of view he divided state activities into the essential and nonessential. Under the "essential" he included protection of the state against external attack, maintenance of internal order, preservation of the national life.   Under the "nonessential" he included "the economic, industrial and moral interests of the people."   The "nonessential" he further

[37] "Reaction in Political Economy"—*Quarterly Journal of Economics*, Vol. I, p. 1, 1886.

[38] Sec. 1273.

[39] See also "Constitutional Government in the United States"; and, "An Old Master, and Other Essays."

[40] "The Nature of the State," 1896; "Social Justice," 1900.

divided into the " socialistic," including the operation of railways and similar public properties, and under the " non-socialistic " he included supervision over labor and education, and duties which if not performed by the state would be left undone. Each function, said Willoughby, must rest upon its own utilitarian basis rather than upon *a priori* theory. He predicted the expansion of the functions of the state in view of the tendencies of modern life.

Garner divided the work of the state into the functions that are " necessary," those that are " natural and normal " but not necessary, and finally those " neither natural nor necessary." The latter he termed doubtful factors.[41] In the last group he included a variety of services mainly economic and intellectual, such as the management of public utilities, tariffs, social insurance, and labor legislation. The general presumption is against such interference, but still the " state should be an instrument of social and economic progress."

Philosophers undertook to show that there is no real conflict between society and the individual, but that they are complementary factors and not contradictory.[42] On the whole, there is no general antagonism between the individual and society. The individual is shaped in and to some extent by society, but there is no inherent ground of opposition between these organic parts of the same whole.

[41] James W. Garner, "Introduction to Political Science," p. 318.
[42] Compare Warren Fite, "Individualism," 1911. Josiah Royce, "The World and the Individual," 1901. J. M. Baldwin, "The Individual and Society," 1911. Edward S. Ames, "The Higher Individualism," 1915.

In almost all of these thinkers there is a definite departure from the type of individualism which had characterized the first half of the 19th century. In fact, they abandoned the earlier idea of the " police state " and substituted in its place the later doctrine of the " general welfare " state. They were not willing to confine the activity of the government to the condition characterized by Huxley as " anarchy plus the policeman." On the contrary, they recognized that under modern conditions the range of governmental activity must be widened in order to meet the new problems arising.[43]

As the question of a governmental program became more acute still further doctrines were developed. Croly[44] protested against what he termed the negative theory of government. " Unless," said Croly, " democracy is a hypocritical delusion, it seeks not human repression, but human expansion."[45] American political organization must therefore be adapted to the realization of the affirmative rather than of negative public purposes. Again he says: " The state lives and grows by what it does rather than by what it is. Its integrity must be a creation rather than a permanent possession." Democracy, therefore, must possess a social program if the promise of American life is to be fulfilled. It must be prepared to follow wherever the democratic ideal leads.

[43] With these writers it is interesting to compare: Michel, " L'Idee de l'Etat," in which he reviews the doctrines of the French individualists during the 19th century, and Barker, " Political Thought in England from Spencer to To-day."

[44] " Promise of American Life "; " Progressive Democracy."

[45] " Progressive Democracy," p. 415.

The government must be flexible enough to adapt itself to new situations under which democracy must suffer, unless the state can readjust its lines of activity.[46]

In the same spirit wrote Lippman.[47] Unless, said he, " a political movement is woven into the social movement, it has no importance." The government must be fitted for a policy of constructive action and be prepared to carry through such a policy wherever it may lead. The indictment against politics, he says, is not its corruption, but its lack of might.

The liberal statesmen likewise formulated new principles of political action. Roosevelt declared for "a policy of more active governmental interference with social and economic conditions in this country than we have yet had." We are face to face, he says, " with new conditions of the relation of property to human welfare, chiefly because certain advocates of the right of property as against the rights of men have been pushing their claims too far." It is important that property should be the servant and not the master of the commonwealth. Citizens of the country must effectively control the mighty commercial forces which they have themselves called into being. Roosevelt constantly emphasized and reemphasized, however, the importance of personal qualities of self reliance, initiative and individual responsibility. He constantly urged not only the activity of the state, but the aggressive action of the individual citizen himself. Of the man who is down he says, " Give him a chance,

[46] See Chap. 5, " The New Economic Nationalism."
[47] "A Preface to Politics"; "Drift and Mastery."

but do not push him up, if he will not be pushed. . . .
If he lies down it is a poor job to try to carry him."

In the " New Freedom " (1913) Wilson discussed the
significance of the democratic spirit rather than the
technique of governmental organization and the details
of a social program. In the main, however, he seemed
to hold that the state should eliminate artificial obstacles
to free competition. The " hindrance of hindrances " he
adopts as the proper policy of the government in the industrial world. The task of the government must be to
prevent an industrial oligarchy by means of the restora-
tion of competition. Obviously this was a broadly
outlined policy, intended to state a very general principle.

Those who favored individualism and those who supported the policy of governmental action as a rule refused
to accept the creed of the Socialists. They adopted a
modified form of individualism sometimes going under
the name of Collectivism.[48] Thus Mr. Bryan, notwithstanding his attacks upon plutocracy, wished it to be understood that he was an individualist. Socialism, said
he, does not sufficiently take human nature into account.
It assumes more unselfishness that can be safely taken
for granted. He believed in the " spur of competition."
The trust system is not a product of individual or industrial liberty, but a perversion of it, caused by the political grant of special privilege. These " privileges "
must be removed, but the system itself is essentially
sound. " Political liberty," said Bryan, " could not long
endure under an industrial system which permitted a few

[48] See Elliot, *op. cit.*

powerful magnates to control the means of livelihood of the rest of the people." [49] The private monopoly, he reasoned, puts unfair odium upon individualism, and should be abolished in the interest of industrial and political liberty.

In many cities public utilities such as waterworks and electric lighting plants were placed under municipal management, while in many others there was a bitter controversy over the traction system in particular. These contests were particularly common during the last half of the period under discussion. In the national field, the difficulties of railway control led to the discussion of government ownership and in this controversy the function of the state was discussed freely. But the tendency was to subordinate the theoretical aspects of the case to more practical considerations regarding financial, engineering and service features of the specific problems.[50] Bryan was the leading theoretical advocate of government ownership of railways but he did not press his argument vigorously after his initial statement on his return from Europe.[51] There were many advocates of government ownership as a means of securing freedom from the political as well as the economic activities of the railway magnates.[52]

Municipal ownership of public utilities was hotly contested, but the theoretical arguments played relatively a

[49] "Speeches," II, 88. Edith M. Phelps, "Selected Articles on Government Ownership of Railroads," 1919.

[50] C. S. Vrooman, "American Railway Problems," 1910; A. Van Wagenen, "Government Ownership of Railways," 1910.

[51] "Speeches," II, p. 92, 1906.

[52] See Vrooman, *op. cit.*

small part in the discussion.[53]   Advocacy of the extension of the function of the city was presented by Bemis,[54] Howe,[55] Parsons,[56] Zeublin,[57] and others.   In general, the theory rested upon the corruption of city government by public utilities, inadequacy of service, the relation between transportation and municipal growth, and the belief that city ownership would make possible more democratic government.   Municipal ownership was opposed by Meyer,[58] Porter [59] and many others whose arguments turned chiefly on the incompetence and corruption of municipal governments.   The general tendency at the close of the period was toward a discussion upon local grounds with relatively little reference to general theories.[60]

[53] Don Lorenzo Stevens, " Bibliography of Municipal Utility Regulation and Municipal Ownership," 1918, p. 221.

[54] Edwin W. Bemis, " Municipal Monopolies," 1899.

[55] Howe, " The City, the Hope of Democracy," 1905.

[56] Frank Parsons, " The City for the People " (1901).

[57] Zeublin, " Municipal Progress," 1902.

[58] Hugo Meyer, " Municipal Ownership in Great Britain," 1906.

[59] R. P. Porter, " The Dangers of Municipal Trading " (London), 1907.

[60] See Beard, " American City Government," Chap. VIII.

CHAPTER XII

THE ecclesiastical organizations reflected the underlying tendency toward broader social interpretation of the duties of the community.[1] Immediately after the War Henry Ward Beecher and other eminent divines had sharply called attention to the serious abuses arising from the rapidly increasing inequalities of wealth. But, in general, the ecclesiastical forces had not actively participated in the struggle for social and political readjustment.[2] The controversy between science and religion following the publication of Darwin's epoch-making theories of evolution attracted wide-spread interest during the early years of this period, and much of the intellectual energy of the day was consumed in this struggle.[2a] Oth-

[1] It is not intended to discuss here in any detail the broad field of religious forms and forces in the United States since the Civil War. This is a subject of great interest and importance which it is to be hoped may soon be fully studied and interpreted. I am indebted to Dr. Shailer Matthews, Father Husslein and Rabbi Hirsch for valuable suggestions, although they are not responsible for what is stated here.

[2] See A. B. Hart, "National Ideals," Ch. XI. "The American Church." H. K. Carroll, "The Religious Forces of the United States," 1893; Leonard W. Bacon, "A History of Christianity" (1897) in American Church History Series, Vol. XIII; Graham Taylor, "Religion in Social Action," 1913.

[2a] Andrew D. White, "The Warfare of Science"; John Fiske's "Life and Letters."

erwise the institutional developments abroad and at home were of chief interest — the growth of foreign missions, the development of the Sunday School, of various forms of Christian fraternal organization, such as the Y. M. C. A., Y. W. C. A., and the Christian Endeavor societies. Religious interests were also divided during this period by the introduction of a much larger element of the Catholic faith and by the infusion of the Jewish element. Some of the clergy mingled in the radical movement of the '70's and '80's and some were allied with the later development of Christian socialism. Many more were actively engaged in warfare upon intoxicating liquors, gambling and prostitution, and in various "reform" movements.[3]

In the course of a generation, however, the attitude of aloofness forward social and industrial problems was gradually changed to one of much more lively interest; and then into a tendency toward constructive participation in the movement for social readjustment. The beginnings of this new movement were seen in the appearance of Christian Socialism in the '80's corresponding to the contemporary development in Europe.[4] This movement made considerable headway in the United States, although its effects were more powerful indirectly than

[3] See Wilbur F. Crafts, "Practical Christian Sociology" (1895), for a complete catalogue of "reform."

[4] See W. H. Freemantle, "The World as the Subject of Redemption," (1883), published 1892 with introduction by Ely. Compare Ernst Troeltsch, "Gesammelte Schriften," I, "Die Soziallehre des Christlichen Kirche," 1912. Paul Monroe, English and American Christian Socialism, *American Journal of Sociology*, Vol. I, 50. George D. Herron, "The Christian Society," 1894, and other works.

directly. Its influence was felt in the attention given to the study of social problems and in the impulses toward social reform.[5] Ely's work in this field was notable. He warned the church of the alienation of the wage-workers, and pointed out that the gospel " is both individual and social." Later there was much more detailed discussion regarding the causes and remedies for social discontent and out of this came the adoption of a much more definitely social point of view. This was early reflected by Washington Gladden,[6] later by Henderson,[7] Rauschenbusch,[8] Taylor, Abbott, and others and vigorously and decisively by Shailer Matthews.[9] These thinkers emphasized the necessity of modifying the individualistic attitude in dealing with problems of social organization and urged with great force the importance of a broad social point of view.

In some instances denunciation of the attitude of the churches was unsparing. Vedder charged that the " bastard, cringing, sycophantic thing that our age calls Christianity is nothing else than the organized worship

[5] See, " The Social Aspects of Christianity," 1889.

[6] " Applied Christianity," 1887; " Social Facts and Forces," 1897; " The New Industry," 1905; Christianity and Socialism," 1905; " The Church and Modern Life," 1908; " The Forks of the Road," 1916.

[7] " The Social Spirit in America."

[8] " Christianity and the Social Crisis," 1907.

[9] " The Making of To-morrow," 1913; " Social Teaching of Jesus," 1897.

[10] See also Charles Stelze, " American Social and Religious Conditions," 1912; " The Church and Labor," 1910; Charles S. McFarland, " The Christian Ministry and the Social Order," 1909; G. B. Smith, " Social Idealism and the Changing Order "; J. W. Buckham, " Progressive Religious Thought in America," Ch. IV.

of mammon ";[11] that Christianity "has been and is the religion of the possessing class " and teaching capitalistic ethics as an inseparable part of their religion.[12]   Others were not far behind him in this spirit.   In 1908 the Federal Council of the Churches of Christ in America adopted a notable program of social activity to which the organization was committed and in behalf of which a widespread agitation was carried on.[12a]

On the other hand a strongly individualistic position was taken by many of the clergy, particularly during the earlier part of the period.   This attitude continued to be evident down to the end of the period under discussion.

Peabody, contending that many changes in social conditions were both necessary and desirable, pointed out that " Religion cannot become a sociological or economic scheme, which substitutes a change in social conditions for a change in human hearts." [13]   After all the chief defects in life according to the teachings of Jesus are not " mechanical, but moral."   Hillis emphasized the importance of individual regeneration with greater force.[14]   A certain controversy arose between the advocates of " Evangelism " and those who contended for a social

[11] Henry C. Vedder, "Socialism and the Ethics of Jesus," 1913; "The Gospel of Jesus and the Problem of Democracy," 1914.

[12] Compare Harry F. Ward, "Social Creed of the Churches," 1912. "Social Evangelism," 1915.

[12a] E. B. Sanford, "Origin and History of the Federal Council of Churches of Christ in America," 1916.

[13] "The Approach to the Social Question," 1900; "Jesus Christ and the Social Question," 1900.

[14] N. D. Hillis, "The Fortune of the Republic," 1906, especially Ch. V.

program. The Evangelists held in substance that the prime purpose of the church was to save the individual soul, and that emphasis should be laid upon the individual will and spirit, while the social reformers contended that the church could not ignore the social and industrial evils of the day. Some Evangelists objected, for example, to ecclesiastical action upon the peace treaties, constitutional prohibition, the social effects of cooperation, the problem of educational betterment, promotion of democracy, the solution of the trust problem, and promotion of political efficiency, all of which they contended were outside the scope of ecclesiastical jurisdiction. "Is it not, then, it was said, of the greatest importance that we guard the pure evangel from accretions that may turn us aside from our great mission and dissipate energies on the perishing things of time when they should be concentrated on and consecrated to the mighty things of eternity?" The objects of the social program while possibly desirable had the effect, they thought, of "turning the forces of the church into many side channels and so weakening the forces of her one supreme call to save men for time and eternity." [15]

At the same time there were notable developments of interest in social problems both in the Catholic Church and in Judaism, both of which were increasingly represented in American life. In both of these religions there were strong social survivals. The Catholic Church in particular, was officially opposed to Socialism, but not to a social program. In both there was a distinct ten-

[15] "The Churches of Christ in Council" (1916), I, 26, quoting action of Presbyterian Church (South).

dency toward a broad social point of view, in dealing with modern industrial and political problems.[16]

Notable in this direction were the writings of Father Ryan, particularly the volume on " A Living Wage " (1906),[17] and Father Husslein on " The Church and Social Problems," 1901.[18]   In general, their position was midway between socialism and individualistic *laissez faire* — criticising both as destructive of religion, morality and social progress.[19]

These developments were in accord with the general Catholic movement in the field of social and industrial relations, [20] although in many instances there was a notable socialistic development.[21]   In 1888 there was held

[16] James MacCaffrey, " History of the Catholic Church in the 19th Century," II, 4, 11, 12; Merwin-Marie Snell, " The Catholic Social Reform Movement in America "; *Am. Journal Soc. V.*, 16–50 (1900). See also the volumes of the *American Catholic Quarterly Review,* 1876–; *The Catholic World,* 1864–; *America,* 1909–, for numerous articles on social problems.

[17] John Augustus Ryan, " The Morality of the Aims and Methods of the Labor Unions," *Am. Cath. Quart.,* 29, 326; and articles in the Catholic Encyclopædia (1907) on " Individualism"; " Labor and Labor Legislation "; " Labor Unions." See also *Central Blatt — Social Justice* for numerous discussions.   In 1913 a Catholic School of Sociology was established.

[18] Joseph Husslein; also the " World Problem," 1918, and " Democratic Industry," 1919.

[19] Compare Wm. J. Kerby, *The Cath. Quart. Rev.,* 28, 227, 521, on " Reform and Reformers " and " Social Reform." Le Socialisme aux Etats Unis 1897.   [20] See also " Political Economy " of E. J. Burke, 1913; S. J. Ming's " The Morality of Modern Socialism," 1909; " The Characteristics and the Religion of Modern Socialism," David Goldstein, " Socialism, the Nation of Fatherless Children," 1903; A. Preuss, " The Fundamental Fallacy of Socialism," 1908.

[21] Francesco Nitti, " The Catholic Socialists," 1908.

the International Congress of Catholic Socialists, but this movement tended to blend into the social reform stream, after the latter had gained headway in the twentieth century.

Likewise Judaism was represented in the general tendency toward the modification of current individualism.[22] Many of its lay representatives were conspicuous in the struggle for social reform and socialism,[23] and prominent representatives of the ecclesiastical organization were a part of the general process by which the function of the state in social and industrial amelioration was widened.[24]

On the whole, there is evident a distinct change in the ecclesiastical attitude toward social and political problems, corresponding to the liberal movement in politics and law. The pressure of economic and social conditions was as clearly traceable here as elsewhere.

Not only was this true of the industrial problem, but in dealing with the liquor traffic, the supremacy of the general welfare over individual interest was distinctly emphasized. Acting under the police power, drastic regulation of individual conduct was demanded and obtained,

[22] Boris D. Borgen, "Jewish Philanthropy, 1917. [23] Cohen, I., "Jewish Life in Modern Times," 1914; Jacobs, J., "Jewish Contributions to Civilization," 1919; Levi, L. N., "The Intellectual and Ethical Development of the American Jew," 1889. [24] David Philipson, "The Reform Movement in Judaism," 1907, p. 492 cites the Rabbinical Conference at Pittsburg, 1885: "In full accordance with the spirit of Mosaic legislation which strives to regulate the relation between rich and poor, we deem it our duty to participate in the great task of modern times, to solve, on the basis of justice and righteousness, the problems presented by the contrasts and evils of the present organization of society."

on a large scale. " Personal liberty " was not accepted as a valid objection to regulation in the social interest, and all theories of individualism yielded to political regulation of the traffic in intoxicants. Nor was compensation for private property used in the business either offered or accepted. On the contrary, property devoted to such uses was held to be employed at the owner's peril, in the face of impending regulation.

The prohibition movement throughout this entire period was an impressive illustration of the willingness to subordinate the individual to the general interest, where a principle was involved. Unquestionably it played a significant part in the modification of general theory, even though it often had no direct connection with the social movement.

The trades union movement which began to develop most rapidly in the '80's was neither revolutionary nor political nor socialistic. Its philosophy and policy were opportunist and its ultimate goal was never clearly formulated. Before the Senate Committee on Education and Labor, in 1883, Strasser, representing the American Federation of Labor, said, " We have no ultimate ends. We are going on from day to day. We are fighting only for immediate objects — objects that can be realized in a few years." [25] The political activities of the unions were limited, their formal legislative program was not elaborate, and they did not rely largely upon political action or gov-

[25] Cited by Commons, II, 309. See the noteworthy document of Ira Seward, " The 8-hr. Movement," 1865; " Poverty," 1873; also John Swintons, " Live Burning Questions," 1885; Adolph Douai, " Hard Times," 1877; Wendell Phillips, " Foundation of the Labor Movement," 1871; " The Labor Question," 1872.

ernmental aid to obtain their demands.   Public ownership of public utilities was endorsed.[26]   Various political
proposals were approved or disapproved, but neither political action as a fixed policy nor Socialism as an economic or political program was accepted.[27]

The Socialist theory of the function of the state appeared early in the United States and was a considerable
factor in public thought, especially during the last twenty-
five years.[28]   Here, as elsewhere, in the 19th century
there were devolopments of Utopian socialism, scientific
socialism, revolutionary and evolutionary socialism, state
socialism, communistic and anarchistic socialism.   Especially in the '70's and '80's these groups, though small
in number, were bitter in their struggles.

Socialism in the United States has passed through a series of phases.   In the first half of the 19th century,
socialism took the form of communistic experiments conducted by various groups.   Among these the most important were the sectarian communities, and the Owenites,
Fourierists, and Icarians.   Of the religious colonies the
best known communities were those of the Shakers, the
Amana and the Oneida.[29]   New Harmony was the most

[26] " Proceedings," 1896, p. 84.
[27] See chart of labor-organization in U. S. in Brissenden, " The
I. W. W.," p. 384.
[28] John R. Commons, " History of Labor in U. S."; Morris
Hillquit, " History of Socialism in the United States," 1903; J. H.
Noyes, " History of American Socialism," 1870; Richard T. Ely,
" The Labor Movement in America," 1886; John Macy, " Socialism
in America," 1916; A. H. Simons, " Social Forces in American History," 1912; Werner Sombart, " Socialism and the Social Movement."
[29] Commons, John R., " Horace Greeley."

pretentious of the Owenite period and Brook Farm of the Fourierists. In the latter movement such men as Horace Greeley, Channing, Dana and Emerson, were deeply interested. These communistic undertakings were the work of religious groups, or of humanitarian idealists who hoped to see the regeneration of society successfully inaugurated on a small scale. In none of these instances, however, were the expectations of the enthusiastic promoters realized.

The struggle over slavery cut across these movements, and after the War they were not revived; their place was taken by "proletarian" socialism. During the early part of this period, Socialism, losing its early hold on native Americanism, allied itself alternately with radical reform movements on the one hand and on the other with various forms of international socialism. In the ranks of the Socialists there were found from time to time those who favored party political action and those who preferred violent revolution, those who preferred direct industrial action, those who favored state socialism, and those who favored anti-authoritarian or communistic socialism.[30] In this way they followed the general European divisions between those who believed Socialism would be brought about largely by trades unions' cooperation, those who held primarily to political methods, and the communistic anarchists who believed in revolution as the means and Communism as the end.

[30] See Hillquit for a narration of the vicissitudes of the Socialist Party from the organization of the Social party in 1868 to the formation of the Socialist Party in 1901; also Commons, Vol. II op. cit.

At the outset, the Liberal Republicans, the Greenbackers, the liberal reformers and the single taxers absorbed the interest and attention of many of the socialists and various combinations were made. From time to time they plunged into political action and, again, were persuaded of the uselessness of the ballot and fell back upon educational propaganda, on direct industrial action, or in some instances upon revolution and violence. In the '80's came the development of Christian Socialism, a movement which endeavored to develop the socialistic program under the auspices of religion.[31]   Since the expulsion of the Socialists from the United Labor Party in 1887 the field of parliamentary action has been steadily cultivated.

During this period the socialistic theory of industry and the state has been expounded by many American disciples of Karl Marx. Among these are Hillquit, Simons,[32] Berger,[33] Kelly,[34] Debs,[35] Hunter,[36] Spargo, Walling,[37] Russell,[38] Nearing,[39] and a long series of others.[40]   In the main, however, there is found in these

[31] John Spargo, "Christian Socialism in America"; *American Journal of Sociology*, Vol. XV, 15.

[32] "Social Forces in American History."

[33] "Broadsides."

[34] Edmund Kelly, "Government or Human Evolution," 1900.

[35] "The American Movement."   "Life, Work and Speeches," 1908.

[36] Robert Hunter, "Poverty," 1904; "Socialists at Work," 1908; "Violence and the Labor Movement," 1914.

[37] "Progressivism and After."

[38] C. E. Russell, "Lawless Wealth," 1908; "Business," 1911.

[39] Scott Nearing, "Social Adjustment," 1911; "The New Education," 1915.

[40] Including Upton Sinclair, "The Industrial Republic," 1907;

writings little variation from the early theories of Marx and such European modifications as had been made from time to time in orthodox Marxian socialism. They believed in the ultimate breakdown of the competitive capitalistic system and were ready to substitute for it some plan of collective ownership of the means of production. There were some here as in the European countries who believed in a socialistic economic and political program as a necessary basis for the " higher individualism." They reasoned that no individual can truly be free unless he enjoys economic rights and liberties, and that this result can come only through the socialist system.

By far the most widely read of the American Socialists was Edward Bellamy, whose volume on " Looking Backward," published in 1888, was very generally circulated and was the basis of the formation of the Nationalist Party.[41] His Utopia rested upon a military organization in which all were obliged to render service. The period of industrial activity extended from the age of twenty-one to the age of forty-five, after which the individual retired from active industrial duties. The government of the society was to be vested in officers and generals selected by the various departments of industry and a president chosen from among the heads of departments by a vote of all the men of the nation who are not connected with the industrial army.

Of the theory of socialism, John Spargo was a leading

A. K. Lewis, " The Rise of the American Proletarian," 1907; Vida D. Scudder, " Socialism and Character " (1912).

[41] See also his " Equality."

exponent [42] and in his numerous writings he expounded with great fluency, force and skill the socialistic doctrine. He held in the main to Marxian socialism, but refused to regard his writings as a " sacred book," preferring an evolutionary view of socialist theory.

In Spargo's theory, there will be no revolution necessary to establish socialistic system, but gradual growth and evolution. The state will not be abolished, but it will cease to be a class instrument and become a genuine agency for general welfare. Private property will not disappear altogether, nor will individual freedom in choice of occupation be destroyed, nor entire equality of wage established. Socialism will not be a vast system of regimentation, oppressing the individual citizen, but will give him a wider range of freedom and choice than he now possesses. Socialism opposes the theory of anarchy that there can be liberty without law, sustained by force, and is hostile to the communistic theory of industrial self-government by groups, independent of state control. Nor is socialism, as he conceives it, hostile either to the family as an institution or to the church, notwithstanding unauthorized individual utterances to this effect. Religion is a private affair for the individual, while the monogamous family is rooted in soil which socialism would not affect.

Walling [43] sharply criticized the proposals of social

[42] " Socialism," 1906; " Common Sense of Socialism," 1908; " The Spiritual Significance of Modern Socialism," 1908; " The Socialists," 1908; " The Substance of Socialism," 1909; " Karl Marx," 1910; " Sidelights on Contemporary Socialism," 1911; " Applied Socialism," 1912; " Socialism and Motherhood," 1914.

[43] Willoughby Walling. See also his interesting study on " The

reform, contending that the purpose and effect of these regulative measures would be to preserve the institution of capitalism, to maintain the system, although in a better and more humane form, nevertheless fundamentally undisturbed. He believed that the reform plans of wider state activity involved nothing more than an intelligent " efficiency system " on a " patriarchal basis." While he did not oppose directly these measures, he did not regard them as fundamental or final. He denounced what he called the " capitalistic reform program " and the activities of the so-called revisionists, reformers and " German social-democrats of the Berger type." The new reform programs, says he, however radical, are aimed at regenerating capitalism, and the net result will be to establish another form of economic feudalism, patriarchism or paternalism.

Edmund Kelly, attorney and man of affairs,[44] undertook an elaborate defence of collectivism, illustrating his arguments with many illustrations drawn from the biological world. The whole purpose of society, says Kelly, is to correct the inequalities of nature, to undo the cruelty and injustice of blind natural forces, to substitute an artificial human society in which equality and fraternity may be genuinely recognized. For this purpose the existing economic machinery is inadequate and it must be replaced by a new order, in which the evils of competition are corrected and restrained, and sounder principles of social justice established.

Larger Aspects of Socialism," 1913; " Progressivism and After," 1914; " Socialism As It Is," 1912.
[44] Cf. " Government."

For a quarter of a century the most militant figure in American socialism was Eugene V. Debs, repeatedly the party choice for President of the United States; and always on the firing line of aggressive action.[45] A conspicuous personality and an able orator, he was not primarily a philosopher, and his speeches embody the usual doctrines of orthodox socialism adapted to political agitation and propaganda. He inclined to the revolutionary, rather than the evolutionary group of the party; and was not hopeful of the methods of the social democracy.

The local and national programs of the socialists called for a wide extension of the work of government. As immediate steps they demanded the public ownership of municipal utilities, the ownership of railways and natural resources, such as mines, forests, and large scale industry. They also put forward a program of social legislation covering the field of working and living conditions, and industrial insurance in its various forms. In many instances socialists scored local successes in elections, notably in Milwaukee, but obviously were unable to undertake a socialistic program on a large scale.

While the socialist theory of the state was at no time or place widely adopted, nevertheless, it deeply influenced the general course of political thought in America. This was particularly true during the last quarter of the century, after the severance of the alliance with international anarchism. In the main it was the doctrine of state socialism — the authoritarian rather than the anti-authoritarian type, following the German model rather more

[45] "Life, Writings and Speeches," 1908; also "Life and Letters" by David Karsner.

closely than any other, just as the trade-unionists were more nearly like the English type, and the Syndicalists resembled the French and Italian form, while the Anarchists preferred the Russian ideal as far as it had been developed at that time.

The anarchistic doctrine that the state performs no useful function and should therefore be destroyed or dissolved has appeared from time to time in America, but has not struck its roots deeply into our soil. Of the three groups of anarchism all have been found here. The type that springs from religious individualism was represented by the Antinomians of Puritan days. The early Antinomians of Massachusetts, a religious sect who held themselves above the law because they believed that the Christian dispensation had set them free from the law, were practically anarchists. Their activities, history relates, proved most embarrassing to their Puritan colleagues of Massachusetts Bay. The Quakers were non-resistant and anti-militarists, but were not opposed to organized government. In the ante-bellum days among the Abolitionists there developed a non-resistant or no-government period, and the sects known as " Come-Outers," Emancipationists and Perfectionists. The immediate occasion of their activities was their unwillingness to co-operate with a government which recognized slavery and made a human being a chattel. They concluded that men must " come out " of the state or any other organization the spirit of which was anti-Christian. Of this creed William Lloyd Garrison was the most striking figure. The noted author, Thoreau, Abolitionist and individualist, who was once imprisoned for refusal to pay taxes, said that a prison was the only home in a slave state in which a free man can abide with honor.[47]

The development of anarchism after the Civil War was based upon economic rather than on political or religious grounds. It was largely a reflection of the European types of anarchy developed by Proudhon, or Max Stirner, the anti-state-ism evident in Karl Marx, and later the doctrines of the Russian revolutionist Bakunin and the Black International.[48]

The anarchist groups were divided from the beginning into the philosophical and the fighting anarchists, one believing in the attainment of anarchy by the peaceful processes of evolution and the other by the employment of force and by revolution. The Black International as the International Workingman's Association was called, after its capture by the anarchists in 1881, was represented in the United States by little known adherents. They

[47] An attempt to apply anarchy to practical affairs was made by Josiah Warren, in Utopia, Ohio. See his volume on "Equitable Commerce," in which he defines labor as the "sovereignty of the individual" and demanded the abolition of all government. "There should be no such thing as the body politic . . . no member of any body but that of the human family. Every man should be his own government, his own law, his own church, a system within himself." Warren's ideas were more fully developed by Stephen Pearl Andrews, in "The Science of Society," or "The True Constitution of Government in the Sovereignty of the Individual as the Final Development of Protestantism, Democracy and Socialism," 1851.

[48] Richard T. Ely, "The Labor Movement in America," 1886; Herbert L. Osgood, "Scientific Anarchism," *Political Science Quarterly*, IV, 1; Morris Hillquit, "History of Socialism in the United States"; Zenker, "Anarchism"; Eltzbacher, "Anarchism"; Ghio, "L'Anarchisme Aux Etats Unis"; Commons and Andrews, op. cit. Vol. II.

adopted the views of the European organization, and held to the doctrines of revolutionary anarchism. Johann Most, expelled from the German Social Democratic Federation, arrived in the United States in 1883, and brought with him the propaganda of revolutionary anarchism in its most violent form. His ideal was a loose federation of groups of producers, each self-governing and without any superior authority over them. He opposed all compromise between capitalism and anarchism, denounced trades unions and political action, and urged revolutionary violence. He believed in the execution of all reactionaries and the confiscation of all capital.[49]

The Pittsburg International Working People's Association, adopted a platform in 1883 in which the most significant planks were (1) the destruction of the existing class rule by all means — that is, by energetic and relentless revolutionary and international action; (2) the regulation of all public affairs by free contract between the autonomous (independent) interests and associations resting on federalistic basis. The Chicago anarchist affair of 1886 caused a general revulsion from the principles and methods of revolutionary anarchism[50] and the influence of the revolutionary anarchists declined, while that of the political Socialists and trades unions increased.

Emma Goldman was a well-known figure among the active anarchists.[51] Her definition of anarchism was

[49] See Most's "Science of Revolutionary War," extracts from which were reprinted in the *N. E. Reporter,* 12, 894.

[50] A. R. Parsons, "Anarchism, Its Philosophy and Scientific Basis," 1887; G. A. Schilling, "Life of Albert R. Parsons," 1903.

[51] "Anarchism and Other Essays," 1910; "The Social Significance of the Modern Drama," 1914; also "Selected Works of Voltairine

" the philosophy of the new social order based on liberty
unrestricted by man-made law." She believed that all
governments rested on violence, and were harmful and
unnecessary; opposed religion, government, and private
property; and expressed the opinion that woman's suffrage would not improve conditions.

Of the peaceful anarchists the leading figure was Benjamin Tucker, editor of *Boston Liberty* for many years.
His ideas were expressed in a volume unconventionally
entitled " Instead of a Book, By a man too busy to write
one," (1893). Tucker acknowledged his theoretical in-
debtedness to Proudhon, Stirner, Warren, Krapotkin, and
others. He bitterly denounced Most and his colleagues,
whom he characterized as pseudo-anarchists, robbers, in-
cendiaries, murderers, and common criminals, using anarchism as a cloak for greed and crime. Tucker urged
the abolition of the state and all organization upon a compulsory basis, asserting their futility and undesirability.
There would remain, he conceded, a defensive association on a " voluntary basis which will restrain invaders
by any means that may prove necessary." Until that day
passive resistance to the government was urged. One
may pay a poll tax just as one submits to a highwayman,
but would not think of asking him for a receipt.[52]

De Cleyre," 1914; Alex Berkman; " Prison Memoirs of an Anarchist," 1912; Dyer D. Lum, " Economics of Anarchy," 1892; D. I.
Sturber (H. A. Krouse), " The Anarchist Constitution," 1903.

[52] Reflecting the influence of Tolstoi, Clarence Darrow, in " Re-
sist Not Evil " (1903), indicted the state as a powerful contributory
cause of harm. He emphasized particularly the evils arising from
the current theories and methods of punishment as a means of
obtaining human justice.

On the whole, anarchism made little progress in America as a political theory. There was widespread disregard for and disobedience of law in many individual instances, but the adoption of a systematic philosophy of no government was not common.[53]

Midway between anarchism and socialism came syndicalism, represented in the United States by the Industrial Workers of the World.[54] Syndicalism grew up in France under the influence of revolutionary conditions of more than a century, with its repeated uprisings of the masses not only to obtain political democracy, but also forms of social democracy, as in the days of '48 and in the Commune of the '70's. Syndicalism adopted the economic theory of the socialist, a political theory distrustful

[53] See Lysander Spooner, "Letters to Grover Cleveland"; William H. Van Ornum, "Why Government at All?"; (1892). See also the Anarchistic publication, "Mother Earth"; Hutchins Hapgood, in "The Spirit of Labor" (1907), gives an interpretation of anarchism; also in "An Anarchist Woman," 1909.

[54] John Graham Brooks, "American Syndicalism; The I. W. W.," 1913; John Spargo, "Syndicalism, Industrial Unionism and Socialism" (1913); P. F. Brissenden, "The I. W. W." (1919); John Macy, "Socialism in America," Chap. IX; Werner Sombart, "Socialism and the Social Movement," Chap. V, on Revolutionary Syndicalism; Louis Levine, "Labor Movement in France," 1912. Bibliography, p. 208; G. G. Groat, "Organized Labor in America," Ch. 25-28 (1916); Robt. Hunter, "Violence and the Labor Movement," Ch. 10; Arthur D. Lewis, "Syndicalism and the General Strike" (1914); R. F. Hoxie, "Trade Unionism," Ch. VI; Levine, "The Development of Syndicalism in America," *Pol. Sc. Quarterly*, 28, 451; W. Walling, "Socialism As It Is," Pt. III, Ch. V-VI; Helen Marot, "American Labor Unions," Ch. 20; J. A. Estey, "Revolutionary Syndicalism," 1913; Proceedings I. W. W. Conventions, 1905-.

of the state as a tool of capitalism, and a modification of
the direct non-political methods of the trades unionists.
The purpose and the methods of syndicalism diverged
sharply from other political movements and ideals. The
goal of syndicalism is the creation of a society made up
of federated and self-governing industries somewhat after
the fashion of the communistic anarchists or the guild
socialists. Their most comprehensive method of action
is the general strike, which it is believed will some day
usher in the industrial revolution and millennium.

Another weapon is sabotage, or the deliberate reduction
of the output by various devices of the laborer, theoretically to be executed without loss of life or the destruction
of material. Syndicalism is marked by indifference to
political action. It largely abandons parliamentary efforts, believing that the results obtained by efforts to control the machinery of government through parties and
elections are not commensurate with the labor involved.
It proposes to exert power " at the seat of production,"
through industrial leverage, which is regarded as more
efficient than the formally political. There are, however,
varying shades of opinion upon this point. The " left "
group is practically anarchistic in theory, while the
" right " is much more distinctly political or governmental in tendency.

In America this movement has taken the form of industrial unionism. It has proceeded by organization of industries, rather than of crafts, including all the workers
of a given plant or industry. Of this group, Haywood
has been the most conspicuous leader in a situation where

organization and leadership have had only the most precarious existence.[55]

The organization and scope of future government is a matter of indifference to this group, although crude attempts have been made to outline such a form. In the main, they propose to ignore the government and " governmentalism," and to obtain their ends through direct exercise of economic power and pressure. Their ideal of a reorganized society is but vaguely depicted as a loose federation of industrial groups, indefinitely organized. When able to overthrow capitalism, they anticipate some form of industrialism under loose group control. But the question regarding the exact type of this organization they are not careful to answer. In the United States, indeed, there has been but little philosophizing on the subject, while in France and Italy there has been a considerable body of speculation.[56] But even here two groups have arisen, one favoring and the other opposing party or political action.[57]

The significance of syndicalism did not lie in the numerical strength of its supporters, but in its revelation of a fundamental disturbance in the social world. It

[55] William H. Haywood, " The General Strike," 1911; Vincent St. John, " The I. W. W.: Its History, Structure and Methods "; " Political Parties and the I. W. W."; Wm. E. Trautmann, " Direct Action and Sabotage "; U. S. Commission on Industrial Relations, Vol. II, pp. 1445–1579; Daniel De Leon, " As to Politics," 1907; Addresses of Ettor and Giovanitti before the Jury at Salem, Mass., 1912.

[56] See Winston Churchill, " The Dwelling Place of Light," based on the Lawrence strike, for a literary picture of Syndicalism.

[57] See Brissenden, op. cit. Appendix II, for Detroit and Chicago plans of industrial unionism.

marked the advent in America of a new spirit which was agitating all the industrial states of Europe. Commonly the disappointments of democracy here had led to a demand for reforms in the machinery,— for more or better organized democratic government: or for a livelier civic spirit or a higher type of leadership. Then there was the demand for social reform, for anti-trust laws, for social legislation. Beyond that came the socialist movement for political action to capture the state for collectivism. Syndicalism was cynical of democracy, suspicious of trade-unionism, profoundly scornful of socialism. It proposed by mass action of the organized workers to create inside the shell of the old state a new order of economic and social justice, and finally to substitute the new shell for the old. These ideas were latent in communistic anarchism and in anti-authoritarian socialism, but in syndicalism they found a new industrial basis and a new technique of action.

It is quite clear that the prevailing theory during this period was strongly individualistic. Yet it is equally plain that material modifications were made in earlier individualism as the twentieth century came on. Urban experience and industrial pressure from the trust and the union, familiarity with new forces and new forms of social and economic life, easily led to a broader view of the work of the government. Hence what would have been termed socialism in 1870 was generally accepted in 1910. The urgent need of railroad regulation, the demand for corporate control, for the restriction of unfair practices in trade, for the protection of workers, to meet the needs of public sanitations, to solve the pressing urban problems: all combined to modify the earlier theories of *laissez faire*. Gen. Walker said in 1889, that the doctrine of *laissez faire* had been more strictly held in the U. S. than elsewhere. The formula was "used to decide whether a man were an economist at all." [58] By 1910, Sen. Root almost agreed with his position. And both were favorable to its modification.

The swift improvement in means of transportation and communication brought men more closely together than before. The massing of employees under the factory system developed the idea of cooperative action, while in all fields organization was rapidly developing. In agriculture this tendency was less marked than elsewhere, but in business, big and little, and in labor, association and organization were widely recognized as basic principles. Men came to work in groups more commonly than ever before. Organized, collective action took the place of individual, isolated action in a large section of human conduct.

Nor can it be forgotten that at all times there were other large fields in which the individualist made no strong or effective protest. In the field of morality, the widest interpretation was given to the function of the state. Laws against gambling and lotteries, against prostitution, against the sale of intoxicating liquors, showed no tendency toward *laissez faire* or any weakness in favor of " personal liberty." On the contrary, sweeping regulations were regarded as necessary restrictions of the individual, and were passed not only for the good

[58] "Discussions in Economics and Statistics," Vol. I, p. 328, on " Recent Progress of Political Economy in the U. S."

of the community but for his own benefit as well. That they were unwarrantable interferences with the rights and liberties of individuals was charged, but not believed, either by the legislature, the courts or the electorate. " Personal liberty " as a slogan was not effective here.

Nor was the plea of *laissez faire* effective as a form of protest against the protective tariff or governmental subsidies, either for manufacturing or for agriculture; or against any other activities designed to promote industrial prosperity upon a large scale. There was no abstract theoretical opposition to these projects as long as they followed the broad line of promoting and fostering trade in private hands. On the contrary it was deemed the duty of the government to promote industry and prosperity. The argument based upon natural law and economic harmony when advanced in favor of free trade was strongly repudiated and while it found theoretical defenders, was never dominant.

Nor was this a period of broad tolerance of conflicting social and political ideals. The evolutionist in the early part of the period and the socialist or radical in the latter part often struggled hard to obtain a hearing and a status in the democracy. In industrial disturbances freedom of speech was sometimes sacrificed. In educational institutions the persecution of scholars for their allegiance to their ideas of truth and social justice was not unknown. Not infrequently those who exalted the doctrine of *laissez faire* in one field of activity quietly ignored the same principle in another. Conflicting standards were often applied to trust regulation and " prohibition," to

" municipal ownership " and to sugar subsidies, to anarchism in theory and lawlessness in practice.

In the case of governmental action conflicting with the interest of industrial groups, the plea of liberty was promptly and more effectively made. The field of social and labor legislation where class interests seemed to clash was indeed the only one where the struggle over liberty was carried on. Here singularly enough the concept of individual liberty was defended by the corporation, a highly compact form or organization, itself often reaching or approaching monopoly. The sharpest application of the " let alone " policy was reserved for this division of legislation.

Generally speaking, in the party, in the corporation, in the union, the principles of association, organization and regimentation were the order of the day. Organization and discipline as well as individual liberty of action were now the standard types of the time. Liberty was a formula to which men adhered, but its application was by no means clear. It tended more and more to pass from a purely negative idea that less government meant more liberty, to a positive and constructive form — to a doctrine of individual and social advantage gained through the government or through organization. Fear of strong government, and unbounded belief in unrestrained competition, both declined; and in their place came the recognition of the need of well organized and equipped government, with broad powers to regulate unfair competition and to promote social efficiency and general welfare.

In America as elsewhere this was the transition process

by which the form of democracy was filled out with a content of social and industrial meaning. It was the reconciliation of liberty not merely with government, but with the grim facts of industrial and social life.

CHAPTER XIII

SYSTEMATIC STUDIES OF POLITICS

DURING the Revolution and in the first generation of the Republic, no little attention was given to the study of politics. The statesmen of the nation were familiar with the best products of the world's political experience and thought, as developed at that time: and they made free use of them in the formulation of their political philosophy and in the practical affairs of state.[1] Jefferson and Adams were equally at home in the field of political theory, and many others shared the same interest with them. These leaders were not attempting to work out a science of politics, but they were acquainted with the results thus far achieved in this direction.

In the Jacksonian era, this interest declined at least in the world of politics, although reviving in the form of social and economic speculation. Theoretical discussions over the nature of the Federal Union, regarding the status of slavery, and upon the ideal constitution of society, were common. Emerson expounded a unique philosophy. Brisbane [2] undertook a science of society. Treatises on states' rights and slavery were frequent, and the beginnings of the study of political economy appeared.

[1] See Merriam, "History of American Political Theories," Chap. II, III.

[2] "Social Destiny of Man: Or Association and Reorganization of Industry," 1840.

But on the whole there was little energy expended in the study of systematic politics, in comparison with the contemporary English and Continental developments in social science, economics and politics, where the rise of the science of society under the inspiration of Auguste Comte, and of Utopian and proletarian socialism, aroused general interest in social problems. Here the juristic aspects of federalism and the discussion of the anachronism seen in human slavery were the social topics most widely discussed. Democracy was taken for granted, and the chief interest was in its practical application to such concrete problems as suffrage, governmental structure, and civil rights.

In the general development of political thought many striking changes were made during this period. Overshadowing all others were those caused by the discoveries of Darwin and the development of modern science. The Darwinian theory of evolution not only transformed biological study, but profoundly affected all forms of thought. The social sciences were no exception, and history, economics, ethics and politics were all fundamentally altered by the new doctrine. Both individualistic and socialistic interpretations and conclusions were derived from the Darwinian theory by various thinkers. Aristocratic and democratic philosophies alike found support in the broad doctrine of the survival of the fittest.[3]

Karl Marx' development of " scientific " socialism, succeeding the Utopian socialism of the first half of the century, also deeply affected all social thinking. Of even greater importance than his more strictly and technically

[3] David G. Ritchie, " Darwinism and Politics."

economic doctrines of surplus value, class struggle, ultimate proletarian success, was his theory of the economic or social interpretation of history. This theory was a challenge to the foundations of all institutions and ideas — legal, political, economic and social — and taken in connection with other parallel movements its influence upon human thought was far-reaching. The work of the Webbs in England, Bebel, Bernstein, Sombart in Germany, Jaures in France, Vandervelde in Belgium, Ferri in Italy, carried further on the Marxian doctrines with modifications in technique, but with substantial agreement in spirit and purpose,[4] Many who repudiated his economic conclusions, consciously or unconsciously followed his social interpretation of history, at least part of the way.

Another notable development of this period was the beginning of a study of society in more formal and systematic manner than ever before. Comte and Spencer laid the foundations of systematic sociology, and their followers undertook to develop and elaborate this system on a broad scale. Their efforts did not result in the creation of a definite science of society, but in the accumulation of vast masses of social material, schemes of analysis and classification, insights into various phases of social activity, and the development of a social point of view. Anthropology, ethnology, social psychology, economic geography, all produced volumes of research and inquiry, joining in the same general direction.

One of the striking features of the last half century [5]

---

[4] Ensor, " Modern Socialism."
[5] See Woodbridge Riley, "American Thought" (1915); L. H.

in America was the greatly increased attention to the scientific study of politics. In the last twenty-five years, particularly, this tendency was very clearly marked. The foundation of systematic study was laid by Francis Lieber, a German refugee, who came to America following the Revolution of 1848, and was for many years a source of inspiration in inquiry and a teacher of methods of investigation.[6] Following Lieber came studies of the type of Mulford's "Nation" (1870), a striking illustration of the intoxicating effect of undiluted Hegelian philosophy upon the American mind. He expounded an entire dialetics of democracy in the abstract and theoretical form of the German mid-century "metapolitics." Brownson's "American Republic"[7] was notable as a careful exposition of American political doctrines.

Beginning about the '80's there was an impetus given to the systematic study of political problems which continued undiminished in force down to the end of this period. Woolsey's monumental work on political science appeared in 1878, Henry George's challenging "Progress and Poverty" in 1879, Wilson's encyclopædic "The State" in 1889, Bryce's comprehensive and illuminating

Haney, "History of Economic Thought," Ch. 32 (1911), "Recent Economic Thought in the United States"; A. W. Small, "Fifty Years of Sociology in the United States — 1865-1915," (1916) ; J. F. Jameson, in the *Am. Hist. Rev.*, 1910, 1-20, traces the first quarter century of the American Historical Association (1884-1909). See also twenty-fifth anniversary of American Economic Association in "Publications," 1910, pp. 46-111.

[6] "Political Ethics," 1838-9; "Civil Liberty and Self-Government," 1853; "Miscellaneous Writings," 2 vols. 1881.

[7] O. A. Brownson, 1866. See also "Constitutional Government," 1842; "Essays and Reviews," 1852.

work on " The American Commonwealth " was published in 1888, and Burgess' formal treatise on " Political Science and Comparative Constitutional Law " in 1891.

The examination of political problems was also undertaken by various scientific organizations during this period. Following the establishment of the English Social Science Association in 1856, the American Social Science Association was formed in 1865. It included in its membership among others Edward Atkinson, Charles Francis Adams, Agassiz, Choate, Evarts, Godkin, Walker, Wines, Lea and political leaders such as General Grant, Garfield, Horace Greeley, and Charles Sumner.[8]

The American Historical Association was established in 1884. A forward step was taken in 1886, when the American Economic Association was founded for the systematic investigation of industrial problems; the American Statistical Association in 1888 (first in 1839), the American Academy of Political and Social Science in 1889, the American Political Science Association in 1903, the American Sociological Society in the same year, and the American Society of International Law in 1907. All of these organizations undertook the task of inquiry into various groups of social problems, with great enthusiasm and energy. In the course of a generation they made notable contributions to the sum total of human knowledge upon questions of political interest.[9]

Johns Hopkins University inaugurated the study of

[8] See Mary E. Sargent, " Sketches and Reminiscences of the Radical Club of Boston," 1880. Among the members were Emerson, Channing, Wells, James, Fiske, Holmes, Higginson, Shaler.

[9] Useful compilations were those of Bliss, " Encyclopædia of Social Reform," 1897; Lalor, " Cyclopædia of Political and Social

"History and Politics" in 1876. The Columbia School of Political Science was founded in 1880. Many other universities, including Harvard, Pennsylvania, Chicago, Wisconsin, followed in the development of departments in which the problems of politics, economics, sociology and history were analyzed and discussed with the greatest activity.[10]   The study of government both in graduate and undergraduate branches of the universities was very widely extended.   However, in high schools and grades popular instruction in the elements of government lagged behind the pace set in the more advanced work.

The undertakings of these institutions were supplemented in the earlier part of the twentieth century by various private foundations on the one hand, and by state activity upon the other.   Among the more conspicuous of the private endowments were the Carnegie Institution and the Sage Foundation, which turned their attention in part to the governmental questions of the community.   In the local field, the New York Bureau of Municipal Research led the way in undertaking detailed inquiries into the framework and function of municipal governments, with constructive studies for their betterment.   New York was followed by Chicago, Boston, Philadelphia, Cleveland, Cincinnati, and other cities.

Furthermore, there were begun far-reaching governmental activities in the collection of systematic data.

Science" (1888–90) ; McLaughlin & Hart, "Cyclopædia of American Government," 1914.

[10] See the series of studies published by Columbia, Harvard, Johns Hopkins, Wisconsin, Iowa, Illinois, California, and other universities.

The Census Bureau was a mighty instrument for this purpose.[11] But other governmental organs and agencies were also freely employed. Here was set up the machinery of social observation on a great scale. Here was made possible the observation, the collection and the classification of political facts on a scale which no individual observer working alone could hope to accomplish. Year by year new schedules were perfected, and the accuracy, comprehensiveness and value of the reports steadily increased. While it cannot be said that full advantage was always taken of the possibilities in interpretation and use of this material, the significant fact is the organization of a gigantic machine for social observation, and the preliminary advances made toward comprehensive inquiry.

Bulletins and analysis of legislation were also prepared in many fields of governmental work. The most elaborate of these were the New York State Library's Review and Digest of State Legislation and Digest of Governors' Messages. This was unfortunately discontinued, however, and was not revived either under public or private auspices.[12] Many bulletins were issued by branches of the Federal Government, however. Legislative reference departments in various states and cities, added very greatly to the classified knowledge available to the lawmaker, the student and the general public interested in special phases of legislation. It goes without saying that the commercial interest in the practice of law soon

[11] John Koren, "History of Statistics"; Richmond Mayo-Smith, "Statistics and Sociology," 1895; "Statistics and Economics," 1899.
[12] 1890–1910.

brought the reporting and digesting of legal cases to a high point of efficiency.

During the last quarter of a century the scope and method of popular government have been subjected to keen analysis from many sides.[13] The historical, social, economic and cultural meanings of democracy have been made subjects of inquiry by many earnest investigators. The list includes interpretations in terms of economics, of ethics, of education, of philosophy, of sociology, and in broad terms of social democracy in the most liberal use of the word. Scientific studies of value were made by many workers in the field of formal political science; and in related fields of statistics, sociology, economics, ethics, history, philosophy and psychology, notable contributions were made to the knowledge of political facts and methods.

The first systematic study on politics was made by Theodore Woolsey, whose ponderous volumes on " Political Science," or " State," published in 1878, were a weighty contribution to systematic politics. Yet these studies were based on lectures delivered by Woolsey in Yale College in 1846 to 1871, and really represented the *ante-bellum* period. His work was broadly divided into three sections dealing with natural rights, the theory of the state, and practical politics, following, as he said, the German classification of *Naturrecht, Staatslehre* and *Politik*. In many ways Woolsey was influenced by Lieber. His method was historical and comparative, and carried

[13] See " Political Economy and Political Science," by Sumner, Wells and others (1881) giving bibliography of suggested readings prepared by the Society for Political Education.

him over the whole field of political speculation. In general his theological training and tendencies led him to emphasize the importance of ethical principles in politics and to dwell upon the great significance of religion and morality in their relations to political thought and action.

Woolsey repudiated the classical doctrine of " natural rights," declaring that rights implied the coexistence of men. Historically the state arises out of custom and usage. Rationally the state is based on the nature and destiny of man, and the fact that unorganized he could make nothing of himself or of his " rights." The state " is as truly natural as rights are, and as society is," and is the bond of both. It is the means for all the highest ends of man and society.

The sphere and ends of the state, he believed, should be limited, but by no means confined to the mere legal rights of man. The state may reach " as far as the nature and needs of man reach, including intellectual and æsthetic wants of the individual, and the religious and moral nature of its citizens." Yet in general the state ought not to overstep the bounds of reason, and Woolsey was particularly emphatic in his denunciation of communism and socialism, which he discussed in a separate volume.[14] He opposed a protective tariff, mightily feared the cities, demanded independence in party affairs, defended the middle class, especially in the rural districts, and looked with alarm upon many of the growing tendencies of the time, such as urban development, immigration, " extreme democracy." [15]

[14] " Communism and Socialism."
[15] Vol. II, 141. With Woolsey compare George H. Yeaman,

Following Woolsey came the systematic work of John W. Burgess.[16] Burgess' method, like that of Woolsey, was historical and comparative, but his training was that of the historian and the jurist. Much of his interest centered in the problems of comparative public law. His fundamental political philosophy was much influenced by the ideas of Hegel, and in general his work showed strong traces of his German training and influence. Burgess followed the current political theory in repudiating the doctrines of natural law and the social contract, declaring that they were wholly contrary to our knowledge of the historical development of political institutions. The social contract theory assumes " that the idea of a state with all its attributes is consciously present in the minds of individuals proposing to constitute the state, and that the disposition to obey law is universally established." [17] These conditions, he maintained, are not found at the beginning of the political development of the people, but at the end of a long process of experience and growth. This theory, therefore, cannot account for the origin of a state, although the doctrine of the consent of the governed may apply to a people politically educated and consciously determining the form of their own government. That there are legal rights and liberties outside of the state Burgess as a good Austinian regarded as inconceivable. The only liberty possible is the liberty found within the political society and protected by the state.

"Study of Government," 1871; Robert J. Wright, "Principia or Basis of Social Science," 1875.

[16] "Political Science and Comparative Constitutional Law," 1891.

[17] Vol. I, 162.

Burgess also developed the doctrine of sovereignty, which he regarded as the " original, absolute, unlimited, universal power over the individual subject, and all associations of subjects," the most fundamental and indispensable mark of statehood. " Really the state cannot be conceived," says Burgess, " without sovereignty, i. e., without unlimited power over its subjects; that is its very essence." There is no other organized power which can be thought of as limiting the state in its control over its own subjects. Otherwise the authority which could exercise such power would itself be sovereign. This unlimited power on the part of the state is not an interference with civil liberty, but on the contrary is the guarantee and protection of liberty, and the more completely sovereign the state is the more secure is the liberty of the individual. It is true that the state may abuse its power and wrong the individual under its control; but on the whole the national state is the human organ least likely to do wrong.

Reasoning in this way, Burgess demolished the federal state which he declared to be an impossibility. What seems a federal state is either a number of sovereign states with a number of local governments and a common central government, or one sovereign state having a central government and several local governments. In any event, the sovereignty is indivisible, and must rest either with the nation as a whole or with each of the several states. In this respect he agreed with Calhoun, but drew the diametrically opposite conclusion.

Burgess also emphasized strongly the mission or purpose of the state. The ends of the state are government, liberty, the development of national genius and world-civilization. These ends must be realized in this historical order, and one cannot be put before the others. The highest form of the state has been reached only by the Roman and Teutonic peoples, whose duty it is to undertake the political civilization of the world. History and ethnology teach, he says, that the Teutonic nations are the political leaders of the modern era, that " in the economy of history the duty has fallen to them of organizing the world politically, and that if true to their mission they must follow the line of this duty as one of their chief practical policies." Americans, he thought, might be unwilling to undertake their own duties and responsibilities, but in the long run their political genius would make it necessary for them to assume their burdens.

In 1885, appeared Woodrow Wilson's " Congressional Government," an epoch-making essay in American constitutional literature. This work was a brilliant criticism of the inefficiency and chaos of the Congressional system, and a plea for more responsible government. " In any business, whether of government or of mere merchandising, somebody must be trusted," he said. Power [18] and strict accountability for its use are the essential constituents of good government. In many ways this essay both in content and in form was one of the most remarkable that had appeared upon a political topic.

In 1889 Wilson published a volume entitled " The State." This was an historical and comparative study of various types of government based, as the author states in the preface, largely upon Marquardsen's " Handbuch

[18] P. 283.

des Oeffentlichen Rechts der Gegenwart." Throughout its chapters run a philosophy of law and government, subordinated, however, to the study of the structure and spirit of the political institutions described. His political ideas were further expressed in " An Old Master and Other Political Essays " (1893), in " Mere Literature" (1896), in "Constitutional Government in the United States" (1907) and "The New Freedom" (1913); and numerous addresses and papers. The chief significance of his method lay in the importance attached to the study of politics as made up of living facts and forces, institutional as well as constitutional, organic rather than mechanical. He constantly called attention to the life and spirit of things political, to the actual workings of political forces, to the vital processes of political life. In this manner he discussed the workings of political parties, the development of the constitution, the organic interrelation of the various parts of government, the importance and purpose of political initiative and leadership in a democracy. The formal, the mechanical in politics, the " Newtonian " system, as he termed it, he repeatedly discussed and always denounced.

In " The State " he had dealt with the objects of government, taking a middle ground between individualism and socialism.[19] Individualism " has much about it that is hateful, too hateful to last." But the remedy is not to destroy competition as the Socialist urges. " It is not competition that kills, but unfair competition — the pretence and form of it where the substance and reality of it cannot exist." The state must control all combinations

[19] Chap. 15.

or monopolies which put or keep " indispensable means of industrial or social development in the hands of a few, and these few not the few selected by society itself, but the few selected by arbitrary fortune." Outside of natural monopolies the state must also equalize competitive conditions where the individual cannot act effectually, as in the case of child labor, unsanitary factory conditions, hurtful employment of women, limitation of hours of labor.

Later in his " New Freedom," as already indicated, he elaborated somewhat the doctrine that one of the chief purposes of the state is to prevent interference with fair competition, to eliminate the obstructions preventing the natural tendencies of men from finding their free expression. Thus it appears that the evils of the industrial world will be eliminated by the destruction of industrial privilege of an artificial character, while the evils of the political world will be minimized by the removal of all mechanisms and forms that prevent free expression of public sentiment and free organization of the public will. This principle is well expressed in the concluding paragraph of his " State." " The rule of governmental action is necessary cooperation: the method of political development is conservative adaptation."

Clearer light on his theory is thrown by " Mere Literature " in which he characterizes the English publicists Burke and Bagehot, and also the great American statesmen from Washington to Lincoln. Burke was an interpreter of English practical utilitarianism and expediency, magnificent in type and form. Bagehot has practical knowledge of conditions, but

" has no sympathy with the voiceless body of the people, with the ' mass of unknown men.' He conceives the work of government to be a work which is possible only to the instructed few. . . . He has not the stout fibre and the unquestioning faith in the right and capacity of inorganic majorities which make the democrat. He has none of the heroic boldness necessary for faith in wholesale political aptitude and capacity. He takes democracy in detail and in his thought, and to take it in detail makes it very awkward indeed." [20]

Among the great Americans he placed Washington, Lincoln, Grant, Lee and chief among all, Lincoln, " the supreme American." [21] That he never ceased to be a common man was the source of Lincoln's strength, with a genius for " insight into the common things of politics, that inhere in human nature and cast hardly more than their shadows on constitutions." The whole country is summed up in him —" the rude western strength tempered with shrewdness and a broad and human wit; the eastern conservatism, regardful of law and devoted to standards of duty." [22]

Through Wilson's political theory runs an unusual note in American political philosophy — the reaction from the formal and mechanical to the human and social. " I do not find that I derive inspiration, but only information," said he, " from the learned historians and analysts of liberty; but from the sonneteers, the poets, who speak its

[20] P. 100.
[21] *Op. cit.*, Ch. 7, " A Calendar of Great Americans,"
[22] P. 208.

spirit and its exalted purpose — who, recking nothing of the historical method, obey only the high method of their own hearts — what may a man not gain of courage and confidence in the right way of politics? " [23]

There is more of a nation's politics to be got out of its poetry than out of all of its systematic writers upon public affairs and constitutions. Epics are better mirrors of manners than chronicles; dramas often may let you into the secrets of statutes. It is not knowledge that moves the world, but ideals, convictions, the opinions or fancies that have been held or followed.[24] Their primal relations are not independent of their way of living, and their way of thinking is the mirror of their way of living.

Keen analyses of American political conditions were made by Theodore Roosevelt in his early " Essays " (1888) and in his later " Autobiography." [25] His political ideas are also expressed in his numerous speeches, messages, and writings. The best summary of his later views is contained in " The New Nationalism " (1910). In the early years of his career he championed civil service reform and honest government, while in the later period he took up the gauntlet for social and industrial legislation, equal suffrage, the initiative and referendum and the recall of judicial decisions; still later the advocacy of universal military training.[26] Among the outstanding features in his quarter-century of public activity was his develop-

[23] *Op. cit.,* 36.
[24] *Op. cit.,* 10.
[25] See also " The Strenuous Life."
[26] " Fear God and Take Your Own Part "; " The Foes of Our Own Household," 1917.

ment of executive power on the side of party and public
leadership, in its technical administrative aspects, and in
relation to the legislative branch of the government. Notable also was his analysis of nationalism as the instrument
of democratic progress, particularly in his later years.
His historic controversy over the courts has already been
discussed, and need not be renewed here. He likewise
furnished the formula of progressivism, in his speeches
of 1912–1914: " The invisible government,"— the combination of political bosses and industrial privilege,—
must be overthrown, more democratic political machinery
provided, and a broader industrial-social program outlined and executed.

" The citizens of the United States," said he, " must effectively control the mighty commercial forces which they
have themselves called into being." Property must become the servant and not the master of the commonwealth.
Human rights and human welfare have been neglected.
They must be put back in their proper place. Socialism
and Anarchism must be combatted, but the most effective
" antidote " is wise and beneficent social legislation eradi-
cating the causes from which these movements spring.
Both capital and labor must be restrained in the general
interest, but at the same time the public must not merely
act negatively, but must energetically root out the causes
of discontent, and build broader foundations of social
welfare.

Most influential was Roosevelt as a preacher of civic
duty to the nation, breathing a sense of responsibility into
thousands, inspiring what Wells declares Americans lack
—" a sense of the state,"— political consciousness and in-

terest expressed in political action for the public weal. To this task his own dramatic personality and his trenchant style of writing and speaking were admirably adapted, and these gifts made it possible for him to wield a far reaching influence on the public mind of America. A great personality is an asset of any state, and great political personality is a treasure in a democracy, living in the *mores* of the people long after the individual life has passed away.

A systematic study of political theory was made by W. W. Willoughby, who wrote in 1896 " The Nature of the State "; in 1900, " Social Justice "; in 1903, " Political Theories of the Ancient World." [27] The method of Willoughby was in the main analytical and followed broadly the ethico-political theory of the English philosopher T. H. Green, developed in his " Principles of Political Obligation," and the Austinian school of jurisprudence. Willoughby analyzed and criticized the theory of a social contract as the basis of government. Rights cannot be maintained outside of political organization and no such rights can be conceded as existing before the state. The state need not justify its existence or its use of coercive power as against the individual, for the state itself is a legal personality and has its own claims to rights and duties.

Sovereignty was interpreted by Willoughby largely in the Austinian spirit. The attribute of supreme power belongs to the state as a person representing the supreme

[27] See also " Constitutional Law of the U. S.," 1910; " The American Constitutional System," 1904. Compare F. M. Taylor, " The Right of the State to Be " (1891).

will of the body politic. This power is indivisible and absolute in its authority. The much mooted question of the location of sovereign power Willoughby solved by finding a habitat in " all organs through which are expressed the volitions of the state," that is to say, in legislatures, executives, courts and all other agencies of state government.

The aims of the state have elsewhere been discussed, and are, broadly speaking, expressed in terms of strongly qualified individualism. The purposes of the government are the maintenance of order, preservation of liberty, and the promotion of general welfare. The precise application of these powers in specific cases will depend largely upon the underlying social and political conditions. The determination, says he, " of just what powers should be assumed by the State is solely one of expediency, and as such lies within the field of Politics or the Art of Government, and not within the domain of political theory." [28] Likewise in discussing the nature of justice and of equality Willoughby concludes that there are no absolute rules by means of which final determinations may be made. Equality he repudiates as an abstract principle of justice and substitutes the idea of proportionality,[29]— that is, proportioning of rewards in each particular case according to some ascertainable conditions of time, place or person.

Systematic studies of the state were made by James W. Garner, in his introduction to " Political Science " (1910), and by Gettel, in his " Introduction to Political

[28] " Nature of the State," p. 338.
[29] " Social Justice."

Science "— and " Problems in Political Evolution " (1918). These works, however, were largely descriptive and explanatory of the principal types of the more important theories, and the writers did not undertake to advance, in most instances, independent opinions. The presentations of politics were designedly encyclopædic rather than dogmatic, and were in fact intended as convenient manuals for study rather than original inquiries into the theory of the state. In this spirit the authors' conclusions regarding the origin, organization and purposes of the state are presented in a moderating and modest fashion.

The leading figure in the systematic formulation and adaptation of political theory during the latter part of this period was Frank J. Goodnow, whose theoretical and practical activities were numerous and varied, and made him a powerful force in both fields.[30] Goodnow approached the problems of politics from the point of view of public administration, of which subject he may be said to have been the first systematic student in the United States. His greatest contributions were made in this field, which he himself developed and organized, using the scattered material of public law, private law,

[30] See " Comparative Administrative Law," 1893; " Municipal Home Rule," 1895; " Municipal Problems," 1897; " City Government in the United States," 1904; " Municipal Government," 1909; " Social Reform and the Constitution," 1911; " Principles of Constitutional Government," 1916; also The Work of the American Political Science Association, " Proceedings," Vol. I, p. 35, " Politics and Administration," 1900; " American Conception of Liberty and Government," 1916; " Principles of the Administrative Law of the U. S.," 1905.

and governmental organization for the purpose of building up a compact body of administrative law.   Significant work was also done by Goodnow in the field of
municipal government, particularly in dealing with legal
and structural problems.

The scope of political science, as conceived by Goodnow, included the expression of the will of the state;
second, the content of the will of the state, and third, the
execution of the will of the state.   Under the first head,
he would include political action, notably that seen in
political parties.   Under the second head he would place
the legal relations of the state as a legal person, the relation of public officers to the legal system, and the study
of comparative legislation.   Under the third branch he
would include the study of various aspects of administration, the theory and practice of the enforcement and application of the law.[31]   In his general attitude Goodnow
leaned toward the study of public law and concrete organization and away from abstract or speculative philosophy, although conceding the necessity of the latter in a
comprehensive system of politics.   Reluctantly philosophical, he somewhat overcame his inhibitions.   He repudiated the doctrine of natural rights and the social contract
as the basis of organized political society, relying rather
upon historical and evolutionary considerations and tendencies.   He rejected Montesquieu's theory of the three-
fold separation of powers, and substituted the dual division into politics and administration.[32]   He emphasized

[31] See Proceedings, American Political Science Association, op.
cit.
[32] See " Politics and Administration," Chap. IV.

strongly the importance of effective organization of political leadership within the government, and explained the abuses of the party system, including the eccentricities of the boss and the machine, by the lack of effective central organization of power and responsibility.

In his later writings he pointed out the discrepancy between current legal theories and the dominant social and political doctrines of the day, and urged the importance of squaring the juristic theories of justice with the contemporary conditions and necessities.[33] Orderly and progressive political development, in accordance with changing economic and social conditions, he regarded as fundamental.

In general, Goodnow adhered to the "pragmatic" philosophy and to the social interpretation of history. "More and more," said he, "political and social students are recognizing that a policy of opportunism is a policy most likely to be followed by desirable results and that adherence to general theories which are to be applied at all times and under all conditions is productive of harm rather than good."[34] In short, he undertook to develop in the midst of the forces of legalism, party conflict, abstract speculation, a domain of political science resting upon an essentially practical and pragmatic foundation. He was neither a legal realist nor a political idealist, but represented the best type of opportunist in theory and in practice. In this respect his work may be said to have been typically English or typically American in its adherence to the principle of common sense as distinguished

[33] See "Social Reform and the Constitution."
[34] *Ibid.*, p. 3.

from speculative idealism or from reactionary formalism.
Comparable with the work of Goodnow was that of
Freund and Pound, whose political theories have already
been considered in connection with the discussion of the
courts and justice. Freund's chief contribution to political science was the development of the theory of
police power.[35] The doctrine of the police power had
appeared earlier in American political development, but
had never been systematized or organized. Woolsey had
discussed the nature and sphere of the police power,[36] and
distinguished between the "detective" and the "pre-
ventive" duties of police; but had urged that the term
"police" should not be applied to this particular function of the state. "Police" is another name, he said,
for public welfare, and its activities should be grouped
together. But as "police" is an odious name, he suggested the term "public economy."[37] Burgess[38] had
also discussed the police power in connection with the
topic of civil liberty. The liberty of the individual is lia-
ble to attack and must be protected by the state. "This is
the police power," said he. "Its realm is therefore the
counterpart of the realm of individual liberty. It is the
guard which the state sets upon the abuse of individual

[35] Ernst Freund, "Police Power," 1904; "Standards of Legislation," 1917; Article on Police Power in McLaughlin and Hart's Cyclopædia of American Government. Compare W. W. Cook, "What
Is Police Power?" in *Columbia Law Review*, VII, 322 (1907). L. P.
McGehee, "Due Process of Law," 1906. Hastings, "Development
of Law as Illustrated by the Decisions relating to the Police Power
of the State," 1900 in Proceedings American Philosophical Society.
[36] Vol. I, p. 235.
[37] See *op. cit.*, I, 237.
[38] Vol. I, p. 216.

liberty." Other writers have considered in a fragmentary way the theory of the police power.

These scattered ideas and principles were brought together by Freund, however, in systematic form, and were developed into a coherent body of rules. The purpose of the police power, said Freund, is "to promote the public welfare and its characteristic methods are those of restraint and compulsion." The principles of justice are ordinarily based on the common sense of right and wrong, of moral responsibility, on the faith of obligations, on the principles of justice, and therefore appear commonly as dictates of reason, not as orders of government. The public welfare, however, is determined more openly and directly by social and economic conditions as the result of which the state prescribes additional rules of conduct. Under these are, first, the primary needs of safety, order, morals and the care of dependents. But in addition to these there is a broad field of economic interests in which the state may interfere for, the protection of the individual and the promotion of the common good. It is these relations and activities of the state which Freund classified, organized and developed into a system.

In his " Standards of American Legislation " he undertook to apply similar methods to the technical processes of law-making.[39] The two chief principles developed are those of "correlation" and "standardization." Under these heads he includes such canons as conformity to scientific laws, standardization of juristic data, definite method in reaching determinations, and stability of policy.

[39] See Ch. VI.

The scientific study of legislative processes and the elaboration of the practical technique of law-making are the goals toward which he moves.

Of the fruitfulness of the studies made by Goodnow, Freund and Pound there can be no question, and their far-reaching effect in the domain of law and politics can readily be traced. They represent a distinct advance from the formalism and legalism of earlier days toward a period of broader consideration of social forces and sharper technique of governmental organization and action.

Progress was also made in tracing the evolution of systematic political ideas, notably by Dunning [40] in his historical studies, also by Willoughby [41] and by Hart in his " National Ideals." [42] Others developed various phases of the growth and differentiation of forms of political thought.[43]

A significant study was that of Ford [44] in the relations between biology and politics — a field to which inadequate attention was given by American students of politics. Surveying the evolutionary process, and reviewing conclusions drawn from biological, psychological, linguistic, and anthropological data, he deduces certain " first principles

[40] William A. Dunning, I, "History of Political Theories, Ancient and Mediæval"; II, "From Luther to Montesquieu"; III, covering later period.

[41] "Political Theories of the Ancient World."

[42] A. B. Hart, "National Ideals Historically Traced," 1907.

[43] Merriam, "History of the Theory of Sovereignty since Rousseau, 1900; "History of American Political Theories," 1903; George Scherger, "The Evolution of Modern Liberty," 1904; F. W. Coker, "Organismic Theories of the State," 1910; H. J. Laski, "Problems of Sovereignty," 1917.

[44] Henry Jones Ford, "The Natural History of the State," 1915.

in politics." [45]   In these are included the proposition that " man is the product of Social Evolution " ; the definition of state and government in biological terms ; and conclusions touching the character of sovereignty and the scope and nature of state activity.   To these are added certain conclusions respecting ethical rights and the meaning of liberty.   All of these are presented as " corollaries of the Social Hypothesis," which he finds in his study of natural science.

The scientific study of politics is also evident particularly during the last quarter of a century in numerous studies, historical and comparative, in various fields of political activity.   Thus the extra-legal organization of the political party has been analyzed by numerous writers, among them Ford, Woodburn, Macy and many others.[46] In connection with these studies are the admirable analyses of European parties, and of public opinion in its relation to government made by Lowell.[47]   In the field a distinct attempt has been made to describe, classify and interpret the political phenomena centering around the group activities outside the formal government.   This movement represents another step away from the formalism and the mechanical discussion of political problems developed in the period of strict legalism and constitutionalism.

To the study of the urban problem no little attention

[45] P. 173 *et seq.*
[46] See Chap. X.
[47] A. Lawrence Lowell, " Essays on Government," 1889; "Government and Parties in Continental Europe," 1896; "Government of England," 1908; " Public Opinion and Popular Government," 1913.

has been devoted. Shaw's brilliant description of the government of European cities stimulated wide interest in the betterment of urban conditions.[48]   In this field Goodnow led the way in the effort toward systematization and organization.   Other notable studies were made by Wilcox,[49] Fairlie,[50] Munro,[51] McBain,[52] Howe,[53] Rowe,[54] Beard,[55] Cleveland,[56] Bruere,[57] and a long series of other writers on the structural and functional aspects of city life.   In the main these studies were concerned with the organization and legal relations of municipalities, but they were by no means confined to this field.   On the contrary, no phase of municipal life was left untouched in the general desire to discover the causes of municipal

[48] Albert Shaw, " Municipal Government in Continental Europe," and " Municipal Government in Great Britain," 1895, published first in the *Century Magazine*.

[49] Delos F. Wilcox, " Great Cities in America," 1910; " The American City," 1906; " Municipal Franchises," 1911.

[50] John A. Fairlie, " Municipal Administration," 1901; " Essays in Municipal Administration," 1908.

[51] W. B. Munro, " Government of European Cities," 1909; " Government of American Cities," 1912; " Principles and Methods of Municipal Administration, 1917.

[52] Howard L. McBain, " Law and Practice of Municipal Home Rule," 1916.

[53] Frederick C. Howe, " The Modern City," 1915; " The City, the Hope of Democracy," 1905; " The British City," 1907; " European Cities at Work," 1913.

[54] Leo S. Rowe, " Problems of City Government," 1908.

[55] Charles A. Beard, " American City Government," 1912.

[56] F. A. Cleveland, " Chapters on Municipal Administration and Accounting," 1909.

[57] Henry Bruere, " The New City Government," 1912. See also Herman James, " Municipal Functions," 1917.

misgovernment and constructive methods for their improvement. During the last fifteen years in particular, no side of American political life attracted a larger number of students than that of municipal government, but the vastness of the field, the novelty of the enterprise, and the rapidly changing character of the situation made it difficult to collect and systematize the material or to organize its principles into definite form.

Munro's "Bibliography of Municipal Government," with its elaborate array of titles of publications, both by individuals and by organizations, illustrates the rapid growth of public interest in urban problems, and the increasing attempt at scientific study, particularly since 1900.

In the field of public law, administration and politics, especially during the last quarter of a century, a formidable array of investigators and thinkers worked indefatigably in special fields. To many of these studies reference has been made in previous chapters, and it is outside the limits of space here to catalogue and classify them all. Taken together they constitute a movement of very great significance in the development of political thought, and their joint product to the sum of political information, analysis, and technique was not inconsiderable. They were the miners and sappers in the advance of democracy.[58]

In the field of international law the earliest advances were made by Lieber. After him came Woolsey, who

[58] A significant summary is found in the proceedings of the St. Louis Congress of Arts and Sciences (1904) under "Social Science."

following the publication of his " Political Science " devoted himself to the problems of international relations. Numerous workers appeared in the same field and substantial studies were made in American diplomacy and in international law by Moore, Scott, Wilson, Hill, Foster and others.[59] A great amount of detailed study of material and of systematic organization was patiently carried on. With the creation of the American Society of International Law this undertaking was still further systematized and supported.[60] Significant studies were those of Reinsch on " Public International Unions " (1911), " Colonies and Colonial Policy " and " World Politics." [61]

The intensity of interest was greater, however, in the direction of the organization of world peace than in the technical conduct of international relations. In the peace philosophy and movement there was widespread participation, while the study of diplomatic history and international relations was confined to a smaller group. Relatively to contemporary European interest in international questions, that of America was almost negligible,

[59] J. B. Moore, "Digest of International Law," 1906. "American Diplomacy," 1905; Elihu Root, "Addresses on International Subjects; George G. Wilson, "International Law," 1910; A. B. Hart, "Foundations of American Foreign Policy," 1901; David Jayne Hill, "History of Diplomacy," 1905-14; "World Organization," 1911; A. C. Coolidge, "The United States as a World Power," 1908; J. H. Latane, "America as a World Power," 1907; John W. Foster, "A Manual of American Diplomacy," 1903; "The Practice of Diplomacy," 1906; Edwin Maxey, "International Law," 1906.

[60] American Journal International Law (1907). Compare Publications, Carnegie Endowment for International Peace.

[61] Alpheus Snow, "The Administration of Dependencies," 1902.

but measured by the preceding half century of our history, American attention to international affairs was rapidly increasing. The turn of the tide of foreign trade, the world-wide missionary movement, the international tendencies in labor and culture, the annexation of overseas territory after the Spanish War, the Hague conferences, all tended to stimulate American interest in extra-Continental affairs. The development of systematic study was a part of this general movement.

Carl Schurz, George William Curtis and others discussed the problems of politics acutely but did not attempt systematic or exhaustive treatment. Contemporary journalists did much toward the keener study of political problems. In this group were included Horace Greeley, Dana, Godkin, and others who molded and expressed public opinion in many ways. Their voices were raised in effective protest against political and economic abuses, particularly against political abuses, but they did not present either a systematic theory of politics or a method of arriving at one.

A keen analysis of the practical workings of democracy was made by Godkin, for many years editor of the New York *Evening Post,* and in close touch with the affairs of the metropolis.[62] In his studies, based in great part upon municipal experiences, Godkin sharply challenged the achievements of democratic government, and reviewed the failures and successes of a century in a striking procession of events. The unforeseen develop-

---

[62] E. L. Godkin, "Problems of Modern Democracy," 1896; "Unforeseen Tendencies of Democracy," 1898; "Fifty Years of Idealism," a compilation of *Evening Post* articles.

ments in the evolution of democracy which Godkin pointed out were the failure of the voters to participate in elections, the disregard of special fitness or qualification for political office and leadership, the decline of legislatures, the grave problems of urban communities, the indifferent development and functioning of public opinion, the general apathy toward political liberty. In Godkin, however, there is relatively little reference to the social and industrial phases of democratic evolution. He represented very well, however, the opinion of those whose theoretical and practical efforts centered around political " reform " in the narrower sense of the term.

Much more radical in temper were the utterances of Lloyd,[63] whose first efforts were directed against monopolies, but who later formulated a more general philosophy. Democracy must be of wider application than government merely; it must be a " positive progressive instinct for the conscious creation of the public welfare." The old freedom must be transformed into the new, including freedom of access to land, to credit, to the tools of industry, to employment, to our fellow men. " Man is forever harmonizing liberty in organizations and breaking up organizations to get liberty," said he.[64] In social organizations there must be individualism as well as socialism, home rule as well as national rule, independence as well as interdependence.[65]

[63] Henry D. Lloyd, "Wealth against Commonwealth," 1894; " Man, the Social Creator," 1906; " Men, the Workers," 1909.

[64] " Man, the Social Creator," p. 231. Society's growth might be mapped out, he said, in a series of alternate " communisms " and " anarchies."

[65] Compare the utterances of W. J. Ghent, " Our Benevolent Feud-

Significant studies of American public life were made throughout this period by thoughtful observers. Among these were Charles W. Eliot,[66] Lyman Abbott,[67] Hadley,[68] N. S. Shaler,[69] Henry Van Dyke,[70] John Graham Brooks,[71] and many others whose names were widely known.

Almost every man of eminence contributed to the common counsel of democracy, from his own experience, observation and reflection. These and other studies, though fragmentary, were often illuminating in their analysis, and rationalizing in their tendency. Their chief significance lay in the aid they gave to the general process whereby the democracy built up its appreciation of the rational and deliberative element in the governing process. Outside of court and council chamber, the greater body of public opinion was constantly forming and reforming amid the clamor of demagogues, fanatics, and the more insidious pleas of special interests. But such men as these rose in the market place and counselled wisdom, prudence, moderation, examination of facts, analysis of causes, sound methods, and statesmanlike

alism"; "Mass and Class"; Henry George, Jr., "The Menace of Privilege," and the early protest of D. Cloud, "Monopolies and the People," 1873, 4th ed.

[66] "American Contributions to Civilization," 1897.

[67] "The Rights of Man," 1901; "The Spirit of Democracy," 1910.

[68] "Freedom and Responsibility" (1903); "Undercurrents in American Politics" (1915); "Standards of Public Morality," 1907.

[69] "The Individual," 1900; "The Neighbor," 1904.

[70] "The Spirit of America," 1910.

[71] "Social Unrest," (1903). Compare Barrett Wendell, "Liberty, Union and Democracy," 1906; J. H. Hyslop, "Democracy," 1899; William Garrott Brown, "The New Politics," 1914.

conclusions.   Herein lay their significance in democratic development.

A thoughtful study of American life was that made by Herbert Croly, who was in the latter part of this period editor of the *New Republic*.[72]   Croly reflects and represents the desire for governmental reorganization coupled with a broader social program.   " Political democracy," said he, " is impoverished and sterile as soon as it becomes divorced from a social program.   A social program becomes dangerous to popular liberty in case it is not authorized by the free choice of the popular will." [73] Croly urged with great force the significance of the nation as the unit of democratic organization, the necessity of simpler political machinery, the development of responsible political leadership.   He emphasized the importance of the national ideal and of a practical program for its application and enforcement.   But the ideal of " social righteousness," he thought, must not be separated from the specific social program.   " The goal is sacred.   The program is fluid.   The pilgrims can trust to the torch only in case they constantly alter and improve it, in order to meet the restless and exacting exigencies of the journey." [74]   Progressive democracy must make its program as it advances.

In general, he stands as an advocate of progressivism both in the form and the function of government, inclining toward concentration of authority and sharpening

[72] " Life of Mark Hanna," 1912; " The Promise of American Life," 1909; " Progressive Democracy," 1914.
[73] P. 212.
[74] " Progressive Democracy," p. 217.

of political leadership, on the one hand, and the broadening of the social and industrial program of the state, on the other. He leaned toward what he called " Rooseveltian Progressivism," as distinguished from " Wilsonian Progressivism." Progressivism must be constructive in the genuine sense of the term. It must be ready to provide " not merely a new method, important as a new method may be, but a new faith upon the rock of which may be built a better structure of individual and social life." Democracy, he held, has been dormant, torpid, preoccupied with the frontier of its own life, accepting uncritically an inherited array of ideas and institutions.

Industrial democracy appears as a significant factor in the new scheme of things political — with social education, the abandonment of the earlier legalism and the substitution of the social spirit in its stead. In brief, we have here a theory of economic and political reorganization, incomplete in details of frame-work and enumeration of specific function, but clear as to the general spirit in which the new enterprise should be undertaken.

Lippman, in a series of brilliant essays, plead for the adoption of a social program adequate to the new needs of society.[75] Here is found a protest against formalism and legalism — a plea for the vital and human as against the mechanical and inflexible. Politics is experimental, tentative, pragmatic, not absolute and final in its conclusions. Its forms are built upon vital forces, whose action and reaction is as significant as — often more significant than — the external mechanisms of order.

[75] " Preface to Politics," 1913; " The Stakes of Diplomacy," 1915. See *ante.*

At the very close of this period Laski outlined a study of sovereignty, which was not then fully developed. He began a siege of the " monistic " theory of the state and the legal doctrine of sovereignty, substituting " pluralism " for " monism," and "relativity for " absolutism."

Weyl undertook an analysis of the relations between plutocracy and democracy, outlining the evolution of plutocratic authority and the beginnings of a constructive program for democracy. The organizing skill of the business magnate in systematizing political corruption has changed it from a local phenomenon to one which is organic and nation-wide.[76] Analyzing the elements of plutocracy, Weyl points out that all real plutocrats are not also rich. Just as some men of fortune are democrats, so on the other hand the plutocracy itself is backed up by millions of like-minded poor men, " penniless plutocrats, dream millionaires." Criticising the theory and practice of the Marxian Socialists, he undertakes to outline a program of democratic activity, under which are included government ownership or regulation of monopolies, government regulation of industry, progressive income and inheritance taxes, and taxation of unearned increments. Democratic political measures include direct nominations, the initiative and referendum and recall, administrative efficiency, increased flexibility in constitutional amendment. Under the democratic social program he would include " conservation," education and the socialization of consumption, all tending to promote " equality and opportunity." The new democ-

[76] Walter Weyl, "The New Democracy," 1912, 2nd Ed., p. 99.

racy must grapple constructively with the submerged world, with the race problem, and with immigration. But after all, no cut and dried program, complete in all of its details, can possibly be outlined. " We seek not a goal but a higher starting point from which to seek a goal." Our Utopia, he thinks, is not a state at all, but a " mere direction."

Numerous contributions to the systematic study of politics were also made by certain of the sociologists.[77] Comte's " Positive Philosophy " opened a new field of social inquiry and boldly attempted a science of social physics. Herbert Spencer's systematic sociology gave an immense impetus to the study of society in America. Spencer's earlier works, in fact, attracted wider interest here than elsewhere, and the publication of his " Social Statics " was made possible only by the interest of his friends in this country. Particularly in the '70's Spencer's ideas had a wide vogue in America; and he was probably read and discussed more than any other writer. Although other attempts had been made before his day,[78] the first scientific student of sociology in America was Lester F. Ward. Ward was a biologist, interested principally in paleontological botany; and his works appeared when the general interest in Spencer was at its height. His " Dynamic Sociology " was published in 1883; " Psychic Factors in Civilization " in 1893; " Out-

[77] Albion W. Small, "Fifty Years of Sociology in the United States " (1865-1915) in *A. J. S.* XXI, 721 (1916) : " Sociology" in Encyclopædia Americana.

[78] H. C. Carey, "Principles of Social Science," 1858-59. John Bascom, " Sociology," 1887.

lines of Sociology " in 1898; " Pure Sociology " in 1903, and " Applied Sociology " in 1906. Ward undertook to construct a complete scheme of social science adding the " dynamic " principle to the " statics " of Spencer. As has already been shown, he repudiated Spencer's biological doctrine of individualism, and strongly defended the possibility of social modification of the human environment, instead of its acceptance as an unchangeable order of things. To the conscious, deliberate, purposeful control over individuals and environment by society he gave the name of " Collective Telesis," and proposed the establishment of a system of scientific government under the name of " Sociocracy." By this he meant " the scientific control of the social forces by the collective mind of society for its advantage." Both individualism and socialism create either artificial inequalities or artificial equalities, but " sociocracy " recognizes natural inequalities and aims to abolish artificial inequalities. Individualism confers benefits on the superior. Socialism confers the same benefits on all alike, while " sociocracy " would confer benefits in strict proportion to merit, insisting on equality of opportunity as the only means of determining the degree of merit.[79]

Democracy has been a great step forward, but still leaves much to be desired because of its unscientific character. True legislation is in reality a process of " invention," and for this the democracy is not competent, unless some scientific method is brought to its aid. Its heart is right but its head is wrong.

[79] See "Outlines of Sociology," Chap. XII. Cf. W. J. Durant, " Philosophy and the Social Problem," 1917.

Following Ward came Giddings, Small, Ross, Patten, Cooley and many others who undertook the elaboration of social science. Giddings [80] and Small were perhaps more concerned with the methodology of the new science than with the development of particular fields. They dealt with the logic and the methodology of social science, struggling to bring order out of the chaos of social phenomena, to find a key method and spirit of social interpretation. At first a journalist and then an economist, Giddings developed his well known formula of "consciousness of kind" as the fundamental social fact, and built around it a sociological system. Later he undertook to sharpen the technique of social observation and analysis, and render methods and results more specific and scientific.[81] Small was especially occupied with the task of social technology, but in particular emphasized the significance of the social point of view, the unity of the social process, the organic relation between economic, political, historical, ethical phenomena, and the impossibility or inadequacy of any form of scientific discussion of one without regard to the other.[82] This social point of view he emphasized with great persistence and power for a generation.

Small also carried through a striking analysis of certain fundamental concepts in his "Between Eras, From Capitalism to Democracy" (1913).[83] He examined the

[80] "Principles of Sociology," 1898; "Inductive Sociology," 1901; "Democracy and Empire," 1901.
[81] "Inductive Sociology."
[82] See especially his "Meaning of Social Science."
[83] See also "The Social Gradations of Capital," *A. J. S.,* XIX, 721; "A Vision of Social Efficiency," *A. J. S.,* XIX, 433; "The Evolution

" Illusion of Capital," the " Fallacy of Distribution," the
" Superstition of Property." He assailed the current
economic theory of the productivity of capital, finding
that the " only producers of wealth are nature and labor "; that " the rewards of human activity should be
distributed solely on the basis of social service." What
he termed " hereditary economic sovereignty " is a " system professedly democratic which permits individuals
through the sheer irrelevancy of blood relationship to other
individuals to take over and exercise the ownership of millions of capital without even counterbalancing conditions
requiring a corresponding return to the community."
There is, said he, no compensating function to which this
privilege corresponds.   Capitalism standing by " Have "
and enforcing hold-up money from " Have Not " is the
most misanthropic enemy left in the path of society.
Under a properly organized social system, he contended,
the functions of labor and capital must both be fully
recognized. Labor must be represented in industrial
control, and the principle of distribution must be that
of social service, fixed by the voluntary agreement of the
participants or the arbitration of the state.   If this is not
done, he predicted, " in another fifty years it may have
been discovered that capitalism is a merger of lottery
and famine."

From the point of view of the study of groups, and
group struggle in society, notable contributions to the
understanding of political problems were made by Ross
and Cooley. A keen analysis of social control was

of a Social Standard," *A. J. S.*, XX, 10; See also his " General Sociology " (1905).

made by Ross,[84] who instituted a comprehensive study of all the social forces that constitute the control of the group over the individual. With this in view, he examined the " grounds " of control, the " means " of control, and the " system " of control. The " grounds " of control include the rôle of sympathy, sociability, the sense of justice, and of individual reaction. The " means " of control are various forces by which society insures social obedience. These agencies are partly legal and include law, belief, ceremony, education, illusion; and partly ethical, under which head he classifies public opinion, suggestion, art, and social valuation. He further discusses class control, the vicissitudes of social control, the limits and criteria of control. Ross asserted that in the future the control of society would be largely insured through education, which would be found to be the most effective agency in repressing the spirit of disobedience. He further undertook to lay down certain principles under which social control should be exercised. For example, social control must conduce to human welfare. It must not lightly excite against itself a passion for liberty. It should not be so paternal as to check the self-extinction of the morally ill-constituted, and finally, social interference should not so limit the struggle for existence as to nullify the selective process. " The Strong Man," said Ross, " who has come to regard social control as the scheme of the many weak to bind down a few strong may be brought to see it in its true light as the safeguard-

[84] Edward A. Ross, " Social Control," 1901; " Foundations of Sociology," 1905; " Social Psychology," 1908; " Sin and Society," 1907.

ing of a venerable corporation, protector not alone of the liberties of living men for themselves, but also of the liberties of bygone men for coming generations; guardian not merely of the dearest possession of innumerable persons, but likewise of the spiritual property of the human race."

Likewise in Cooley are found quietly fruitful studies of public opinion, social classes, interaction between classes and institutions, and of the nature and meaning of democracy.[85] Democracy, insisted Cooley, is not merely a political type, but instead is a principle of breadth in organization. " It involves a change in the character of social discipline not confined to politics, but as much at home in one sphere as in another."

Democracy does not suppress personality, but on the contrary welcomes it. That public opinion is necessarily average opinion is not essentially true. He reasons that the collective judgment may be and often is superior to the average judgment, the originality of the masses consisting in their sentiments and the fact that they are close to the springs of human nature. The critical faculty of the democracy is most effectively used, however, when its range is limited; and is more accurate in its judgment of persons than of measures. The significance of leadership in a democracy is examined and appraised by Cooley.[86] Public opinion must on the whole be re-

[85] Charles H. Cooley, "Human Nature and the Social Order," 1902; "Social Organization" (1909).

[86] "Human Nature and the Social Order," Ch. 8 and 9; see also Dealy, J. Q., "Sociology," 1909; Ellwood, C. A., "Sociology in its Psychological Aspects," 1903; also E. Hayes, "Introduction," 1915; Blackmar, "Elements," 1915; A. F. Bentley, "Process of Govern-

garded as "a latent authority," generally exercised by the public only when dissatisfied with the judgment of a specialist in exercising some function. On the whole, he concludes that government is only one agent of the public will; "merely one way of doing things, fitted by its character for doing some things and unfitted for doing others." It is likely to be too mechanical, too rigid, costly and inhuman, but has the counter-balancing advantages of power, reach and definite responsibility. The number of instances of state regulations, he pointed out, is rapidly increasing, but whether state control is increasing relatively to the new conditions, he questioned.

Patten undertook to lay the foundations of a new system of economics, politics and sociology.[87] The basis of his philosophy lay in the distinction drawn between what he termed the "pain economy" or period and the "pleasure economy" or period, in the history of mankind. In one — the "pain economy" — men are influenced chiefly by fear, and in the other by desire for some pleasurable end. Let us picture, he says, a social commonwealth in which there are no enemies to avoid and where the greatest evils to be met are those arising from intemperance, disease and crime. Under these conditions, social impulses would be developed adequate to the purpose of maintaining social life. In the economic field groups of

ment," 1908; Compare J. M. Baldwin, "Social and Ethical Interpretations," 1897; Sumner, "Folkways," 1907; Thomas, "Race Psychology," *A. J. S.*, XVII, 725; "Source Book for Social Origins, 1909; "The Polish Peasant in Europe and America," I, pp. 1–86 on Methodology of Social Science; Stuckenberg, J. H. W., "Sociology," 1898; Davis, M. M., "Psychological Interpretations of Society," 1909.

[87] Simon N. Patten, "The Theory of Social Forces," 1896.

producers would be automatically brought together. In the social field esthetic ideals would be substituted for the moral. In the political world he suggests something like the medieval guild system. State socialism, he thought, is an ideal of those suffering under the " pain economy," but " pleasure economy " would be that of a loosely organized social commonwealth, not an all-inclusive, all-regulating state. Citizens of such a commonwealth " would not understand what a state is if the word were used in its present sense."

Numerous other studies were made by sociologists, bordering on the field of politics. Conspicuous among these were Henderson,[88] with a long series of others, notably in the field of public philanthropy.

Specific studies were made in the field of the delinquent, defective and dependent, and notable progress was made in the practical amelioration of conditions.[89] Of special significance on the side of method was the development of the " social survey," a local study of social problems designed as a basis for intelligent community action.[90]

A unique study was that of Shailer Matthews, whose part in the social movement has already been noted. In an incisive inquiry into the relations between social, polit-

[88] " The Social Spirit in America," 1897; "Dependent, Defective and Delinquent Classes," 1893; "Social Duties from the Christian Point of View," 1909; "Modern Methods of Charity," 1904; E. T. Devine, "Spirit of Social Work" 1911; "Social Forces," 1910.

[89] Breckinridge and Abbot, "The Delinquent Child," 1912. Flexner and Baldwin, "Juvenile Courts and Probation," 1914.

[90] Russell Sage Foundation Publications, Department of Surveys and Exhibits.

ical and religious ideals, he traced many fundamental but little noticed connections between political theories and theology.[91] Doctrine is the " result of a dominant social mind at work in religion," and can be understood only in the light of social and political forces and theories. In this spirit he traced the influence of the Independent, the Feudal, the Nationalist, the Bourgeois and the Modern social mind upon " doctrine," with special emphasis upon the effect of political terms and concepts upon theology. His conclusion is a plea for a doctrinal system reflecting or incorporating the passion of the modern democratic social mind for justice.

Political economy during this period attained independent recognition as an academic study. Perry, Dunbar, Bowen, Sumner and Walker early in this epoch occupied chairs of instruction in political economy. In the early part of the period, economics was chiefly a continuation of the English classical economy, while its practical efforts were devoted to international free trade and general *laissez faire*. Later, the modern social forces were felt, as well as scientific tendencies.

Henry George's " Progress and Poverty " (1879), gave a violent impetus to public discussion of fundamental economic doctrines.[92] His wide vogue depended not merely on his advocacy of a special form of public revenue — the single tax — but on his keen and vigorous attack upon orthodox political economy. Socialistic theories had thus far made little impression, but the tax doc-

[91] Theology and the Social Mind, *Biblical World*. Vol. 46 (1915).

[92] P. A. Speck, " The Single Tax and the. Labor Movement," U. of Wis. Bulletin No. 878; A. N. Young, " The Single Tax Movement in the United States " (1916).

trines of George were widely popular and influential, arousing not only interest but deep enthusiasm. The element of deepest interest was his evident sympathy with the widespread social and industrial unrest, and his courageous attempt to find a way out. His sweeping and confident diagnosis of social disease was the key to his power.[93]

One of the most striking figures in the early field, and in fact throughout much of the period, was Sumner, a student of theology, politics, economics and sociology in the order enumerated.[94] His early study on " What Social Classes Owe To Each Other " was the highwater mark in the let-alone theory of government, and this doctrine was forcefully continued by Sumner for a generation. His study in " Folkways," a quarter of a century later, was notable in the field of sociology.

In 1885, the foundation of the American Economic Association gave a great impulse to the scientific study of economic questions.[95] The Quarterly Journal of Economics was established in 1890, the Yale Review in 1892, and the Journal of Political Economy in 1893. General Walker published his " Political Economy " in 1883, Professor Clark his " Philosophy of Wealth " in 1885, Laughlin his " Elements of Political Economy " in 1887, and Ely the " Introduction to Political Economy " in 1889.

[93] See his " Social Problems," 1883.
[94] See H. E. Barnes, " Two Representative Contributions of Sociology to Political Theory," A. J. S., XXV. With Sumner compare Edw. Atkinson, " Addresses upon the Labor Question," 1886; David A. Wells, " Practical Economics," 1888.
[95] See Small, " Fifty Years," p. 779.

The political economists of this period were concerned partly with the problems of the older " classical " economic theory, as modified by later English developments and by Austrian and German thinkers; and partly with the current questions of public policy and administration.[96] Under the latter head the chief interest lay first in the discussion of the tariff, later in the currency question, then in corporation control and in taxation. In the latter part of the period, increasing attention was given to the problems of industrial organization and education. The general tendency of economists was toward a modified theory of individualism, although upon this point there were wide differences of opinion. In the earlier part of the period there was a disposition to follow certain so-called " natural laws " whose uninterrupted operation, it was assumed, would automatically produce the best results. This argument was conspicuous particularly in the discussion of the tariff, where many economists advocated " free trade." To some extent the same doctrine was applied to economic evolution. In the latter part of the period, however, there was a strong tendency to emphasize the importance of state action, although this was sometimes justified merely as a removal of artificial obstructions to the natural action of industrial forces.

Far-reaching studies on the border line between economics and politics were made by Veblen.[97] In his earliest work, Veblen analyzed with classical irony the

[96] Haney, "History of Economic Thought."

[97] Thorstein Veblen, "The Theory of the Leisure Class," 1899; "The Theory of Business Enterprise," 1904; "The Instinct of

useless expenditures occasioned by the desire for distinction, and scored the useless types of expenditure, which
he characterized as "conspicuous waste." In an ingenious study later, Veblen undertook to find the origin
of natural rights and natural liberty in the period of the
handicraft industry. Natural rights he defined as "an
institutional by-product of workmanship under the handicraft system." [98] He reasoned that under the craft system the individual workman was thrown back upon his
own resources, where it appeared that the most sacred
right was that of property in what he individually produced. This right was thus made by usage and "inalienable right." But the system of capitalism which
grew up later was used against the workman under different conditions. When these natural rights were fully
established, trade fell into the hands of the capitalist or
the large-scale producer, so that the workman found
himself free "to dispose of his labor only to the capitalist
and at the same time the full right of ownership property
fell to the capitalist also."

In his "Theory of Business Enterprise" he undertook
to show that the essential motive power of business to-
day is not social efficiency, but ability to secure pecuniary
reward or profit without any necessary regard to the
character or quantity of service rendered to the community in return therefor. Government, he maintained,
represents and reflects in general the desires of business.

Workmanship," 1914; The Place of Science in Modern Civilization, in *A. J. S.*, XI, 585 (1906) ; The Preconceptions of Economic
Science, *Quarterly Journal Economics,* XIII, 121, 396; XIV, 240.
[98] "Instinct of Workmanship," p. 341.

Constitutional government he characterized as "a department of business organization guided by the advice of the business man." Modern politics is business politics in the literal sense of the term.[99]

Of still more fundamental importance was his analysis of the relation of modern civilization to the machine process. The machine, he asserted, has become the master of the man who works it, and controls the cultural fortunes of the community into whose life it has entered. The machine technology tends constantly to produce a standardized intellectual life in which regularity of consequence, mechanical precision and measurements in terms of pressure, temperature, velocity and tensile strength are likely to drive out other ideas. Habits of thought and methods of reasoning tend to shift from the conventional, the pecuniary, the legal, the mechanical, the industrial, to reasoning in terms of causation — from the *de jure* to the *de facto*. Accompanying this process he found a general tendency toward the weakening of the traditional ideas of piety, allegiance, conviction. " The ubiquitous presence of the machine with its spiritual concomitants — work-day ideals and a skepticism of what is only conventionally valid — is the unequivocal work of Western culture to-day as contrasted with the culture of other times and places." [1] Thus the machine system, as he interprets it, fundamentally affects the family, religion and the state. It affects the whole range and scope of human thought in the most fundamental

[99] "The Theory of Business Enterprise," Chap. VIII, on " Business Principles," in Law and Politics.

[1] *Op. cit.,* p. 323.

way. The cultural growth dominated by the machine industry is " of skeptical, matter-of-fact complexion, materialistic, unmoral, unpatriotic, undevout." [2] Veblen discovers a connection in " point of time, place and race between the modern machine technology, the material sciences, religious skepticism, and that spirit of insubordination that makes the substance of what are called free or popular institutions." [3] Thought is fixed or tends to fix not on " first causes," not on the final outcome or distant purpose of things, but on the actual process as it goes on with the results that develop from day to day, and the effect upon the welfare of the time present rather than of the golden age in the past or future.[4]

Notable contributions to the clearer understanding of industrial problems and their relation to politics were made by Ely,[5] Wright,[6] Commons [7] and many others. Ely was a courageous pioneer, who undertook the scien-

---

[2] *Op. cit.,* p. 372.

[3] "Instinct of Workmanship," p. 201.

[4] See also "The Nature of Peace," discussed in Ch. IX.

[5] "Past and Present of Political Economy," 1884; "Recent American Socialism," 1885; "The Labor Movement in America," 1886; "Social Aspects of Christianity," 1889; "Problems of To-day," 1888; "Socialism," 1894; "Studies in Evolution of Industrial Society," 1903; "Monopolies and Trusts," 1900; "Property and Contract," 1914.

[6] Carroll D. Wright, "Relation of Political Economy to the Labor Question," 1882; "Industrial Evolution of the United States," 1895.

[7] John R. Commons, "Social Reform and the Church," 1894; "Distribution of Wealth," 1893; "Documentary History American Industrial Society," 1910, 1911; "Labor and Administration," 1913; "Principles of Labor Legislation," 1916 (with Andrews); and other works.

tific analysis of social and political facts in the face of vigorous opposition and persecution. He established the principle of free inquiry into social problems, and for a generation served as an inspiration to the scientific study of industrial-political problems.[8] Of special value were the studies made by Commons, likewise a courageous explorer of social territory, in the field of industrial history.

Much of the time of economists was spent in refuting the doctrines of Socialists — a topic to which much attention has been devoted during the last generation in particular. One of the first volumes was that of Woolsey, in 1880, on " Communism and Socialism." To this initial attack was added an argument by practically all of the leading economists either as a part of some general treatise or in more specialized form. General Walker's spirited reply to Bellamy's " Looking Backward " was an interesting feature of his day. This was followed by many criticisms of Socialism, ranging from technical economic theory to broader considerations of social and political policy.[9] The systematic presentation of Socialism by its advocates has already been discussed, and need not be rehearsed here. In general, it followed Marxian lines, without as much " revision " as was found on the Continent or in England.

The study of public finance was greatly stimulated by

[8] Compare Eugen von Phillipovitch, " Social Political Ideas in German Economics," *A. J. S.*, 17, 145.

[9] Among the more searching of these were Veblen, The Socialist Economics of Karl Marx and His Followers, *Q. J. E.*, 20, 575, 21, 299; Simkhovitch, " Marxism vs. Socialism," 1913; Small, Socialism in the Light of Social Science, *A. J. S.*, XVII, 804; Le Rossignol, "Orthodox Socialism, A Criticism," 1907.

the thought of Seligman,[10] Adams,[11] Plehn,[12] and many others.[13] To the problems of taxation both theoretical and practical much detailed attention was given; and a persistent effort made to outline a constructive program of tax reform. Seligman in particular emphasized the importance of the income tax, based on ability to pay, as a just measure of democratic contribution to the support of the state. Practically all united in condemnation of the current taxing system as unjust and undemocratic.

Scientific study of the vital immigration problem was begun during this period, and pushed forward by many inquirers. A Federal inquiry was made in 1890, and a far more elaborate investigation was begun in 1907 and published in 1911.[14] From 1882 when the first Federal immigration law of this period was enacted to the passage of the Act of 1917, there was animated discussion of the relation of immigration to the social, economic and political life of the nation.[15] A battle center was the literacy test, vetoed by President Cleveland in 1897, Taft in 1913, Wilson in 1915 and 1917, but finally made effective notwithstanding.

Among the more significant studies were the early work of Mayo Smith on " Emigration and Immigra-

[10] " Essays in Taxation," 1895.

[11] " Science of Finance," 1898.

[12] " Public Finance," 1896.

[13] " Proceedings National Tax Association," 1908–; S. F. Weston, " Principles of Justice in Taxation," 1903.

[14] Senate Doc. 747, 61st Cong., 3rd Sess, 42 vols. of especial value is Vol 1; the Report of the Massachusetts Commission of 1913 is of exceptional value.

[15] A good general summary is contained in Mary K. Reely's " Selected Articles on Immigration," Ed. 1915.

tion " (1890), those of Jenks and Lauck, the " Immigration Problem " (1911); Hourwich, " Immigration and Labor " (1912); Commons, " Races and Immigrants " (1907); Abbott, " The Immigrant and the Community " (1917); Woods, "Americans in Process "[16] (1902). These studies, based upon observation and personal experience, were directed toward more scientific treatment of what had been a typical and fundamental problem of national life for three-quarters of a century. The resources of investigation and statistical interpretation were brought into play in the effort to find a solid basis of fact for a policy.

Still broader in scope were the inquiries in anthropology and ethnology of which this period saw the beginning. Morgan's studies early attracted wide attention in the scientific world.[17] Ripley published his " Races of Europe " in 1899, stimulating interest in the study of origins, already long developed in Europe. Boas,[18] Thomas,[19] Sumner,[20] and others [21] undertook investigations in special fields. At many points these inquiries

[16] See also E. A. Steiner, " The Immigrant Tide," 1909; P. F. Hall, " Immigration," 1906; E. A. Ross, " The Old World in the New," 1914. For the earlier and less critical type see Joseph Cook, " Unamerican Immigration," 1894.

[17] L. H. Morgan, " Ancient Society," 1877; " The League of the Iroquois," 1904.

[18] Franz Boas, " Anthropology," 1908; " The Mind of Primitive Man," 1911.

[19] W. I. Thomas, " Sex and Society "; " Social Origins," 1909, with bibliography.

[20] W. G. Sumner, " Folkways," 1906.

[21] Webster, H., " Primitive Secret Societies," 1908; " The American Anthropologist," passim.

touched the field of political institutions and the theory of the state.[22]

In the field of formal philosophy, and notably in the province of ethics, significant contributions were made to the development of political thought.[23] Varied influences were operating in the field of philosophy. Some of these were German in their nature, and particularly Hegelian. Others were of English origin and of these by far the most influential were the doctrines of Darwin and Spencer.

Royce, representing the idealists, discussed the relation between the world and the individual (1901) in absolutist style. Politically he was influenced by Mill and Spencer, but on the whole he arrived at moderating conclusions, as far as the doctrine of the state was concerned.[24] Baldwin, in connection with his suggestive studies in social psychology, discussed the problem of the individual and the state.[25]

But by far the most striking and significant studies were those made by William James,[26] and John Dewey,[27]

[22] See Eben Mumford's "Origins of Leadership," 1909.

[23] See Woodbridge Riley, "American Thought," 1915.

[24] See his "Spirit of Modern Philosophy," 1892.

[25] James Mark Baldwin, "Mental Development in the Child and the Race," 1895; "The Individual and Society," 1911; "Development and Evolution," 1902; "Philosophy and Science," 1902; "Darwin and the Humanities," 1909; "Social and Ethical Interpretations in Mental Development," 1897; Daniel G. Brinton, "The Basis of Social Relations," 1902.

[26] "The Will to Believe," 1897; "Pragmatism," 1907; "A Pluralistic Universe," 1909; "The Meaning of Truth," 1909.

[27] "The School and Society," 1899; "Influence of Darwin on Philosophy," 1910; "Democracy and Education," 1916.

two striking figures in American philosophy, and a group associated with them under the name of " Pragmatists." [28] With this group were allied others who were engaged in the common task of creating social ethics, endeavoring to reach a basis appropiate to a democratic society and state. Among these were Tufts,[29] and Mead,[30] and less closely, Jane Addams; [31] and others who blazed the way for democratic ethics.

" Pragmatism " as a philosophy was less concerned than " Rationalism " or " Absolutism " with first causes or principles, or with equally absolute ultimate aims or purposes.[32] Pragmatism is essentially experimental, looking toward " fruits, consequences, facts "— a trial balance system evolving its philosophy as it goes. " The idea and the ideal to which it pins its faith," says Moore, " and from which it draws its inspiration are those which are wrought out and tried out in our world of struggle, of

[28] See the valuable summary by A. W. Moore, " Pragmatism and Its Critics," 1910. Compare criticism by C. M. Bakewell, " Latter-Day Flowing Philosophy," 1904.

[29] James H. Tufts, " Our Democracy," 1917; Why Should Law and Philosophy Get Together?, *Int. Journal Ethics*, XXV, 188, and other writings.

[30] George H. Mead, Natural Rights, *Journal of Phil. Psych. and Scientific Methods*, XII, 141 (1915) ; " The Social Self," Ibid., X, 374 (1913) ; Social Psychology, *Psych. Bulletin*, VI, 401 (1909) ; " Scientific Method and Individual Thinker " in " Collective Intelligence," 176–227.

[31] " Twenty Years at Hull House," 1910; " Democracy and Social Ethics," 1902; " Newer Ideals of Peace," 1907; " The Spirit of Youth," 1909; " A New Conscience and An Ancient Evil," 1912; " The Long Road of Woman's Memory," 1916; see Harvard Guide to Reading in Social Ethics and Allied Subjects, 1910.

[32] R. B. Perry, " The Present Conflict of Ideals," 1918.

defeats and victories." Pragmatism is a tentative philosophy of developing life. Its basis lies in the broad historical background of modern life, in the central place of evolution in the scheme of modern thought, in the social character of consciousness —" in short, it bears many of the resemblances of the general theory of things adapted to a democratic era." In ethics its followers applied it to the evolutionary theory of morality, although they did not originate this point of view.

Dewey applied the doctrine to the problems of democracy, particularly in connection with the study of the educational process, but by no means confining it to this field. " When a theory of knowledge," said Dewey, " forgets that its value rests in solving the problem out of which it has arisen, viz., that of securing a method of action . . . it begins to cumber the ground. It is a luxury, hence a social nuisance and disturber." Democracy requires a new philosophy and a new psychology. " Democracy, the crucial expression of modern life, is not so much an addition to the scientific and industrial tendencies as it is the perception of their spiritual or social meaning." [33] This necessary philosophy cannot be found in the worn-out systems of earlier days, but must be developed in accordance with the demands of modern conditions. This philosophy may be furnished by pragmatism with its experimental, tentative, day-by-day and problem-by-problem method. It will supply the standards and sanctions rapidly disappearing under the dissolving tendencies of modern life. Social ethics should not be isolated from the practical world, nor should politics become merely a

[33] " Influence of Darwin," p. 59.

refined statement of tribal traditions.   They should both attempt to translate philosophy from a general and therefore abstract method into a working and specific method. " I believe," said he, " that philosophy in America will be lost between chewing a historic cud long since reduced to woody fiber, or an apologetics for lost causes (lost to natural science), or a scholastic, schematic, formalism, unless it can somehow bring to consciousness America's own needs and its own implicit principle of successful action." [34]

The need may be met by means of " a deliberate control of policies by the method of intelligence."   But this " intelligence " is not that " honored in text books, and neglected elsewhere," but is " the sum total of impulses, habits, emotions, records and discoveries, which forecast what is desirable and undesirable in future possibilities, and which contrive ingeniously in behalf of imagined good." [35]   Without such a principle we tend to combine loose, ineffective, optimistic idealism with a practical realistic acceptance of the theory of " take who take can." All peoples have been " narrowly realistic in practice," and then employed " idealization to cover up in sentiment and theory their brutalities."

Democracy, said Dewey, is more than a form of government.   It is primarily a mode of associated living, of conjoint communicative experience.   Its essential characteristics are the wider " area of shared concerns " and " the liberation of the greater diversity of personal ca-

[34] " Creative Intelligence," p. 67.
[35] See " Creative Intelligence " (1917), by Dewey, Moore, Mead, Tufts and others.

pacities." In this spirit he discusses the problems of education developing in a state where popular rule is the fundamental and accepted principle.

A great end of education is " social efficiency," but this must not be interpreted merely in economic terms of material output. It involves also " civic efficiency," " capacity to share in the give and take of experience." It involves " nothing less than socialization of mind." [36] Its chief constituent is sympathy and good will.

Education is a social process to be carried out in a social spirit. Democratic education, unless it is to be " a farcical yet tragic delusion," must open the doors of opportunity wide, and must so far modify traditional ideals of culture, subjects of study, and methods of teaching and discipline as to make youth master of its economic and social career. Democratic education must give individuals " a personal interest in social relationship and control, and the habits of mind which secure social changes without introducing disorder." [37] The philosophies of the 19th century made the national state the agency for development, but narrowed the conception of the social aim to members of the national unit, excluding all outside, and reintroduced the idea of the subordination of the individual to the institution.[38] But a democratic society must allow for full intellectual freedom and the play of diverse gifts and interests — the individual variations developed where there is mental freedom and growth.

The practical influence of Pragmatism was great. Af-

[36] " Democracy and Education," p. 141.
[37] P. 115.
[38] See Ch. 22, " The Individual and the World."

fected by its general spirit were Roscoe Pound, in sociological jurisprudence; Goodnow, in public administration;
Croly and Lippman in their political enquiries; and to
some extent, Veblen. Broadly speaking, its tendencies
and methods coincided with the spirit and purpose of the
liberal-conservative, critical constructive movement characteristic of the time. Philosophically its range was made
wider than this, aiming at a reconciliation of materialism
and idealism, of science and philosophy.

A unique figure during the latter part of this period
was Jane Addams, whose long and intimate experience
with urban, industrial, cosmopolitan conditions was
summed up in fragmentary but significant social studies.
The concepts of social ethics are applied to charity, to
domestic relations, to industrial situations, to educational
methods and to political reform with keen insight into
actual conditions and sympathy with democratic ideals.

Democracy must be more broadly constructed; it must
afford " a rule of living, as well as a test of faith." The
identification with the common lot is the essential idea
of democracy, and also the source of social ethics. Her
conclusion is that while the perplexities of the new situation are most keenly felt by the educated and self-con-
scious, the " actual attempts at adjustment are largely
coming through those who are simpler and less analytical." [39] But the acceptance of democracy brings a certain life-giving power with its own sanctions and com-
forts — the most obvious of which is that " a certain
basic well-being can never be taken away from us whatever the turn of fortune."

[39] " Democracy and Social Ethics," p. 12.

Contributions to political philosophy were also made by a great group of historians during this period. The greater part of the historical writing of the time was political and constitutional in its scope and centered closely around the essential problems of the state. There was seen, however, a general tendency toward the broadening of the field of historical inquiry beyond the constitutional and the political to the economic, social, religious and cultural. This general tendency toward social history, although not fully carried out, was one of the most striking features of historical writing during this time.

A notable statement of this doctrine is contained in Turner's presidential Address, of 1911,[40] and likewise by Jameson[41] and Robinson.[42] Seligman[43] elaborated the economic interpretation of history in a notable monograph. Beard's[44] studies in economic interpretation of political events were significant developments in historical treatment.

Of equal significance was Ellen Semple's[45] study of

[40] F. J. Turner, Social Forces in American History, *American Historical Review*, XVI, 217.

[41] J. F. Jameson, The American Acta Sanctorum, *Am. Hist. Rev.*, XIII, 286.

[42] "The New History" (1912).

[43] E. R. A. Seligman, "The Economic Interpretation of History" (1902). Compare the early work of John W. Draper, "Thoughts on Future Civil Policy of America" (1867).

[44] Charles A. Beard, "An Economic Interpretation of the Constitution," 1913; "Economic Origins of Jeffersonian Democracy" (1915). Compare Gustavus Myers, "History of the Supreme Court of the United States," 1912.

[45] "American History and Its Geographic Conditions," 1903; "Influence of Geographic Environment," 1911.

geographical influences in history. Brooks Adams undertook an interpretation of social revolutions in terms of the economic forces in society [46] elaborating his conclusions with great enthusiasm and energy.

The chief tendencies exhibited in the systematic study of politics during this period were the development of the historical and comparative method, a broader social outlook, and the beginnings of the use of statistics and psychology. Beginning with the '80's, the social sciences taken together occupied the interest of many workers who covered a wide field of inquiry, and followed their pursuits with great enthusiasm and interest. That they solved the problems of methodology cannot be contended, but that material progress was made towards sounder types of investigation cannot be disputed. At best the machinery of political and social research was too inadequately manned to operate the mechanism and show its possibilities. Organization and action on a large scale was not possible under conditions effectively testing the apparatus of scientific social inquiry. Notwithstanding this, notable additions were made to the progress of the time.

Valuable analyses and interpretations of political forms and forces are everywhere evident. These were fragmentary and imperfect, but possessed a distinct social utility, characteristically incomplete, with wide gaps and many ups and downs. Yet in comparison with the development of the preceding half century, the scientific study of politics had made appreciable headway, and the last

[46] " The Law of Civilization and Decay," 1903; " The Theory of Social Revolutions," 1913.

quarter of a century had far surpassed the period preceding it. During the first generation of our history, the politics of America was fully abreast of the best political thought of that time, and, indeed, as the writings of Adams and Jefferson show, of all times. In the next generation this technical advantage was largely lost, during the " Jacksonian " democracy. During the last generation, the earlier position was regained under leaders like Roosevelt and Wilson, reenforced, indeed, by the more broadly democratic education of the new time. The technique of inquiry made progress with the aid of history and statistics, the methods of legislation were advanced somewhat, while the organization and principles of public administration were set ahead in theory and in practice. At the same time the technique of jurisprudence tended to become somewhat more scientific and its underlying spirit more broadly social. It is easy to exaggerate the advance of the rational and scientific spirit in politics, but it is equally easy to underestimate the progress of education in political affairs. A break-down in government, as seen in mob rule or the treason of a public official, is widely heralded, but the silent advance of scientific methods in public education, in legislation, in administration, in the ways and means of democratic rule, is less spectacular and less observed. It would not be difficult to formulate a critique of methods and results, but in viewing the historical evolution of politics, the significant feature is the beginnings of improved technique in political methods, and more scientific processes in politics and the allied social studies. Broadly speaking, this was a period of beginnings rather than of conclusions, of tentative and often timid advances rather than of dogmatism and finality in the field of systematic politics. The influence of class was relatively strong and the influence of modern scientific method relatively weak.

CHAPTER XIV

POLITICAL IDEAS IN AMERICAN LITERATURE [1]

Significant were the political tendencies traceable in the literary output of the time.[2] In the earlier days a great part in the social development of the time was played by Emerson and the highly developed individualism of his writings. Whittier, Lowell and Harriet Beecher Stowe had been important factors in the anti-slavery movement. They had by no means cultivated systematic political philosophy, but they had profoundly influenced the political thinking of their day, just as the English writers of the type of Dickens, Thackeray, Elliott and Ruskin had made their influence felt in reformation of English social conditions.

At first the literary world was dominated by the powerful group of New England " Brahmins " as they were called, including Emerson, Longfellow, Lowell, Whittier, and Oliver Wendell Holmes.[3] These remarkable

[1] For a portion of the material in this chapter I am indebted to one of my students, Mr. Clyde Hart, who is writing a fuller discussion of this topic.

[2] See "Cambridge History of American Literature" and studies cited there; Vida Scudder, "Social Ideals in English Letters"; Bliss Perry, "The American Spirit in Literature"; Van Wyck Brooks, "America's Coming of Age"; Woodrow Wilson, "Mere Literature," 1896; Percy Boynton, "A History of American Literature."

[3] See Howells' delightful study, "Literary Friends and Acquaintance."

figures, however, were the product of the first half of the 19th century, and they reflected the spirit of that time. To the later development of social, industrial and political conditions, after the Civil War, they did not so readily respond. The themes they chose did not commonly center around the urban and industrial forces now working so powerfully on the lives of men. These distinguished writers were essentially patrician in their views of life; and their political ideas, while by no means consciously undemocratic, were the thoughts of an earlier day. Their fight for liberty was completed with the emancipation of the slave.

Of this group Lowell was the most politically minded and in his " Essays " discussed and defended democracy.[4] This volume was based on his addresses while Ambassador to England, and constituted a type of apologetics. His theme was chiefly a defence of democracy. He plead the newness of popular rule and the growing pains that must naturally accompany its advance to maturity. There may be much " rough and tumble " in the democratic process, but on the whole it is educational in tendency and value. " Government by discussion " is, all things considered, a desirable alternative to that of force. Great evils had sprung up in democracy, including the " enormous inequalities " in his day. These must be corrected, he believed, though Socialism he considered a menace to society. The work of Lowell was characterized by a grace and charm which give it an exceptional value in the literature of American democracy.

The fundamentally democratic forces in the literature

[4] James Russell Lowell, " Democracy," 1884.

of this period began with Walt Whitman, " the good gray poet " whose rough, plebeian form contrasted sharply with the polished finish of the literary leaders of his day.[5] Whitman's writings breathed a spirit of democratic comradeship and sympathy that was without precedent in American literature. " Not till the sun excludes you, do I exclude you " sums up his attitude toward his fellow men. The influence of his ideas and his sentiment was far-reaching and profound, and tended to increase rather than decline as time went on.

To Whitman it appeared that democracy was not merely a form of government. " If ever accomplished," he said, " it will be at least as much (I think likely double as much) the result of democratic literature and arts (if we get them) as of democratic parties." [6] It seemed to him that democracy must have its own art, its own poetry, its own schools, and even its own " sociologies." [7] " Literature," he said, " has never recognized the people, and whatever may be said, it does not to-day." He found three stages in the evolution of democracy — the political foundation, the basis of material prosperity, and finally what he termed religious democracy. " Taste, intelligence and culture (so-called) have been against the masses and remain so. There is plenty of glamour about the most damnable crimes and hoggish meannesses, special and general, of the feudal and dynastic world over

[5] " Democratic Vistas "; " Chants Democratic "; " To a Foiled Revolter or Revoltress." With Whitman compare the southern poet, Sidney Lanier, in his " Poems." Of note is that on " Corn," and others in which contemporary commercial ideals are criticized.

[6] Prose Works," p. 323.

[7] " Democratic Vistas," p. 205.

there . . . with its personnel of lords and queens and courts so well dressed and so handsome. But the People are ungrammatical, untidy and their sins gaunt and ill-bred." Culture, therefore, must be given democratic meaning and expression. "Democracy must have at least as firm and as warm a hold in men's hearts, emotions and beliefs as the days of feudalism or ecclesiasticism." [8]

Whitman was distinctly the champion of the common man. "It is doubtful," he said, upon one occasion, "whether the State is to be saved either in the monotonous long run or in the tremendous special crises by its good people only." Help comes from strange quarters. He thought it might be necessary to "cure the bite with a hair of the same dog." He looked and hoped to see the official personnel of the government changed. He would like to see some "qualified mechanics" in Congress and a blacksmith or a boatman for president.

The purpose of the government Whitman believed to be not merely to repress disorder but to develop "the possibilities of all beneficence and manly outcroppage and of that aspiration for independence and the pride and respect latent in all characters." [9] Whitman's idea of a democracy's security was that of the "safety and endurance of the aggregate of its middling property owners." [10] "Democracy," he said, "asks for men and

[8] Emerson he considered to have "a dandified manner — all sugar and butter." He praised Hegel's idea, saying, "It is strange to me that they were born in Germany or the Old World at all." See also his interesting "Russia and America," 316.

[9] P. 218.

[10] P. 221.

women with occupations, well off, owners of houses and acres, and with cash in the bank, and with some cravings for literature, too." [11] The urban and industrial tendencies just coming into view he did not fully recognize as essentially democratic. On the contrary, the spirit of democracy, he thought, was found mainly in the agricultural regions.

For almost a generation, however, Whitman had no successor, and there was no great voice raised in defence of the broad doctrines of human fellowship he had so vigorously championed. The literary form of his works offended many, and for a long time tended to overshadow his broad humanitarianism.

In 1889, Edward Bellamy's " Looking Backward," was published and quickly attained a surprising circulation. Inspired by his doctrines Nationalist Clubs were formed, even a Nationalist Party, which, however, was short-lived. Bellamy depicted a socialistic state organized upon the basis of universal industrial service with a hierarchy of officials arranged in military form. It was the most widely read social treatise of the day, with the possible exception of Henry George's " Progress and Poverty." But the effect of this effort was soon lost, although its indirect influence was no doubt considerable.

In the early '90's came a remarkable break in the conservative line, when the stately Howells, now dean of American literature, published " A Traveller from Altruria " (1894).[12] In this work Howells, influenced by

[11] P. 221.

[12] See also " Through the Eye of the Needle," 1907; " World of Chance," 1891.

Tolstoi and Morris, produced the sharpest satire yet written on American economic and social life. He pictured a state of affairs in which " there is as absolute a division between the orders of men and as little love as in any country on the globe." He reproduced in detail the standard defences of the established social order, and readily demolished them. Finally in a glowing description of Altruria, he portrayed a socialistic Utopia.

Aside from the significant works of Bellamy and Howells, Utopias of all types appeared, running the whole gamut of the radical, reactionary, middle class, anarchistic and individualistic. Aside from those already described, most of these had no great circulation or influence, but they possess some historical significance as types of speculation, cropping out at widely scattered points. In comparison with the Utopian ferment of the ante-bellum period, the output was relatively small and unimportant.[13]

In the last generation increasing attention has been given to the description of American political conditions including urban and rural types and covering all sections of the country. An early example was Crawford's " An American Politician " (1885), describing the mysterious industrial-financial Council of Three, and concluding with the doctrine of Independency. A widely read volume was Ford's " The Honorable Peter Stirling " (1894)

[13] Interesting types of these are Philip Dru, Administrator, 1912, published anonymously, and David Lubin's, "Let There Be Light," 1900. See also among many others: S. B. Welcome, "From Earth's Center," 1895; Frank Rossiter, "The Making of a Millennium," 1908; Henry Olerich, "A Cityless and Countryless World," 1893; C. W. Wooldridge, "Perfecting the Earth," 1902.

— an interesting account of politics in New York City in the nineties, detailing the methods and spirit of Tammany, and the social and economic basis of machine rule in a great urban cosmopolitan community. Lewis' "The Boss" centered around the same theme with Croker as its dominating figure.[14]   "I have yet to meet," says the cynical boss, "that man or that corporation, and though the latter were a church, who wouldn't follow interest across a prostrate law and in the chase of dollars break through ordinance and statute as a cow walks through a cobweb."

Lincoln Steffens with his great power of vivid portrayal led the way and turned the spot light on the dark places of government and industry.[15]   But he did more than photograph. He undertook the formulation of a philosophy as well. The fundamental cause of political corruption he found in the relation between government and special industrial privilege, between the political boss and the business beneficiary. To this all trails led him. But his final conclusion was that both the boss and the beneficiary are the products of a system which must answer for them both. Of like import were the notable stories of Judge Lindsey, "The Beast" (1910), Brand Whitlock's [16] "Forty Years of It" (1914) and Samuel

[14] Compare George Vickers, "The Fall of Bossism," 1883, and Rufus E. Shapley's "Solid for Mulhooley," 1881, stories of Philadelphia; and the keen satire of Champernowme (D. M. Means) "The Boss" (1894); W. L. Riordan, "Plunkitt of Tammany Hall" (1905).

[15] "The Shame of the Cities," (1904); "The Struggle for Self-Government," (1906), and many short articles.

[16] See also his "Gold Brick" (1910); "The Turn of the Bal-

Blythe's "The Price of Place" (1913).[17]   C. K. Lush's "The Federal Judge" (1897) describes the relation between a country judge and an industrial magnate.

Of all these the most widely influential was Winston Churchill, whose volumes vividly portrayed the economic and political situation.[18]   In the first of these studies he described the early stages of political and industrial development in which railroads struggled for consolidation and centralization.   In the second, he depicted a more fully developed and highly organized system, in the third, the riper product of business and political growth, and in the fourth, the development of industrial unionism.   The discrepancy between the forms and the facts of repreance" (1907).   Compare Elizabeth B. Bohan, "The Drag Net," 1909.

[17] See also Hamlin Garland's "A Spoil of Office," 1892, describing Populism in Iowa; Francis Lynde, "The Grafters" (1904), dealing with Populism in a mountain state; Booth Tarkington, "The Gentleman from Indiana" and "In the Arena" (1905) on Indiana politics; D. G. Phillips, "Light Fingered Gentry" (1907), covering the New York insurance investigations; Clifford Raymond, *American Magazine*, 73, 469, 523, 651 on Illinois; Will Payne, "Money Captain," on the Chicago gas case, 1898; and Flower's "The Spoilsman," also based on Chicago public utilities; J. W. Linn, "The Second Generation," an Illinois story (1902).

[18] Coniston, 1906; "Mr. Crewe's Career," 1908; "A Far Country," 1915; "The Dwelling Place of Light," 1917; P. V. Mighel, "The Ultimate Passion" (1905) and J. K. Friedman, "The Radical," tracing the relation between federal politics and business; M. L. Luther, "The Mastery," 1904; J. A. Altsheler, "Guthrie of the Times" (1904), a story of a Southern legislature; H. R. Miller's "The Man Higher Up" (1910), a description of Pennsylvania municipal politics; William Sage, "By Right Divine" (1907), and Holman Day, "The Ramrodders" (1910) center around state politics and industry.

sentative government was dramatically outlined by Churchill —" Democracy in front, the feudal system, the dukes and earls, behind, but in plain clothes; democracy in stars and spangles and trappings and insignia. . . . Proclamations, constitutions and creeds crumble before conditions. The Law of Dividends is the high law, and the Forum an open vent through which the white steam may rise heavenward and be resolved again into water." [19] The growth of central organization in business and natural control in politics is also a topic of extended consideration. The "Banker Personality," presumably Morgan, was sketched by Churchill, and his far-reaching power examined. "Wherever commerce reigned — and where did it not? — he was king and head of its Holy Empire, Pope and Emperor at once. What I did not then comprehend was that he was the American Principle personified, the supreme individual assertion of the conviction that government should remain modestly in the background, while the efficient acquired the supremacy that was theirs by natural right; nor had I grasped at that time the crowning achievement of the unity that fused Christianity with those acquisitive dispositions said to be inherent in humanity. In him the Lion and the Lamb, the Eagle and the Dove dwelt together in amity and power." [20]

The conclusion of his philosophy is that democracy is still in an experimental stage, struggling for more perfect development. Democracy, says the author, "Is still in a far country, eating the husks of individualism, material-

[19] "Mr. Crewe's Career," p. 141.
[20] "A Far Country," p. 367.

ism. What we see is not true freedom, but freedom run to riot, men struggling for themselves, spending on themselves the fruits of their inheritance; we see a government intent on one object alone — exploitation of this inheritance in order to achieve what it calls prosperity. And God is far away." [21]

Broader in scope came studies penetrating beyond the industrial and the political to the deeper social relations of democracy. One of the earliest of these was Elizabeth Stuart Phelps, " Silent Partner " (1871)— a story of a New England mill town. Keener in analysis and more finished in form were the studies of Herrick,[22] White and Poole.[23] These writers undertook to picture the web of American life as it was woven by the industrial and urban forces of our time. Their analysis showed the complex and confusing relations of democracy under the new environment, with its weakness and its perils, its strength and its hope. They showed cross sections of the social democracy behind the formal equality and democracy of government; and they took no pains to gloss over the glaring discrepancies between political, industrial and social democracy.

[21] *Ibid.*, 481.
[22] Robert Herrick, " The Common Lot " (1904) ; " A Life for a Life " (1910) ; " The Web of Life " (1900).
[23] William Allen White, " A Certain Rich Man " (1909) ; " The Old Order Changeth " (1910) ; Ernest Poole, " The Harbor " (1915) ; H. S. Harrison, " Queed " (1911) ; J. M. Patterson, " A Little Brother of the Rich," 1908; see also such works as those of Bliss Perry, " The Plated City," 1895; Hutchins Hapgood, " The Autobiography of a Thief," 1903; Donald Richberg, " The Shadow Men " (1911) ; Frank Norris, " The Octopus," 1901, " The Pit," 1903.

This period was rich in sketches of many races and regions, and social types of all descriptions. North and South, East and West, among old inhabitants and newest arrivals, the eager seekers went searching for fresh types to portray. Many of these like Tourgees's " Fool's Errand " (1879), Cable's " John March, Southerner " (1894), Dixon's " Clansman " (1905), Helen Hunt Jackson's " Ramona " (1884) are valuable interpretations of a spirit and a time. Mary Antin's " Promised Land " and Lillian Wald's " The House on Henry Street " are invaluable for their appreciation of urban cosmopolitan conditions, and their political philosophy is by no means a negligible quantity in a period when political formalism often overlooked the realities of life.[24]

Among the Socialist writers the best known were Jack London and Upton Sinclair.[25] The former developed the orthodox Socialist doctrine in his numerous writings, notably in the " Iron Heel " (1908)— a picture of the final triumph of the plutocratic " oligarchy." Sinclair first wrote " The Jungle " (1906), a widely read story based upon the conditions in the packing industry of Chicago, and later undertook to outline a constructive program in his " Industrial Republic " (1907). London was the more picturesque and more popularly effective. An interesting compilation of democratic appeals from all lands was made by Sinclair in his " Cry for Justice," in

[24] See also Angelo Pietri, " The Schoolmaster of a Great City "; Jacob Riis, " An American in the Making "; Rebecca Schneider, " Bibliography of Jewish Life in the Fiction of America and England," 1916; Benjamin Brawley, " The Negro in Literature and Art."

[25] Katherine Pearson Woods, " Metzerott, Shoemaker " 1890.

which he brought together the protests of liberty-lovers
of all the world.[26]

On the other hand, there were not wanting literary
works in defence of the existing politico-economic order.
Of this type was John Hay's "Breadwinners," published
in 1883-4.[27] The inspiration of this fiction was the
great strike of 1877. Apparently deeply influenced by
the terrorism of that period, the writer held up to ridicule
and scorn the labor agitator and organizer and the tactics
of organized labor in general.[28] His unfriendly pictures
of the personality of the leaders of organized industry
and his discussion of their methods of operation were of
such a type as to produce distrust and dislike of the labor
movement.

Critical and somewhat cynical in its attitude toward
free government is a volume called "Democracy" whose
author was probably either Clarence King or Henry
Adams (1880). The thinly veiled references to the
President of the United States and leading public officials
and the outspoken criticism of the methods and purposes
of democratic government were, if not distinctly hostile
to democracy as such, at least doubtful and hesitating.
They were not calculated to inspire confidence either in
the present or the future of democracy.[29]

In his "Voice of the Machines" (1908) Gerald S. Lee
undertook to write the poetry of the machine process,

[26] See also "King Cole" and other stories.
[27] First appearing anonymously in the *Century Magazine*.
[28] Chap. V. "A Professional Reformer."
[29] Compare Francis Hodgson Burnett, "Through One Administration," 1883 — dealing with industrial political relations in Washington; Mrs. Atherton, "Senator North," 1900.

and in his " Inspired Millionaires " (1908) to interpret the business magnate and give him literary shape and form.[30] " How can a machine-made world," he asked, " be run in the spirit of a hand-made world? " The answer is that there are two spirits in the machine, that of weariness and weakness, and on the other hand that of conquering, moving mountains, accomplishment. " Perhaps Religion in the twentieth century is Technique — Technique in the twentieth century is the Holy Ghost." [31]

Crowds produce a real aristocracy. They " speak in heroics." " There is a kind of colossal naked poetry in what Pierpont Morgan has done which I cannot but acknowledge with gratitude and hope." [32] Millionaires are " the bellows of great cities, the draught of the creative forces and the latent energies of men." [33] " Labor unions are conspiracies of poor men for not working so hard and for intimidating men who want to work hard." Our choice is " between the socialized millionaire and Socialism." Our salvation lies in the Aristocrat who " is the man who is more of a democrat than the other people have the brains to be, the man who can identify himself with the interests and with the points of view of the most kinds of people."

An interesting type is " The Scarlet Empire," by David M. Parry, President of the National Association of Manufacturers (1906).[34] " The Scarlet Empire " is a social-

[30] " Crowds " (1914), p. 38.
[31] *Ibid.*, p. 188.
[32] *Ibid.*, p. 310.
[33] " Inspired Millionaires."
[34] Compare Richard Michaelis' " Looking Further Forward," 1890, an answer to Bellamy. Octave Thanet, " The Heart of Toil," 1898.

istic government; described somewhat after the manner
of Bellamy's " Looking Backward." The excesses of democracy and socialism are delineated and discussed at
length. The evils arising from the suppression of the individual and the tyranny of the majority under a system
of state socialism are vividly depicted. The socialistic
empire is painted as a land of " social petrifaction." " In
its infatuation for what it called equality, it had taken
every vestige of independence from the individual units
and had made the State into a Frankenstein, which, while
crushing in its grasp the souls of the people, was itself
without a soul." [35] " Individual energy and ambition
had been discouraged and stifled. Sympathy, charity and
self-sacrifice had become unknown. The spiritual in man
had ceased to be manifest and the physical had become
dominant to such an extent that the people had sunk under
the vicious use of the aletha weed." " The whole race
had been placed on the same dead level as that of the peni-
tentiary. Governed by a few men for selfish purposes,
the State had become a despotism of laws."

Sometimes nearer to the average American philosophy
of things political than court decisions, or political platforms or systematic treatises were the informal philosophies of the humorists. They could not be reversed, re-
manded, reelected or recalled, and their playful sayings
often struck close to the mark. The quaint and widely
noted remarks of Mr. Dooley [36] often revealed in a flash
a widely accepted theory, as when he said that whether

[35] Chap. 17.
[36] Finley Peter Dunne, " Mr. Dooley in Peace and War " 1898,
and continuation of series. An amusing type is David Starr Jordan's satire on the tariff system in " The Fate of Iciodorum," 1909.

the Constitution follows the flag or not, the Supreme Court follows the election returns. The underlying spirit of Mark Twain [37] was democratic, but was focussed against political aristocracy and autocracy rather than on questions of social and industrial democracy. It is not possible to understand American democracy by reading Nasby,[37a] Bret Harte, Artemus Ward, Mark Twain, but who can understand America without appreciating them? If Mr. Ostrogorski, for example, could have understood them how differently he might have written of our political parties.

Whitman had no successor for a generation, but at the end of that time a new school appeared breathing again the democratic spirit.[38] Triggs, in his " Changing Order," [39] endeavored to apply Whitman's principles under all conditions, including democratic criticism, canons of beauty and pleasure, and education, in place of the military, priestly and cultural, which he held essentially non-social. In somewhat the same strain wrote Charles Zeublin, in his " Religion of a Democrat."

Many of the later poets hurled a protest against political and social conditions, but although they were inspired by democratic ideals presented no particular program.[40]

[37] Especially in "Innocents Abroad," 1869, and "A Yankee at the Court of King Arthur," 1889; "The Man that Corrupted Hadleyburg," 1900.

[37a] "In Search of the Man of Sin," in "Struggles of Petroleum V. Nasby," p. 687, 1872.

[38] Percy Boynton, "American Poetry." Louis Untermeyer, "The New Era in American Poetry" (1919).

[39] Oscar Lovell Triggs, "The Changing Order" (1905).

[40] Alice B. Curtis, "Modern Industrialism and the Struggle between Capital and Labor, in American verse, from 1865 to 1913."

Of these none was more notable than Edwin Markham's
"The Man With the Hoe," written after seeing Mil-
let's famous painting:

> "Oh, masters, lords and rulers in all lands,
>   How will the Future reckon with this man?
> How answer his brute question in that hour
>   When whirlwinds of rebellion shake the world?
>
> "How will it be with kingdoms and with kings,
>   With those who shaped him to the thing he is —
> When this dumb Terror shall reply to God —
>   After the silence of centuries?"

Underlying the poems of William Vaughn Moody
there is the same passionate protest against social injustice and the same plea for a broader brotherhood.[41]   In
the new school of Masters,[42] Sandberg[43] and Lindsey[44]
is found the same resentment against political and social
wrong, and the same reflection of profound unrest.   Urban and industrial subjects were not omitted in their efforts to interpret and express their ideals of human fellowship.   These writers unquestionably exercised a deep
influence on the political thought of America, spurring
the conscience and intelligence of the community to

[41] "The Brute" and the "Breaking of Bonds." Compare the
earlier writings of Sydney Lanier, notably "The Symphony" (1875).

[42] Edgar Lee Masters, "Spoon River Anthology" (1914); "Songs
and Satires" (1916).

[43] Carl Sandberg, "Chicago Poems" (1916), dealing with the
urban-industrial problem.

[44] Vachel Lindsey, "General William Booth" (1916) and other
works; Webster Bynner, "New World" 1915; Arturo Giovanitti,
"Arrows in the Gale," 1914.

sharper thought on the new problems of democracy under new conditions.

On the whole it may be said that the literary attitude was one of indifference to political and social problems during the first part of the period, passing over to vigorous championship of social justice in the last quarter of a century. Howells' " Altruria " seemed to mark the parting of the ways. There was always the tendency to accept the *status quo* of polite indifference to social facts and forces. But if we consider the frequently reactionary attitude of courts, of statesmen and philosophers, the literary group was certainly not unprogressive in the interpretation of the democratic ideals of America.

The literature of this period clearly reflects the swift changes in economic, social and political conditions, the growing interest in social problems, and the new response to the challenge of the new world to the old democracy.

Yet in the field of literature, much more than in that of political theory or practical politics, the influence of European writers was felt.   The internationalists, James, Dickens, Ruskin, Carlyle, Morris, Shaw, Chesterton, Bennett, Galsworthy, Kipling, Tennyson, with their varying interpretations of social ideals, were widely read and their ideas sunk deep.   Likewise Tolstoi, Ibsen, Zola, Victor Hugo, were read by large groups and political and social effect was not wanting.   To smaller groups the whole range of the French, German, Italian, Slav and Scandinavian literature was open, and they absorbed the ideas embodied in the fiction of other lands, and assimilated their interpretations of social and political life under modern conditions.

Whitman was rediscovered, Howells, Steffens, Churchill, White, Herrick, and others went behind the forms of government and were powerful preachers of a democratic spirit that swept through America in the twentieth century. Their influence was profound and far-reaching in shaping democratic political and social ideals. The voice of the later poets was equally insistent, and still more fervid and forceful, but the circle of their direct influence was not so wide.

CHAPTER XV

SUMMARY

IT now remains to summarize and characterize as concisely as possible the broad tendencies of political thought during the last half century. Unquestionably the most significant features of this period were the gradual tendency toward concentration of political and economic institutions, and toward the socialization of the state. The tendency toward centralization, developing slowly at the outset, swept forward as the end of the century approached with increasing momentum. In city, state and nation, and in the industrial world as well, the trend was toward closer integration of the institutions of control, economic and political. The development of nationalism in the nation as a whole, the growth of " bosses " and organizations within the political party, and the appearance of the " trust " in the commercial world, the consolidation of powers in the form of the commission government in the city, the development of central control in the state, were all evidences of the same general drift toward more compact organization. Again, the broadening of the purpose of the state was a conspicuous feature of the time. Beginning with a theory of the limited function of the government, the new conditions and the new spirit of the time forced a gradual departure from

450

the original position and the organized political society took up new duties on a much broader scale than ever before. Concentration of power and broadening of the scope of authority were typical of the institutional development of the period. On the theoretical side, the abandonment of the doctrine of weak government as the necessary defence of liberty was forced as the urgent need of more vigorous government began to be evident, while the early doctrine of *laissez faire* tended to retire before the theory of the broader social function of the political society. Taking the period as a whole, it was characterized by comparative weakness of government and limitation of function, but considering the tendencies of the time, it is clear that the broad movement was toward strengthening government and broadening its function. Decentralization was on the decline, and non-interference as a political dogma was on the wane as the period came to a close.

Broadly speaking three philosophies of action and interpretation were in competition during this time. They were the old time doctrine of conservatism, centering around the unimpeded operations of the assumed " natural laws " of trade; the liberal or progressive theory demanding popular control of the most threatening features of the new industrialism in the interests of the many as against the few; and the collectivist philosophy demanding industrial democracy in the broadest sense of the term. Of these the first reigned without much opposition during the greater part of the time; the second rose to power as the middle of the period approached, and the third had no status until toward the middle of the period but gained in strength as the end of the period drew near.

Examining the features of change in greater detail, it appears that significant alterations were made in the fundamentals of government. The suffrage was broadened by the inclusion of the colored voter although this was subsequently taken from him in the Southern states; and by the grant of the right to vote to large numbers of women, particularly in the Western part of the country. The number of elective officers was somewhat diminished, particularly in the cities, and the tendency to increase the list was everywhere checked. At the same time the electorate was given a veto over legislation in large sections of the country by means of the initiative and referendum, in addition to which the recall of certain officials was provided for in many sections, notably in local elections. The underlying theory was democratic in that it predicated the grant of voting power to all adult citizens, and broadened the circle of democratic determination of policies. The short ballot tendency seemed to foreshadow a more effective organization of leadership and responsibility in the democracy, than it had been possible to obtain hitherto.

With reference to the various powers of government, popular practice and theory underwent important changes. In many instances the powers of government were brought much more closely together, notably in cities. At the same time the theory of the balance of powers as a fundamental of free government was abandoned in many quarters. The mechanical theory of "equilibrium" as a guarantee of liberty was attacked by many students of politics and toward the end of the period was very widely discredited, especially as a dogma upon which democracy must necessarily rest. On the contrary, greater emphasis was laid upon the desirability of closer coordination and cooperation between the various branches of the government, on the assumption that separatism in the government was undesirable for the community. Montesquieu's doctrine of the separation of powers had never existed in the English constitution from which he borrowed it. Its crystallization in the constitutional law of the several states had caused many practical difficulties; and the defence of the three-fold classification as the end of this period came on, was relatively weak.

Of the three powers of government, the executive was the greatest gainer in public esteem, in practical and effective organization and in political theory. Executive leadership emerged as a definite feature and was supported by a strong body of sentiment and theory. When Woodrow Wilson said that he intended to assume the initiative in the government of New Jersey, if elected governor of the State, and that if that was unconstitutional, he intended to be an unconstitutional governor, he stated the whole situation in a nutshell. The " municipal dictator " theory of the mayoralty in many of the large cities was an evidence of the same general tendency working in the public mind. Not only was the executive supported as against the other branches of the government, but during this period began to acquire the permanent and skilled staff and force imperatively necessary for the proper administration of executive office, but which it had lacked up to this time. "Administration" began to appear, expert and technically qualified, as an aid to executive leadership.

On the whole the executive emerged from the half century with distinct leadership, rooted in public opinion and reenforced by sundry constitutional provisions. Only in the city did the legislature regain some of its lost prestige and authority. The commission and the commission manager forms of city government were illustrations of the revival of the power of the legislative branch of the government although under new and changed forms. Their permanence either as institutions or as indications of a new form of thought could not be assumed at the end of this period, however; and in any event their significance was local rather than national. The organization of political leadership, and the means of holding leaders responsible to the will of the democracy were still a mooted point in the theory and the practice of the democracy.

The legislative branch of the government suffered throughout this period from lack of popular confidence in its integrity, in its competence and in its impartiality. Councils and legislatures were frequently under the ban of popular suspicion as to plain honesty, while Congress was often considered insufficiently responsive to popular opinion — a conviction that found expression in the movement for the direct election of the Senators and in the insurgency against Cannonism. Only toward the end of the period was begun the formulating of more scientific methods of law making, bill-drafting, of mature consideration of facts, and of elaboration of principles of legislation.

The courts suffered through the period from a lack of confidence in their impartiality. The judiciary failed to satisfy the democracy as to the representative character of many of the decisions rendered in cases involving the rights of the many and the few, and while the power of veto over legislation was continued, it was subjected to severe attacks and important limitations were threatened and in some instances carried through. As the doctrine of the independence of the judiciary was more clearly stated and more generally understood by the community, the possibility of its continuance was more and more clearly conditioned on the limitation of this authority to cases in which broad public policies were not called in question; and of a very discreet and circumscribed employment of the power in a very small number of cases. The judicial development of private law was also an object of hostility in so far as through that indirect process old principles of private law were introduced in situations where broad questions of public policy were concerned. No searching examination was made, however, of the underlying rules and principles of jurisprudence from the point of view of a democratically organized society. The body of the common law was recognized by leading jurists as frankly individualistic and as the outgrowth of an ancient and outgrown régime, but this did not fully penetrate the popular consciousness and no pronounced change was made at this point. But the development of sociological jurisprudence threatened to accomplish notable transformations, and the end of the period saw the lines drawn for a sharp battle upon this field.

Both the institutional and the theoretical developments regarding the area or unit of government were notable. The general tendency was toward nationalism as against the state in accordance with the decision reached in the Civil War and with the economic and social tendencies of the time. Broader powers were conferred upon the nation by the Fourteenth Amendment to the Constitution, and these powers were often broadly construed by the courts, while the state lagged behind in ideals and organization. The state was no longer the rival of the nation, but tended toward the position of a subordinate though powerful agency. Powerful social and industrial forces constantly worked in the direction of the national unit as against the state. Commerce demanded a greater degree of uniformity in the commercial code, and a general sentiment urged the need of uniformity at many points. The theory of national supremacy was more sharply formulated than ever by Burgess and others who assailed the commonwealth as a unit of government. There were some *post-bellum* statements of the state sovereignty doctrines, but these were more in the nature of historic justifications of the " lost cause " than serious advocacy of living principles of political action. The devotion to local self-government, notable in earlier years, declined during this period. It revived around the municipality, but even here the sentiment was by no means unanimous. Local self-government as a fundamental and necessary guarantee of liberty was not much in evidence, except for that de-

velopment of the idea of local autonomy centering around
the demand for broader powers of self-government for
the city. Nor were these municipal powers asked as
guarantees against some dangerous and centralized
power, but as desirable means for the self-development
and self-expression of communities with distinct local
interests. Liberty was no longer regarded as primarily
local in character, in danger of losing its soul if extended over too broad an area. Conceptions of liberty,
justice, democracy were to a large extent interpreted in
terms of the nation, rather than of the state or the city
or the rural local government. Toward the end of the
period the international obligations of the nation began
to enter into popular thought — first in relation to the
development of imperialism and colonialism, and then in
relation to the international guarantees of permanent
peace. The earlier isolation of the nation tended to
disappear and to give place to the broader problem of
the position of America among the other powers of the
world. " Manifest destiny " which had been a strong
belief since Puritan days, but had received no concrete
formulation except in the Monroe Doctrine, began to
take on a more tangible form, although the exact shape
could not be foreseen even by the clearest-eyed.

The institutional development of the political party was
one of the striking features of the period under discussion. Its ramifications and elaborations were the object
of intense interest at home and lively curiosity in other
countries of the world. The development of the boss,
the machine, the spoils system, were structural contributions to institutional democracy, while the alliance of boss

and trust was characterized as the "invisible government." One of the striking features of the development during this time was the extension of legal control over many of the party activities and the gradual absorption of the party by the government as an organic part of its general structure. What had been voluntary associations became subjects of the most detailed legal regulation with reference to organization and to many of the most important of the modes of their activity. The political thought of the time recognized the significance of the party system in the general workings of the democracy, and not only began the process of regulation, but the more difficult task of providing a philosophical interpretation of the party in the general scheme of things political. For parties were not contemplated in that simple state of affairs described in the "state of nature" conceived by Locke and the 18th century theorists; nor were their activities covered by those who discoursed of the natural rights of man and the social contract. The attempts to explain the party system, whether in terms of the structure of the government, or of the industrial and political forces of the time, or of the aggressive tendencies of the "organization" in political or other institutions, were all helpful in the fundamentally necessary process of securing a deeper insight into the forces and the forms of democracy; of anchoring those public understandings upon which all government rests, below the surface of superficial phenomena upon the solid rock of democratic appreciation of basic forces and tendencies. The party is an effort to formulate leadership in the great cooperative enterprise of democracy, and obviously that is not the undertaking of a day. The transfer of power and responsibility from a small hereditary group to the many brings with it no greater problem than the formulation of the ways and means by which the latent power of the community shall be organized and energized for effective action. The party was one of the ways attempted; and that it failed to carry out this ideal purpose fully, and that very grave abuses arose in its management may occasion chagrin, but not surprise. Diligent practical and theoretical inquiry was necessary to allocate the blame in proper proportions between the system itself, the individuals who administered it, and the general intelligence and interest upon which it rests and above which it cannot long rise, and to construct a superior type of system. That this task was completed during this period no one believes; but that substantial progress was made in the statement of the problem and in the first steps toward a constructive solution is equally clear.

The proper scope of state activity, as a theoretical and practical field of political discussion, witnessed notable changes during this time. The period opened with an intense individualism dominant in all fields; — in the business world where the economic doctrines of *laissez faire* coincided with the theory of the survival of the fittest, and both with the tendencies of strong and determined men to conduct their affairs without let or hindrance; in the legal field with the crystallization of the common law and the application of early common law theories to the problems of public law administered by an almost irresponsible judiciary. Mobility of population, mobility of occupation, mobility of land, labor, and capital, all combined to make this doctrine supreme in spite of the sweeping changes in the industrial and urban worlds. Toward the middle of the period there came a change both in theory and in practice. Free land disappeared. The economic theory of the benevolence of competition was shattered by the sudden appearance of monopoly and unfair competition; the sociological theory of Spencer was matched by that of Ward, who urged the " efficacy of effort " as a legitimate interpretation of the Darwinian theory, and on the legal side a little later legal individualism by the assaults of the sociological school of jurisprudence. Meantime the steady pressure of conditions in cities and in industry had forced the practical recognition of many changes, if not because of a new theory, then at the imperative demand of intolerable human relations. A flood of social legislation followed in city, state and nation, sweeping into almost every way of life and every form of activity where the public developed an interest. Where the *laissez faire* doctrine was not abandoned, it was materially modified in actual practice. Its complete defence could no longer be made even by the greatest enthusiasts for the principle. The most stubborn case for the old principle was made against organized labor under the plea of " freedom of contract," and the " industrial liberty " of the citizen; but even here the battle was a losing one; for the tide turned strongly toward the relief of conditions that could not be tolerated on a democratic or even a human basis. The industrial and urban revolution took heavy toll of the doctrine of non-interference, whether in regulation of competition in trade, in limitation of the rights of persons and property through the varied forms of the convenient " police power," or through the slow broadening of the purposes of the state beyond the earlier function which Huxley once characterized as " anarchy plus a policeman." To say that individualism was abandoned as a general theory during this period would be incorrect and misleading; but that the function of the state was largely expanded in practice and almost equally so in theory is undeniable. The collectivist doctrine in the form in which taught by the socialists was generally rejected, but the practical necessity for broader action by the government overcame all scruples and compelled relief in the urgent situations precipitated by the urban and industrial revolutions. Ours was not a doctrinaire collectivism; but its advance, regardless of the spirit in which made or the goal toward which it moved, was none the less evident and important. Nowhere was a tougher texture of legal and economic individualism encountered than in America, but for that very reason nowhere was the advance of a conscious social policy more marked and conspicuous and significant than here. Next to the tendency toward integration of the government the socialization of the work of government was the most striking tendency of the time in theory and practice alike.

The method of political thought was notably altered during this period. On the one hand there was a crude and brutal rapacity speaking the language of corruption and intimidation — making a mockery of law, justice and democracy — the crude tactics of the new industrial oligarchy. America had not known so cynical a defiance

of genuine democracy.   But on the other hand there came
at the end of the period liberal statesmen of the highest
type, men of the character and ability of Roosevelt and
Wilson, who revived the best traditions of English and
American public life, and raised the hopes of sound
democratic leadership and fruitful statesmanship.   The
study of politics took on a new interest and vigor in the
last quarter of a century, and significant advances were
made in the investigation of the forms and forces of political life, and in the allied regions of economics and
sociology.   Parties, cities, administration, legislation, began to receive serious and systematic consideration.   It
would be easy to overestimate the value of such research,
but the more common error is to undervalue it, forgetting that the rationalizing process is not spectacular or
swift.   It deals with deep-rooted tendencies and its pace
is slow, but the gains in the technique of political study
are appreciable and the ultimate results are not negligible
in a study of great states.   That part of the process of
social control centering around the state left much to be
desired, but it also showed signs of promise and progress.
Parts of such studies are phases of the elaborate process
by which the authentic traditions and ruling purposes are
woven into the social mind and to that extent they are
elements in the governing process of society and the
state.   But other portions of these inquiries touch the
underlying problems of social science in its technical and
systematic aspects, toward the solution of which our
limited intelligence gropes its way, and which still lies
far ahead.   The small number of workers in the field
of scientific politics and the inadequacy of their ap-

paratus, makes scientific progress of necessity slow. Of the great forces of industrialism, urbanism and feminism, which have so powerfully affected our life during the last half century, that of industrialism has been the most notable. Here the major problems of human life which the state must interpret were found and here America struggled hardest and against the greatest odds to find an equitable and reasonable way through institution and idea toward the future without breaking wholly with its legal and political past. Urbanism also precipitated great problems which were frankly left unsolved, even in the simplest elements of protection of persons and property, while the larger constructive problems were just reached. The lights and shadows of American political life were nowhere so clearly marked as in the urban communities where specialized vice and virtue elbowed each other for living room. Urbanism and industrialism, which went together, revolutionized the lives of men, and compelled fundamental readjustments of ways of action and of thought which were so far reaching as almost to escape full realization. At the risk of tiresome reiteration, it may be said once more that these basic changes in the course of human thought were of prime importance in the political as in all other branches of human thought here and elsewhere.

Feminism left its mark upon social and in less conspicuous ways upon political theory. Jane Addams' sympathetic studies rank among the fruitful thoughts of a progressive time; and exemplified the finest application of woman's sympathetic instinct and constructive reason in the world of public affairs. That a method or a spirit rather than a schematic philosophy was presented in no way altered the value of the contribution. The influence of women in the socializing of the government has been significant, particularly during the last quarter of a century. This has been especially evident in the care of children, in the scientific care of the defectives and the dependents, in the development of the schools, especially upon the social side, in the pursuit of constructive policies of public recreation, in public sanitation and housing, in the restriction of vice, and in the amelioration of the conditions of working women. The feminine impulse and contribution in all these fields was so great as to stamp it as of fundamental value in any survey of American political ideas.

Considering the quick interchange of ideas and the many fundamental resemblances in the culture of western nations, it is not easy to assign a specific result to a particular nation. Yet the various outside influences affecting American political thought can be broadly sketched. French influence was conspicuous in our history in the period following the American Revolution, as seen in the adoption of Montesquieu's theory of the three-fold separation and balance of powers, and in the lively sympathy with the revolutionary democracy of the time. It was not conspicuous thereafter to the same degree. At the end of the period the French syndicalist influence was reflected in the industrial unionism of the United States, although the French refinements of the theory were not closely followed. The influence of French criminologists, jurists and economists was also evident, although not on a large scale, while the broad philosophical doctrines of Bergson's Creative Evolution were influential in shaping the fundamentals of human thought. The fiery Eugene Debs was of French origin. Large numbers of Germans settled in the United States and indirectly affected the course of life and thought.[1] In the third quarter of the century the influence of Francis Lieber, a German refugee, in systematizing the study of political science was notable. Later many Americans studied in German schools or familiarized themselves with the results of German thought. This was particularly true of social science, philosophy, education and natural science. Bluntschli, Gierke, Jellinek, Ihring, Kohler have all left their impress upon the study of politics. Wagner and Schmoller and the Austrians headed by Böhm-bawerk and Wieser in the domain of economics; Schaeffle, Ratzenhofer, Gumplowic, Simmel in the province of sociology were widely studied in the United States by special students of sociological problems. In the broader field of philosophy Kant, Hegel, Schopenhauer, Nietzsche have deeply influenced the workings of thought throughout the domain of Christendom and America has been no exception to the general movement of the world. Wundt, Haeckel, Virchow and others were of great influence in their various fields. The German influence was especially noticeable in the adoption of thorough methods of inquiry, and subsequently in the growth of the social spirit and point of view.

On the practical side the effect of German social legislation was pronounced and in the field of municipal government, the German cities received much attention from

[1] See A. B. Faust, "The German Element in the U. S."

American students of the urban problem. The city manager has many resemblances to the burgomaster who presided over the German municipal administration. The compact social organization of the German people, although undemocratic at the top, was not without its effect, as a type of highly centered and energetic political-social structure.

Socialism in the United States was largely of German origin. Its first great philosopher, Karl Marx, was a German Jew who lived much of his life in London. The earlier Socialists were almost all Germans and the active work of propaganda was in their hands. In the later part of the period Marx's philosophy deeply influenced political activity and speculation throughout America. His influence could not be accurately measured by the weight of the political movement known as the Socialist party, for its deeper effect was exercised in the slow formation of the texture of economic and political philosophy, which lies beneath the surface activities of the struggling groups. Whether Marx should be attributed to German origin, the Jewish race or English environment is not material for the purpose of this inquiry.

The social forces working in England were in many ways different from those in the United States, as is evident in the different political positions held by large owners of land, the established religion, groups of hereditary rulers, international relations, both commercial and political. But at many other points there were close contacts and common bonds. The close parallel between the English common law and the subsequent development of it in both countries was a fundamental tie of political unity. The general tendency in both countries toward universal suffrage and responsible democratic government was another point of similarity. In both the two-party system flourished. The decisions of the English courts were cited daily in American tribunals. Bryce's " American Commonwealth " was as common in our schools as Blackstone was with the lawyers. The leading personalities in English public life were well known in the United States. The political economy of Adam Smith and Mill, the ethical theories of Bentham, the sociology of Spencer and the science of Darwin, the Austinian theory of positive jurisprudence were all known and current here. The Fabian socialism of the Webbs was widely spread and frequently followed. English trades unionism rather than Continental socialism supplied the model of organization and action for American labor. Gompers, the chief figure in the American labor world, was born in England, and followed broadly the English tactics in the development of the industrial movement, both as against Socialism on the one hand, and independent political action on the other hand. Dicey, Holland, Anson, Pollock, Maitland, the great English commentators on common law and constitutional law in England, were widely read and of great influence among the ranks of lawyers and students. The literature of English social and political reform and reaction, from Dickens down to the days of Chesterton, Shaw, Wells and Galsworthy, was circulated as widely here as in England. In brief, the private and public law and social and political theories of England were as influential during this half of the century — and particularly during the last

quarter of the 19th century — as at any time since the
days of Locke and Blackstone.   The Canadian and Australian political tendencies also played a not unimportant
part in the shaping of American thought, as witness the
Australian ballot, proportional representation, the initiative and referendum, and industrial arbitration.

Russian influence was evident in the form of revolutionary anarchism as taught by Bakunin and later by
Krapotkin, who visited the United States, and whose
writings were well known in scientific circles.   Far wider
in range and depth of influence were the ideas of Count
Tolstoi, whose opposition to militarism was profoundly
felt in this country.   Bryan, for example, frequently
quoted Tolstoi, and was evidently influenced by his opinions, while Jane Addams was also much affected by the
Tolstoian philosophy of life; and Howells, the dean of
American literature, was deeply impressed by the social
doctrines of the great Russian theorist and writer.   The
Slavic influence was one among the many factors which
combined to shape the character of American thought.

Of other influences, the Italian was expressed chiefly
in the field of art and literature and religion, but on the
political side was represented by the flaming spirit of
Mazzini, whose democratic liberalism and breadth of
social vision were well known here.   Lombroso's work
on criminology was given wide vogue.   Ferri was later
well known in the same field.   Economists of the type
of Loria, Cossa and Pantaleoni were also of significance
in economic thought, as was Ferrero in history, and many
other thinkers in special fields.

The culture of many other peoples was represented

here and all were mingled in the great melting pot of
nations, but their specific contributions are not so clearly
traceable in literature or in the detailed development of
our political institutions, although all possessed an influence in determining the form of thought and the type
of government.

Any attempt to trace the fundamental democratic tendencies discloses many striking contrasts between the
economic, the educational and the political forces, forms
and ideals. The economic evolution of the last half
century tended superficially toward industrial control by
the few, but fundamentally in the opposite direction.
Educational development in the main was profoundly
democratic, unterrified by the barriers of sex, class or
race. The tendency of political institutions was left in
doubt, while the evolution of political and social ideas and
ideals was again distinctly democratic. The reduction of
the hours of labor and universal compulsory education
were democratizing influences of vast and little realized
significance. One gave leisure to the adult, which meant
eventually emancipation. The other developed the productive intelligence of the race, and created a basis
and standard for democracy. The shorter working day
and the universal educational system were powerful democratic forces, driving forward regardless of parties or
bosses or governments or court decisions or of the ebbs
and flows of surface opinion. If democracy as a whole
could learn to think and had time to think, it was inevitable that it would in the long run draw its own
democratic conclusions, whatever might happen in the
short time; while ignorance and labor to the point of

exhaustion on the part of the mass of the people inevitably mean rule by a few over the many regardless of what the form of government may be.

The ideals of democracy during this time were only imperfectly represented by its institutions and by their actual operation. Democratic faith was stronger than democratic works. Capitalism developed at an amazing pace and, because of the weakness of the government and the general surviving prejudice against strong government, was able to escape effective control. The absence of clear-cut ways and means of effective mastery over economic consolidation made this easier. There was no tendency to abandon democratic theories of government; on the contrary, the general faith in the ultimate triumph of democratic principles and institutions was never stronger. But there was grave difficulty in making the transition from earlier theories of weak and inactive government to the later doctrines of strong and aggressive government. In the meantime the old formulas of democracy were at work to prevent the formulation or adoption of a program adequate to deal with the altered situation.

Here as elsewhere through the Western world, Conservatism, Liberalism and Socialism were all obliged to make important alterations in their general strategy. Conservatism apparently intended to abandon bribery, corruption and irresponsibility and assume the decent garb of moderate social progressive leadership after the English Tory model. Liberalism tended to abandon its earlier extreme individualism and its earlier indifference to a constructive industrial program and adopt a thorough-going social democratic program. Socialism tended to cut loose from revolutionary anarchism and to adopt an evolutionary and parliamentary program. The smouldering discontent with political methods and results, and with orthodox trades unionism flamed out in the newer type of Syndicalism, challenging all previous forms of social control.

America had not fully thought out its democracy. It was working out its urgent tasks of territorial settlement, of industrial development, of race assimilation, secure in the faith of democracy but troubled often by its wayward and unwelcome developments. Yet the common denominator of all sections, parties and classes was democracy. No voice was raised to challenge the democratic goal, although there were many who doubted the way, and a few who were not sorry to see the public confusion.

A land of immense vitality and profound faith in its destiny, America struggled to realize its ideals of liberty and democracy and equality, to make practically effective its faith and hope in human capacity for self-government. Graft and greed, bosses and trusts, spoils machine and predatory privilege did not reflect the ideals that gleamed before the eye of the American as he looked forward into the future of his nation. The Yankee mind hesitated to speak its hopes and dreams, reserving them in silence; or suffering unrebuked some raucous counterfeit, some blaring, blatant utterance; listening to every vagary, but shrewdly difficult to convince; conscious of abuses, yet slow to act, but powerful when fully roused to action. The American preferred his shirt sleeves to a uniform, but was not incapable of donning military garb, and offering the " last full measure of devotion." He preferred personal and national individualism and isolation, yet was not incapable of collective action in internal or international affairs, with unexpected impulse and determination where a principle was involved and the way was clear. America's greatest gift to humanity has been the establishment of a democratic government over a wide extent of territory during a long period of time — a phenomenon with which the world was unfamiliar; and the persistent advocacy of high ideals of democracy, liberty and equality, immensely effective even when only in part realized.

The latent but not always dominant ideal of the period, expressed in political philosophy, in legislation and administration, in the institutions, tendencies and characteristics of our people, was essentially to translate the hope and faith of democracy into more effective form under the new social and economic conditions:— to organize, energize, mobilize the forces of the great democracy, awakening men to the need of responsible leadership, sounder law, more skilful administration, and broader social justice; to raise governmental methods to a plane nearer our ideals of democracy; to vitalize and humanize the work of government by contact with social needs and through constructive social policies; to preserve and progressively develop and apply its democratic ideals to the changing situations, ensuring the rule of the many under the forms of law, and liberty through that self-restraint and control without which democracy cannot survive.

Sometimes national personalities interpret better than its philosophies or institutions the inner spirit of its life. If we were to look for a personal embodiment of the typical American spirit, by whom was our national ideal more faithfully reflected than by Abraham Lincoln, with his lowly origin and his lofty words; his mingling of strength and gentleness; of caution and courage; of unpreparedness and attainment; of reconciliation of reverence for the forms of law with the vital facts of human life; of hatred of special, privilege and love of practical liberty; yet with shrewd ability to discern and indomitable courage to act upon the overshadowing issue — the maintenance of the nation's life,— paramount to forms of law and privileges guaranteed under the law, and vital to democracy and liberty?

INDEX

Abbot, Edith, cited, 16
Abbot, Grace, cited, 421
Abbot, Lyman, cited, 401
Adams, Brooks, on social revolutions, 429
Adams, Henry, cited, 45, 443
Adams, H. C., on sphere of state, 335
Addams, Jane, on pacifism, 260; on democracy, 427
Administration, See Executive
Agriculture, relation to political problems, 18 et seq.
American Economic Assn., 334, 414
American Historical Assn., 374
American Political Science Assn., 374
American Social Science Assn., 374
American Society International Law, 374
American Statistical Assn., 374
American Sociological Society, 374
Amidon, Judge, on amending constitution, 220
Anarchism, in U. S., 358
Aristocracy, in industry, 51
Australian ballot, 278

Baldwin, J. M., cited, 422
Barnes, Wm., on individualism, 319
Beard, C. A., cited, 221, 396, 428
Beecher, H. W., cited, 59
Bellamy, Edw., collectivist, plan, 354, 436

Bemis, E. W., on public ownership, 342
Berger, V., cited, 353
Blythe, S., cited, 439
Boas, F., cited, 421
Boss rule, theory of, 300 et seq.
Brewer, Justice, cited, 147
Brooks, J. G., cited, 401
Brooks, R. C., on party system, 300
Bryan, W. J., on plutocracy, 60; on imperialism, 250; on socialism, 340
Bruere, H., cited, 396
Burgess, J. W., on judiciary, 155; nationalism, 234; constitutional amendment, 218; state interference, 321; theory analysed, 379 et seq.
Business, rise of, 17; new type of, 24 et seq.; rule of, 25 et seq.
Butler, N. M., on recall, 123; on constitutional amendment, 223; on individualism, 320

Capitalism and democracy, 8-9
Carnegie, A., on individualism, 322
Carter, J. C., theory of law, 169; opposition to codification, 200
Catholicism and social reform, 347
Catt, Mrs. C. C., on suffrage, 89
Church and state, 33
Churchill, W., on democracy, 439
Cities, See Urbanism

475